The Wines of Hungary

How does a country with once-proud wine traditions reinvent itself after forty-five years of Communism, during which the entire structure of grape-growing and wine production was changed out of recognition? This book explains how the painful process of readjustment, which still continues, has progressed through privatization, foreign investment, and the dedication of small producers struggling to achieve quality standards in the face of a chronic lack of capital. It surveys the problems that remain to be overcome, and charts the progress already made, giving profiles of the leading producers in each of the country's twenty-two wine regions, with assessments of their wines. Special emphasis is placed not only on famous regions such as Tokaj and Villány, where significant results of these changes have already occurred and some remarkable wines are now being produced, but on the little-known and as yet undeveloped region of Somló – once equal in renown to Tokaj – which, in the author's opinion, also has the potential to make world-class wines. The resulting picture of the present Hungarian wine scene offers a fascinating account of a national industry in transition, poised eventually to re-establish its place as a major player among European wine-producing countries.

The Wines of Hungary

Alex Liddell

MITCHELL BEAZLEY

This book is dedicated to all those who are working
hard to raise the quality of Hungarian wine.

The Wines of Hungary
by Alex Liddell

Published in Great Britain in 2003 by Mitchell Beazley, an
imprint of Octopus Publishing Group Limited, 2–4 Heron Quays, London E14 4JP.

A CIP catalogue record for this book is available from the British Library.

ISBN: 1 84000 789 3

The author and publishers will be grateful for any information
which will assist them in keeping future editions up-to-date.
Although all reasonable care has been taken in the preparation
of this book, neither the publishers nor the author can accept any
liability for any consequences arising from the use thereof, or the
information contained therein.

Phototypeset in Berkeley Book by Intype London Ltd

Printed and bound by Mackays of Chatham

Contents

List of Maps

Acknowledgements

There is not enough space to thank individually the hundreds of people who have contributed, in one way or another, to this book. First and foremost, I should like to thank all the winemakers, producers, and wine firms – more than 300 of them – who gave me their valuable time so unstintingly. Many, I am sure, will be disappointed to receive no more than a mention in the text of my book. I would like to assure them, however, that the time they spent with me was never wasted because, without their help, my understanding of Hungarian wine would be much less detailed than it is.

I should also like to thank the army of interpreters, from school-teachers and priests to civil servants and relatives on holiday from their adopted English-speaking countries, who made communication with the winemakers possible. Without them, quite simply, there could have been no book. Had I realized in advance the immensity of the task of research-ing a subject without any knowledge of the relevant language, I would probably never have got started; that I managed to survive was entirely due to the linguistic proficiency, good humour, and eagerness to help of everyone concerned.

A number of people not directly connected with winemaking also deserve my thanks, including the many politicians, government func-tionaries and civil servants who agreed to be interviewed, and who assisted in other ways. Among these I should like to give particular recog-nition to József Urbán of the Hungarian Agricultural Marketing Centre, who arranged my visits to winemakers with great efficiency, cheerfulness, and patience, and to whom no request for help was too much trouble. With my thanks to him go my thanks to his colleagues in the Agricultural Marketing Centre, many of whom gave me invaluable help from time to time. At the same time I should like to thank the Hungarian Government for having made a generous grant towards the expenses of my research, and I am also indebted to Henkell & Söhnlein Hungária for kind hospitality at Balatonboglár.

I first learned about Tokaji when I read Hugh Johnson's fascinating book *Wine* in 1966, and not long afterwards I purchased Aszú Esszencia of the 1964 vintage: the first post-war import of Aszú to the United Kingdom by Berry Bros & Rudd. I therefore take a very special pleasure in thanking Hugh Johnson, not only for so kindly agreeing to write an introduction to my book, but for having stimulated my interest in this nectar so many years ago.

I also have to offer my thanks to András Kató, formerly the editor of the wine magazine *Borbarát*, for having read this book in manuscript, and for vetting my eccentric Hungarian orthography. His wide knowledge of Hungarian wine enabled him, through his comments, to make this a better book than it would otherwise have been. I am equally indebted to Julian Jeffs, who was the general editor of the *Faber Books on Wine* series when this volume was first conceived, and whose perceptive and sage advice, always unstintingly given, nurtured its earliest life. His supportive encouragement also sustained me through the frustrating delays that attended the transfer of ownership of the series from Faber & Faber to Mitchell Beazley, whose excellent editorial team led by Hilary Lumsden took over the project and brought it to final fruition. My very special thanks go to all concerned. Needless to say, the opinions expressed in the book are my own, and neither András Kató nor Julian Jeffs has any responsibility for them, or for any errors which the book contains.

For various specific kindnesses I should like to acknowledge my thanks to László Bakonyi, Ernő Péter Botos, Roger Fisher, Lajos Gál, Patrick Gooch, Susan Gorka, Julia Grexa, John Gueterbock, Judit Gueterbock, Barnabas Kalina, István Kopenczei, Miles Lambert-Gócs, Gabriella Mészáros, Péter Módos, Kenan Nashat, András Németh, Alan Ponting, Alex Pravda, Gábor Rohály, and Ferenc Tólgyes.

July 26, 2002
Alex Liddell

Introduction by Hugh Johnson

This may be the most important account of Hungarian wine ever published. I can think of no other that comes close, either in content or in timeliness. Alex Liddell is an unusual writer: a wine-lover extremely aware of quality, eloquent when he finds it, but totally, sometimes chillingly, clear-eyed and objective.

He is telling the story of a great tradition brought to its knees by twentieth-century history, and being rescued and reinventing itself at this very moment. He writes with admirable clarity about the Hungarians of today and their wines, good or bad. But the future is unclear, as Hungary stands on the threshold of a more or less united Europe.

To be definitive and tentative at the same time is a tall order. Liddell handles it with magisterial authority. He has asked all the questions and digested all the answers in a startlingly comprehensive account, which makes only one assumption: that Hungarian wine is worth such a sustained effort. It would be over the top to chronicle the wines of Romania or Bulgaria, or (dare I say) even Italy or Spain, in such dispassionate detail – if only because so much can be taken for granted. But Hungary is a creature of marvellous pedigree – wounded, bewildered, and in need of nurture.

If wine can be made with such skill, care, and discrimination that it bears comparison with works of art, why have so few nations, or regions, or individuals in history taken it this far? I always ask myself this question when I visit the Côte d'Or. Out of all France's (or the world's) thousands of hillsides with soil to suit vines, why do we only know the full potential of every corner of this one?

History provides the answer: human history – the needs and opportunities of the inhabitants, their contacts with others, their energies, and their tastes. In Burgundy, it started with Gallo-Romans capitalizing on the passing traffic; in Bordeaux, with the best sheltered port on the west coast for supplying northern Europe – and dry, gravel soil of the Graves. The French followed their national genius in elaborating consistent styles in astonishing variety, by choosing grapes to fit their many *terroirs*. The Rhinelanders, within the constraints of their marginal climate, did the same. And the Hungarians likewise. From the seventeenth to the nineteenth century, Hungary, for the quality and individuality of its wines, for their international fame and their prices, led the rest of Europe.

In *A History and Description of Modern Wines*, published in 1833, Cyrus Redding wrote: "The French wines are the best and purest, and not these alone, but the German and Hungarian wines are, besides their purely vinous qualities, among the most delicate and perfect in character."

Why Hungary, rather than Italy, or Austria, or Romania, or Portugal, or Greece? History has not been kind to any of these countries (Austria, perhaps, excepted). To Hungary it has been especially cruel, submitting the Hungarians to centuries as vassals of the Turks and Austrians – and, latterly, Soviets.

Part of the answer lies in the genes. The brawny founders of Hungary – they can be admired, formidable in bronze, in Heroes Square in Pest – were Magyars, a race famous for intelligence and resilience. From the founding of the Magyar kingdom in 1000 AD wine-growing was given pride of place, privileged and regulated.

In a country with few natural resources, the perfecting of wine, adding value to a basic commodity, was an intelligent measure. Free-draining soils, especially fertile ones of volcanic origin (there are many in Hungary), are famously propitious for wine-grapes. Hungary's gallery of indigenous grapes is another of her great resources, adapted over centuries, offering flavours as different from Chardonnay and Cabernet as Budapest is different from Paris.

Even more important, though, is Hungary's latitude, on a par with that of northern France. It provides the slow ripening conditions, allied with high summer luminosity, that give fruit its maximum flavour and aroma.

Hungary lies between the same parallels as Paris and Lyon. It is different from France in having a Continental climate; the summers can be relied on for the heat that in northern France arrives only four years out of ten. There is less cloud-cover and less autumn rain. Combining the qualities of a northern, almost marginal, climate with warm summers gives Hungary exceptional opportunities.

In its glory days, Hungary's taste was for sweet white wine, and its export customers concurred. It was wine of a kind that is almost extinct today, depending as it does on small crops and slow stabilizing in cold cellars. Tokaji is now almost the sole survivor, yet the great Riesling wines of the Rhine once had much the same qualities. Fashion has moved away from them towards wines that are lighter, drier, more abundant, and faster-moving. Certainly more profitable.

The old, generous style was not wine to quench thirst, but to put hair on your chest. "Stiff" was a favourite word of approval – not only in the sense of a stiff drink, but meaning a liquid that was dense, almost oily with extract. "Fiery" was another; its concentrated flavours seemed almost to burn your mouth. It made an explosive mixture with paprika, leaving you in need of a drink. The flavour most sought-after was the flavour of honey – whether the wine was sweet or dry. And the general notion was the sweeter the better.

These wines were great survivors. They lived for many years, taking on mellow flavours as they gradually oxidized. They were the antithesis of today's crisp, dry white that depends on chilling to be palatable. Cellar temperature, even café temperature, suited their mouth-filling flavours. I remember a Hárslevelű from Debrő, near Eger in Hungary's northern hills, bought at Budapest airport in the 1980s, that had survived years of maltreatment to emerge golden, aromatic, viscous, exotic, and thrilling.

Are there modern wines of this stature but in the idiom of today? There are many, and more appearing all the time. I'll leave aside Tokaji – although this book does not: its extraordinary qualities and complexities make much the longest chapter. Having immersed myself in the past decade in the revival of this legendary wine, I am partial. There are plenty of others to invoke. The best wines from the north shore of Lake Balaton have the intense mineral drive, the palpable energy that only great vine-yards project. The best reds and whites of Sopron, whites of Somló and reds of Pécs show the vitality of old, classic wine regions, and the reds of Villány and whites of Etyek include excellent examples of styles new to Hungary. Eger, the country's most famous red-wine region in the past, is perhaps not sure at present exactly what is expected of it – although its best reds are fine, crisp, and highly appetizing, and its whites are attractive.

In old Hungary white wine was generally preferred, generally better, and certainly in the majority. Seventy per cent of Hungary's wine is still white. All Hungary's native grape varieties (or at least grapes unique to Hungary) are white. But it is only history that says they should be. Ripening and soil conditions could not be better for intense-flavoured but not over-strong wines, white or red: the very kind of wine that makes Australians and New Zealanders move their vineyards further south, and South Americans move theirs higher into the mountains.

These are the comparisons that matter today. The past is vital evidence of Hungary's potential, both human and topographical, as a source of great wines. But Hungary has lost her old markets: first the demanding ones of old, aristocratic Russia and Poland, then the easy ones that came with Comecon (the Soviet bloc countries would buy anything). What counts now is how Hungarian vineyards and winemakers shape up to a global market that has little patience with tradition and ignores borders.

This book is the first serious assessment of the new situation. It is an astonishing feat of research, appraisal, recording, and balanced judgement. Alex Liddell is Hungary's candid friend. Without a passion for the country, he could never have launched himself on such a comprehensive and detailed survey. Everything is here, from the sometimes grisly politics to the pros and cons of malolactic fermentation in grape varieties rescued from oblivion. The sustained energy needed to compile such data in a tongue as strange as Magyar is a wonder in itself.

But that Hungarian wine is worth it, Alex Liddell is not in the slightest doubt. And nor am I. Nor do I doubt that it will surmount its present difficulties to be admired again as a great original in a world of ever-growing conformity.

Foreword

This book tries to give the reader some understanding of the Hungarian wine industry at the start of the twenty-first century, still struggling to re-establish itself thirteen years after the end of Communist rule in 1990. Its main problems are threefold. Firstly, there are the direct consequences of policies adopted under Communism: a legacy arising from state control, repression of initiative, neglect, underfunding, and general economic mismanagement. Secondly, there are difficulties created within the last ten years by political and economic policies aimed at the structural change necessary to transform a command economy into one based on free enterprise, and to regulate a new and burgeoning industry. And lastly, there is what, at the moment, is the most serious and least tractable problem of all: a chronic lack of the capital necessary to deal effectively with these other problems.

To be able to understand such issues, the reader needs to see them in context, against the circumstances which have produced them. So, while not attempting to be in any sense a history book, or wishing to dwell on a past that most Hungarians only want to forget, this volume must inevitably give some consideration of what occurred during the Communist period. Other historical information in the book has been confined to providing background information in the sections on each wine region.

I first visited Tokaj in 1994, and have been back to Hungary many times since. The main research for this project, however, was carried out between April 2000 and May 2001. The result, therefore, may be regarded as a snapshot (warts and all) of the Hungarian wine industry as seen by an independent, foreign observer during this period of just over a year. The reader should also bear in mind that the subject of the snapshot is a continually developing one; by the time this book appears in print (with Hungary poised to join the European Union), some of its detail will inevitably have changed.

Because the post-Communist Hungarian wine industry is so young, writing about it poses problems not usually encountered when dealing with a classical wine-producing area with a stable structure and settled traditions. The last thirteen years have, in effect, given birth to what is, in most respects, a completely new industry, with a new set of winemakers. Most of them are just beginning to show what they can achieve, but as yet, they lack a track record of sufficient depth to justify much generalization. As Aristotle's wine merchant might have said, "One swallow doesn't make a drink"; equally, a single bottle of excellent wine does not necessarily indicate a consistently able vintner. On the other hand, the reader naturally wishes to find guidance here as to the best producers, and some indication of the character and quality of their wine. I have, therefore, adopted a pragmatic policy of giving (sometimes tentative) generalizations where I think they can be justified, while avoiding too many detailed tasting notes of individual wines, because this will only frustrate the reader when he discovers that they are no longer obtainable.

Part Three of this book, in which the twenty-two official Hungarian wine regions are considered in detail, also offers profiles of individual wine producers. For simple reasons of space, it has not been possible to deal with all of them in the same amount of detail. Those that have been selected appear for a variety of reasons: most for the excellence of their wines, or the evidence of potential they show; some for their undoubted importance within a region, and because an account of the region would therefore be incomplete without them; and some simply because they make an interesting story, or illustrate in an apt way some aspect of the current situation. I have also tried to give some prominence to younger winemakers in whose talent I have faith, sometimes at the expense of more famous producers whose talent I doubt. For completeness, the section on each wine region ends with a list of wine producers it has regrettably not been possible to discuss in detail, but who, except in a handful of cases, were kind enough to receive me in their cellars during my most recent visits to Hungary.

Happily, there is plenty of evidence of individual high achievement and of generally improving quality among many winemakers. There are also exciting native grape varieties, almost unknown in the west, from which interesting new wines are being made. Although too frequently the best Hungarian wines are still available only on the domestic market, given the increasing interest shown by foreign importers, it can only be a matter of time before most readers will be able to test the truth of these assertions for themselves.

Unhappily, there is a downside. Too many Hungarian wines are unworthy of the attention of serious wine-lovers – although, equally, the same can be said of almost all famous wine-producing countries. Many Hungarian winemakers need little prompting to tell you how aware they are of the poor quality image of Hungarian wine in western Europe. "You find it on the bottom shelves of supermarkets," they say. As far as I am concerned, however, these wines are not the main problem; in general, they are of marketable quality or they would not be found there. A bigger problem for the present and future is the still larger quantity of wine that is not even up to this minimal standard, and the fact that many of its pro-ducers appear to be blissfully unaware of just how poor it is. Hungarians have a word for wine like this. They call it "crawling wine" – that is, wine so awful that, to avoid the risk of being seen by your neighbour and invited by him to sample it, you crawl on hands and knees under his window.

In attempting to diagnose the current ills of the Hungarian wine industry, this book will sometimes have harsh things to say that not everyone will be pleased to read. I wish to emphasize, therefore, that criticism is offered only in the hope that the honestly expressed views of an independent observer may be of assistance to the Hungarian wine trade in making further progress. If I did not have a fundamentally positive view of Hungarian wine, I would not have wanted to write this book.

Independence, intelligence, determination, and industriousness are important parts of the Hungarian character, and it is to these qualities that progress in overcoming many present difficulties is and will be due. Sometimes a streak of pessimism can get in the way – although it is said that Hungarians regard a pessimist simply as a well-informed optimist. Pessimists in the wine trade may take comfort in the reflection that other eastern European countries face problems similar to those of Hungary, but even more difficult to solve. When I mentioned to a German winemaker working in Romania that I had heard that its wine production is twenty years behind that of Hungary, his reply was, "Oh no: much more than that."

PREFATORY NOTE

The reader may find it helpful, before starting to read this book, to look at Appendix I to become familiar with matters such as Hungarian usage regarding proper names, units of measurement, and other conventions adopted herein. Appendix IV provides a guide to Hungarian pronunciation. The reader is also invited to use the index as a cross-referencing system. Principal references are printed in bold type. In this way, footnotes have been kept to a minimum.

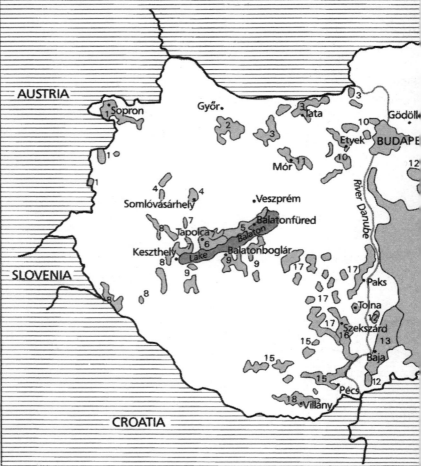

Key to Regions

1	Sopron	7	Balatonfelvidék	15	Mecsekalja
2	Pannonhalma-Sokoróalja	8	Balatonmelléke	16	Szekszárd
		9	Balatonboglár	17	Tolna
3	Ászár-Neszmély	10	Etyek-Buda	18	Villány-Siklós
4	Somló	11	Mór	19	Eger
5	Balatonfüred-Csopak	12	Kunság	20	Mátraalja
		13	Hajós-Baja	21	Bükkalja
6	Badacsony	14	Csongrád	22	Tokaj-Hegyalja

The Wine Regions of Hungary

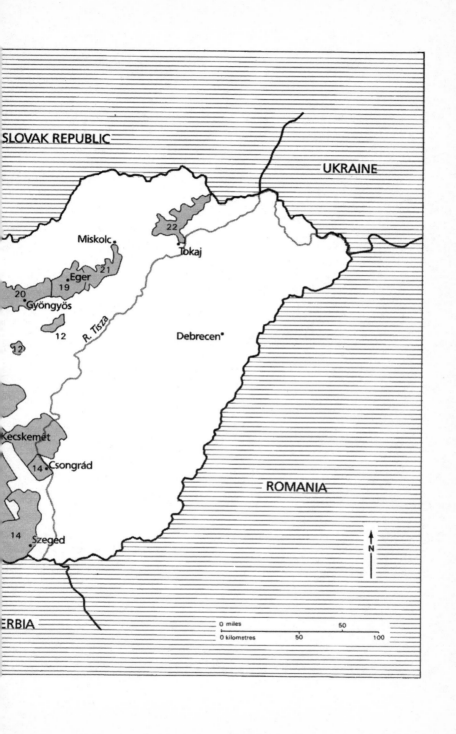

SLOVAK REPUBLIC

UKRAINE

Miskolc

22

Tokaj

21

Eger

20 19

Gyöngyös

12 R. Tisza

12

Debrecen

Kecskemét

14 Csongrád

ROMANIA

14 Szeged

N

ERBIA

0 miles   50
0 kilometres   50   100

part I

Recent History

1

Winemaking Under the Communists

THE BACKGROUND

Hungary became a nation on Christmas Day, 1000. Situated within the Carpathian Basin, close to a succession of militarily and politically powerful states, its geographical position has shaped its destiny, and for half of its thousand-year-long history it has been under the influence of its neighbours. Scholars debate whether vestiges of viniculture survived down the ages from the Roman occupation of the region – then known as Pannonia – at the beginning of the Christian era, when winemaking flourished. More probably, when the Magyars arrived from the Turkic Caucasus and settled in the region at the end of the ninth century, they brought with them a knowledge of winemaking. They certainly brought with them the word used in Hungarian for wine – *bor* – derived, it seems, from Turkish. Whatever its remoter origins, viniculture rapidly established itself in the new kingdom, nurtured at first by the church, then under a feudal system, and finally by German, Walloon, and Italian settlers. Concomitantly, trading in wine with neighbouring countries gathered momentum, and by the beginning of the sixteenth century, Hungary had as flourishing an export trade as any other Continental wine-producing country. Then, suddenly, everything changed.

Defeated in 1526 by a Turkish army at the battle of Mohács, Hungary struggled until 1541 to stem the Ottoman advance, but in vain. For over 150 years, Turkey occupied central and southern Hungary, while only the eastern part – Transylvania – retained a degree of independence under a vassal. Although some viticulture continued during the occupation, there was a decline, and when Austria eventually evicted the Turks in 1699, it took control of the entire (but unwilling) country, inaugurating a period of Austrian rule (eventually developing into a dual monarchy) during which Hungary was subordinated both culturally and economically to Austrian interests. The emperor rewarded his allies' generals with grants of land, much of which had been forfeited to the Turks by the Hungarian nobility, and during the eighteenth century, a manorial wine culture started to develop. Throughout the 1700s, there was an influx of Swabians, who settled mainly north of Lake Balaton and in the south, and later of Romanians, Slovaks, and Slavs, who repopulated the Great Plain. By the end of the eighteenth century, only thirty-five per cent of the population was of Magyar origin. Nevertheless, the settlers gave a huge boost to Hungarian viniculture, and by the 1780s, when Joseph II (1780–90) carried out a national land survey, the area of vineyards was found to be 571,838 hectares.[1] Bearing in mind that Hungary was then three times larger than it is now, this is proportionately twice today's figure.

The end of the eighteenth century and the beginning of the nineteenth was a time of reforming landowners with a genuine concern for the advancement of agriculture. On their estates viticultural progress was made. Vines began to be planted in rows, and trained around stakes instead of being grown promiscuously as bushes. Pruning to the base bud was replaced by spur-pruned head-training. Such advances in viticulture, however, took place against a background of continuing serfdom, and it was not until 1848 that this was officially abolished. In some areas, such as the south, serfdom survived until 1882; in any case, enfranchised serfs were usually transformed into landless peasantry, paying rentals as onerous as their previous tithes.

Winemaking suffered a severe setback with the arrival in the 1870s of phylloxera, the louse that attacks *Vitis vinifera* vine roots. Exports came to a virtual halt, and by 1891, the country had become a net importer of wine from Italy. By 1897, sixty per cent of the vines had been devastated,[2] although some areas suffered more than others. Hungary entered the twentieth century still trying to cope with the consequences, and some regions never fully recovered. Neszmély, for example, had to wait until the 1960s before replanting started seriously.[3] Then, just when new hope

---

[1] Halász (2), p. 43.

[2] *Ibid.*, p. 47.

[3] *Ibid.*, p. 67.

for the wine trade seemed to be in sight, the First World War dealt it another near-fatal blow.

Allied to the losing side, Hungary paid a heavy price during and after the war: the death or destitution of hundreds of thousands of its citizens, the destruction of its economy, and occupation by foreign troops. In October 1918, the dual monarchy was replaced by a national republic, and under the Treaty of Trianon of July 4, 1920, to satisfy nationalist aspirations within its old borders, Hungary lost two-thirds of its land. With it went valuable wine-producing areas to Croatia, Romania, and Slovakia. In the same year, after a short Communist regime, Admiral Horthy became "regent" of a re-established kingdom. It was effectively a right-wing dictatorship, run by a so-called Government Party, which consolidated the interests of landowners and the Roman Catholic Church. A radicalized workforce and a destitute peasantry were kept in check by a repressive police force. As the depression of the 1930s deepened, conditions for the masses got worse. Resentment towards the former allied powers transformed itself into admiration for Hitler's "successful" Germany, and Nazi and anti-Semitic sympathies began to develop at all levels of national life.

During the 1920s, the wine trade again struggled to rebuild its fortunes. In the 1930s, annual exports hovered between 200,000 and 300,000 hectolitres – as compared with over 2 million hectolitres (admittedly from a country three times bigger) early in the nineteenth century.[4] The structure of the Hungarian wine trade as the Second World War loomed was not greatly different from that of other major European wine-producing countries. Apart from a multiplicity of tiny rural plots mainly supplying domestic needs, the cultivation of vines and the making of quality wine for commercial purposes remained in the hands of medium-sized estates belonging to the gentry, and smaller, family-owned farms and wine firms. The marketing and export of wine were controlled by independent merchants who, in Hungary, were predominently Jewish. Their trade was to a large extent based on Budafok (a riverside suburb of Budapest). At the end of the war, all this was to change.

[4] Cf. *ibid.*, pp. 43 and 199.

THE START OF THE COMMUNIST ERA

In 1939, at the beginning of the war, Hungary adopted a posture of non-alignment, but in June 1941, Horthy openly allied Hungary to the Axis powers. Later, realizing that he had backed the likely losers, Horthy attempted to change sides, thereby exposing Hungary sequentially to the wrath and vengeance first of Germany, then of Russia. Hitler occupied Hungary in March 1944, expelled Horthy, and installed a Fascist puppet government. A reign of terror ensued. In fewer than six months, 400,000 Jews had been deported to extermination camps, while intellectuals, labour leaders, and politicians were imprisoned or sentenced to hard labour. In mid-October, Russian troops began an invasion from the east, and by Christmas, Budapest was under siege, suffering enormous damage. The Germans were finally driven out in April of the following year, a provisional government was declared, and a Soviet army of occupation took control of the country.

Soviet interference began at once. In the free elections held at the end of 1945, the Independent Smallholders' Party got fifty-seven per cent of the vote. The Communists and Social Democrats, with only seventeen per cent between them, nevertheless joined the government under Soviet direction. Two years later, in 1947, fresh elections were held under a new electoral law, but were manipulated by the Communists so that their candidate, the Stalinist Mátyás Rákosi, won. The Social Democrat and Communist parties were then merged to form the Hungarian Socialist Workers Party, and by 1948 overt Communist rule had been established.

This was a period of social turmoil deeply affecting wine production. In 1946, by international agreement, a large proportion of the German population of Hungary was forcibly repatriated. The basis of selection was the 1941 census. Many whose forebears had emigrated to Hungary in the eighteenth century still thought of themselves as German, and had responded to the census by claiming German nationality. In those areas with large German immigrant populations engaged in winemaking, the short-term effect was cataclysmic.

The new government immediately carried out a comprehensive nationalization programme covering all forms of commercial activity from manufacturing industry down to the smallest shops. Much of the mining, transportation, and telecommunications industries was already under state control. Then, in 1947, the (not-yet-Communist) government embarked on Hungary's first Three Year Plan (1947–9), with the intention of overcoming the legacy of the war and setting the country on the path to economic prosperity.[5]

Even before this, however, Imry Nagy, the Communist minister of agriculture (later to become prime minister), had sponsored far-reaching proposals to dismantle agricultural estates and redistribute land on a large scale. In 1945–6, land belonging to *kulaks* (peasants working for personal profit) and to the church was seized. This did not just mean the large estates of the nobility, because a *kulak* was defined as someone who owned fifteen hectares of arable land, or three hectares of vineyards. Estates larger than this were broken up and redistributed to the peasants who worked on them. In 1946, 2 million hectares were distributed among 642,000 people – each getting an average of three hectares – thereby creating a new class of small farmers. Something close to a tithing system was also imposed. Peasants had to give a certain amount of their produce to the state; ex-*kulaks* had to give a larger quantity. In return, according to the amount you gave, you got vouchers that were exchangeable for necessities, such as clothes and shoes.

As privatization in the 1990s has again demonstrated, agricultural estates designed to be run as a single entity are generally quite unsuited to being run as a number of separate units. Some peasants responded to the new situation by forming small, voluntary cooperatives. For example, twenty-five peasants who had worked on the local nobleman's estate in Gyöngyöstarján formed such a cooperative entirely for practical reasons. This was a lesson the government was also quick to learn: that replacing *kulaks* with peasant farmers paid few dividends in terms of the efficiency required for the realization of its main economic aims. In 1948, therefore, the Communists abruptly changed direction and introduced a policy of enforced collectivization of the three-year-old private peasant holdings that was to continue for the next three years.

[5] My debt to Tőkés in this chapter will be clear. His lucid and detailed explanation of the stages in the development of the Hungarian economy from 1945 to 1990 can be recommended to the reader in search of more detail, as can Berend's.

COLLECTIVIZATION – COOPERATIVES AND STATE FARMS

Two types of organization were involved: the *szövetkezet* (cooperative) and the *állami gazdaság* (state farm). Some small cooperatives, both productive and marketing, had existed before the war. New cooperatives were started in 1949. In general, cooperatives were made up of the land of peasants – that is, areas of less than three hectares. Every village had its cooperative, and this meant that there were between 3,000 and 3,500 cooperatives across the country. The size of a cooperative depended on the village on which it was centred but, typically, it would be between 400 hectares and 600 hectares.

Cooperatives were of two types. The most common form was the *mezőgazdasági termelő szövetkezet*, (agricultural producing cooperative) abbreviated as MGTSZ or TSZ, where the members put their own land into the cooperative. This land, as well as buildings and equipment, and any land subsequently acquired by the cooperative, was all owned communally. Very uncommon, and mainly to be found in the Kunság (Great Plain) region, was the *szakszövetkezet*, (shared cooperative). In this kind of cooperative, members continued to own their land privately and, except in Kiskunhalas, there was no upper limit to the amount they could own. Shared cooperatives made and sold wine from grapes produced by their members, and also coordinated the selling of wine from other sources. The reason for having this type of cooperative was administrative rather than ideological; in the Great Plain, farms were often small and scattered, and consequently too difficult to organize centrally.

State farms were much larger units, and could comprise anything from 500 to 10,000 hectares. They began to appear around 1950, and had as their nuclei church lands and those parts of estates or institutions which, because of their specialized character, had been deemed unsuitable for redistribution – for example, nurseries, equine centres, etc. They also incorporated land that had been abandoned by peasants who had opposed collectivization: in fact, only twenty-five per cent of the peasantry had voluntarily joined cooperatives.[6] State farms, like most cooperatives, engaged in forms of agricultural activity as diverse as arable

[6] See Berend, p. 2.

farming, nursery-based horticulture, cattle breeding, horse breeding, forestry, fishing, and, of course, viticulture. Which activities were included depended on local conditions, so many state farms did not deal with viticulture at all; of those that did, some confined themselves to viticulture while others also produced wine.

It is possible to exaggerate the comprehensiveness of the cooperative and state farm system. In the 1970s and 1980s, when the system was at its most flourishing, cooperatives occupied sixty per cent, and state farms sixteen per cent, of the total land area. The remaining land was either unexploited, or remained in the hands of specialized institutions or in private hands.

The way the system worked was that the Central Committee of the Communist Party determined goals and targets that were embodied in economic plans and decrees. Where cooperatives were concerned, these plans and associated budgets were diffused downwards through a chain of command: first to the Ministry of Agriculture, then to the National Association of Cooperatives – a private, rather than state, institution – which, in turn, passed them down to regional cooperative associations, which finally communicated them to individual cooperatives. A system of reporting back, application for special permissions, etc, operated in the opposite direction through the same chain.

State farms, on the other hand, were controlled both financially and technically by the National Centre of State Farms. The farms were included in the national five-year agricultural plans, which set them specific goals and how they were to be achieved. State farms, therefore, worked strictly within the parameters set by each plan – although Hungarian five-year plans were not as minutely detailed as those in the USSR. Their officials were nominated by the state.

By contrast, the law said that cooperatives belonged to their members, and that their officials were to be elected by them. How they achieved the targets set out in government economic manifestos was, to a large degree, left to local management decisions. Cooperatives, for example, arranged their own credits with state banks. In practice, however, there was often little difference between the functioning of cooperatives and state farms. Presidents of cooperatives, like those of state farms, were nominated in Budapest from party cadres. In the case of one cooperative in Kecskemét, the result of the "free" vote of its members was known one month before it took place. The independence of managers was often compromised by political interference. At first, the cooperatives were run by people without any specific knowledge of wine (and, sometimes, even of management). Specialists were excluded because they had served the previous regime.

This new system provided the model for wine production for the next four decades, and in 1949, the national wine law, which had existed since 1893, was revoked because its structures had become redundant. The most significant difference between cooperatives and state farms was, in the end, with regard to their budgets. Up until 1982, the cooperatives got less subsidy from central government than the state farms, which tended, therefore, to be net beneficiaries of investment. This gave them an edge, with better and more modern technology, as well as (latterly, at least) better-qualified direction.

From the late 1940s, marketing was handled by a state-owned cellar system. The cellars in Budafok had all been nationalized, and here the *Magyar Állami Pincegazdaság*, (Hungarian State Cellar Organization) was set up. Across the country, similar commercial cellars, for which the term *borkombinát* (wine combine) was often used, were created. These included Hungarovin (also based on Budafok); Egervin in Eger; Pannonvin in Pécs; Kecskemétvin, originally the *Közép-Magyarországi Pincegazdaság*, (Mid-Hungarian Cellar), in Kecskemét; the *Badacsony-vidéki Pincegazdaság* (Badacsony Region Farm Cellar) in Balatonfüred; and the *Dél-Alföldi Pincegazdaság* (Southern Great Plain Cellar), in Szeged. Broadly, the cooperatives and state farms sold to them, and they distributed wine throughout Hungary. Wine for export was dealt with by another state monopoly called Monimpex. It, too, was located in Budafok, and it was also complemented by regional cellars.

Just as collectivization was being completed, the party introduced its first Five Year Plan (1950–4), the aim of which went beyond restabilization of the economy. Hungary was faced with crippling post-war burdens, such as war reparations and the cost of garrisoning Soviet forces. The goal, therefore, was to change the country into a modern industrialized power whose economy was no longer based almost entirely on agriculture. This involved cutting back on living standards and targeting investment on industrial development (including armaments production); such investment went up by 462 per cent within the period,[7] while investment in agriculture stood still or actually diminished.

On the one hand, the wholesale changes to the agricultural system brought with them a degree of social discontent; on the other, the inefficient way in which the system was run had disastrous economic consequences, which the policy favouring industrialization only made worse. In 1953, Imre Nagy (now the prime minister) tried to defuse the political rumblings and improve matters economically by introducing yet another policy change (called the New Course) that actually sanctioned partial decollectivization of the agricultural sector. Some commentators believe that this timely step reduced political tension among farmers so successfully that they remained on the sidelines during the 1956 revolution.

Wine exports had begun again in 1949, the year in which Stalin established the Comecon system within the Soviet bloc as the economic counterpart of the Warsaw Pact. Under this system, member countries were to trade with each other to their mutual benefit. Despite the shortcomings of the cooperative system, by 1956, the pre-war wine export average was being comfortably exceeded.[8] Opinions differ about the quality of the wine being made at this time, except that it was of a generally higher standard than was later to be the case.

Nagy proved to be too liberal for the party and was ousted from office in 1955, to be replaced by the repressive Ernő Gerö. Popular demonstrations in 1956 against the new government and the USSR prompted the withdrawal of Soviet troops. Nagy, back in power on a wave of popular nationalist sentiment, appointed a non-Communist cabinet and tried to withdraw from the Warsaw Pact. Subsequent events happened quickly and, with the return of Soviet troops, the Hungarian Revolution, which had started on October 23, was over by November 4. Nagy was replaced by János Kádár and later executed, and a new Communist regime was imposed. One hundred and ninety thousand Hungarians took the opportunity to flee the country, many of them to return to their homeland only after the collapse of Communism in 1990.

---

[7] *Ibid.*, p. 87.

[8] Cf. Halász (2), p. 199. Exports averaged 350,000hl between 1955 and 1960.

VINEYARD DEVELOPMENT

Immediately after 1956, Kádár took a firm line on re-collectivization, using a pragmatic mixture of intimidation and financial incentives to bring those peasants who had taken advantage of the 1953 liberalization back into the fold. By 1961, seventy-five per cent of all arable land was within the cooperative system. A second Three Year Plan (1958–60), followed by a second Five Year Plan (1961–5), aimed at raising industrial output still further, and more resources were directed towards this goal. Paradoxically, because it was a corollary of this policy that agriculture also had to contribute towards increased industrialization, viticulture reaped some benefits. For example, greater mechanization improved agricultural efficiency, and this released agricultural workers to swell the ranks of those engaged in industry. Between 1960 and 1965, the agricultural population dropped by ten per cent and, between 1965 and 1976, by a further twenty-seven per cent.[9] Initial results were considered satisfactory because industrial output almost doubled, but the results for the wine sector were mixed.

In 1962, the USSR enforced restrictive agreements on members of Comecon, limiting the production of its satellite members and forcing them into economic dependence on the USSR. Instead of each country having to stretch its manufacturing resources to produce the same range of goods, a system of specialization developed. Wine became a significant export under what was essentially a barter system, whereby it was exported in return for commodities in which Hungary was not self-sufficient or which it completely lacked – latterly, oil and gas. This led to the extension of cooperative vineyards between 1962 and 1965 – generally on land acquired after the original nationalization – and to further development of state farm vineyards.

At this time, some areas (in Mátraalja, for example) had as much as eighty per cent of their vineyards planted with grape varieties such as Noah and Othello. These were reluctantly jettisoned, as were traditional Hungarian varieties, in favour of easily cultivated, large-yielding varieties. Increasingly, the emphasis was put on quantity rather than quality.

[9] See Hare *et al.*, pp. 226–7.

On the positive side, exports to the west began to gain in momentum, and this saw the introduction of so-called "western" varieties such as Chardonnay to enable Hungarian wines to compete on these markets.

In 1966, under a scheme known as the Nádudvar Plan, a development of considerable future significance to the wine trade took place. Every member of a cooperative was given the opportunity of renting and working a 0.3 hectare household plot (known as a *háztáji*), and of using (for a nominal payment) cooperative equipment to cultivate it. This led to the establishment of small vineyards: hobby plots, as they were called. Some chose to sell grapes, and some to make wine, but at first there was effectively only one potential purchaser, and that was the cooperative itself – although, even from the beginning, one could shop around for the cooperative that paid the best price, or with less delay, or with interest added to delayed payments. These plots constituted a sort of hidden continuation of old winemaking traditions, and countless wine producers now in business learned or honed their winemaking skills on such hobby plots.

By 1965, however, before this had happened, it was clear that expansion of the industrial sector had run out of steam, but whether from mismanagement or because of flaws endemic to the system was unclear. A full-scale examination of the command economy, raising questions about over-centralization and poor planning, was started by Kádár in 1965, and the result of this debate, the New Economic Mechanism (NEM), came into effect in 1968. It proved to be a damp squib, because it did not address the intrinsic flaws of the system; instead, if anything, it reinforced control from the centre and politicized agricultural management still further. Managerial decisions were motivated more by the need to satisfy political orthodoxy, or protect oneself within the system, than by economic efficiency.

For some time, agricultural pay had lagged behind that of blue-collar workers, forcing many of those living in the country to supplement their incomes not only from household plots, but also by doing industrial jobs. The Hungarian saying "One needs more than one leg to stand on" puts the point very neatly – and the economic reality behind it is as true today as it was thirty years ago. By 1970, every fifth industrial worker and every third construction worker was a peasant commuter trying to earn more money.[10] The NEM spurred the government to devise various schemes to motivate agricultural workers, as well as to supplement their earnings. Cooperatives were permitted to make additional profits by undertaking off-season work (often not clearly related to agriculture), and many paid wages to their members as well as dividends. More significantly, in 1971 the maximum size of household plots for crop-fields (although not at this stage for vineyards or orchards) was raised to 0.6 hectares, and the restriction on selling produce only to cooperatives was removed. It became possible to sell wine direct to bars and restaurants, although surprisingly few appear to have taken advantage of this particular relaxation. Nevertheless, initiatives like these became a creeping form of rudimentary market capitalism, and the foundation of much later private enterprise. Quite quickly, agricultural incomes, thus supplemented, overtook average industrial earnings.

The NEM also brought about more centralization of cooperatives. Between 1970 and 1972, small village cooperatives were merged (often six at a time) to form larger and, it was hoped, more efficient units. At the same time, the hitherto clear-cut production-marketing division of function between cooperatives and state farms on the one hand, and state cellars on the other, became blurred. The latter began to get involved in production, while the former began to sell their own wine themselves.

As production began to increase, benefiting from planting carried out during the 1960s, the consolidated cooperatives undertook further vineyard development. Increased mechanization was exploited to the limit to reach production targets by working day and night shifts. Unfortunately, however, the specialized production system within the Comecon countries impinged adversely on the way that vineyard development was carried out. A decision was made in 1972 to stop production of tractors in Hungary in favour of buses, which were imported by other Comecon countries. In the same way, Czechoslovakia specialized in making lorries, and tractors became a Russian monopoly (although, curiously enough, imports of American John Deere and Italian Fiat tractors were permitted). Whereas planting carried out in the early 1960s had had a distance of 2.4 metres (almost eight feet) between the rows because they were worked by narrow Hungarian tractors, those made after 1972 had to have

[10] Tőkés, p. 100.

rows at least 3.5 metres (eleven feet) apart, and perhaps as much as 4.5 metres (fourteen-and-a-half feet) apart, because Russian tractors were so wide. Intermediate rows were removed from existing vineyards to increase the distance to 4.8 metres (fifteen-and-a-half feet).

At a time when the policy was to increase wine production, this all seems rather silly, but (like the export of wine, as discussed below) such matters have to be seen within the context of the large-scale management of the Comecon economies. The consequences of this particular policy are, sadly, still with us. All currently existing state-planted vineyards have widely spaced rows – 3.5 metres or more apart – with consequent densities within the range of about 2,500 to 3,300 vines per hectare. Indeed, most new plantations in the 1990s are probably the same, because the majority of growers either still use, or only have access to, wide tractors.

The mechanization of the vineyards had another effect, greatly increased by the use of wide tractors: the abandonment of vineyards, not just those on high, rocky, terraced ground – traditionally considered to be prime-quality vineyard sites – but also those on comparatively gentle slopes. These abandoned vineyards, most of which have still to be reclaimed, are often easy to identify from the large number of acacia trees they contain – although why acacias have such an affinity to old vineyards is hard to say. Many of the new vineyard developments, on the other hand, were on easily mechanized flat ground with inferior soil, poor exposure to the sun, and, very often, other drawbacks such as a greater risk of frost.

LIBERALIZATION

When the first phase of the NEM finished in November 1972, the party came under pressure from other Comecon countries to rescind the small economic liberties introduced four years earlier. They were considered ideologically unacceptable and seen as eroding party control. Profit-making was frowned upon, and successful agricultural cooperatives were stigmatized as profiteers. Nevertheless, economic problems, exacerbated by increased energy costs and falling foreign trade (including the deterioration of economic relations with the USSR and its withdrawal of extended loans), made fundamental economic policies such as fixed annual wage increases unsustainable. By 1978, economic reform had become more pressing than ideological orthodoxy, and government measures progressively became a form of hand-to-mouth pragmatism designed to keep the show on the road.

Economic necessity suddenly required that all forms of productivity should be harnessed, and the Politburo reluctantly decided not only to legitimize but also to expand private agricultural and artisan activity. The gravity of the economic situation required immediate action, but so moribund was the bureaucratic system that it took forty-six months to push through what had been intended as a crash programme.[11] It was approved and implemented only in 1982, by which time Hungary's foreign debt (at $14.7 billion) was the highest per capita in eastern Europe, and inflation was approaching thirty per cent a year.

This new freedom had remarkable effects. In 1978, the permitted size of vineyard hobby plots was raised to 0.6 ha, and relatives of members of cooperatives, many of them town-dwellers, were also allowed to own household plots. After 1982, cooperatives were expected to pay more and more, in the form of social security and other levies, towards the state budget and, from year to year, pressure increased on the agricultural sector to support the rest of the economic system. To reduce these financial burdens, cooperatives, under various local initiatives quite separate from hobby plots, began to rent more and more of their land to members to work privately. This gradually led to quite large organizational changes in cooperative production. By 1990, when it became officially possible to rent another 1.5 hectares of land, some cooperative members were working as many as five hectares each. At the *Mátrai Egyesült MGTSZ* (Mátra Amalgamated Cooperative), in Gyöngyöstarján, for example, only eight out of its total 1,000 hectares of vineyards remained as conventional cooperative vineyards. In the context of wine production, when privatization came in the 1990s, it was almost as much a regularization of what was already developing into a system of private production as it was an extension of it.

[11] *Ibid.*, p. 113.

THE END OF AN ERA

During the 1970s, Törley (part of Hungarovin in Budafok) exported 5 million bottles of sparkling wine each year to the USSR under the Comecon system. Each bottle cost thirty-five Hungarian *forints* to produce but was sold at HUF25, and because this was known to the managerial workforce, there was no incentive to cut costs or to try to aim at real profits. On the other hand, in 1971, the average price obtained for *Ausbruch* (sweet) wine exported to West Germany was 272 Deutschmarks (DM) per hectolitre (when the exchange rate was HUF17 to DM1) – a slightly higher price than it fetches today.

Small wonder, therefore, that the regime began to develop more western-oriented, trade-driven policies. Nevertheless, throughout the next ten years, despite efforts to change direction and an increase in export activity, the Hungarian economy remained decisively dependent on Eastern bloc markets. In 1985, when Mikhail Gorbachev took power in the USSR and initiated the policies of *glasnost* and *perestroika*, exports were at their peak. Out of an export total of 3.27 million hectolitres of wine, 2.4 million went to the USSR. That this amount diminished almost to vanishing point within the next six years was due to a series of adverse circumstances.

First came Gorbachev's all-too-successful anti-alcohol campaign in the USSR. Another blow came in 1989, when the barter export system with the USSR was changed to a hard-currency system. Had this been phased in gradually, it might have worked better, but change came abruptly, and the Soviet importing companies did not have enough money to maintain their imports at their previous levels. The wine sector, it turned out, was particularly vulnerable to these upsets. Because the export market had been so buoyant, nobody appears to have noticed what had been happening on the domestic market. At the beginning of the 1960s, wine consumption was around forty litres per capita, but by the late 1980s, it had decreased to twenty-four litres per capita. During the same period, however, beer increased from fourteen litres to over one hundred litres per capita.

When the political and economic crash occurred in 1991, Comecon markets disappeared overnight, and bankruptcy loomed. Political change, however, had already taken place. Kádár had been ousted in May 1988, and thereafter reformists steadily gained ground. In October of the following year, the Communist Party reconstituted itself and, in anticipation of free elections, opposition parties became legal. Almost immediately afterwards, in November 1989, the Berlin Wall fell, and in 1990, the recently declared Republic of Hungary elected to power a centre-right coalition dominated by the Hungarian Democratic Forum (MDF) under József Antall as prime minister, in conjunction with the Independent Smallholders' Party (FKgP) and the Christian Democratic People's Party (KDNP). It became the immediate task of this government to deal with the economic mismanagement of the previous forty-five years.

WINE QUALITY

What was wine really like during the Communist period? Was the quality as low as is frequently asserted? These are questions I have often asked winemakers who worked within the system, and this is a summary of their responses.

At the lowest level was wine that was shipped to the USSR. What the Soviet market required was fortified, sweetened wine, and the product manufactured for it was, according to one description, "a sort of artificial wine". This type of wine was mainly produced on a quota system by state farms (and only by them); with seventeen per cent alcohol and 120 grams of sugar per litre, it was called *erősitett csemege bor*, (fortified dessert wine). It was exported in non-returnable wooden barrels, and at the peak of the export trade made up twenty per cent of the entire export market. It was not wine to be proud of, but it supplied a market demand. When people talk about how bad the wine was that went to the east, this is generally the product they have in mind. It was quite different from wines supplied to other markets, including the domestic one.

The quality of these wines was not as bad as it is often said to have been. It was neither the best not the worst produced, but an average – literally so, because until the mid-1980s, most winemakers were instructed to blend their best musts with the rest so as to raise the general quality. Dénes Gádor of Balatonboglár explains:

"During the command economy, the emphasis was on quantity, with exports mainly to the USSR and East Germany. However, this emphasis

on quantity did not necessarily mean that the quality was deplorable; winemakers tried to produce clean flavours and healthy wines. The varieties that were most common here in Balatonboglár were Sémillon (which went to the USSR), Muscat (to East Germany), and Olaszrizling. However, temperature-controlled fermentation came into use only in the mid-1980s (before privatization), and then only in a few favoured wineries. Although wines were sold under varietal names, they were frequently made from mixed varieties. In spite of everything, however, winemakers did make grape selection experiments, and in general tried to make decent wines."

Despite what must have been a dull uniformity in the vast majority of wines, it is clear from museum stocks of old wines that a few of high quality were undoubtedly made during the Communist period. They were not, as one might think, produced mainly for the Politburo and top party members, although for some cooperative managers judicious gifts of good wine were undoubtedly a passport to political patronage. The making of these wines was largely dependent on the policies of local cooperative managers, some of whom would reserve musts from the best vineyards expressly for this purpose. These wines served a number of aims, but were usually made for prestige purposes rather than profit. Some were sold in the best hotels and restaurants in Budapest to help create a quality image for Hungarian wine. Others were used to enter international wine competitions, or served at important international receptions, or given as presents to colleagues in the wine sector to show the level of quality their producer was able to achieve.

2

The Market Economy

PRIVATIZATION AND COMPENSATION[1]

One of the first tasks facing the post-Communist authorities was the replacement of the old command economy with one based on a free market. The slow erosion of the command economy through the 1970s and 1980s had obviously helped to lay an informal basis for these changes, but the problems of selling off state-owned companies and assets were nevertheless immense. These were not just problems of devising a machinery for the transfer of assets, but of devising one that would be fair to all citizens. Whatever one may say about the appropriateness of the solution to the former problem, it is impossible not to think that the scheme failed dismally on the second count.

As far as agriculture and winemaking were concerned, the system of transfer was as follows. The assets of state farms were to be sold off, either as a whole (as going concerns) or in part (with, for example, the sale of vineyards), much of this taking place through public auctions. Under the Cooperative Law of 1992, the land assets of cooperatives were to be returned to their original members or their descendants – called "insider members" – in proportion to their original land contribution to the cooperative when it was formed, while other chattels (such as buildings, machinery, and vehicles) were to be inventoried and valued, with each insider member able to withdraw his share of these in cash or kind should he so wish. So-called "outsider members" – ex-employees of cooperatives who had worked for at least five years but

---

[1] A more detailed account can be found in Farkas, Z.: "The Antall Government's Economic Policy", in Gombár et al., pp. 162–177.

who had never contributed land to the cooperative – were included in this inventory and were given a written valuation of their shares, but they were initially frozen (and will have lost their value if, since then, the cooperative has gone bankrupt). Workers on state farms, who (unlike the original members of cooperatives) had not contributed assets towards their establishment, were allocated benefits according to criteria such as the length of time they had worked at a state farm.

Added to this was a scheme to recompense citizens (or their descendants) for real estate that had been nationalized by the state. Land had originally been registered in accordance with property values in 1948, in terms of gold crowns, each nominally worth HUF1,000. Thus, one hectare of good-quality land was valued at around twenty-seven gold crowns, whereas one hectare of poor land had a value of about fifteen. The Compensation Act of 1990, which became effective in 1991, embodied the machinery for implementing this scheme. Vouchers designated in gold crowns were issued in proportion to the 1948 value of the assets, such vouchers being exchangeable (for example, on the stock exchange, or at auction) either for assets of a similar kind, or of quite a different kind. Thus, a wine producer might use vouchers in recompense for his father's furniture business to purchase vineyards. On the other hand, because the vouchers were freely negotiable, if a recipient had no interest in acquiring tangible assets (because he was already a pensioner, for example), he might decide to spend half of them on household furniture, or sell them to the highest bidder.

Initially, vouchers to the value of HUF54 billion were distributed to more than 800,000 people. Later, a second distribution was made equal in value to HUF8.5 billion.[2] Unfortunately, while land values rose steeply, traded compensation vouchers decreased in value, and had depreciated by sixty-five per cent by 1996.

In some cases, where there was not enough land available to satisfy demand, it was sold at above its official valuation, or it was subdivided into smaller lots so that everyone managed to get something. Where there was insufficient competition, it was sold off on a Dutch-auction basis, the valuation being reduced until a buyer was tempted to bid. Auction rings,

[2] See Gombár et al., p. 172.

collusion between the auctioneer and favoured bidders, and various forms of horse-trading were frequent.

Quite apart from the obvious inequalities of distributing actual assets (such as cooperative vineyards) or potential ones (in the form of compensation vouchers) on the basis of property distribution in 1948 – thereby leaving out of account sections of the population that had no claims to lodge – these privatization and compensation schemes were complicated by what had taken place before they were introduced.

In 1988, when the last Communist government withdrew from direct management of the economy, what occurred was tantamount to a breakdown of law and order. Unofficial, highly corrupt privatizations occurred as officials, nicknamed "red barons", took the opportunity provided by economic breakdown to implement various schemes of self-privatization such as management buyouts. Here is how one government official described to me what happened:

"In effect, the managers of state enterprises were able to ensure that they were the beneficiaries of privatization. In some cases, they cynically made their enterprises bankrupt, so as to drive down the price of acquisition. In others, they were able to use party connections to obtain preferential treatment for their purchase bids, while they often had well-established links to banks, which gave them unsecured credit at uncommercially low rates of interest. They bought up compensation vouchers at low rates to gain leverage for their bids to gain control of state organizations."

The government supinely acquiesced in what was happening:

"A [government representative] insisted that, irrespective of evidence of widespread abuses associated with many cases of self-privatization of state enterprises, the process had to continue . . . In doing so, the outgoing regime, in effect, gave the green light to the systematic embezzlement of state assets . . . [and in] deliberately turning a blind eye to the quiet takeover of substantial portions of the country's productive resources by the incumbent captains of industry, banking, and commerce, much of the real power in Hungary remained in the hands of the Kádár regime's economic nomemklatura elite well beyond the 1990 elections."[3]

[3] Tőkés, p. 340.

It all boiled down, in the end, to who you knew – and that mostly meant who in the Party you knew. The Hungarians have a wonderful way of putting it: "To succeed in business and in life, you have to stand close to the fire." Some people emerged from this property feeding frenzy as multimillionaires; others, who did not have the right party connections and were not standing close enough to the fire, emerged with nothing.

THE CONSEQUENCES OF PRIVATIZATION AND COMPENSATION

Almost everyone has reservations about the consequences of privatization. One minister of state told me:

> *"I envisaged the growth of small producers dedicated to quality, and I am dismayed that most of the investment (both foreign and national) has been directed at churning out wine of minimal quality for mass markets."*

Foreign investment was, of course, inevitable, because at the outset of privatization, only a few Hungarians had the capital necessary to start new commercial enterprises. The government encouraged foreign investment in two forms: the setting up of wholly foreign-owned companies, and the formation of joint ventures, partly funded from abroad and partly by Hungarian entrepreneurs. What developed was a raid on Hungarian land, available in 1990 for about a tenth of its value in Germany. Alarmed at the way in which agricultural land was falling into foreign hands – and this included prime vineyard land – in 1993, the government, through the Act on Land, placed an embargo with effect from 1994 on land ownership, apart from housing land, by foreign nationals personally, and by all companies, whether Hungarian or foreign.

As a consequence, only wine firms that had acquired land before the embargo can grow grapes in their own vineyards. Other firms may claim in their publicity material that they farm their own vineyards, but normally they are the personal property of the firm's directors, or they are former state farm vineyards leased from the state. In a few cases, foreign companies appear to have been able to pose as joint ventures, using their Hungarian directors as front-men holding the company's vineyards only nominally.

The various methods of implementing privatization took time and often conflicted with each other, resulting in quite long-term uncertainty about the true ownership of land and property. It took until 1995–6 for these problems to be sorted out, and in the meantime, this resulted in considerable vineyard neglect. People were unwilling to work, let alone invest in, land which they might later find belonged to someone else. The situation was exacerbated by the collapse of the export trade, and because not only the actual but the future profitability of grape-growing was in doubt, there was widespread abandonment of vineyards.

Unfortunately, between 1990 and 1997 the maintenance of proper statistics of land use was in abeyance, so there is no official record of the decline in vineyard areas over this period. Even between 1997 and 2001, returns of land usage often failed to distinguish properly between actual and previous vineyard utilization. Consequently, not only are there no statistics for the first seven years of the 1990s, but subsequent figures are not completely reliable, either. Only the National Vineyard Register currently being compiled will finally give us accurate information. To determine the decline in vineyard area during the first part of the decade, therefore, one is dependent on informed guesswork, and the figures most generally mentioned are in the range of twenty-five to forty per cent, with the Great Plain even worse affected.

Apart from issues arising from land ownership, there have been many other undesirable consequences of cooperative privatization. One of the most obvious of these has been the fragmentation of vineyards designed and planted to be run as an integrated whole. In such cases cooperative members received, say, eight rows of vines on a twenty-hectare plantation as their share of land. Where a cooperative remained a strong one, it tried to reach agreement with its actual or ex-members to tie their vineyards into its production, and to ensure that spraying and other treatments could be carried out professionally and economically by the cooperative on behalf of all the owners. But this has not always been possible, and many vineyards suffer from inefficient, ad hoc spraying and maintenance, and even from partial abandonment. Some owners wish to be independent of their old cooperative. Some people who (perhaps through inheritance) have been allocated a part of a vineyard have not known what to do with it, or have simply abandoned it. Some growers, disillusioned by the poor prices paid for grapes, have walked away from their rows. And, of course, when part of a vineyard is not properly looked after, the rest can only suffer.

History repeats itself. Just as collectivization solved the impracticality of running uneconomic units resulting from the breakup of estates in the late 1940s, the task now is to find a way of stitching broken-up vineyards back together again. Slowly, a certain amount of consolidation is beginning to take place. One helpful related development has been the encouragement by the government of so-called "integration contracts". These are contracts – in principle long-term, but often renewable year by year by the grower – whereby a company offers certain price guarantees to the grower, as well as advice on cultivation and/or the actual carrying out of mechanical and spray treatments, in return for commitments regarding crop volumes, harvesting dates, sugar levels, and so on. It is heartening to report that such contracts work well and appear to be on the increase.

Wine producers who wish to expand their firms, and therefore their vineyards, have to buy small plots on the best vineyard sites as and when they can. It is not at all unusual, therefore, to find that a small producer, who has been in business for about ten years, has built up a holding of some four or five hectares, split into a score of plots scattered over an area spanning a distance of as much as twelve kilometres (seven miles) from end to end. Working such a holding economically and efficiently is well-nigh impossible. Moreover, further consolidation becomes a problem because sellers of strategically placed plots place unrealistically high prices on them.

The situation for the cooperative shorn of its land is just as bad. Most wine-producing cooperatives have become just that. Those members who have chosen to remain members may sell their grapes to the cooperative, but if they can get better prices elsewhere, they may not. The cooperative is then obliged to buy in grapes from other sources to reach viable quantities for the efficient use of its vinification facilities. It may be unable to raise enough money to make such purchases; even if it does, this may lead to cash-flow problems, especially if it has trouble selling its wine. Either way, it is unlikely to make enough profit to embark on the systematic replacement of its outdated facilities. It then finds itself in a vicious circle: no modern equipment equals poor-quality wine;

poor-quality wine equals no buoyant sales; no buoyant sales equals no profits; no profits equals no investment in better technology; no investment in better technology equals inability to increase quality; inability to increase quality equals poor-quality wine; poor-quality wine equals no buoyant sales, and so on. Some cooperatives, as the reader will find out in Part Three of this book, struggle on manfully, and divert wafer-thin profits to whatever modernization they can fund; others have members who take all the profits in dividends, eschew modernization, and seem headed for disaster. More than three-quarters of the cooperatives operating in the 1980s have already disappeared, and only a handful of those that remain are in anything other than an extremely fragile state.

THE ECONOMICS OF MAKING AND SELLING WINE

The economics of making and selling wine are interdependent, but hardly ever as clearly so as in Hungary, where wine production is the art of the economically possible.

It is a matter for amazement how, in the past ten years, many private producers, starting virtually from scratch, have managed to get themselves a reasonable amount of vineyard land and some halfway respectable vinification equipment. For most of them, it has been a hard struggle, and has involved real sacrifices by their families. It has to be said, however, that those who started in the early 1990s were in a much better position than any aspiring winemaker starting today.

Land prices have increased tenfold in as many years, and in the early 1990s there were state incentives on offer, including cheap loans, that are no longer available. Many benefited from compensation vouchers as their families rallied round to get them set up, and those who invested in land in the early 1990s – a once-only golden opportunity – have done well. For the young winemaker starting a career today, however, the situation has changed. Whereas, previously, the state would provide a fifty-percent subsidy towards the planting of new vineyards, this has recently been effectively curtailed to between thirty and forty per cent. In any case, to benefit from any such subsidy, you have to be able to raise the balance of the total cost. Depending on what part of the country you are in, and on what sort of terrain you are planting, it is estimated that the average cost of planting one hectare of vines is around HUF4 million (£9,600) – ranging from HUF2.5 million (£6,000) on the Great Plain to HUF6 million (£14,400) in Eger or Tokaj. That is a vast amount to all but the richest Hungarians, and only large firms or wealthy producers can afford to take advantage of such state subsidies. Interest on bank loans currently runs at between nineteen and twenty-seven per cent per year.

Another factor that has changed in the last ten years is the cost of vineyard and vinification equipment, fuel, and labour in relation to the selling price of wine. Producers make various comparisons to drive the point home: in 1988 you had to sell 200 hectolitres of wine to buy a tractor, but now you have to sell 800; in 1988, the cost of a litre of petrol was the same as that of making a litre of wine, but now it costs as much as making three; at the end of the 1950s, one litre of wine would buy four kilograms of bread, but now it will buy only one. Whatever the accuracy of such comparisons, it is clear that there is an increasing mismatch; as production costs steadily rise, the profitability of making wine steadily drops. This is, for the Union of Hungarian Wine Producers, the most important single issue facing the wine trade today.

Of course, a few privileged producers can command high prices for their wine not only on the export market but on the domestic market, too. There is a small group of relatively affluent people in Budapest and other large cities who provide them with a niche market. Between this group and the rest of the population there is something of an economic gap; there is not yet an extensive middle-class income group. For other producers – growers, cooperatives, and small artisan producers – the profits available are, therefore, wafer-thin. For them, the limiting factor in producing wine is what their customers can afford to pay. We may take as our starting point, therefore, some typical wages. In 2001, the legal minimum wage was HUF40,000 (£96) a month; in 2000, it was HUF30,000 (£72). This would have been earned, for example, by a trainee nurse. In 2000, a manual labourer or a vineyard worker in Mátraalja, for example, earned HUF270 (£0.65) an hour, or about HUF50,000 (£120) a month; a policeman or a schoolteacher would have earned about the same, while a senior bank clerk would have earned about HUF90,000 (£215). This is close to the official government figure for the average monthly earnings of employees across the country in 2000: HUF87,645 gross (£210) and

HUF55,785 net (£134). Without having to go into detailed household and living expenses, it will be immediately obvious (especially when it is remembered that some consumables, such as petrol, are the same price in Hungary as they are in neighbouring Austria) that the average Hungarian lives on a tight domestic budget and has little spare cash to spend on commodities such as wine.

Go into a foreign-owned Hungarian supermarket – the principal large-scale distributive medium of bottled wine in Hungary – and you will find that the cheapest 75cl bottle of the lowest-grade wine (emanating from the Great Plain) will be about HUF270 (£0.65). More than seventy-five per cent of what is on offer will be under HUF600 (£1.44) a bottle. Between HUF600–1,000 (£2.40) the market is almost non-existent. Over HUF1,000 one finds a tiny market; people, it seems, who can afford to pay more than HUF600 a bottle can in fact afford to pay more than HUF1,000, and prefer to do so to obtain what they perceive as incomparably better value.

The price of a bottle of wine includes the cost of the bottle and the label (HUF60–120 (£0.14–0.29) depending on quality), transport and distribution costs, HUF5 per litre duty, and VAT at twenty-five per cent. The cost of bottling is such a crucial factor that it is customary to recycle wine bottles (on a deposit basis), because this saves about HUF40 (£0.10, or between eight and fifteen per cent) on the overall cost to the consumer. However, where possible, well over half of all consumers will buy their wine in bulk (in a plastic container) direct from a local winery, where the lowest price will be around HUF170 (£0.40) a litre. Wine sold to pubs and restaurants (for example, in Sopron) starts at HUF140 (£0.33) per litre for a white wine like Zöld Veltelini, and HUF190 (£0.46) per litre for a red like Kékoportó, and it is generally sold over the counter with a mark-up of one hundred per cent. A better-quality white wine (say, Olaszrizling) can be had for as little as HUF150 (£0.36) in Tolna, while in Pannonhalma, it is sold to restaurants at HUF170 (£0.41), with a red wine such as Kékfrankos costing HUF220 (£0.53). Naturally, these are generalizations: wine costs reflect living standards across the country, with the east being much less affluent than the west.

Grape-growers feel that they are being squeezed out of business. Cooperatives used to provide an assured purchaser at a fair price. Now

that so many cooperatives have disappeared, in many regions the growers
are at the mercy of large national producers who offer such low
prices that, faced with increases in the cost of chemicals, fuel, and
other materials, many are beginning to think there is no worthwhile
profit available to them. In fact, prices for grapes rose in 2000 by
about five per cent for white varieties, and on average around fifteen
per cent for red. In some regions, quality varieties such as Cabernet
Sauvignon showed as much as a forty per cent increase over 1999
prices – a reflection of their scarcity, not of production costs. In general,
the hike in prices reflected the reduction in grape volumes in 2000 compared with the previous year rather than a real, overall profit increase to
the grower.

The following table shows some typical prices.

PRICE PER KILOGRAM TO THE GROWERS IN HUF

	Sopron	Mátraalja	Kunság
Zöld Veltelini	35		
Olaszrizling		38–45	55–65
Rizlingszilváni		65–97	45–55
Hárslevelű		70	
Zweigelt		70–105	35
Kékfrankos	80		70
Cabernet Franc			140
Cabernet Sauvignon	170	120	

Bearing in mind that it takes about 1.3 kilograms of grapes to produce
one litre of wine, it will be clear from the bulk-wine prices quoted
above that the average producer in Hungary, such as a cooperative,
makes very modest profits. In 2000, the cheapest wine made in the
Great Plain cost about HUF90 (£0.21) a litre to produce from grapes
costing HUF35 (£0.08) per kilogram. Added to this would be
HUF28 (£0.07) of administrative costs, leaving a profit of about
HUF20 (£0.05) per litre.

In global terms, here is the balance sheet for a cooperative
(Visontai Mezőgazdasági Szövetkezet) in Mátraalja. Wine makes up two-
thirds of its economic activity, the remaining third consisting of cereal
production, provision of agricultural services, and the operation of retail

shops (including wine shops). The breakdown of the wine sector, producing 25,000 hectolitres a year, is, in broad terms, along the following lines:

Total earnings (HUF)	500,000,000
Disbursements:	
purchase of grapes	200,000,000
running costs	200,000,000
wages and dividends	50,000,000
amortization and interest	20,000,000
development	30,000,000

This cooperative is at the moment in a stable position, because in 1996, with help from the World Bank, it purchased a bottling line for HUF30 million. Before that, it sold all its wine in bulk to Hungarovin. Its directors believe that the extra income generated by selling wine in bottle will keep its head above water. Many cooperatives, however, do not have bottling equipment, and they have to solve their problems differently. This often takes the form of exporting to eastern countries, still a large and important market, except for Russia, where the requirement that Quality Wine has to be two years old now acts as a deterrent. Profit margins are often as low as HUF4 or 5 (around £0.01) per litre. Speaking cruelly, but accurately, of such cooperatives, one eminent wine producer remarked to me: "The people who work there do so not to make money, but just so that they may feel tired when they go home at night."

Many cooperatives, even prosperous ones, have been continuously and adversely affected since the changes in the political system by the incidence of fake wine. Trained chemists assist in its production, and its deceptiveness is steadily improving. The wine is made by using the lees or pressings of real wine, adding water, citric and tartaric acids, colouring compounds, and flavouring agents. This is blended with real wine in the ratio of two parts to three, and is sold to pubs and restaurants in five- or ten-litre containers at HUF120 a litre, thereby undercutting genuine wine and providing publicans with higher profits. Nobody knows how much fake wine is made. Some is imported from Romania, but most is made by apparently reputable producers in the Great Plain, whose legitimate activities mask what they are doing. As an example, one cooperative in the Ászár-Neszmély region believes that it has lost up to fifty per cent of its trade during the last five years because of the circulation of fake wine, and wine community officials in the Kunság region estimate that 40,000 families have had their livelihoods damaged by it.

In 1998, 25,000 hectolitres of fake wine were found in the Kunság region, but so far there has been no prosecution. Government officials have mentioned the names of suspect firms to me, but nothing is done to curb their activities. The truth is that bribery and corruption protect the powerful people behind the production of fake wine, and it remains a time-bomb waiting to damage the entire Hungarian wine trade (as a similar scandal damaged Austria), because Hungarian fake wine has already been detected in the Czech Republic and Austria. It has been claimed that new customs regulations introduced in 2001 will help to eradicate this trade, but few of those damaged by it seem to think so. I know full well that many in the Hungarian wine trade will be dismayed at my giving any publicity whatsoever to this delicate subject. I have decided to do so in the hope that publicity may create the political will to stamp it out before the time-bomb explodes.

Another factor that may undermine the trading position of many cooperatives in the future is a recent government decision to implement the payment to outsider members of their frozen shares of assets. Few cooperatives could meet such claims out of income, and the sale of assets will tip many of them into bankruptcy. In the summer of 2001, the matter was being challenged in the country's constitutional court, and was unresolved at the time this book went to press.

This, then, is the daunting background against which Hungarian winemakers who want to rise above the depressingly low quality level of the industry have to work and from which they have to escape. Shortage of funds is their common enemy. It prevents them from expanding their vineyards, from replanting their vines, from improving their vinification equipment and, worst of all, constrains customer choice to the extent that, unless they strike it lucky, there is no point in making better-quality wine that almost nobody can afford to buy. Yet, as Part Three of this book will show, many winemakers are facing up to this challenge, and despite the obstacles, slowly, slowly some of them are beginning to win the battle.

part II

The Hungarian Wine Culture

3

Structures and Knowledge

REGIONS

Hungary is divided into twenty-two wine regions. These regions are legally defined by the parishes noted for wine production that are included in them. For most of the twentieth century there were only fourteen delimited regions, but the number has grown in recent years, mainly through the sub-division of larger ones. Many believe that there are now too many regions, and that some amalgamation – for example, of those on the north shore of Lake Balaton – should take place. Most of these regions give recognition to wine-producing areas that have had a long and celebrated history. Fifteen of them are in Transdanubia – that is, the area south and west of the River Danube. The other seven are in the part of the country east of the River Danube and (apart from a small part of the Kunság region) to the west of the River Tisza. The regions vary greatly in size. In terms of vineyard area, excluding household plots, Somló is the smallest, and Kunság – more than eight times its size – is the largest. The larger wine regions contain districts and sub-districts.

WINE COMMUNITIES

A system of local regulation that developed after 1271 endured until its abolition by the Communist regime in 1949, but has recently been revived. Then as now, if we exclude the Great Plain, which did not enter the picture at this time, the main wine-producing areas of Hungary were all situated in hilly parts of the country. In each of these the vine-growers formed a group, somewhat like a guild, called a *hegyközség*: literally, a mountain community. Nowadays, to avoid the slightly quaint suggestion of alpine dwellers, this is generally translated as "wine community". They were, for their time, surprisingly democratic organizations, and each wine community was administered by a freely elected "hill judge". Gradually, through them there evolved purely local systems of regulation for the selling of vineyards, fixing the date of the harvest, the conditions for the marketing of wine, and the settlement of disputes. The powers of these communities were often explicitly recognized and supplemented by the crown.

Largely as a response to the havoc created by phylloxera at the end of the nineteenth century, a national wine law was enacted in 1893, and this not only recognized the wine communities, but gave them a national legal framework within which to operate. The system functioned well until the politico-bureaucratic control system of the Communists made it redundant. Act No 102 of 1994, however, reinstated wine communities, and was based on their historical precedents (and even on living memory of how the system had operated in the past).

The new system is arranged as a pyramid. At the bottom (the local level), there are currently 321 autonomous wine communities. Membership of a wine community is compulsory within each wine region for grape-growers owning a vineyard of 0.05 hectare or larger, for wine producers, and for wine merchants. Each wine community covers a vineyard area of at least fifty hectares. The members make up the general assembly of the community, and they elect a committee and a president. The second level of the pyramid is composed of regional councils of wine communities – one for each of the twenty-two regions – organized in a similar way. Each has a general assembly consisting of the presidents of, and a number of delegates from, the wine communities within the region, and each elects its own committee, president, and secretary. At the top of the pyramid is the *Hegyközségek Nemzeti Tanácsa* (National Council of Wine Communities). This meets three times a year, and consists of the twenty-two presidents of the regional councils and twenty-two delegates, from which a president, a vice-president, and various committees are elected. Its secretary-general is an employee.

The duties of the wine communities and their councils are broadly twofold. Some are legal (for which the government provides funding), while the others concern members' interests (and are funded out of locally determined membership fees). The main legal functions of the system, all carried out at local level, are to collect data about grape and wine production, to issue certificates of origin (legally necessary for selling grapes for wine production), to participate in the licensing of wineries, to issue permits for planting or grubbing up vineyards, and to ensure compliance of members with the law. The more general issues dealt with include protecting and representing common interests, providing technical information, services and advice, formulating local rules about quality and limitation of yield, overseeing specific plant protection or training methods, and (in a few cases only) setting minimum prices for grapes. The wine communities also provide a forum for the discussion of issues relevant to their members.

The national council performs a mainly consultative and co-ordinating function, and has no legal coercive powers over the lower communities. It acts as the government's partner in all questions regarding grape production and wine, and transmits information and opinions between government and local communities in both directions. Opinions vary about the efficiency with which the system works. On the whole, growers seem satisfied, although one hears a few grumbles. Criticisms by growers seem to be directed more towards government policy than towards the wine-community system.

LEGAL REGULATION

As mentioned above, the first national wine law was promulgated in 1893. During the course of the next half-century it was revised and supplemented from time to time, but suffered no fundamental alternation until it was summarily abolished in 1949. Various laws were made during the Communist period, the most significant being Act No 36 of 1970 on Grape and Fruit Production and Wine Management, which, with subsequent amendments, was repromulgated on September 15, 1994. Act No 121 of 1997 on Grape Cultivation and Wine Management has now replaced all but Sections 1–3 of the 1970 Act, but has itself been modified by Acts Nos 99, 111, and 142 of 2000. The Minister of Agriculture is permitted to supplement the wine law by issuing periodic decrees. Mandatory provisions regarding the production, marketing, use, and analysis of wine are contained in a publication called *A Magyar Borkönyv* (*The Hungarian Wine Book*). There is space here only to indicate the most important of its provisions. In general, we may say that the 1994 law was based on a fusion of elements in German and French wine law, and that recent changes have been intended to harmonize Hungarian laws with European Union norms.

Vineyards. For the purposes of legal regulation, only vineyards with an area of 0.05 hectare (500 square metres/5,380 square feet) or more are considered, smaller ones being regarded as household vineyards. (The area of a household vineyard was briefly increased to 1,500 square metres/16,140 square feet under Act 99 of 2000, but has since reverted to its original 500 square metres.) In a wine region, the vineyard area must cover at least seven per cent of the total agricultural land. Besides regions, there are wine-producing areas – over thirty of them, scattered over eight of Hungary's nineteen administrative counties – in which vineyards occupy less than seven per cent of agricultural land. Vineyards are assessed in terms of quality as Class I, II (i), or II (ii). A total of 400 points is awarded across eighteen different factors, such as type of soil, exposure, altitude, slope and so on. Since January 1, 2000, vineyards with American direct producers are not permitted. Permission for planting new commercial vineyards is subject to conditions such as survey, consent of all competent authorities, and use of permitted propagation material. Subsidies to establish new plantations depend on more stringent criteria, including propagation of recommended varieties only. Cultivation and the planting of vineyards must be in accordance with the regulations laid down by OMMI (*Országos Mezőgazdasági Minősítő Intézet*), the National Institute for Agricultural Quality Control, and overseen by the competent wine community. Grapes intended for winemaking must have a certificate of origin issued by the local wine community.

Wine. Wine comprises the following six categories: (1) Table Wine (wine made from must with a minimum natural sugar content of 13MM°;[1] (2) Country Wine (wine from a specified [non-appellation] wine-producing area, made from authorized varieties, with a minimum natural sugar content of 15MM°); (3) Quality Wine (wine from a delimited [appellation] region, made from authorized varieties harvested at not more than one hundred hectolitres per hectare, with a minimum natural

[1] See Appendix I under "Measurement of Sugar".

sugar content of 15MM°, and possessing the organoleptic characteristics of the region and variety); (4) Superior Quality Wine (wine from a delimited region or wine producing area, made from ripe, overripe, shrivelled or botrytized grapes harvested at not more than seventy-five hectolitres per hectare, with a minimum natural sugar content of 19MM°, possessing the organoleptic characteristics of the region, variety, and winemaking techniques employed, and "deserving high distinction on account of its place of origin and vintage"; (5) Wine of Protected Origin (Quality or Superior Quality Wine, as defined above, where the the region or area of origin has been granted protected status); (6) Museum Wine (Quality or Superior Quality Wine, aged for a minimum of five years in bottle, worthy of distinction due to a specific feature). With regard to the second category (Country Wine), this may reach the standard of Quality Wine but, because it is not from a delimited region, can only be sold as Country Wine.

The natural sugar content of must, when it is less than 19MM°, can be raised (by adding beet or cane sugar, or enriched or concentrated must) by up to 3MM°, or up to 19.5MM°, provided that this does not increase the total alcoholic strength of the wine by more than two per cent by volume. Sweetening a must cannot alter the quality category of the resulting wine. Except in the case of Superior Quality Wine, the acid content of either must or wine may be raised, by decision of the wine community, by the addition either of 2.5 grams per litre to the former or 1.5 grams per litre to the latter, but not to both. The blending of white, red, rozé (rosé), or siller (see Glossary), or of different types of sparkling wine, with each other is not permitted.

Superior Quality Wine must correspond one hundred per cent to the origin, variety, quality, and vintage claimed for it. Quality Wine must correspond eighty-five per cent to the variety and vintage, and one hundred per cent to the origin and quality claimed for it. Other still wines require a seventy-per-cent correspondence to the origin, variety, quality, and vintage claimed for them. In the case of sparkling wine, a reference to a vineyard site or variety is permissible if a minimum of eighty-five per cent of the base wine derives from the site or variety.

Quality control. Containers used for storing wine must be unambiguously marked to identify their contents, and cellar documentation must correspond. The act lays down the permitted types of container for use in selling wine, and the information to be given on labels. When wines are blends, all the varieties must be printed on the label in the order of greatest to least volume. Bikavér, apart from within the region of production, must be sold in bottles. Some regions (such as Tokaj-Hegyalja) producing Superior Quality Wines are considered as closed regions and are subject to rules concerning the circulation of must and wine within the region. Specifically, to protect the reputation of such wines, the grapes from the region (unmixed with those from any other region) must be made into wine, and that wine must be matured, in the region.

On August 1, 2000, a consumption tax of eleven per cent of the sales price of wine (payable by the consumer at time of purchase) was replaced by a flat-rate excise duty of HUF5 per litre (payable by the producer at time of bottling), while VAT on the sale price of wine was maintained at twenty-five per cent. On the same date, a complex system of cellar accountability, operated by VPOP (*Vám és Pénzügyminisztérium Országos Parancsnoksága*), the National Customs Authority, came into force. It is similar to those used elsewhere in Europe to enable stringent checks to be carried out on the origin, storage, and eventual disposal of the contents of producers' cellars.

GOVERNMENTAL AND NON-GOVERNMENTAL AGENCIES

Grape-growing and winemaking are regulated by acts of Parliament, which it is the responsibility of the FVM (*Földművelésügyi és Vidékfejlesztési Minisztérium*; Ministry of Agriculture and Regional Development), to implement in conjunction with other governmental departments such as the *Pénzügyminisztérium* (Ministry of Finance), through its *Adó és Jövedéki Főosztály* (Tax and Fiscal Department) and VPOP (National Customs Authority). The FVM, under a minister of state (a politician) who is assisted by two state secretaries (civil servants), administers the following departments (among others): (1) the *Mezőgazdsági Főosztály* (Department of Agriculture), which controls the OMMI (*Országos Mezőgazdasági Minősítő Intézet*; National Institute for Agricultural Quality Control); (2) the *Állategészségügyi és Élelmiszerellenőrzési Főosztály* (Department of Animal Health and Food Control), which controls the OBI (*Országos Borminősítő Intézet*; National Wine Qualification Institute); (3) the *Jogszabályelőkészítő Főosztály* (Department of the Preparation of Acts), which drafts acts and ministerial decrees; and (4) the *Jogi Főosztály* (Department of Law), which provides legal supervision of the system of wine communities.

We may particularly note two agencies that are easy to confuse: OBI and OBB. OBI, mentioned in the previous paragraph, is responsible for the maintenance of general quality standards, supervising technical standards of production, and labelling. It also oversees imported wine. All Hungarian wine intended for the market has to be submitted to OBI for laboratory analysis to ensure that it conforms to legal standards. Certificates of origin of the grapes and of the wine (obtainable from the producer's local wine community) have to be submitted at the same time; if all is in order, OBI issues a commercial distribution permit.

OBB, on the other hand, stands for *Országos Borminősosítő Bizottség* (National Wine Qualification Board). It is the body that authorizes wines of superior quality (signified by a special neck label). Tokaji Aszú and Bikavér can only be sold if they have qualified as Superior Quality Wines. Other wines are submitted voluntarily by their producers to OBB if they wish to sell them in this higher category.

Several other government agencies impinge, more or less directly, on the wine trade. The *Állami Privatizácós és Vagyonkezelö* (Hungarian Privatization and State Holding Company) results from the amalgamation of two organizations in 1995. It answers to the prime minister's office and, at the moment, administers twenty-seven former state farms. Eight of these, of which Tokaj Kereskedőház is the only one concerned with wine, are earmarked for long-term state ownership (although this will be reviewed in 2003). The only other wine company it controls is Komáromi MG, which is at present for sale.

An agency that has been of some importance in the past is the *Ágrár Intervenciós Központ* (Agricultural Intervention Centre). Distillation of surplus grape crops was aided between 1998 and 2000, with a minimum price for grapes being fixed by decree. The extent of the intervention was that, out of 4 million hectolitres produced, 200,000 hectolitres (five per cent) were distilled. The government had the intention of discontinuing such intervention on the grounds that Hungary is now under a full market regime. However, in 2000 the government made separate intervention arrangements in Tokaj-Hegyalja, and when it did the same thing again in 2001, this caused such a howl of protest from the trade that it was induced to promise HUF2 billion to the rest of the wine industry for distillation and the production of concentrated must.

An important department in the Ministry of Agriculture is the *Európai Integrációs Főosztály*: (Department for European Integration). Hungary declared its wish to join the EU in 1996. In the wine sector, after similarities and differences between Hungarian and EU law had been identified, a Harmonization Working Group on Wine was set up in 1998. Chaired by the minister of agriculture, it works conjointly with similar groups with shared interests (e.g., food safety, genetics). The entry negotiations, still incomplete as this book goes to press, have been beset with problems. Delay by the EU in implementing regulations proposed in its Wine Law 1493 of 1999 left the group unclear about precisely what it had to respond to, and the EU initially rejected many requests on Hungary's wish list for exceptional exemption from EU standards, especially as regards Tokaji. Other thorny issues, not entirely resolved, include the following: ownership of agricultural land (Hungary wants a continued limitation on land purchase – particularly by foreigners – and on leasing for ten years after accession to the EU); the compulsory distillation of *marc*[2] (Hungary does not have the capacity to meet EU standards); and parity of EU subsidies to farmers (although those available to the wine sector will not be discriminatory). Currently the relation between Hungary and the EU regarding wine and spirits is regulated by Council Regulation (EC) No 678/2001 of February 26, 2001. Hungary's original objective was to become a full member of the EU on January 1, 2003, but delays caused by Ireland's initial rejection of EU enlargement, uncertainty about reform of the Common Agricultural Policy, and disagreement about how enlargement is to be funded mean that accession cannot now take place before 2004.

PROMOTIONAL ORGANIZATIONS

A number of organizations exist either to promote the interests of different sectors of the wine industry, or to advance the cause of Hungarian wine in general. The *Magyar Borgazdaság Szövetsége* (Union of

---

[2] The name refers to grape skins left after pressing and also the strong-smelling brandy that is made from them.

Hungarian Wine Producers), started in 1988. It has 120 members, representing eighty per cent of the largest winemakers in the country – all big companies – and it lobbies the government on matters of concern to its members. According to its president, "It does a lot of work but without a lot of success." It maintains links with similar organizations in other wine-producing countries.

A *Pannon Bormíves Céh*, (Guild of Pannonian Wines), was established in 1999 with ten founder members. Its object is to promote the national wine heritage, to raise the quality level of regional wines, and to elaborate an ethical code of wine production. The guild, now with eighteen members, includes winemakers in five regions, with one sub-guild in Eger and four others planned.

In the heady days of 1992, the *Magyar Borakadémia* (Hungarian Academy of Wine) was founded by a group of intellectuals, academics, journalists, artists, and cultural figures as an entirely civil organization to re-establish and promote the reputation of Hungarian wine. With ninety-nine members representing all aspects of professional life, it organizes various forms of wine publicity, provides wine courses, and formulates opinions on wine-policy matters. It also provides moderators in regional and national wine competitions and, since 1992, has sponsored the nomination (after a vote) of the Hungarian Winemaker of the Year. Its first women members were elected in October 2001. However, women wine-lovers (mainly from the catering and wine trades) have already organized their own *Első Magyar Borbarát Hölgyek Egyesülete* (Women's Association of Friends of Wine), which has branches in different towns in Hungary.

Producers' wine guilds and brotherhoods, all of recent foundation, are part of the image of many regions and wine areas. At the moment there are twenty-four such organizations, coordinated by a central association that liaises with similar bodies abroad.

EDUCATION

Education in horticulture and winemaking occurs at school, college, and university level. In addition, a few commercial organizations offer courses on wine appreciation and professional (sommelier) training. Children enter secondary school, having completed eight years of primary education, without any qualifying examination. Secondary education normally lasts for four years and usually includes an element of vocational training, which may be winemaking. The aim is to qualify children to undertake a post-secondary technological college course of three years, should they wish to do so. Particularly noteworthy is the *Soós István Élelmiszeripari Szakközépiskola* (István Soós Food Industry Vocational School), in Budafok. Founded in 1901, it provides a secondary education followed by a two-year vinicultural course, and is supported financially by the wine industry. It has 150 pupils (of whom forty-five are girls) and twenty teachers, so classes are small; it also has its own vineyard, and a modern winery and cellar built in 1995–6, so well-equipped that it must be the envy of a number of Hungarian producers. Many currently famous winemakers were educated here, and their children often follow in their fathers' footsteps.

University courses last for five years. The main vini- and viticultural university is now the *Szent István Egyetem* (Szent István University) of Gödöllő. Until 1999, there were two universities covering the wine sector: the Agricultural University of Gödöllő and the Horticultural University of Budapest. The latter had three faculties: horticultural engineering, landscape design, and food science. However, as part of a hotly disputed move by the government to integrate certain institutions of higher education to create larger, American-type universities with many faculties, these two formerly independent universities have now merged, and we have the Szent István University of Gödöllő with a faculty of horticulture in Budapest.

Similar amalgamations have affected previously independent centres of higher education in other parts of the country. Thus, Keszthely's Georgikon Faculty of Agriculture (which produces agronomists) is now linked to the University of Veszprém, and the Horticultural College at Kecskemét has become a faculty of Kecskemét University College. The Szent István University of Gödöllő has also absorbed the Faculty of Horticulture of Gyöngyös University. The Agricultural College at Kaposvár, however, remains independent.

The Georgikon Faculty of Agriculture at Keszthely requires separate mention. György Festetics founded the Georgikon at Keszthely in 1797. It was Europe's first higher-educational institution of agriculture, and besides undertaking teaching and research into plant breeding, animal husbandry, and viticulture, it also offered practical training courses. An experimental station, which still exists, was established at neighbouring Cserszegtomaj. The Pannon University of Agricultural Sciences is the direct descendant of the Georgikon; The Georgikon faculty of agriculture was founded in 1949 by Dr Károly Bakonyi, the propagator of Cserszegi Fűszeres (see page 58), and its link to the Georgikon is perpetuated in its name.

Courses on wine are provided by the *Magyar Borok Háza* (House of Hungarian Wine), in Budapest, and the *Borkollégium* (College of Wine). The first of these is discussed in Chapter Seven. The second, founded and run by Gabor Rohály and his wife Gabriella Mészáros, offers both general and specialized courses on wine, and publishes *Rohály's Wine Guide Hungary*, an annual publication (in Hungarian, German, and English) that provides tasting notes and other information on wines currently on the Hungarian market – although, in my opinion, its assessments are insufficiently rigorous. *Birtokok és Borok Magyarországon* (*Estates and Wines of Hungary*), a rival guide published by Borbarát (see below), first appeared in November 2001, with a future English version planned.

Hungary has several wine periodicals. *Borbarát* (*Friends of Wine*) is a well-established quarterly, published in Hungarian and English, and therefore the most accessible way for foreigners to keep themselves abreast of developments on the Hungarian wine scene. Its only real rival is a new bimonthly journal, *Bor és Piac* (*Wine and the Market*), which first appeared (in Hungarian only) in 2001. More of a newsletter than a periodical providing in-depth coverage, *Bor és Világ* (*Wine and the World*) appears bimonthly in Hungarian, covering wine in all its aspects (gastronomy, tourism, etc). The Union of Hungarian Wine Producers has its own house journal, *Magyar Szőlő- és Borgazdaság* (*Grape and Wine Production*).

RESEARCH

The Ampelographical Institute established in Buda in 1896 was the first wine and vine research unit independent of university patronage to be founded anywhere in the world. It was started in order to replant the wine regions after phylloxera, and dealt first with plant propagation and protection. Later, it broadened its interests to cover a wider range of oenological and viticultural topics, such as varietal selection, breeding, and plant physiology. During the twentieth century, the Institute had a good network of field stations in Eger, Tarcal, Kecskemét, Badacsony, Mór, and Pécs. The basic laboratory research, however, was done in Budapest. This set-up survived until 1978, when it was decided to move the headquarters of the Institute to Kecskemét. By this time, urban development had displaced grape-growing in Buda, whereas Alföld (the Great Plain) had become a mass-production area, and this may be why it was preferred. In 1982, the institute was linked to the Horticultural University of Budapest, and the remaining stations were linked to larger firms (such as Egervin and Pannonvin) with the intention of offering a less academic and more practical type of help to producers. It was a strategy that failed, and this linkage ended in 1991, when the stations became independent research institutes. Kecskemét became independent of the university in 1994.

Three research institutes, each with state funding and independent research programmes, survive in Kecskemét, Pécs, and Eger. Mór disappeared in the 1960s; Badacsony has become an eighteen-hectare field station of the Pécs institute. The Tarcal station still exists with a staff of four, but is virtually dormant because the Tokaj Kereskedőház, which controls it, has insufficient funds to run it properly. Kecskemét retains a certain coordinating role to avoid duplication of effort.

The institutes are chronically underfunded, and research workers at Eger (for example) are paid only the minimum legal wage. Eger and Pécs produce and sell wine in order to supplement their budgets – a distraction from their proper research role – while Kecskemét undertakes activities over and above its research role in the form of self-funded national and international projects. Research reflects both local interests (such as determination of clones and rootstocks best suited to local conditions) and national interests. All have joint research projects with other national and international bodies, both academic and commercial.

Research at Kecskemét covers grape breeding, clonal selection, virus freedom, plant protection, *in vitro* fertilization, agro-agricultural problems, wine chemistry and biology, and export market conditions. In 2001, the institute was also given the task of compiling Hungary's new vineyard register. Pécs carries out research on clonal selection, interspecific varieties, regional varieties, rootstock affinity, training methods and pruning for hillside grape production, and soil fertility. A very important part of the institute's work is the maintenance of its grape-gene bank, which contains 1,112 varieties. At Eger, research topics include grape breeding and physiology, production technology, experimental wine-making technology, barrel-ageing, and *terroirs* in relation to protection of origin.

In 1971, the Hungarian Academy of Sciences created five regional units covering the nineteen administrative counties in Hungary. These are situated in Pécs, Veszprém, Miskolc, Debrecen, and Szeged, and their role is to coordinate and enhance scientific research in the regions, and to ensure that the results of academic research filter down to the most basic levels of economic activity.

TRADITION

The proper understanding of Hungarian wine culture requires an insight into matters less tangible than laws and research institutes. Wine is in the soul of many Hungarians. It has, for some, an almost sacramental quality. Indeed, when tasting one day, I asked, because I was driving, if I might spit out the samples I was being offered. "Wine," came the reply, "is the blood of God, and to spit it out is sacrilege." And, indeed, wine is used to seal contracts and to accompany solemn events in family life. In some parts of the country, having your own little plot of vines is a matter of self-respect. You are hardly part of things without one, and people arriving from other parts of Hungary (even from towns), who have had no previous experience of grape-growing or winemaking, often acquire a plot as a badge of citizenship and an *entrée* to their new community.

Much of this can be guessed from the large numbers of private cellars to be seen around the country. A legacy of the Austro-Hungarian Empire, similar cellars can be found in Austria and Moravia. They are often arranged in rows, tucked into a rock face or hillside, but they can also be found as a street in the centre of a town, having once been on the fringes before urban growth swallowed them up. In villages, they can exist in parallel streets, or banked up on a hillside, row behind row. Hajós and Nemesnádudvar are famous wine villages, the latter with 800 cellars and no houses for living in. Palkonya, in the Villány region, originally had sixty-three cellars, stacked up in seven rows – although, unfortunately, the top rows are now incomplete.

These traditional cellars, which in some regions are also situated in the middle of vineyards, are built with a press-house at ground level, either with the cellar as an inner sanctum built into the hill on the same level, or with a trapdoor with steps leading down to a cellar underneath the press-house. Sometimes, under a steep, inverted-V roof, one or more small rooms over the press-house provide basic accommodation for the family during the harvest. Some press-houses boast elaborately decorated wooden doors, and are adorned with alpine fretwork boarding and verandahs. If, as you wander around, you see an open cellar door with a wine container standing on a box or chair, this indicates that the cellar is open for business, and you will be welcome to taste the wines.

Competitiveness among winemakers has become an important and healthy tradition of local winemaking within the last ten years. Wine competitions are organized at wine community level, as well as at regional and national levels, and top wine producers increasingly enter their wines in international competitions. Winning a gold, silver or bronze medal is a matter not only of personal pride, but sometimes also of commercial significance. To have listed the many awards won by producers mentioned in this book would have left little space for anything else, so prolific have been their successes. Sadly, these medals seldom have significance to the world at large, and local wine shows are usually very provincial affairs; many of the wines are of an abysmal quality, and such competitions are usually more revelatory of how low general standards are than evidence of real achievement. But they do have an important role to play, particularly in newly recognized wine regions. Where economic incentives to improve quality are completely lacking, recognition by one's peers becomes a powerful motive towards improvement.

Finally – and sadly, because it continues to have a baleful influence on so much Hungarian winemaking – mention must be made of the Hungarian palate. Wine tastes are generally not at all sophisticated, and much wine is simply a vehicle for the alcohol it contains, as the small, dumpy glass usually used for drinking and tasting (filled to the brim) rather suggests. Your glass of wine is likely to be accompanied by a plate of pogácsák (small cheese scones).

Hungary is full of borozók (wine houses), as well as sörözők (beer bars). These are not pubs, but drinking dens of a fairly basic kind. The wine served in a wine house will usually be of very low quality, never out of a glass bottle, and all too often fake. The popular taste is for semi-sweet wines, so this is the style in which most wine for the home market is produced. I have a theory about why this is so, one which many Hungarians are apt to confirm, which is that during the Communist period, and possibly before, many winemaking faults were disguised by sweetening wine to make it more palatable.

Another very popular taste is for drinking *fröccsök* (spritzers), white wine to which an equal amount of carbonated water has been added. Fairly acidic wine is needed for this, otherwise the addition of the water makes for total blandness, and this fashion means that over-acidic wine finds a ready market. In fact, this appears to be a long-standing tradition, spritzers having become a substitute for beer in the nineteenth century as a widespread reaction to the custom (I have been told) of Austrian army officers swigging beer while overseeing the executions of Hungarian patriots. Like Italian coffee, spritzers appear in various forms. A *kisfröccs* (small spritzer) consists of a decilitre each of wine and carbonated water; a *nagyfröccs* (big spritzer) is two decilitres of wine to one of carbonated water; and a *hosszúlépés* ("long step") is one decilitre of wine to two of carbonated water.

4

Viticulture and Viniculture

SOIL

Soil types are indicated in more detail in the sections dealing with each region. In general, we may say that virtually all types of soil can be found somewhere in Hungary. Sandy soils typify the Great Plain; volcanic soil is found in the north of the country, particularly north of Lake Balaton, and in areas like Eger and Tokaj-Hegyalja. Loess, gravelly clay, and brown forest soil (an alkaline soil formed under forest vegetation containing humus and clay) are found all round the country, and chalky soil is also common, as is tufa.[1]

GRAPE VARIETIES

Hungary has a truly astonishing range of grape varieties in its vineyards. The National Council of Wine Communities records ninety-three varieties of which there are ten or more hectares to be found. Most of their names are completely unfamiliar even to knowledgeable westerners, and there is no possibility of doing them justice here. I confine myself to commenting only on those most commonly met with and the wines they make.[2]

There are between twenty and thirty varieties in most medium-sized wine regions, with fifteen to twenty varieties in small ones, and up to forty in Kunság. In general, there are too many (frankly nondescript)

[1] More detailed information about the geology and soil types of Hungary can be found in Rohály, *passim*.

[2] There is no space, alas, for detailed ampelographical discussion of them. For more detailed consideration of those varieties also found in Austria, the reader is referred to Blom, pp. 41–58.

varieties in Hungary, and this is unlikely to change in the medium term. Without money to replant, producers make do with what is available, and regions are expanding their lists of authorized varieties to capture as much of the market as possible. For example, in Mátraalja in 1977, there were five recommended varieties and seven permitted varieties. In 1994, the recommended varieties remained at five, while the number of permitted varieties had grown to nine. By 1997, however, there were ten recommended varieties, and an astonishing fifteen permitted varieties – a doubling of the total number of varieties within twenty years.

Although some "western" grape varieties such as Szürkebarát (Pinot Gris), Cabernet Sauvignon, and Pinot Noir were to be found in Hungary before the Second World War, by a very long way most of the varieties grown until about twenty-five years ago were Austrian, Transylvanian, Balkan or native Hungarian. The most widely planted red variety until after the war, for example, was Kadarka, a Hungarian variety seldom heard of in the west. Even today, in spite of the impetus given by export demand for planting western varieties like Chardonnay and Merlot, it is still true that traditional varieties account for considerably more than half of total grape production. Kékfrankos (9.1 per cent) is the most widely planted of all varieties, with Olaszrizling (8.8 per cent) the leading white variety. Of the red varieties, Zweigelt (three per cent) and Kékoportó (1.7 per cent) outstrip Cabernet Sauvignon (1.4 per cent). Similarly, with the white varieties, we have Furmint (4.6 per cent), Rizlingszilváni (Müller Thurgau: 4.4 per cent), Ezerjó (4.2 per cent), and Zalagyöngye (four per cent) before we get to Chardonnay (3.9 per cent). The top eight varieties account for 39.8 per cent of the total planted area.

The *Vitis vinifera* grape varieties met with in Hungary may conveniently be considered under four groupings. First, there are those ubiquitous varieties commonly found in most areas of the wine-producing world which are known by the same names in Hungary as elsewhere. Of these we have, as white varieties, Chardonnay, Sauvignon Blanc, Pinot Blanc, Chasselas, Vognier, Favorita, Muscadelle and Sémillon; and as red varieties, Cabernet Sauvignon, Cabernet Franc, Merlot, Cinsaut, Syrah and Pinot Noir.

Secondly, there are those varieties that are almost as ubiquitous, but which hide their identities under Hungarian names. Among these we have the following:

Hungarian name	More usual name
White varieties	
Olaszrizling	Welschriesling
Ottonel Muskotály	Muscat Ottonel
Rajnai Rizling	Rhine Riesling
Rizlingszilváni	Müller-Thurgau
Sárga Muskotály	Muscat de Lunel or Yellow Muscat
Szürkebarát	Pinot Gris
Tramini	Gewürztraminer
Zöld Szilváni	Sylvaner
Zöld Veltelini	Grüner Veltliner
Red varieties	
Kékfrankos	Blaufränkisch or Blauer Limberger
Kékoportó	Blauer Portugieser

These varieties will be referred to by their Hungarian names in this book.

Thirdly, there are those varieties that are less well-known to the world at large but are relatively common in neighbouring Austria, Transylvania, and the Balkans, although some of them also have purely Hungarian variants of their names. I call these, purely for convenience, "eastern" varieties. Some, like Ezerjó, Kéknyelű, Kövidinka, and Hárslevelű, appear to be of purely Hungarian ("Hungaricum") origin. Some of these also have German names, but their English translation is probably more interesting (and amusing) to English readers:

Hungarian name	English translation
White varieties	
Aranysárfehér	Golden Muddy White
Budaizöld	Green Buda
Cirfandli	
Csabagyöngye	Csaba's Pearl
Ezerjó	Thousand Good Things
Furmint	
Gohér	
Hárslevelű	Linden Leaf

	Hungarian name	English translation
White varieties contd.		
	Juhfark	Sheep's Tail
	Kéknyelű	Blue Stem
	Kövérszőlő	Fat Grape
	Kövidinka	
	Kunleány	Girl from Kunság
	Leányka	Maiden
Red varieties		
	Kadarka	

Lastly, there are crosses, both natural and cultivated, to be considered. Many of those most frequently met with have been developed in Hungary itself. The following list shows their immediate parentage, although many of the parents are themselves crosses.

Blauburger	Kékfrankos x Kékoportó
Corvinus	Olaszrizling x Ezerjó
Cserszegi Fűszeres	Irsai Olivér x Tramini
Irsai Olivér	Pozsonyi Fehér x Csabagyöngye
Királyleányka	Köverszőlő x Leányka
Koróna	Juhfark x Irsai Olivér
Magyar Rizling	Olaszrizling x Ezerjó
Medina	Seyve-Villard x Kékmedoc
Nektár	Judit x Cserszegi Fűszeres
Pátria	Olaszrizling x Tramini
Rozália	Olaszrizling x Tramini
Valentin	Nektár x Zenit
Zeusz	Ezerjó x Bouvier
Zenit	Ezerjó x Bouvier
Zéta (Oremus)	Ezerjó x Furmint
Zweigelt	Kékfrankos x St-Laurent

Surveying these four groups, I offer brief comments on some of the varieties and their potential for making high-quality wine in Hungary. In the first group, we have "western" varieties. Chardonnay made its first modern appearance in Hungary in 1961, although it was already known in the nineteenth century under the name of *Kereklevelu"* ("Round Leaf").

It is planted more for its export potential than because it is particularly suited to growing conditions in any part of Hungary, except perhaps Etyek. Even the best that is produced, with few exceptions, only competes with run-of-the-mill Chardonnays from the New World. Sauvignon Blanc is, for most producers, a non-starter because, even with reductive vinification, they mostly fail to capture the gooseberry/herbaceous character of the variety. Pinot Blanc, however, appears to do well, giving round, flavourful wines (although, unfortunately, they are hard to find), while Sémillon is now so uncommon it does not really have a track record at all.

As for red varieties, my firm conviction is that Cabernet Franc is the one that appears to offer the highest potential when planted on suitable sites and well-vinified. Sadly, ninety per cent of all Cabernet Sauvignon grown in Hungary comes from clones from the Eger Research Institute. All too often, the wine it produces is green and harsh, although growers will swear that they picked the grapes when they were ripe. The problem lies not entirely with the climate, but with what Tamás Dúzsi has aptly christened "cash-shortage disease" – that is, premature harvesting. September is a warm month, and soils are often very rich, so sugar levels increase quite quickly to adequate or high levels before the grapes have reached phenolic maturity and the tannins have properly ripened. Cabernet Sauvignon seems to be fully at home only in Villány (and possibly on the Tihany Peninsula), and there are many among researchers and producers who believe it will never give first-rate results elsewhere in the country. I incline to the same opinion.

Merlot is sometimes called the "queen of wines" in Hungary. It is almost always disappointing, indeed wishy-washy, lacking the characteristics of Merlot from France and the New World. I believe that, until recently, most of the clones planted came from the Veneto, and wise producers now seek new planting material from France. Pinot Noir was not uncommon in Hungary before the war, but established plantings are of clones used during the Communist period for the production of sparkling wine, and they are not suitable for making wine of high-quality. Recent plantings, just beginning to mature, have used planting material from France. For example, Tibor Gál (in Eger) has planted eight different clones across five different rootstocks. I think the jury is still out on whether or not Pinot Noir will have a successful future in Hungary, but first vinifications have been quite promising.

In the second group, Olaszrizling and Szürkebarát are relatively late-ripening varieties, capable of making really good and sometimes exciting wines showing more power than finesse. All depends on the quality of the grapes and the technology used to vinify them. Both varieties seem to respond well to barrique maturation. Rizlingszilváni, early ripening and very prone to rot, makes low-quality wines that, in my opinion, are fundamentally boring and characterless. Ottonel Muskotály is an early variety, and fairly rot-resistant. It is generally used to make easy-drinking, low-acid, semi-sweet or sweet wines. They can occasionally reach a higher plane. A few producers, bucking the market demand for semi-sweet wine, make attractive dry aperitif wines from it.

Rajnai Rizling is sensitive to rot, and its success depends on how it is trained, mid-height arched canes being best. Wine from it is made in an approximation to an Alsace style, but usually lacks depth, and producers see it mainly as a cheap bulk seller rather than as a serious wine. Tramini, a mutant variety rather than a true Gewürztraminer, is an early variety, moderately prone to rot. It is made as a fresh, often semi-sweet, summer thirst-quencher and, as such, it can be momentarily charming. Serious, weightier versions are few and far between, and only in a few cases successful. Zöld Szilváni is a weak variety and relatively unusual; I have encountered it only once or twice, and I have no opinion about it. On the other hand, Zöld Veltelini, which in Hungary is a workhorse grape making lowly (though usually pleasantly drinkable) wine for the masses, is a variety with huge potential. One or two producers have seen the light and are making delicious, complex wines, which are often ageworthy.

Kékfrankos and Kékoportó, with Zweigelt (from the fourth group), are the most common red varieties in Hungary. Of the three, Kékfrankos is reckoned to be capable of giving the best quality. For the most part, however, it is over-cropped and picked too early. When made from weak musts, it is a lightish-coloured, cherry-flavoured wine of no distinction whatsoever. It is also a variety with high acidity, and early harvesting results in crude wine. However, when it is made from low-yielding, properly ripened grapes, and is given a malolactic fermentation, it can be a wine of complexity, with depth of colour and flavour, showing peppery, rich, blackberry fruit, and a hint of liquorice. It also responds well to barrique treatment. Kékoportó has quite similar characteristics to Kékfrankos, except that it is one of the varieties most prone to rot. As generally made, it has the same light, cherry-cordial character as average Kékfrankos. However, it does not appear to have the same capacity to make complex wines, although when grown and vinified with care, it just begins to look like a serious wine.

In the third group we have a very mixed bag. In many cases, the style of vinification depends on the winemaker. One of the most interesting varieties is the late-ripening Kéknyelű, at one time threatened with extinction and presently accounting for a mere ten hectares throughout the country (mainly in Badacsony). It is one of only two out of 6,000 grape varieties that are entirely female, the other being the Italian Picolit. Kéknyelű is difficult to fertilize because of a dwindling bee population, and grower-enthusiasts resort to bizarre alternative expedients. I wish I could say that I think the wines I have encountered justify the effort.

Ezerjó is particularly associated with Mór, Cirfandli with Pécs, and Juhfark with Somló. Neither of the first two appears to me to justify its local reputation, nor to have much potential to do better. Ezerjó is a problematic variety, tending to be difficult to ripen, giving low sugar musts in all but the best vintages, and being rot-prone. Cirfandli is a late-ripening variety, averse to drought and prone to rot. Wine made from it needs several years of ageing, after which it develops a distinctive apricot flavour that is something of an acquired taste. Juhfark is a high-acid, late-ripening variety prone to disease. It is, however, capable of making complex, high-extract wines despite its low sugar musts; in Somló, it occasionally does. Csabagyöngye and Aranysárfehér were widely planted in the Great Plain to make base wine for sparkling wine, and have no interest as wines for the table.

Furmint, Hárslevelű, Kövérszőlő, and (unofficially, at the moment) Gohér are varieties used for Tokaji Aszú wines, when they are over-ripened and allowed to develop botrytis. The first two are also used for making wines for the table, not just in Tokaj, but in other regions. Hárslevelű, although drought-prone, yields abundantly in the right conditions. It is most famous in Debrő, but is not yet being made there to a standard to justify its previous celebrity. However, there are examples of Hárslevelű, both sweet and dry, which exploit its limey fragrance and exhibit a honeyed charm on the palate, and it is clearly an interesting variety. Furmint is an awkward grape, tending to very high acidity. This acidity balances the sweetness when it is made into a late-harvest or Aszú wine. When made as a dry wine, it is usually harsh, thin, and unappealing – because it is harvested too early – although one or two barrique versions suggest that something interesting may be made of it. Leányka ripens at the end of September, and is harvested early because of its proneness to rot. It makes undistinguished but acceptable wine, and is far outshone by its daughter, Királyleányka (considered below).

Kadarka has obscure origins, possibly Balkan (related to the Gamza variety), possibly Turkish. What is certain is that it has been grown in Hungary for many centuries; during the nineteenth century, it accounted for two-thirds of Hungary's red-grape production. Even as late as 1960, it was the most widespread variety in the country, its 47,000 hectares making up 23.4 per cent of the total vineyard area. Today, there are fewer than 1,000 hectares of it. It disappeared because it was unsuited to the methods of cultivation adopted by the cooperatives (it does best when stake-trained), it is very prone to rot, sensitive to frost, an unreliable ripener, and has poor colouring. A little of it used to be found in Austria, but has been dying out there because it is perceived as a poor variety. In Hungary, however, it still has its fans, especially in Szekszárd. One "traditional" producer there believes it should spearhead Hungary's assault on export markets, and that it will one day re-establish the reputation of Hungarian wine. I can tell him that he is wrong. It makes a soft, blush wine, with a spicy, fruity entry, a hollow mid-palate, then an explosion of flavour in the throat, but a short finish. A good wine for blending, perhaps, to complement a wine with upfront fruitiness – it used to be the foundation of the *Bikavér* (Bull's Blood) blend both in Eger and in Székszárd – but it is always, in my experience, undistinguished on its own. A variety called Bibor Kadarka, with all the intense colour that ordinary Kadarka lacks, is used as a tinting wine for other reds.

The fourth group consists of crosses, some of which are well-established and some not. Among the whites, several stand out. Irsai Olivér, developed in 1930 by Pál Kocsis, ripens early and is generally made into light, fresh, and fruity wines with a hint of muscat. Zéta – originally baptized Oremus – is becoming an important Tokaji grape, but is seldom made into a single-varietal wine. Zeusz is a successful variety in making dessert wines. Királyleányka – literally "Royal Maiden" – is a Transylvanian cross first introduced into Hungary after the Second World War. It ripens quite late and gives wines that are round, rich, and slightly

Muscat-flavoured. It is prone to rot. Of all the "eastern" varieties that might, when well-made, have a good export future, this is it. I have encountered splendid wines, full and complete, with fine acids, and wish that more producers would take this variety, as well as Zöld Veltelini, more seriously.

Zweigelt is the Cinderella of the three most common Hungarian red vines, although in Austria it is the most widespread red variety of all. As Zweigelt is a hardy workhorse variety, few Hungarian producers make much effort to exploit whatever potential it has. Weak musts produce boring, rather bland wines, and if this were all the variety had to offer, it would be easy to write off. However, in the few cases where Zweigelt has been made as a serious wine from restricted yields and matured in barriques – as, for example, by Vylyan in Villány – the results can be startling. It is possible, therefore, that Zweigelt may in future cast off its rags and get to the ball. Blauburger, on the other hand, never will; its use is confined to adding colour to blended wines.

Crosses are of interest to Hungarian growers for the following reason. Ripening conditions in many parts of the country are less than optimal, resulting in musts with low sugar levels, and making chaptalization in these areas a normal occurrence. There is, therefore, an interest in breeding crosses that can produce reasonable levels of sugar, coupled with balanced acidity and suitable depth of flavour, from which good-quality wine can be made. If they are resistant to rot, so much the better. The Georgikon Faculty of Agriculture at Keszthely has been foremost in researching this field. Two of its crosses (Cserszegi Fűszeres and Nektár) are already state-approved, while Rozália, Pátria, Koróna, and Magyar Rizling have been nominated for qualification. Among those not yet recognized, Corvinus (which normally gives 19° to 20° MM [henceforth this is implicit] of sugar) and Valentin stand out for quality. Of all these crosses, however, Cserszegi Fűszeres has been a runaway success ever since Hilltop's "Woodcutter's White" 1997 Cserszegi Fűszeres was nominated White Wine of the Year among supermarket wines in Britain in 1998 – as almost every Hungarian in the wine trade will remind you as soon as the variety is mentioned.

ROOTSTOCKS

One of the most influential figures in the development of rootstocks after the phylloxera crisis was a Hungarian, Zsigmond Teleki (1854–1910). Teleki began searching for phylloxera-resistant rootstocks in 1881. At one time, his firm in Villány prepared 250,000 grafts each year, and it continued in business until 1944. After nationalization in 1949, a state farm was established. By 1969, it had become the largest rootstock supplier in Hungary.

Teleki began by importing seeds of American vinestocks. From these he grew 40,000 seedlings, from which he selected 3,000 which he then split into ten groups. The first three groups were discarded because they were too similar to *Vitis vinifera*. The next three were *Vitis riparia*, and these were coded "A"; 5A was selected as the best from this group. The next three groups were *Vitis berlandieri*, and these were coded "B"; 8B was selected as the best from this group. The final group was *Vitis rupestris*.

5A and 8B proved to be the best performers, and from these further rootstocks have been developed. From 5A are descended K.5BB and T5C. Five of Teleki's rootstock varieties have become world varieties: (1) *berlandieri* × *riparia* T.4A, S04 is used in France; (2) *berlandieri* × *riparia* TK.5BB is common in Italy and Austria; (3) *berlandieri* × *riparia* T.5C is common in Germany; (4) *berlandieri* × *riparia* TK.125AA is found in France and occasionally in Austria; (5) *berlandieri* × *rupestris* T.10A is used in north Africa.

In Hungary, *berlandieri* × *riparia* T.8B was the rootstock used until after the Second World War. From then until 1990, T.5C and TK.5BB were the most commonly used (that was all there was) and they presently constitute ninety per cent of all rootstock in Hungary. They are reckoned to be the best in terms of climate. Formerly, TK.5BB predominated, but T.5C is now dominant. Since 1990 there has been a little further research on rootstocks, and now Fercal 504 is more and more widely used. Merlot is being replanted with rootstock 3309 Couderc from Italy. Choice of rootstock now depends on factors such as the lime content and physical structure of the soil, drainage, and the extent to which the stock has limited vigour (thereby curtailing the vine's vegetative growth). In spite of these efforts the development of appropriate rootstocks still has some way to go in Hungary. Many growers rely on the results of international research, and choose to import their materials when possible.

VINE TRAINING

Until cooperatives and state farms began to plant their own vineyards, the traditional method of vine training in Hungary was stake training – that is, the shoots are tied to a stake round which they grow, the vine having been horn pruned. This is a form of head-spur pruning, whereby successive years of pruning have resulted in a knob of old wood on the trunk, close to the ground, leaving truncated, antler-like spurs from which the next year's shoots grow. Kadarka, Kövidinka, Ezerjó, and Olaszrizling were all traditionally pruned and trained in this way, as was Aranysárfehér on the Great Plain. Vineyards of this kind were typically densely planted, with up to 10,000 vines per hectare. These methods still survive to some extent in small household vineyards.

In general, the most favoured training system in the 1970s was Lenz Moser with a high (1.60-metre/five-foot) cordon. It had originally been designed to assist in the mechanization of vineyards, and its use was a response to the appearance of Russian tractors at this time. It has survived mainly through inertia, although many growers profess complete satisfaction with it. More progressive growers changed to single-curtain training in the 1980s (also with a high cordon), and to umbrella (ernyő) training, using either one or two (medium-height) arched canes, in the 1990s. Current practice depends on the production goal (quantity or quality), the variety planted, and what mechanization is available. Single-curtain is suitable for manual-labour maintenance, while Lenz Moser is more suitable for mechanization and mass production (as is Geneva double-curtain). Both systems tend to produce an excessively large number of buds, and are generally over-productive. Neither is really suitable for varieties prone to rot. For high quality, umbrella or medium-cordon training are currently favoured, although the latter cannot be regarded as a traditional Hungarian system. A very few growers are beginning to favour low, single-cordon Guyot, with which a greater stock density is obtainable, while the stock tends to produce fewer buds.

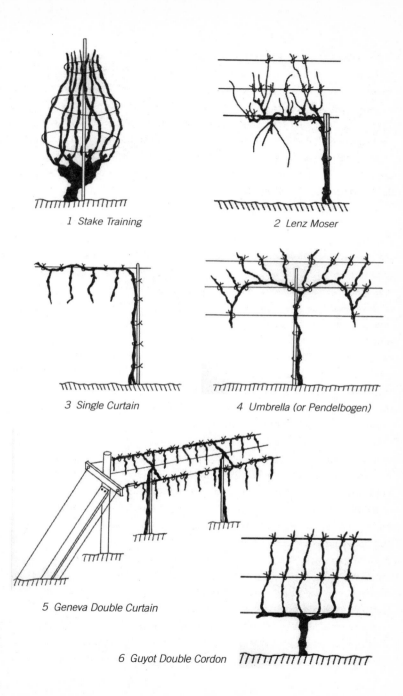

1 Stake Training

2 Lenz Moser

3 Single Curtain

4 Umbrella (or Pendelbogen)

5 Geneva Double Curtain

6 Guyot Double Cordon

Lenz Moser and Geneva double-curtain have the disadvantage of the greatest canopy-shadow factor. Single-curtain and umbrella offer the easiest green pruning. Canopy management in Lenz Moser is carried out by fanning the shoots out above the cordon between double wires, and this is done during the spring or summer pruning. Umbrella training, on the other hand, involves tying down the shoots to the wires. All that said, however, there are many local training systems, or local adaptations of standard training systems. This is especially evident in parts of the Great Plain, such as Soldvadkert, Kiskörös, and Kercal.

The density of vineyards used to be determined by the wide rows necessitated by the large Russian tractors used in them. A typical planting scheme would be rows three metres (almost ten feet) apart, with vines one metre (three feet) apart, giving a density of 3,330 vines per hectare. Examples can still be found, however, of schemes with rows four metres (thirteen feet) apart and vines 1.20 metres (almost four feet) apart, giving a density of just over 2,000 vines per hectare. These densities can, in practice, be further reduced by unreplaced missing vines. In making new plantations, 5,000 vines per hectare (or more) is now regarded as optimum, depending on factors such as gradient and exposure. Planting is often done on a north-south alignment so that the vines benefit from some east and west exposure to sunshine. However, despite this, perhaps the majority of new plantations continue to have densities of 3,330 vines per hectare, because the determinant is that they are still worked with old wide tractors.

It is particularly important to remember all this – and I urge the reader to keep it constantly in mind – when figures indicating crop yields are being bandied about. A yield that might appear quite reasonable from a high-density vineyard can indicate considerable over-cropping when it refers to a low-density vineyard. For this reason, it would be less confusing to indicate a yield per vine, but such an approach is unusual. As a generalization, it would be true to say that in Hungary, three litres per vine is regarded as quite restrictive, and appropriate for good-quality wine; a few people believe that two litres per vine is more appropriate; and a mere handful aim at only one litre or 1.5 litres per vine.

Pruning, of course, is one of the main determinants of individual vine yield. Most pruning in Hungary on vines trained using posts and wires is spur pruning. It is not at all uncommon to leave eighteen to twenty buds, although a certain amount of green pruning reduces this later in the summer. Serious producers limit themselves to about eight buds. Peasant growers are happy to take all the grapes that God sends, and over-cropping is the Hungarian grape-grower's besetting sin.

Many varieties in Hungary are rot-prone, and with September rain, this is a major problem, prompting premature picking. Vineyard owners have to guard against familiar diseases and pest afflictions, such as downy and powdery mildew, leaf mites, and moths. Many old plantations have considerable problems with viral diseases. Less commonly, precautions have to be taken against birds close to Lake Balaton, deer and woodland animals where vineyards are situated near forests, and (increasingly) theft of grapes where vineyards are situated far from village habitations.

WINE TECHNOLOGY AND VINIFICATION

In Hungary we have to consider two main types of vinification: traditional, which is basically oxidative, and reductive, which uses modern technology (or affordable substitutes for it). There are, of course, some small regional variations in traditional methods of vinification – like the use of mud to prevent air contact with the wine after fermentation (described in detail in the section on Szekszárd) – and, in Tokaj, traditional techniques for making Aszú wines stand by themselves. It is, however, possible to give a general characterization of the traditional approach to winemaking, and useful to do so here in order to avoid constant repetition later in the book.

The simplest form of traditional vinification was and is carried out entirely in wood. In the smallest operations, grapes are crushed with a wooden crusher with two rollers, sometimes lined with rubber, rotated by means of a handle under a small wooden hopper. More often, they are pressed in a basket press. In Mór and a few other parts of the county, it is still possible to find screw and beam presses, relics of the nineteenth century, still going strong. Very occasionally, the grapes are not destalked. Sometimes, for fragrant white varieties, the must will be left in contact with the skins for a short period. However, if (as is not infrequently the case) the berries are not healthy, the skins are separated from the must as soon as possible. The must is put into casks varying in size between 200 and 500 litres, and is fermented without the addition of commercial yeasts, and without any form of temperature control. This is not as serious a drawback as may at first appear, because ambient temperatures between the middle of September and the end of October, when wines are being made, can be very cold. In any case, the casks in which the fermentation takes place are in underground cellars with a temperature, typically, of around 12°C. Fermentation takes place until it comes to a natural stop, during which time the cellar may often become uninhabitable because of the gas being given off. Sulphur is added (about two grams per litre), and the wine is racked off into clean barrels in November. A second racking follows in January, and possibly a third in February. The wines thus made are designed for immediate consumption.

In the case of red wine, the grapes and skins are put in wooden fermenting tubs in the press-house. If the weather is really cold, it may be necessary to heat the must to get the fermentation started – not an easy matter. The *cap* (the skins and crushed pulp) is pushed down under the must with a paddle about four times a day. Fermentation continues for a week or ten days, after which the wine is racked and the pomace is pressed, the pressings generally being added to the wine. Maceration after fermentation is unusual, or at any rate short, except in the south of the country. The wine is placed in casks in the cellar, after which it may or may not be racked again like the white wine. Fining by using egg whites or gelatine may or may not be carried out. The cellars being so cold, malolactic fermentation does not normally take place.

In practice, these basic traditional methods are modified in many ways. Instead of wooden fermenters, concrete tanks and plastic tubs are now common. Some growers have acquired an electric destemming and crushing machine. For white wines, many growers now prefer to hold the wine in plastic tanks instead of putting it into wood. While red wine-making is entirely oxidative, all makers try to exclude oxygen from the wine after it has been made.

Another kind of old-fashioned winemaking is carried out in almost all the old cooperatives, or by private companies using old state wineries. As huge quantities used to be the order of the day, large-volume tanks are standard. The worst-case cooperative will still have continuous presses and fermentation tanks in the open air, without any chilling or temperature-control facilities, made from fibreglass, aluminium, galvanized metal, or metal painted with a plastic paint. Storage in the cellars will be in large, old casks that no longer impart any wood character to the wine, or in concrete tanks whose insides have either been painted with epoxy resin, or (more frequently) lined with glass or ceramic tiles. Stainless steel is conspicuous by its absence. The owners of such wineries are normally making valiant attempts to upgrade their plants, but are almost always hampered by lack of money.

At the other end of the scale, Hungary can boast some of the best-equipped modern wineries to be found anywhere. State-of-the-art technology for white wines will comprise computer-controlled weighing of grapes at reception, pneumatic presses, chilling prior to must separation by flotation or sedimentation, and use of nitrogen or carbon dioxide (CO_2) to cover the must in all subsequent operations. Reductive fermentation for both white and red varieties takes place in computer-controlled stainless-steel tanks with chilling/warming facilities for fermentation. The design of fermentation tanks is often sophisticated, with cylindrical tanks having a depth equivalent to their circumference becoming popular for red-wine fermentation, and with various forms of must pump-over and circulation being used. Prolonged skin contact for red wine after fermentation is fairly common now, but pre-fermentation maceration of red grapes is very uncommon.

Fixed systems of piping to minimize use of flexible connectors are becoming more common. Stainless-steel storage is located in acclimatized cellars, and the latest earth and micropore filtration systems are used, as are chilling facilities for white-wine stabilization. Wineries like this will use enzymes and selected yeasts prior to fermentation, and will generally clean the wine by using bentonite. This is the sort of winery I describe as "state-of-the-art".

One or two wineries boast special technology. Pieroth and Balatonboglár, for example, use flash heating of grapes, a process in which red grapes are heated up to 85°C for one minute, then chilled to 40°C in an insulated tank, where they stay for from four to six hours. They are then pressed, and the must is fermented (off the skins) as usual. This system is used mainly because of lack of capacity when the vintage is at its height. The colour produced by this technology is excellent, but the wine itself is – well, "OK" is how one winemaker describes it.

Only one company that I know of – Lesence – uses a reverse-osmosis filter. In general, however, must concentrators have not yet made their appearance, although one hears winemakers talking about them, so their day, perhaps, is not far off. The oxygenation of mature wine – what the French call *microbullage* – has not yet arrived, either. If the claims made for it are true – that it softens tannins, improves fruit character and depth, and reduces the length of maturation – one might hope that such techniques reach Hungary soon.

Just as the old, simple oxidative techniques of traditional winemakers are being modified with items of better equipment (often in line with what their pockets will bear), so in the majority of cases the wineries of commercial wine producers aspire to the modern technology described above. The first priority is usually to have stainless-steel fermentation tanks, then to have an adequate press. Pneumatic presses are relatively uncommon, but so (mercifully) are continuous presses, Vaslin horizontal presses being the type most frequently found. The next most important *desideratum* is some form of cooling system, followed by stainless-steel storage tanks to replace the often motley array of plastic tanks. Where a built-in cooling system is lacking, running cold water over the outsides of tanks (known as a "water curtain") can be a cheap and effective substitute.

Below "state-of-the-art" wineries come most middle-of-the-road wineries, and they will have quite a lot of this sort of equipment. I call a winery "modern" or "well-equipped" if its vinification technology is almost up to the state-of-the-art level, and "reasonable" if it has at least got stainless-steel fermentation tanks and is not obviously deficient in other respects.

Barrique technology has become something of a fashion for even quite small wine producers. Even the most staunchly conservative old-school winemakers feel obliged to experiment, although they will tell you that they dislike wood tastes interfering with the natural flavours of the wine. When you sample their barrique wines, it is easy to agree with them, because they are more often than not disfigured by a green, woody astringency that is foreign to well-handled barrique maturation. In my opinion, this is due mainly to the use of inadequately seasoned oak by some Hungarian coopers, and some of the more serious producers, in apparent agreement with this view, are now buying oak staves so that they can supervise their seasoning themselves before having them made into casks. Few producers can afford French barriques, although those who can usually swear by them. American barriques are also found occasionally. The two principal Hungarian cooperages are Trust Hungary and Kádár. My own tasting experience tends to favour the former, but at least one experienced large-scale producer of well-made barrique wines much prefers the latter.

Hungarian barriques are mainly manufactured from a close-textured oak found in the Zemplén forests in the Hegyalja. I am not convinced that it is ideal for barriques, because even at its best, it imparts very strong flavours to the wine. I miss the gentler accents and elegance imparted by French oak. Defenders of Zemplén oak point out, however, that large amounts of it are imported into France – without bothering to spell out the implication they clearly have in mind.

VINTAGES

Vintages during the 1990s have run to much the same pattern in most of the regions. In general terms, odd years have proved to be better than even years, with 1999 a fitting climax to the century, followed in quality terms by 1993, especially in Villány and Szekszárd. The 2000 vintage proved to be the strangest in living memory, when a long, dry, and hot summer led to forced ripening of the grapes in all regions, bringing the normal harvest dates forward by anything up to five weeks. Must sugar levels were abnormally high, but acid levels plummeted, and only those who managed to harvest in good time were able to make reasonable wines. In those areas where excessively high acidity is normally a problem, the reduction in acid sometimes led to rounder, better-balanced white wines than usual.

Red wines from this vintage will turn out, perhaps, to have more ripeness and body in the lesser quality regions than is usual, and – reader, be warned – may present a more flattering impression of standards than the average would warrant. While it is too early to tell how the better-quality red wines will turn out, producers seem to be agreed that 1999 may, in the end, show itself to be the better vintage, with less sheer power and richness, perhaps, but more finesse and suppleness. In Tokaj, 1993 was the best vintage of the decade, followed by 1999 and then by 1995.

The 2000 vintage, in Tokaj as elsewhere, proved exceptional, with the best yield of high-quality Aszú since . . . well, someone mentioned 1811, but how could they possibly know that?

part III

The Wine Regions and Their Producers

PRELIMINARY EXPLANATION

In this part of the book much of the information regarding the regions and individual producers is conveyed in summary form. That relating to the areas of commercial vineyards within the region is derived from the national vineyard survey carried out in 2001, about which fuller information is provided in Appendix II. That regarding wine communities relates to the situation on January 1, 2002, and has been provided by the National Council of Wine Communities. Information about individual producers has been supplied directly by them and relates primarily to the period during which this book was researched. Readers should bear in mind that the Hungarian wine scene is a rapidly developing one. For that reason the realities behind statistics can change quickly – particularly those regarding individual producers' vineyards, which are continually in flux as planting and replanting take place – and figures given here must be regarded as essentially indicative.

Wine regions

The entry after each regional heading shows:

(1) *Total area of vineyards officially under productive cultivation, in hectares, excluding household plots and those producing table grapes.*
(2) *Area of vineyards planted with white varieties.*
(3) *Area of vineyards planted with red varieties.*

(4) *Number of wine communities in the region.*

(5) *Number of wine community members (growers and producers).*

Producers

The entry for each individual producer indicates the registered name of the enterprise. Alternative trading names are given in brackets. Thereafter follow its registered address(es), and telephone and fax numbers. Occasionally the address of the winery, when different, is also included. Then comes the following information.

(a) *The owner of the enterprise.*

(b) *The area, in hectares, of vineyards under cultivation, followed by the areas of each grape variety, using the abbreviations shown below. No distinction is made between the vineyards belonging to a company (outright or rented) and those belonging to its owners. Occasional rounding up or down of parts of a hectare may result in slight discrepancies between the total vineyard area and its breakdown into areas by variety. Where an area has several varieties, this is shown by separating them with a forward slash: /.*

(c) *The average annual production of wine in hectolitres. Where this is clearly more than can be obtained from the hectarage held by the producer, or a wine is produced from a variety not mentioned in the section, this is an indication that grapes (and, occasionally, must or finished wines) are purchased by the producer. Because of annual variation in aszú berry production, no figures are provided in the case of Tokaji producers.*

(d) *The name(s) of the winemaker(s).*

(e) *The types of wine produced. (Note: cuvée is used by Hungarian winemakers to indicate a blend.)*

(f) *The percentage of annual production currently exported and the most important foreign markets.*

Occasional but easily understood variations in the above layout may be made to accommodate the special circumstances of an individual producer, or to present complex information in a clearer way.

GRAPE VARIETY ABBREVIATIONS

White grapes

B	Bianca	Mo	Mondeuse
Bz	Budaizöld	Mus	Muscadelle
Cg	Csabagyönge	N	Nektár
Ch	Chardonnay	OM	Ottonel Muskotály
Chas	Chasselas	Or	Olaszrizling
Ci	Cirfundli	P	Pintes
CzF	Cserszegi Fűszeres	PB	Pinot Blanc
E	Ezerjó	RR	Rajnai Rizling
Ez	Ezerfürtü	Rs	Rizlingszilváni
F	Furmint	SB	Sauvignon Blanc
Fav	Favorita	Sem	Sémillon
G	Gohér	Sk	Szürkebarát
H	Hárslevelű	SM	Sárga Muskotály
I	Izsáki	T	Tramini
IO	Irsai Olivér	V	Viognier
J	Juhfark	VF	Vegyesfehér
Ker	Kerner	Z	Zeuzs
Kn	Kéknyelű	Zef	Zefir
Kir	Királyleányka	Zen	Zenit
Kör	Köraipirosveltelini	Zt	Zéta
Köv	Kövidinka	Zgő	Zengő
Kun	Kunleány	Zg	Zalagyöngye
Kv	Kövérszőlő	ZV	Zöld Veltelini
L	Leányka		

Red grapes

BK	Bibor Kadarka	Ko	Kékoportó
Bl	Blauburger	Kad	Kadarka
Car	Cardinál	M	Merlot
CF	Cabernet Franc	Med	Medina
Cin	Cinsaut	PN	Pinot Noir
CS	Cabernet Sauvignon	Sy	Syrah
Kf	Kékfrankos	Zw	Zweigelt

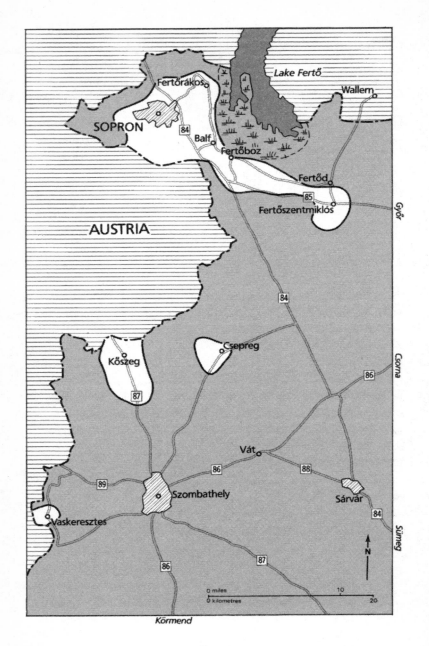

Sopron

5

The Northwest

SOPRON

1,800 hectares: 317 white, 1,483 red
Eight wine communities, with 4,204 members

The Sopron region, surrounding the attractive little town of the same name, is situated next to the Austrian Burgenland, curving around the southern part of Lake Fertő (known in Austria as the Neusiedlersee). Its history goes back to Roman times, when it was known as *Scrabantia* and formed part of the province of Pannonia, even then famous for its wines. Given a tax-free wine trading status as early as 1297, Sopron's location saved its commerce with the west from Turkish interference during the Middle Ages, and it continued to flourish as the capital of the important Burgenland during the Austro-Hungarian Empire. Until 1920, it formed part of a larger wine region – Ruszt-Sopron-Pozsony – recognized in the 1893 Wine Law, but reduced by the Treaty of Trianon.

Today, Sopron is prospering again. Many residents work in Austria at Austrian wage levels, while, reciprocally, many Austrians take advantage of Sopron's bargain-priced housing and its many, but cheap, dentists. The town is rapidly becoming a prominent conference centre, and its cellars, located in the town rather than in the surrounding vineyards, doubtlessly help Sopron's burgeoning wine tourism, as do a local wine route and an annual wine festival in May.

Many of the wine producers are of German origin, and are known as *Poncihter* (*Bohnensucher*, or "bean-seeker") families, thus nicknamed because they grew vines and beans together on posts to shade the beans (traditional in Sopron cooking) under the vine leaves. These families suffered greatly from forced repatriation at the end of the Second World War, when almost half of Sopron's large German population was expelled.

The main vineyard areas are east of the town, between Balf and Fertőrákos, where the ground rises to 233 metres (765 feet) above sea level on the west bank of Lake Fertő. Thirty per cent of the vineyards face south, twenty per cent face northwest, and the rest face mainly eastwards. Kőszeg, Csepreg, and Vaskeresztes, up to seventy kilometres (forty-three miles) to the south, with over one hundred hectares of vineyards, were added (oddly, in view of their distance) to the Sopron wine region in 2000.

Half of the entire vineyard area is made up of plots of 0.3 hectares, effectively the minimum size, owned by grape-growers who tend to sell their produce rather than to make wine from it. There are fifty to sixty private producers who own between two and ten hectares. Some companies have more, with Sop-Vin the largest owner at one hundred hectares. For those who like bizarre comparisons, I have been told that in the seventeenth century, each family in the area owned on average 0.51 hectare; in 2000, the average was only 0.44 hectare.

The soil is predominantly chalky, with clay, loess, brown forest soil, and crystalline shale all to be found. By common consent, the best vineyard area in the region is the Spernsteiner, overlooking the lake. With heavy lumps of heat-retaining shale giving much of it a Portuguese Douro-like appearance, this is probably the stoniest vineyard area to be found in Hungary, and certainly one of the best.

Spring is mild and frost-free, summer is cool and rainy, autumn is dry and sunny with long, warm evenings and cool nights, while winter is mild and wet. Sunshine averages 1,826 hours a year, and the temperature (ranging from −14°C to 34°C) averages 10.21°C. South of Sopron, about fourteen kilometres (nine miles) from Lake Fertő, the climate is sub-alpine, suitable for Sauvignon Blanc and Pinot Noir (sourced here by Hilltop). At lake level, the climate is Continental (1.5°C higher), and on the slopes above the lake it is sub-Mediterranean (1.5°C higher again). Precipitation averages 654 millimetres (twenty-six inches) a year. Hail damage is a hazard every three years or so.

When the previous large buyer, the Sopron State Farm, stopped purchasing grapes, its place was taken by large producers from other parts of the country, such as Hilltop, Egervin, Hungarovin, Danubiana, and Varga.

These set what are locally perceived to be excessively low price levels, and growers now lack the security and the easy sales that the state farm provided.

In the 1990s, the main problem was overproduction, especially of white grapes. At present, only twenty-one per cent of the grapes grown in the region are white varieties. The much-underrated Zöld Veltelini is the local favourite, but no one seems to want to make it seriously, so it is sold, semi-dry and unbottled, in local pubs. Sopron is, therefore, now essentially a red-wine area – possibly the Hungarian *locus classicus* of Kékfrankos, which is the dominant variety. Over-cropping is a chronic problem, and one wishes more growers would cross the border to see for themselves (and then copy) the vineyard management of their Austrian neighbours. The chalky soil makes for very hard red wines, whose high acidity long ago got the region a bad name. However, winemakers are trying to respond to market preferences, and malolactic fermentation, first (consciously) used here in 1997, is carried out by those producers who have sufficient storage capacity to undertake it.

Compared to Austrian Kékfrankos wine, that of Sopron usually lacks depth and sophistication, but can often be more rounded. Weninger – significantly, perhaps, an Austrian – is presently far and away the best producer here, but year by year, the general standard is getting better. The best wines of the two largest producers, Sop-Vin and Vinex Borászati, are of a decent commercial standard, but generally lack distinction. However, there are several individual producers making good, reliable wines that hint at further future achievement, among them Ferenc Princzes, Arnold Jandl, Zoltán Iváncsics, and Péter Roll. Sadly, getting their wine bottled is one of their main problems, and, lacking wider distribution, this impedes recognition further afield. Nevertheless, Sopron in my not-too-widely-held opinion is a region with the potential to outperform its Austrian rivals, and could certainly become, in quality terms, one of the six best wine regions in Hungary.

WENINGER SOPRON-BALF KFT (WENINGER BORÁSZAT)

H–9494 Sopron-Balf, Fő u. 23. Tel/fax: +36–99 339049. *(a)* Franz Sr and Franz Jr Weninger. *(b)* 17ha: Kf 7.5ha; M 1.5ha; Sy 1.5ha; PN 5ha; CF/CS 1.5ha. *(c)* 400hl in 2000. *(d)* Franz Weninger Jr. *(e)* Kf and (shortly) a cuvée. *(f)* 20% (Germany, Switzerland, and Austria)

This company was founded in 1997 by the Austrian winemaker Franz Weninger Sr, following his successful joint venture with Attila Gere in Villány. Although the company is jointly owned by father and son, Franz Weninger Jr (hereafter referred to without the "Jr"), has had full responsibility for running it since 2000. Trained in oenology at Klosterneuburg, Weninger later sought winemaking experience in the Alto Adige in Italy, and in the Sonoma and Napa valleys. He also worked a vintage in the Hunter Valley in 2001.

The company is fortunate to have ten hectares of its vineyards on one of the stoniest parts of the Spernsteiner, seven of which are planted with thirty- to forty-year-old Kékfrankos. With wide rows and originally Lenz Moser trained, their cordon has been lowered to a height of fifty centimetres (twenty inches). However, there is enough nitrogen in the soil here for close planting, and some Syrah planted in 1998 has a density of 5,000 vines per hectare, the vines being single-cane umbrella-trained. The anticipated yield will be a maximum of from twenty-one to twenty-eight hectolitres per hectare.

The winery, in the main street in Balf, a charming small spa town seven kilometres (four miles) from Sopron, was constructed in 1997 with up-to-the-minute vinification technology. Fermentation of the Kékfrankos is in temperature-controlled, stainless-steel pump-over tanks, while open stainless-steel fermenters are used for Cabernet Sauvignon and Merlot. Weninger avoids too much crushing and likes to use natural yeasts to obtain a slow fermentation and good extraction. A small amount of sugar added just as the fermentation is coming to an end apparently increases the glycerine content. After fermentation, the wines are put into barriques and undergo malolactic fermentation. A third of the barriques are French and the rest are Hungarian. All the wines are bottled in the cellar.

Currently, three types of Kékfrankos are offered. The first is matured in 2,700-litre oak casks, and shows a surprising amount of wood on the palate; the second is matured in barriques; and the third, "Selection", is made from selected grapes and selected barriques. The barrique wines are normally aged for eighteen months, and then given two months in bottle before release. Generally offering more concentration than other reds from the region, the wines reflect their grading in terms of weight, richness, and complexity, the Selection having enough backbone to be worth cellaring for a few years.

The wine is marketed mainly (seventy per cent) in Hungary, but sells well in Germany. Increased exports will, it is hoped, secure future expansion. A long-term agreement has been made to market some wine under the Monarchia brand, but the eventual aim will be to sell exclusively under the Weninger label. The next development will be a blend called Spernsteiner Cuvée (which will include Cabernet Sauvignon and Merlot). There is no doubting that Weninger is well-trained and ambitious, and I predict that he is destined for a starry winemaking career.

SOP-VIN KFT

H–9400 Sopron, Ady E. ut 31/B. Tel: +36–99 322063; Tel/fax: +36–99 313175. (a) Ten owners, all previously on the management of Sopron State Farm. (b) 100ha (78 in Sopron; 22 in Fertőszentmiklós). Sopron: Kf 20ha; CS 11ha; M 9ha; PN 6ha; Ch 12ha; SB 4ha; ZV 12ha; Kir 4 ha. Fertőszentmiklós: Kf 22ha. (c) 15,000hl. (d) Zoltán Iváncsics. (e) Varietals, rozé. (f) 72% in bulk (Austria, Japan, Canada, Switzerland, Scandinavia)

The largest producer in the region, Sop-vin was started in 1995. Its winery, previously owned by the Sopron State Farm, was rebuilt in the 1970s on the Algerian model, with concrete pump-over tanks that are still in use. The company also has cellar storage of 31,500 hectolitres and bottling facilities just outside Balf.

Half the production comes from the company's own vineyards, and half from grapes purchased locally. Yields vary from forty-nine to eighty-four hectolitres per hectare. Sixty per cent of the production is red wine. Only ten per cent of the production is bottled. The rest is sold in bulk, eighty per cent being exported and twenty per cent being sold to two large Hungarian producers. The bottled varietal wines are sturdy and characterful, and generally of a very acceptable commercial standard. The winemaker here does a good job with very out-of-date equipment.

VINEX BORÁSZATI KFT

H–9400 Sopron, Rákóczi u. 39. Tel: +36–99 312351/311787; Fax: +36–99 312351. (a) Miklós Szita, György Bacskay, Miklós Sárosi. (b) 49ha: Kf 15ha; M 10ha; CS 5ha; PN 7ha; ZV/SB/T 12ha. (c) 15,000hl. (d) Miklós Szita. (e) Varietals. (f) 1% (Japan, Germany)

Founded in 1989 by three former Sopron State Farm staff members, Vinex owns a former cooperative winery in Balf and a cellar in Sopron. Fifteen hectares of the company's vineyards have been replanted since 1998, all high-cordon trained. Despite some investment, the winery has inferior equipment and insufficient fermentation capacity. This adversely affects production standards. Only five per cent of the production is bottled, mainly for sale in supermarkets, and the rest is sold in plastic containers to the public, or in bulk to other companies. Miklós Szita is the conservative, old-style winemaker. Ákos, his son, on the other hand, with winemaking experience in California, has more go-ahead ideas. He is keen to improve the standards of the company and, in the meantime, has founded his own wine company – Dr Szita és Fia – with eight hectares of vineyards and modern vinification technology.

LUKA JÓZSEF PINCÉSZETE
H–9400 Sopron, Zerge u. 19. Tel: +36–99 316379. Winery: H-9400 Sopron, Balfi út, 93. *(a)* József Luka. *(b)* 2ha: CS 0.8ha; Kf 0.4ha; Zw 0.4ha; PN 0.4ha. *(c)* 75hl. *(d)* József Luka. *(e)* Varietals, rozé, cuvée. *(f)* None

Luka, originally a typewriter mechanic (now retired), is one of the most interesting self-taught winemakers I have encountered. He restarted his grandparents' business in 1995, and began production with very modern equipment in 1997. Luka is motivated by a restless urge to experiment. Having abandoned closed fermenters in 1998, he made his next two vintages in open tanks. In 2001, he progressed to a pump-over tank modified to give the must periodic air contact. He was the first person in Sopron to put his red wines through malolactic fermentation. He also experiments with barrique technology. Currently, he favours a cooper in Tet who uses Slavonian oak dried for five years, but plans to move on to French barriques.

Luka's Zöld Veltelini is impressive: green and Chablis-like, plenty of fresh gooseberry on the nose, racy acidity, and big, untamed flavours with a long finish. But it is the reds that show most potential. The colours of his 1999 red wines made in open fermenters are sensational by Hungarian standards – Grange depth and density best describe them – and the accompanying richness of their ripe fruit puts them among the best I have encountered in Hungary. Sadly, they are marred by some woodiness on both the nose and palate. However, using reserves of the same wines which have not seen wood, Luka hopes to create blends in which awkwardnesses will be smoothed out.

[Very sadly, news of Luka's death reached me just as the book was going to press. He was a talented, kind, and modest man, and I was convinced that his experiments – what the family used to call his "stupidities" – would one day result in even more remarkable wine. I have left the entry as originally written as a memorial to him. Happily, his business will be continued by his daughter, who will be assisted by the Villány firm Vylyan. Monarchia will be the sole distributor of his 2000 Zöld Veltelini and his 1999 Bálint Cuvée.]

JANDL BORÁSZAT

H–9421 Fertőrákos, Patak sor 26. Tel: +36–99 355048. *(a)* Arnold Jandl.
(b) 3.7ha: Kf 2.6ha; ZV 0.5ha; Kör 0.2ha; CS 0.2ha; Sy 0.2ha. *(c)* 400hl.
(d) Kálmán Jandl. *(e)* Varietals. *(f)* None

The Jandl winery, registered in the name of his son (for tax reasons), is effectively run by Kálmán Jandl. Having made wine at the Balf Cooperative prior to privatization, he now works as a professional winemaker in Austria, and looks after his own business in his spare time. In conjunction with winemaking, Jandl runs a bar that he built in 1995 in Fertőrákos, with his cellar alongside. Equipment is basic. White wines are fermented in open-air plastic tanks, while red wines are open-fermented in large plastic tubs or in sunken pits in the cellar, covered with plastic to protect against oxidation. Despite the higher cost, Jandl prefers French to Hungarian oak, because the results are more uniform and predictable.

His wines, three-quarters of which are bottled, are sold only at the cellar door and in his bar. It is a pity they do not get more exposure, for I find them attractive – not least his Cabernet Sauvignon Barrique. Jandl is quietly serious about what he is doing, and has so far achieved very good, reliable quality.

GANGL JÁNOS TERMELŐI PINCÉJE

H–9400 Sopron, Hunyadi u. 24. Tel: +36–99 329816. Winery: H–9400 Sopron, Lehár Ferenc u. 58–62. Tel: +36–99 335343. (a) The Gangl family. (b) 6ha: Kf 3ha; Zw 0.8ha; M 1.5ha; SB 0.8ha. (c) 500hl. (d) János and Zóltán Gangl. (e) Varietals. (f) None

The Gangl family has been making wine for five generations, and three of its members are presently involved in the business. Carried out in a fascinating shell-damaged, 200-year-old cellar, which it has taken the family five years to rebuild, the winemaking here is entirely traditional. All fermentation (except the Sauvignon Blanc, which is fermented in plastic) is in forty-hectolitre open fermenters, and all maturation, including whites, is in large casks. At the moment, only about two per cent of the wine is bottled (for sale to tourists), but a planned bottling line will shortly increase this to fifty per cent. What is not bought by tourists is sold to a large national producer.

Their white wines, very attractive when a year old, lose their vibrancy when matured in large casks, but the Gangls' reds are very good. Their 1993 Cabernet Sauvignon is a serious wine by any standards, with a ripe, old-fashioned Portuguese bouquet, and one hopes that more recent vintages will develop similarly.

PRINCZES FERENC

H–9400 Sopron, Prinyő Borozó, Koronázó domb. Tel: +36–99 334042. (a) Ferenc Princzes. (b) 2.6ha: Kf 1.41ha; ZV 0.3ha; T 0.3ha; CS 0.25ha; Zw 0.16ha; M 0.18ha. (c) 100–150hl. (d) Ferenc Princzes. (e) Varietals, rozé, cuvée. (f) None

Formerly a railway worker, Ferenc Princzes decided to focus his career on winemaking as early as 1987. By 1989, he was already bottling his own wine and, while developing his wine business, he built a restaurant and cellar on a hill overlooking Sopron. He also runs a wine shop in the town.

Red wines are made traditionally in concrete open fermenters and matured in oak barrels; the whites are fermented in plastic tanks at cellar temperature (13°C–15°C). All his wine, a third of which is bottled, is sold through his restaurant, his shop, or locally. The wines are consistently good. The Tramini has depth and aromatic allure, the Zweigelt (cropped at twenty-eight to thirty-five hectolitres per hectare) is elegant, and the

Kékfrankos is outstanding. His Soproni Cuvée Princesse (forty per cent Kékfrankos, forty per cent Zweigelt, twenty per cent Cabernet Sauvignon), which he began in 1997 and which was the first cuveé to be produced in Sopron, is a well-judged blend, but needs time in bottle to round out its tannins.

IVÁNCSICS & ROLL VALLAKOZÁS

Roll: H–9400 Sopron, Afónya u. 8. Tel: +36–99 315145. Iváncsics: H–9400 Sopron, Szegfű u. 30. Tel: +36–99 317262. *(a)* Péter Roll and Zoltán Iváncsics. *(b)* 7.5ha: ZV 2.5ha; Kf 2ha; M 1.2ha; CS 0.8ha; Zw 0.6ha; PN 0.4ha. *(c)* 750–800hl. *(d)* Péter Roll and Zoltán Iváncsics. *(e)* Varietals, rozé, cuvée. *(f)* None

This is a double act; two friends who formerly worked for the Sopron State Farm have in practical terms combined their individual, home-based enterprises to produce wine under a single label. Roll was a quality-control technician and Iváncsics a winemaker – a role he still has with Sop-Vin. Of the total production, two-thirds of which is red, only fifteen per cent is bottled, the rest being sold locally in bulk.

Whites are made in double-wall stainless-steel tanks cooled with well water. Half the red wine is made in open sixty-hectolitre galvanized tanks, and half in stainless-steel, temperature-controlled pump-over tanks. The wines are of a decent quality. The whites are usually semi-dry, but a bone-dry Zöld Veltelini shows how good wine from this variety can be. The reds, uncharacteristically for the market for which they are destined, are all very dry because the partners refuse to compromise the integrity of their wine. Their barrique wines offer big mouthfuls of fruit discreetly tempered by oak. All the reds have a notably tannic spine, and need a couple of years in bottle.

OTHER WINE PRODUCERS

Taschnervin Borászati és Kereskedelmi Kft (Taschnervin Termelői Pincéje). H–9400 Sopron, Virágvölgyi út 55. Tel: +36–99 314894. *Vincellér MPS Szõ lészeti, Borászati Kft.* H–9400 Sopron, Balfi u. 121. Tel: +36–99 316336

PANNONHALMA-SOKORÓALJA

679 hectares; 653 white, twenty-six red
Seven wine communities, with 1,105 growers

Pannonhalma is a small village in Sokoróalja, the geographical region south of the charming baroque city of Győr. Although the name echoes that of the original Roman province of Pannonia, it is to its abbey that the region owes its present-day wine traditions. A Benedictine foundation, the abbey was consecrated in 1001, and its deed of foundation already mentions winemaking. Until 1949, when they were nationalized, the abbey's vineyards made it the largest local proprietor. Wines from the region enjoyed some fame at the end of the nineteenth century, when the vineyards were three times their present size and some red wine made from Othello and Isabella (planted in the wake of phylloxera) was exported to the United States. In 1977, the region was declared a quality wine area, and in 1990, it was recognized as a separate wine region. It consists of unspoilt, rolling agricultural land surrounding thirteen small villages, much of it dominated by the abbey on top of *Szent Martinhegy* (St Martin's Hill) (282 metres, or 936 feet).

There are four main vineyard areas, the most important of which are southwest of Pannonhalma on the slopes of two long, low hills lying parallel to each other on a NW–SE axis, with heights ranging from 150 to 200 metres (293 to 657 feet). All these areas are capable of giving good-quality grapes. The soil is mainly brown forest soil on top of loess, with some adobe. The moderate precipitation (543 millimetres/twenty-one inches per annum) and warmth (2,050 sunshine hours, with temperatures ranging from −15°C to 34°C, averaging 10.46°C) are more or less the average for Hungary, while winters are mild. Every four years or so, botrytized berries are produced.

In the 1980s, the region had seven cooperatives, but there was no state farm. Vineyards are planted with wide rows and have almost universal single-curtain high-cordon training, although some Lenz Moser and a little umbrella training can be found. Two cooperatives survive (without vineyards), but are financially ailing. The Pannonhalma Cooperative, for example, which had 600 members in 1992, now has only 201 active

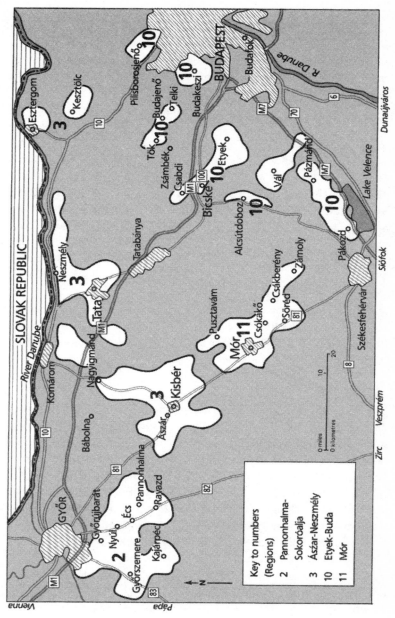

Northwest Hungary

members and is saddled with run-down 1970s technology. Its 500-metre-long cellar (1,642 feet), built in 1670 for the abbey, currently holds only 2,000 hectolitres of its 30,000 hectolitres capacity. As the cooperatives have lost members and revenue, there has been a parallel development of small family cellars.

The region, with only 679 producing hectares out of an officially estimated vineyard potential of 3,234 hectares, is the second smallest in Hungary. The main varieties grown are white. In order of extensiveness they are Olaszrizling, Rizlingszilváni, Rajnai Rizling, Tramini, and Chardonnay. However, tiny amounts of red grapes are grown, mainly Kékfrankos, but also some Cabernet Sauvignon and Merlot. The white wines are generally light, undemanding, soft, and fruity and, despite primitive fermentation equipment, usually quite well-made and consistently pleasant to drink. They are essentially wines for immediate local consumption. The reds have little to be said for them and are best avoided. Sadly, there are only a few wines at present likely to interest wine-lovers with international standards.

Most of the registered grape-growers make wine mainly for their own use. The average holding is between 0.1 hectare and 0.5 hectare, but one farmer controls five per cent of the region. Six makers produce more than 1,000 hectolitres, and around eighty produce between ten hectolitres and 1,000 hectolitres. Large Hungarian producers purchase about half the crop: about thirty per cent as grapes, and twenty per cent in the form of bulk wine. The wine of the remaining producers, apart from what is kept back for family use, is sold to bars and restaurants, or at the cellar door in plastic containers. Less than one per cent is bottled, and virtually none of that appears outside the region, which remains unknown even to Hungarian wine-lovers.

The area of cultivation has decreased from 1,080 hectares in 1990, partly on account of encroachment by house building. An estimated eighty-five per cent of existing vineyards are cooperative plantings made between 1964 and 1982. Since 1988, lack of capital has prevented new planting – "one or two hectares at most" – so the most recent extensive vineyards are now thirteen or fourteen years old. Yields of seventy hectolitres per hectare are considered normal.

Although replanting is perceived as urgent, the region at present has no defined development plan, and its potential, which appears to me to be greater than that of several other small regions, remains unexploited. However, there are moves to develop the touristic possibilities of the area, and several wine routes are being developed. The first is as part of a large-scale joint effort to launch southeastern Austria and northwestern Hungary as an important tourist region aiming at Europe-wide exposure, and wine tourism will be a part of it. A plan for a regional wine route with about forty participants is not yet off the ground. Nyúl, however, more enterprising than the other wine communities, plans to develop its own wine route, with eighteen participants.

PANNON-BORHÁZ–BORÁSZATI VÁLLALKOZÁS

9083 Écs, Hegyalja u. 12. Tel: +36–96 473092. (a) László Vaszari. (b) 25ha: Or 7.5ha; Rs 3.75ha; RR 3.75ha; Kir 3.75ha; Ch 6.25ha. (c) 3,000hl plus. (d) László Vaszari. (e) Varietals, cuvée. (f) None

László Vaszari worked in the Pannonhalma Cooperative for more than twenty years. In 1992, after he and other friends tried unsuccessfully to privatize it, he decided to strike out independently. He bought his vineyards between 1992 and 1995 and started serious wine production in a home-based winery and cellar in 1996. Modern equipment provides excellent facilities for reductive winemaking (only Olaszrizling is matured in wood) and a bottling unit is planned for 2003. Vaszari also buys in both grapes and finished wine, and his production is sold to restaurants and bars within a thirty-kilometre (nineteen-mile) radius. A sandstone cellar on the outskirts of Écs, dating from 1829, has been refronted and is destined for probable tourism use. Vaszari's wines are, in my opinion, the best in the region. The Olaszrizling and Királyleányka are the stars, with considerable depth of flavour, rounded acidity, and good balance.

SZEMENYEI CSALÁD BORÁSZATA

9082 Nyúl, Héma u. 218. Tel: +36–96 364044. (a) Gyula Szemenyei. (b) 4ha: Or 2ha; Rs 1ha; L/RR/Kf 1ha. (c) 350hl. (d) Gyula Szemenyei. (e) Varietals. (f) None

Gyula Szemenyei is a plumber and heating engineer by trade and, although he is teetotal, winemaking is his hobby. Behind his house there is a compact but efficiently laid-out winery with modern reductive equipment, and under it there is a cramped but adequate cellar. His production is sold in bulk to local restaurants and pubs, although bottling is done on the premises on request. A barrique Kékfrankos is unsuccessful, but Szemenyei's rather light white wines show attractive fruitiness and freshness.

BABARCZI LÁSZLÓ-VÁLLAKOZÓ
9081 Győrújbarát, Ersébet u. 19. Tel: +36–96 456734. *(a)* László Babarczi. *(b)* 45ha (5 of them rented): RR 14ha; Rs 12ha; Or 11ha; T 8ha. *(c)* 2,000hl. *(d)* László Babarczi. *(e)* Varietals. *(f)* None
Babarczi's family ranked as *kulaks*, and suffered accordingly during the Soviet purge. Although he had only had an elementary education when, in 1959, he joined the local cooperative, he later managed to graduate as an agricultural engineer and managerial economist, and finally became director of a cooperative in Győr, which he left in 1992.

In 1993, when loans were easy to get, Barbaczi started to buy land seriously, and he currently owns forty hectares of vineyards and rents a further five hectares. This makes him the largest vineyard proprietor in the region. He started making wine in 1993. However, his very outmoded vinification equipment is in urgent need of replacement – at a cost of HUF100 million that he cannot afford. His completely white-wine production is fermented without temperature control at between 20°C and 25°C, and is mainly sold in bulk to large national producers. None is bottled. Given the poor technology, the wines are remarkably acceptable.

OTHER WINE PRODUCERS
Pannonhalmi Szövetkezet Pince (Pannonhalmi Mezőgazdasági Borászati Termelő és Kereskedő Szövetkezet). H–9090 Pannonhalma, Mátyás Király u. 1–3. Tel: +36–96 470161. *Nyúli Mezőgazdasági Szövetkezet.* H–9082 Nyúl, Kossuth u. 44. Tel: +36–96 540058. *S & S Nouvotechnika Kft.* H–9082 Nyúl, Kápolna u. 41. Tel/fax: +36–96 361211. *Salakta Családi Borpince.* H–9081 Győrújbarát, Mátyás Körúti Pincesor. Tel: +36–96 527217. *Borbirodalom Pannonhalma Borpince.* H–9090 Pannonhalma, Szabadság tér. Tel/fax: +36–96 471240

ÁSZÁR-NESZMÉLY

1,601 hectares: 1,484 white, 117 red
Thirteen wine communities, with 2,269 members

This region, on the northern Danube border of Hungary, consists of six separate areas grouped into two main geographical parts. The first, and largest, is on the west, but it was never a particularly well-known production area until Hilltop Neszmély recently put it on the Hungarian wine map. The second, much smaller part of the region lies further east, between Esztergom and Kesztólc. Here there is a cooperative, the Pilis MGTS. Nowadays it simply provides agricultural services to other growers, and its ex-members sell mainly to Hilltop. Apart from the cooperative's original plantings, there are some small private plots which, in 2001, still had American hybrids (now-banned) such as Noah, Othello and Isabella.

Originally two wine regions, Ászár and Neszmély are at the geographical extremes of the present single region. They were combined only recently, their union consummated in 1997 with the founding of a wine brotherhood. Neszmély, in the northeast, is vastly the more important of the two. It is situated on the gently undulating Gerecse Hills, contrasting with the relatively flat area stretching southwest towards Ászár. Their climates reflect this difference to a small extent, but the region as a whole is cooler than average and fairly wet, with only very moderate sunshine and quite severe winters. The soil is a mixture of sandy loess and brown forest soil.

The development of the region under Communism was ill-judged. While Neszmély and Ászár were recognized wine areas, the land in between, where the Komárom State Farm (now Komáromi MG) is situated, was never much of a wine area. Formerly church land, it is more suited to cereal crops. The land here is only 110 metres (357 feet) above sea level and is subject to heavy frosts, while in September a local lake keeps the relative humidity high, and fog is frequent. Rot and botrytis, therefore, are rife. The state farm's vineyard development proceeded contrary to professional advice and, consequently, 200 hectares of vines had to be taken up in 1986 and 1997. The wines produced here have very high acidity, and much was therefore previously sent to Hungarovin to be used as a base for sparkling wine. All this may partly explain why Komáromi MG is the only state farm winery still awaiting privatization – apart from Tokaj Kereskedőház which remains state owned for quite other reasons.

There are only three major wine producers in the region, all in the north, where there has been a lot of new planting. By contrast, in the south, there has been none at all. The main producer in Ászár, the curiously named *Aranykalász Borászati Szövetkezet* – "Golden Ear of Corn Wine-Producing Cooperative" – is in terminal decline and cannot afford to buy the grapes it needs. Like Komáromi MG, its local sales have suffered severely from competition from fake wine. According to local estimates, sixty per cent of the vineyards in the south of the region have been abandoned because grape prices are too low to be profitable. The vineyards that survive are getting into a worse and worse state; the most recent are between twelve and fifteen years old, the oldest from twenty-five to thirty. For the small growers, the outlook is indeed bleak.

HILLTOP NESZMÉLY RT
Budapest office: H–1013 Budapest, Attila u. 35, IV/3. Tel: +36–1 457 3232; Fax: +36–1 214 674. Winery: H–2544 Neszmély, Meleges Hagy Pf. 4. Tel: +36–34 550 455/450; Fax: +36–34 550 451. *(a)* Eva Keresztury, Imre Török, Judit Storicz and Ákos Kamocsay. *(b)* 350ha – but see details in text. *(c)* 68,900hl. *(d)* Ákos Kamocsay, Ágnes Dezsényi. *(e)* Varietals and cuvées totalling about 60 products each year, some of which are the same wine under different labels. *(f)* 98% to the UK, and a little to Scandinavia, the US and Canada

Hilltop, as the name suggests, is on top of a ridge behind Neszmély, looking across the Danube at extensive views of Slovakia. The company has had an enormous success, not just in terms of commercial growth, but in terms of the quality of its wine: Ákos Kamocsay was Hungarian Winemaker of the Year in 1999. Part of that success, however, must be due to the fact that, uniquely, an established market existed before the winery was built, and the operation was thus able to tailor itself to fit in with pre-existing commercial conditions. For other Hungarian producers, the sequence has been the other way round: the creation of a product, then the search for a market.

Eva Keresztury, a founder-owner of Hilltop and the dynamic force behind it, was the UK representative for Hungarian state farms in 1989. This is how she first came into contact with Kamocsay, who, at that time, made wine for the Mór State Farm. Suddenly, just when her export business was expanding, the political and economic system at home began to unravel and her job disappeared. Not wanting to lose the export market she had built up, Keresztury created her own business – Interconsult – in 1990. She commissioned five or six wineries to produce (under Kamocsay's supervision) wine suitable for sale in the United Kingdom, and Interconsult acted as distributor. Hilltop is historically the same company as Interconsult, but as its own winemaking increased and its agency activity diminished, the name was changed in 1998 to the apt and easily remembered Hilltop.

Actual winemaking started in August 1993 in a rented cooperative cellar in Neszmély, but wasting no time, they began to build a new winery in 1994. Designed by Dezső Ekler, a prize-winning Hungarian architect, it blends beautifully into the Neszmély landscape. Hilltop's production grew rapidly from 1.3 million bottles in 1993 to over 9 million bottles in 1999. It is now working at capacity, and specializes in making white wine. In 1998, an additional winery to make red wine was purchased at Császár, some thirty kilometres (nineteen miles) away. Instead of further expansion, the company is now aiming to reduce its dependence on bought-in grapes (purchased in six wine regions), which account for ninety per cent of its production. Starting with 110 hectares of vineyards in bad condition, Hilltop now has a total holding of around 350 hectares. Gradual replanting has so far taken care of just over 200 hectares (eighty of them in April 2000). Despite this, the sourcing of high-quality grapes from independent growers will never entirely disappear, the company's aim being to buy grapes of the quality it requires when and where it can.

The replanting policy is to concentrate on varieties that have proved most saleable, matching varieties to site conditions. The proportion of white to red varieties is 7:3, because Hilltop believes it can compete much better in the market with its white wines. The new vineyards now have a density of 5,000 vines per hectare, and umbrella training is preferred. Use of chemicals is minimal, and great pains are taken to avoid possible residues in the grapes. Vigour is controlled by normal pruning, making green pruning unnecessary. There is an unbreakable rule of same-day-as-delivery processing, which eliminates problems of oxidation even when grapes travel relatively long distances.

The winery equipment is basically French and state of the art. Gravity is used to carry chilled must underground to the press-house, where all operations are done under protective CO_2. Two must-separation drums offer varied treatment (maceration and chilling) for each variety. Half of the must is obtained without pressure, and only must obtained by pneumatic pressures not exceeding 1.00 bar is added to the rest. The winery proper is largely underground, behind a boomerang-shaped office block. The fermentation hall has a total computer-controlled capacity of 45,000 hectolitres. Adjacent to the fermentation hall is a cellar, built in 2000, with an additional 10,000-hectolitre storage capacity.

Opposite the offices a similarly shaped building houses a bottling hall and an air-conditioned storage area, adjacent to which is the cask and barrique cellar. Only Chardonnay – and Cabernet Sauvignon and Kékfrankos at the other winery – receive wood treatment, and only Hungarian oak barriques are used. Chardonnay fermentation is started in tank; when it is half-completed, the must is transferred to barriques, where it remains for four months. Casks are used three times over two years – the third fill being for oak-ageing – and are all replaced at the same time. Tank and barrique Chardonnays are very seldom blended, and oak chips are used only for wines made for Tesco.

There are around sixty products each year, some sold under several different labels. Some of Hilltop's wines, such as the Duna range, are technically Country Wines – that is, from non-appellation regions. Hilltop's largest volume wine is Chardonnay, which it markets under four or five labels, then come Sauvignon Blanc, Pinot Gris, Irsai Olivér and "the unpronounceable grape" Cserszegi Fűszeres. There is one organic wine: Bianca. The UK market, which absorbs ninety-eight per cent of production, is complex. Different outlets operate in different price categories; some wines are found in several outlets, and some are unique to a particular retailer. A number of own-label wines are supplied. Hilltop has its own subsidiary company, Demijohn, to handle its two-per-cent Hungarian distribution through supermarkets, specialist wine shops and restaurants.

Having established Hilltop at a certain level in the UK market, the present policy is to improve quality and increase price categories. The quality of the Virgin Range (made from first vineyard crops) already shows promise, and as the new plantings get older and the materials get better, Hilltop hopes that the quality of its wines – already dependably good, and sometimes excellent – will increase commensurately. Hilltop is also interested in producing small quantities of premium wine; some possible wines of this calibre are awaiting selection and market release.

NESZMÉLY-VIN KFT (SZÖLLŐSI PINCÉSZET)

H–2890 Tata, Agostyáni u. 25. Tel/fax: +36–34 487199. Winery: H–2544 Neszmély, Kásáshegyalja út 6. Tel/fax: +36–34 451254.
(a) Mihály Szöllősi. *(b)* 20.5ha: Ch 9ha; Rs 3ha; CzF 3ha; Kir 2ha; Or 2ha; SB 1ha; OM 0.5ha. *(c)* 1,500hl. *(d)* Mihály Szöllősi. *(e)* Varietals, cuvées. *(f)* Small amounts (Brazil, Germany, and Holland)

After a varied career, first as an agricultural engineer, next as a teacher in an agricultural institute, and then running an accountancy business started in 1989 (currently managed by his wife), Mihály Szöllősi now devotes his time to his winery. Winning a Hungarian gold medal with a Chardonnay refocused his interest in wine, and converted him from being a hobby winemaker into a professional. In 1998, he purchased and refurbished an 1830 wine cellar in Neszmély, once the property of the Gyürky family. To this he has added a new winery equipped with very sophisticated French reductive technology. The business started officially in 1999.

With 10.5 hectares of vineyards purchased in 1996 and ten hectares planted in 1998, not to mention an additional twenty hectares awaiting planting, Szöllősi expects to become self-sufficient by 2005. The wines are made to be sold within the year and are distributed mainly to regional restaurants. Szöllősi's first vintage (1999) was problematic. The wines had high levels of unremittingly raw acidity, and lacked varietal character. His 2000 wines, however, are very balanced, with lots of juicy fruit – helped, perhaps, by a vintage that was hot enough to reduce the acidity of the grapes before the harvest.

GIMESKÖVIN (BORÁSZATI KERESKEDELMI SZOLGÁLTATÓ ÉS IDEGENFORGALMI KFT)

H–2517 Kesztölc, Klastrom út 2. Tel: +36–33 484 397. Tel/fax: +36–33 484 308. *(a)* Károly Gimeskövi, Béla Benedek, and a distillery in Győr. *((b)* 18ha: Ch 6ha; Cz F 4ha; Sk 6ha; Kf 1ha; CF 1ha. *(c)* 1,000hl. *(d)* Iván Gazda. *(e)* Varietals, rozé. *(f)* Small amounts (the US, Japan)

Kesztölc is a sleepy village on a hillside just off the road between Esztergom and Budapest. The Gimeskövin winery and restaurant, in a bright, contemporary architectural style, are situated at the far end of the village. Gimeskövin (a play on words based on the name of one of the owners) was started as a family enterprise in 1996, but is now a relatively big winemaking company with the capacity to become even bigger. The company's vineyards (originally those of the local cooperative, the Pilis MGTZ) were planted in 1986 in broad rows, with a mixture of high-cordon Lenz Moser and umbrella training.

The well-designed winery, which is on a hillside and works on the gravity principle, was built in 1998 and is equipped with up-to-date reductive vinification facilities, although open stainless-steel fermenters are used for a small quantity of reds made from grapes purchased in Mátraalja. There is a modern bottling line. The winemaker and viticulturalist is Iván Gazda, a 1999 graduate of The Horticultural University of Budapest. Half the production is bottled, and sold through supermarkets and restaurants. The rest is sold in bulk to large drink-distribution companies in the area. The wines are well enough made – of a good supermarket standard – and without faults, except that the Cabernet Franc seems too light for successful barrique treatment.

OTHER WINE PRODUCERS

Komáromi MG Rt. H–2911 Mocsa-Boldogasszonypuszta. Tel/fax: +36–34 349523. *Aranykalász Borászati Szövetkezet.* H–2881 Ászár, Jászai Mari u. 20. Tel: +36–34 352848

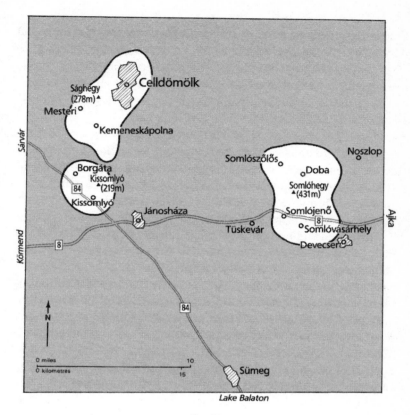

Somló

SOMLÓ

315 hectares: 311 white, four hectares red
Four wine communities, with 4,994 members

This region consists of Somlóhegy (Somló Hill), after which it is named, and two adjacent smaller areas, Sághegy and Kissomlyó. It is the smallest of the twenty-two wine regions, and less than half the size of the next smallest, Pannonhalma-Sokoróalja. But, although a small area, Somló has had an important history since the twelfth century, and was long celebrated for its wines. Their high acidity stabilized them sufficiently for successful export, and at one stage their reputation rivalled that of Tokaji. In the eighteenth and nineteenth centuries, Somló wine became a royal favourite, appreciated among others by Maria Theresa, Joseph II and Queen Victoria. Dealt a crippling blow by phylloxera, the region's fame had largely evaporated by the start of the twentieth century and has never recovered. However, I believe that Somló still has the potential to make really world-class wines, and might, in time, regain its once-golden reputation.

Situated in the southern Kisföld, Somló Hill is an extinct volcano rising in splendid isolation out of an otherwise flat landscape. As early as the eleventh century, the first Hungarian king, István I, founded a convent of the order of St Benedicta in Somló. The order was by far the biggest vineyard proprietor on the hill, but was disbanded in 1511 for "unrestrained unruliness". Its vineyards then passed briefly to the Premontai order of nuns in Szeged, until the nuns fled to Vienna in the face of the Turkish invasion of 1526. The vineyards apparently survived Muslim rule, and in the following century they were given by the Habsburgs to the order of St Clara in Pozsony (now Bratislava). This continued until the partial abolition of religious orders by Joseph II in 1780, when their lands were appropriated to the crown and thereafter administered by state commissioners – a situation that lasted until 1945. Apart from the church, of course, aristocratic landowners in the eighteenth and nineteenth centuries also had vineyards on the hill, among them the Erdödy, Zichy, Esterházy and Fehérvári families.

This history is worth recounting to drive home how changed the situation is now. Until the middle of the twentieth century, most of the vineyards on Somlóhegy were fairly large, often with massive stone terracing. One would certainly not have seen so many of the small plots, each with its tiny house, that now jostle each other on the slopes. When collectivization took place after the Second World War, many of the best vineyards on the hill were abandoned, especially near the top, and a few still await recovery. At the same time, up until 1990, the area around Ajka (close to Veszprém) was an industrial and coal-mining zone, and Somló became a weekend haven for the workers. It soon became fashionable to build small summer residences on the slopes. The progressive inroads this made into prime vineyard land means that much of it has been lost for ever. A little consolidation of the small plots is beginning to take place.

Not only were the vineyards bigger, they were very different in character. Cultivation was by staked vines, and propagation was by layering. Many (perhaps most) of the vineyards had an indiscriminate mixture of varieties, effectively giving a naturally blended wine. Today, Juhfark, Furmint and Hárslevelű are considered the characteristic varieties of the region, and they have certainly been grown here for centuries. However, in 1792 a priest wrote that there were forty-six varieties in Somló; more recently, Dr Elmer Fornady, in a book published in 1930, records a traditional form of planting that was common before phylloxera. This consisted of precisely calculated mixed plantings of forty different varieties per hectare, producing a traditional wine called Somlai Bor (not to be confused with Somlói Bor). During the Second World War, however, farmers left the region, and nobody tried to save the original Somló grape varieties. The situation became worse after the vineyards were appropriated by the state and administered by the *Badacsonyvidéki Pincegazdság*, (Badacsony Region Farm Cellar). Only a few of the smallest vineyards remained in private hands, and the cooperative's crop was sold mainly to Hungarovin to become Somlói Pezsgő (sparkling wine) or acidless, sweet wines for the Communist bloc. Growers were paid on the basis of grape-sugar levels, and soon adapted to this situation by changing over to varieties uncharacteristic of the region that gave three times the customary yield (such as Attila, Ezerjó and Szlanka). Some of these still survive. As late as 1985, big, mechanizable plantings were made by the Noszlop Cooperative on level ground on the eastern perimeter of the hill.

Recent block plantings are generally of the traditional varieties – in order of popularity Hárslevelű, Furmint and Juhfark, with Olasrizling, Tramini and Chardonnay also permitted. Stake training is still quite common, but I have noticed a wider selection of training systems in use in Somló than in any other region. As can be seen from the number of growers, vineyard plots are tiny, most being not much more than 0.05 of a hectare. Only about fifty growers have more than one hectare, the biggest being Tornai Pincészet, with thirty. The old cooperative has disappeared, but a new cooperative of three growers was recently started.

The other parts of the region deserve more discussion than space permits. Sághegy is about three kilometres (almost two miles) along the Mesteri road from the town of Celldömölk while, further south,

Kissomlyó lies close to Borgáta. Both are sisters to Somló, being smaller hills of identical volcanic origin, with similar cultivation and varieties, producing wines of similar character. Because of their relatively small size, large vineyards never developed here – in Kissomlyó the largest plot is only 0.5 hectare – and, being so small and awkward to work, they were never collectivized.

Kissomlyó producers claim that its microclimate makes it a better growing area than either Sághegy or Somlóhegy. The topsoil has less depth, and the basalt rock beneath holds the heat of the sun well. This reduces the acid content of the wines by between 1.5 and two grams per litre below the regional average, which is seen by the locals as a benefit. There are no producers bottling their wine or marketing their wine individually in either place, and what is not used by each family is sold at the cellar door, or in bulk either to local pubs or to one large Balaton producer. However, one Sághegy grower is experimenting with early-ripening crosses conjointly with the Georgikon Faculty of Agriculture at Keszthely (q.v.). Enterprisingly, both share a wine route, while Somlóhegy has one of its own.

The special character of Somlóhegy wines arises from the volcanic nature of the soil, formed through the degradation and erosion of ancient lava flows with a high basalt and varied mineral content. The best vineyards are traditionally those highest on the hill, where the basalt predominates, or on identifiable lava streams on its slopes. The surrounding flat land, by comparison, lacks the same degree of volcanic and mineral content, and vineyards here make slightly inferior wine. The biggest difference between Somló wines and others is in their high acid content. This is not, as it frequently is elsewhere in Hungary, the result of premature harvesting, because high levels of sugar and acidity can coexist. Thus, it is possible to have musts with up to 23° of sugar and eight or nine grams per litre of acid, combined with high levels of dry extract, sometimes in excess of thirty grams per litre. Climatic considerations play a part in this. The climate gives just enough sunshine to ripen the grapes (making chaptalization standard procedure in normal years) but, being very windy, is only moderately warm and therefore helps to preserve high levels of acidity in the grapes. The ripening period is relatively short, beginning at the end of September with Chardonnay and Juhfark, and finishing at the middle to end of October with Hárslevelű. In 1999, autumn was unusually long, whereas in 2000, only forty millimetres (one-and-a-half inches) of rain fell between April and August, and the summer heat made for wines with untypically high sugar levels and lower acidity.

How, then, given their former celebrity, do modern Somló wines shape up? The answer: not terribly well. A handful of dedicated producers make fairly minuscule quantities of high-quality wine – Fekete, Györgykovács, Osvald and Végh among them. Unevenness of quality characterizes many of the rest. Some good, if often rather commercial and undemanding, wines are made by Indovin, Somlóvin, Károly Fehérvari, Gyula Schmall, Tornai Pincészet and Csordás-Fodor Pincészet.

The best wines are traditionally made, using oxidative techniques, and their obvious high acidity when young is unpleasant. Until one has been able to taste wines with five or more years of development, in which the elements have got into a better balance, it is difficult to understand what all the fuss is about. When the wines are mature, however, the high acidity gives them a steely spine, around which the extract develops depth, with a wealth of complex and subtle mineral, pebbly flavours, while the bouquet takes on a sometimes petrol-like intensity reminiscent of mature Rhine Riesling.

Even so, wines with this sort of bottle-age (which are exceedingly difficult to obtain) only hint at why the wine was formerly held in such esteem. It was not until I had tasted a series of really astonishing wines from the private reserve of a Kissomlyó grower that I really began to understand why Maria Theresa and Queen Victoria so favoured Somló. A 1994 Olaszrizling was a revelation: complex and developed, but with no loss of finesse or style . . . perhaps the best wine made from this variety I have ever tasted. A 1994 cuvée was even more sensational: again, enormous complexity was allied to breeding and refinement. Sadly, there are only a very few bottles of such wines in existence. They are never for sale, but are treasured for drinking on special family occasions, and I was privileged to be able to taste them.

I subsequently discovered that, before the Second World War, Somló wines by law had to be matured for five years in cask before being sold. This longer wood maturation seems to add extra layers of flavour and still more depth to the wine, and although only a few of the artisan producers appear to keep their wine in small, old oak casks for this length of time, the results certainly justify the extra trouble. Sometimes these wines become mildly oxidized and a little fino-like (more by chance than design) and many producers seem to accept this style as a legitimate part of the Somló wine culture. When wines are kept in cask for as long as twenty years, they become like Virgin Marsala, both in colour and in nutty flavours, and are offered to special guests or drunk on celebratary occasions. They are not commercially available.

It is worth mentioning that Somló wine has always had a reputation for medicinal qualities, being recommended for ailments such as high blood pressure, anaemia, lack of stomach acid and liver complaints, while it is used in Swiss clinics for the treatment of paralysis. It used to be stocked by Hungarian pharmacists. The wine has also become the subject of legends, such as that its use promotes longevity and increases the likelihood of children being born male. A comparison of regional and national statistics appears, surprisingly, to give these claims some circumstantial backing.

One day, perhaps, a very rich perfectionist with a talented and experienced winemaker will try to recreate the old style of Somló wine. For the sake of the wine world, I earnestly hope so. In 2000, a group of bank directors created what may become just such a firm. It is as yet unnamed, but has ten hectares for replanting, and is managed by István Inhauser, the owner of Indovin.

GYÖRGYKOVÁCS IMRE

H–8400 Ajka, Verseny u. 9. Tel: +36–88 200 116. Cellar: in Somlóvásárhely.

(a) Imre Györgykovács. (b) 0.5ha – in three plots: T/Rs/H/F/Or/J. (c) 40–plus hl.
(d) Imre Györgykovács. (e) Varietals. (f) None

Imre Györgykovács has not achieved recognition as one of the top Somló producers without a struggle. At first, following the family wine tradition, he worked in a cooperative, later becoming a radio mechanic for Videoton. In 1979, he bought his first vineyard for hobby winemaking and, shortly afterwards, left Videoton to become a gardener. He continued to make wine in a quiet way until, in 1992, at a time when he could not afford to bottle his wine, an unfiltered Tramini was chosen as one of twelve wines served at the foundation dinner of the Hungarian Academy of Wine (q.v.). The following year, a Budapest lawyer whom he had never met, but who had drunk and admired some of his wine, offered

Györgykovács a subsidy to enable him to bottle it. This disinterested sponsorship continues, and has enabled Györgykovács to give up gardening in favour of winemaking.

Györgykovács cultivates his vines and makes his wines with scrupulous care. Largely self-taught, he thinks he benefited from a visit to Napa Valley in 1998. The oldest of his vines, which he planted himself, date from 1985, and are double-cordon trained. He prunes one bud in two and crops about eighty hectolitres per hectare – a surprisingly high amount in view of his wines' concentrated flavours. He buys from a neighbour, whose plot he manages, and from others in good vintage years. Grapes are rigorously selected in the vineyard and are picked before 10AM. The must is fermented, 500 litres at a time, in oak casks in the 1828 cellar below his house. There is no temperature control, and natural yeasts are used. After fermentation, the wine is filtered (no finings are used) then settled and racked into casks, or, failing that, plastic containers. The wine is bottled before the next harvest, then given up to two years of bottle maturation before sale.

Györgykovács is experimenting with barriques, but thinks that fruity wines do not benefit from wood treatment. His general philosophy is to take the utmost care in fermenting his wine, and to interfere with it as little as possible afterwards. He deliberately makes five varietal wines to show wine-lovers the range Somló can produce. His wines are particularly noted for their purity of flavour, and right from the start, they combine power with refinement and finesse. The available quantity is so small that it is sold only through the Budapest Bortársaság (Budapest Wine Society), and one other outlet. Györgykovács would like to expand his production, but only on the best terroir. Quality, for him, remains the prime consideration.

FEKETE KFT

H–8200 Veszprém, Látóhegy u. 3. Tel/fax: +36–88 327 407. (a) Béla Fekete. (b) 3ha: H 0.86ha; F 0.72ha; J 1.08ha; Ch 0.34ha. (c) 90hl. (d) Béla Fekete. (e) Varietals. (f) None

Béla Fekete is passionate about his wine. Born in 1926, and having grown up in Somló, he began making wine at the end of the 1960s from purchased must. This led to his buying a 0.13-hectare vineyard on the east of Somlóhegy in 1968. He replanted it and began to learn about winemaking. After two years, he thought (mistakenly, he admits) that he knew everything on the subject. At this time he worked in Veszprém, where he now lives, as head of the agricultural planning department at the local institute. Retiring at sixty, he later sold his original plot and moved to his present one in 1992. Here the soil is so good – a one-metre (thirty-nine inch) deep, gravelly mixture of sand and basalt over very large, degradable basalt rocks – that he soon bought a neighbouring plot to form a single, south-facing 2.5-hectare area. In 2001, he planted another half-hectare of Juhfark.

Despite his age, Fekete does ninety per cent of the vineyard work himself, helped, from time to time, by his son. This is perhaps more by necessity than by choice, because reliable local help is hard to find. Grapes are fermented in wooden barrels. After two rackings in November and May, the wine is thereafter transferred to stainless steel to avoid further oxidation, and after two years is taken to Veszprém for filtering and bottling.

Fekete has no cellar-door sales, but does have a tasting cellar on Somlóhegy where he is happy to receive guests. He sells to Gundel's restaurant and two other agents in Budapest, and also markets some wine through Monarchia. His wines are very unapproachable when young. They are a little rustic in character, and have rather broad flavours when mature. Like the wine of Györgykovács, they are imbued with the complex minerality that characterizes the best Somló wine.

OSZVALD LAJOS

H–1161 Budapest, Szilágyi Dezsőu. 12. Tel/fax: +36–1 405 6839. Winery: Somlóhegy. *(a)* Lajos Oszvald. *(b)* 7.5ha: 3ha of mixed plantings; J 1.3ha; F 1.3ha; Or 1.3ha; H 0.5ha. *(c)* 60hl in 2000. *(d)* Lajos Oszvald and Zsolt László. *(e)* Varietals, a projected cuvée. *(f)* None

Lajos Oszvald is a Budapest-based architect. In 1984, he bought a 0.25-hectare hobby vineyard in Balatoncsicsó and started winemaking as a complete amateur. In 1997, however, a series of accidents brought him to Somló, where he purchased an old house and cellar with a one-hectare vineyard. Having to employ a caretaker encouraged him to expand, and now he has a holding of 7.5 hectares, mainly halfway up the hill, made up of twenty-seven plots in three different areas – Doba, Somlószőlős and Somlósjenő. What started as a hobby is now a business, yet he is just at the beginning. Now he has to invest in proper equipment and possibly in a new winery.

Oszvald's three hectares at Doba are possibly unique. They consist of a traditional forty-variety-per-hectare vineyard in which the vines are over fifty years old, and therefore pre-date the 1949 nationalization. They are in need of restoration: some vines are missing (and have been replaced with Furmint); some are stake-trained, some are on cordons; and there are gaps. However, Oszvald is very conscious of his responsibility in having something so rare, and he is determined to cherish it. It has to be worked entirely by hand and, at the moment, it gives a yield of only ten hectolitres per hectare. There is one Juhfark vine which has an enormously thick trunk, and this has been used for taking cuttings for propagation for the last twenty years (since Juhfark made its reappearance in the region).

Oszvald buys in grapes for the time being. He uses traditional cask fermentation techniques, and is in no hurry to sell his wine, storing it in oak casks and bottling (by hand) only when necessary. He eventually plans to have stainless-steel storage, and to bottle the wine after one-and-a-half to two years (to avoid oxidation).

Oszvald's wines are perhaps consistently the best I have tasted in Somlóhegy. They are paradigms of the traditional mineral and acid character. A 1999 Olaszrizling (low-cordon trained and unfiltered) is delicious, refined, and sophisticated, with a pronounced riesling-type aroma. The 1998 Somlai Bor is revelatory. Balanced and flavoursome, it is complex on both the nose and palate and, at the same time, supremely elegant. The bouquet is developing nice Riesling notes. No wonder Queen Victoria got hooked, and what an eloquent testimony this is of past glories! At last, one can genuinely span backwards across the Communist regime and have some insight into what pre-war wines were like.

VÉGH REZSŐ

H–9545 Jánosháza, Szent István u. 14. Tel: +36–95 450624. *(a)* Rezsó Végh. *(b)* 1ha: Or/Chas 0.5ha at Balatonszentgrót; Kir/Sem/OM/ZV/Or 0.5ha at Kissomlyó. *(c)* Not disclosed. *(d)* Rezsó Végh. *(e)* Varietals, cuvées. *(f)* None

Rezsó Végh, a retired forester, demonstrates with his Kissomlyó wines that Somlóhegy has no monopoly of quality. Purchased in 1971 and replanted in 1972 to enable each variety to be harvested separately, his vineyard – the biggest in Kissomlyó – uses Lenz Moser training, and a middling yield is aimed at. He chose the five varieties so that they would make an interesting cuvée if put together. His cellar dates from 1929 and is suitable for receiving up to twenty people at a time. He makes his wine traditionally, but ferments free-run juice separately and then blends it back into pressed-must wine. I consider his wines among the best in the region. His 2000 wines, tasted from cask, all had the mineral character of the locale stamped on them, but (perhaps because of the vintage) showed less-assertive acidity than I had expected. His Zöld Veltelini, in particular, beats hands down anything I have ever found in Sopron, while the Királyleányka is outstanding. His older wines sing like larks. Végh also makes unusual wines, such as a dry aperitif Ottonel Muskotály and a sweet, red vermouth, whose recipe requires thirty-two different herbs. Only a little wine is bottled for friends.

SOMLÓVIN KFT (FAZEKAS BORPINCE)

H–8481 Somlóvásárhely, Ady E. u. 2. Tel: +36–88 236287. (a) András Fazekas.
(b) 10ha: J 3ha; H 3ha; F 3ha; Or 1ha. (c) 400–500hl. (d) András Fazekas.
(e) Varietals, sparkling wine. (f) 10% (Denmark, Japan)
After a varied career as a mechanic, András Fazekas ended up teaching in a technical school in Ajka. From 1980 he made wine part-time in a rented vineyard, and found it paid ten times more than he got for teaching, so he turned to full-time winemaking in 1986. Fazekas now has ten hectares of his own vineyards, with plantings dating from 1991, but he buys in both grapes and wine. His fermentation equipment is good and getting better, and he ferments in both reductive and oxidative styles, the latter being matured in cask for one year before being transferred to stainless-steel storage. Fazekas, uniquely in Somló, also makes dry and demi-sec tank-fermented sparkling wine from Chardonnay, Furmint, and Tramini. The first private producer in Somló to have his own bottling plant (in 1993), Fazekas commissioned a large custom-built bottling plant in Somlóvásárhely in 1998. He bottles all of his own wine, and that of some other producers as well. In general, Fazekas

makes good wines showing strong mineral characteristics, those from the 2000 vintage being particularly good. They are sold in Somló and in Budapest.

TORNAI PINCÉSZET
H–8460 Devecser, Vasút u. 29. Tel/fax: +36–88 224040/2014886. Winery: Somlóvásárhely. *(a)* A T Tours. *(b)* 30ha: Or 10ha; F 8ha; J 8ha; H 2ha; T 2ha. *(c)* 3,750hl. *(d)* Cecilia Simon. *(e)* Varietals, cuvée. *(f)* Variable amounts (the US, Taiwan, and Holland)

This, the largest producer in Somló, is one of several enterprises (including a textile firm) belonging to the Tornai family. Started in 1946 with 0.7 of a hectare, it remained private throughout the Communist period. The winery was established on its present site, south of Somlóhegy, in 1997, and has sophisticated equipment, partly Italian and partly Hungarian. After grape delivery (using the company's unique, fully automatic technology of computer-identified harvesting sacks on a suspended conveyer belt), fermentation is in a completely closed system. Fermentations are long and slow, and the wine is matured in large, wooden casks. When new plantings come on-stream, the present production level – half of which uses bought-in grapes – is set to double. The wines are of a good commercial standard, but, being reductive, not wholly typical of the region.

OTHER WINE PRODUCERS
Csite Antal. H–8400 Ajka, Alinka u. 15. Tel: +36–88 210874. *Csordás-Fodor Pincészet.* H–8400 Ajka, Május 1. tér 3. Tel: +36–88 3111753. *Danka Imre.* H–9500 Celldömölk, Arany J. u. 30. Tel: +36–95 421842. *Fazekas József.* H–1027 Budapest, Bem J. u. 14. Tel: +36–1 202 1521. *Fehér Tamás.* H–9500 Celldömölk, Deák F. u. 25. Tel: +36–95 420806. *Fehérvári Károly.* H–8200 Veszprém, Egry J. u. 45. Tel: +36–88 320738. Fax: +36–88 420737. *Hartmann József.* H–9500 Celldömölk, Sági u. 28. Tel: +36–95 420330. *Héjjas-Jeszenszky Pincészet.* H–1053 Budapest, Kossuth L. u. 17. Tel: +36–1 337 6166. *Indovin Kft (Inhauser Pincészét).* H–8483 Somlószőlős, Somlóhegy. Tel: +36–30 562741; Fax: +36–94 358228. *Molnár Pince.* H–8477 Tüskevár, Rózsa u. 1. Tel: +36–88 259182. *Schmall Gyula.* H–9700 Szombathely, Szűresapó u. 22. Tel: +36–94 316451. *Somogyi Lajos Kertészmérn és Szőlőbor Termelő (Hegykapu).* H–8481 Somlóvásárhely, Somlóhegy. Tel: +36–88 236306. *Somló-Trade Kft (Bogdán*

Családi Pince). H–8500 Pápa, Szent István u. 22. Tel: +36–89 312068. *Stubán Zsigmondné–Somlói Bortermelő.* H–8500 Pápa, Korvin u. 24. Tel: +36–89 313516. *Szolnoki Gyula.* H–8400 Ajka, Vörsmarty u. 13. Tel: +36–88 201863. *Vathy Gyula.* H–8400 Ajka, Újélet u. 14/C. Tel/fax: +36–88 311635

6

Lake Balaton

BALATONFÜRED-CSOPAK

2131 hectares: 1,900 white, 231 hectares red
Eighteen wine communities, with 5,264 members

Lake Balaton, seventy-eight kilometres (forty-eight miles) from end to end and at the heart of the former Roman province of Pannonia, is the largest lake in continental Europe. Its entire north bank is classic Hungarian wine territory, the regions being contiguous and not dissimilar to each other. Wine traditions are deep-rooted, and owe much to the Swabian communities that put their roots down here in the eighteenth century. It is especially celebrated for its Olaszrizling, generally considered the best in Hungary, and for long its signature variety.

Balatonfüred is a spa town, and like the whole of the lakeside, it is very busy during the summer with holiday-makers. Tourism really started in the Balaton area after the First World War, when Hungary lost so much of its territory. Budapestians regarded the lake as the Hungarian seaside, but between the wars it remained relatively quiet and rural. However, tourism got a further boost after the Second World War, when Hungary supplied a holiday venue where German families separated by the Iron Curtain could be temporarily reunited.

This German link has continued since the change of regime and has, if anything, grown stronger. Now, during the high season, the area is a hive of activity, and so many Germans have bought summer residences here that in some villages they outnumber the locals. This flourishing tourism has repercussions on the wine trade. On the positive side, it provides an affluent market, but on the negative side, because tourism pays better, it

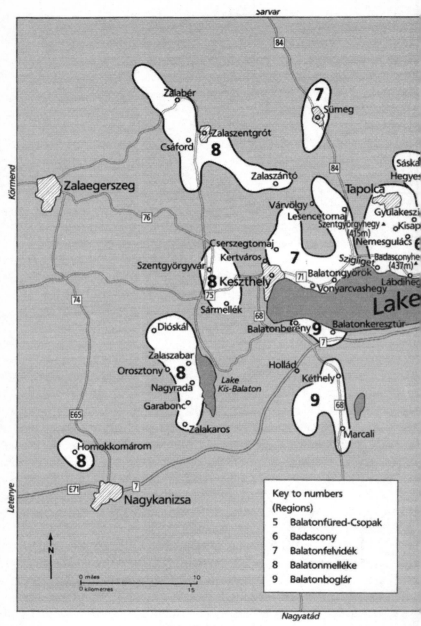

Lake Balaton

Key to numbers (Regions)
5   Balatonfüred-Csopak
6   Badascony
7   Balatonfelvidék
8   Balatonmelléke
9   Balatonboglár

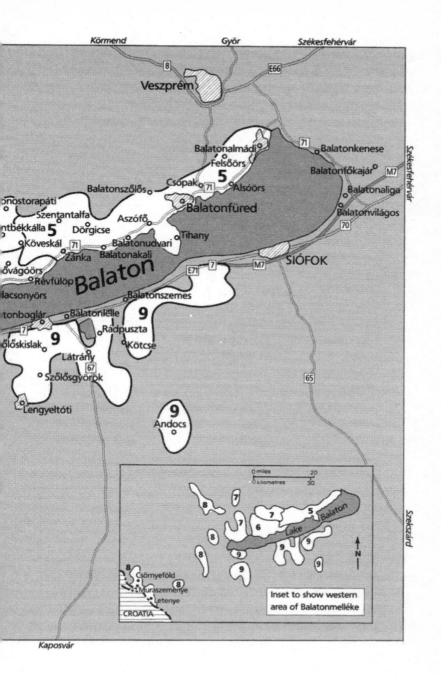

Körmend   Győr   Székesfehérvár

Veszprém

Balatonalmádi   Balatonkenese
Felsőörs
Csopak   Balatonfőkajár   M7
Balatonszőlős   Alsóörs   Balatonaliga
önostorapáti   Balatonfüred   Balatonvilágos
Szentantalfa   Aszófő
ntbékkálla 5   Dörgicse
Köveskál   Tihany
Balatonudvari
Zánka   Balatonakali
övágóörs   Balaton
Révfülöp
lacsonyörs   Balatonszemes   SIÓFOK
tonboglár   Balatonlelle   9
Rádpuszta
őlőskislak   9   Kötcse
Látrány
Szőlősgyörök

Lengyeltóti   9
Andocs

0 miles   20
0 kilometres   30

8   7
7   5   Balaton
7   6   Lake
8   9   9   9
8   9
Csörnyeföld   9
Muraszemenye   8   N
Letenye
CROATIA

Inset to show western
area of Balatonmelléke

Kaposvár

lures the local labour force away from the vineyards. Not even high wages can compete, and many producers have had to resort to bussing casual labour from villages forty or more kilometres (twenty-five-plus miles) away.

Very much a white-wine region, Balatonfüred-Csopak consists of rather scattered vineyard areas, some of them close to the lake – like Balatonalmádi, Alsóörs, Balatonakali, and Zánka – but many of them around inland villages scattered among low-lying hills, most notably at Dörgicse, Csopak, and Felsőörs. However, the region also includes Tihany (added only in 1997) a peninsula that stretches out into the lake and makes it possible to reach the other side by means of a short ferry crossing. Blessed with a very favourable microclimate, with vineyards protected by belts of forest, and excellent basalt-based soil with a high humus content, Tihany is becoming notable for its red-grape production, of which there are around eighty hectares. Tihany produces musts with high acidity and extract, and long ageing potential. With its prolonged hot autumns, it is perhaps the only place in mid-Hungary where Cabernet Sauvignon can be fully ripened.

Csopak was associated with János Ranolder, bishop of Veszprém during the second half of the nineteenth century. He had family vineyards here and in Badacsony, and was said to have the best wines in central Hungary. In 1892, shortly after his death, phylloxera reached Csopak and the rest of the north Balaton area, and all but ten per cent of the vines were lost. Many of the inhabitants left to settle at Helvécia (q.v.), and the area was not replanted until well into the new century. During the Communist period, winemaking here was dominated by the Csopakvin Cooperative, but this went bankrupt in 1999.

The lake exercises a moderating influence on the climate of all the regions on its north bank. The average annual temperature is 10.8°C, veering between 34°C and −14°C, with the lake freezing over during the winter. There is an average of 2,069 sunshine hours a year. The Csopak area has a special microclimate, a little warmer than the rest of the lake, with a slightly larger share of sunshine. The soil is red sandstone over a crystalline base, and stretches from Csopak to Balatonalmádi. It differs from the brown forest soil characteristic of Balatonfüred. Because of the lake, birds present growers with a big problem just before harvesting. One grower compares their attacks to scenes from Hitchcock's film *The Birds*, and losses can be very serious. "If a grower tells you that he does not have a problem with birds, you know that he picks too early."

FINE WINE BORÁSZATI VÁLLALKOZÁS

H–8230 Balatonfüred, Siske u. 44/b. Tel/fax: +36–87 343557. Winery: Csárda utca, Balatonfüred. *(a)* Mihály Figula. *(b)* 10ha: Or 4ha; Ch 1ha; Sk 1ha; SB 0.7ha; Sem 0.7ha; OM 0.5ha; T 0.5ha; red varieties 1.6ha. *(c)* 500–600hl. *(d)* Mihály Figula. *(e)* Varietals, rozé, cuvées. *(f)* 20–30% (Germany, Benelux, Finland, and Japan)

Mihály Figula was born in the east of Hungary, a part of the country without any wine. A graduate of the Horticultural University of Budapest, he was a director of the Győr State Farm from 1979 until 1985, when he moved to Csopakvin, the local cooperative, where he remained until January 1999.

Figula works as a private individual, but was joined by his son in 2001. He first entered the market in 1993 with the aim of making wines that show clear varietal character. His vineyards are situated in Balatonfüred and Balatonszőlős. Most are old Lenz Moser-trained state plantings, bought for their prime location, but two were planted by Figula in 1991, with a density of 3,900 vines per hectare and umbrella training. The crop is restricted to fifty-six hectolitres per hectare from the new plantings, and to between thirty-seven and forty-nine hectolitres from the old.

Figula concentrates mainly on reductive white wines. Because of its local reputation, he takes special care with Olaszrizling, of which he offers a barrique version that is unusual in Hungary. His Tramini is made as a dry wine with a little residual sugar, although in the best years he makes a semi-dry wine with eight to fifteen grams per litre of residual sugar. His cuvées are made by fermenting two varieties together rather than by subsequently blending them. He is not interested in making late-harvest wines (he says that there is a real risk of the grapes being stolen!), but to give his winery an image, he tries to make an "astonishing wine" (like his barrique rozé) every year. Interestingly, he considers that the region produces wines that are a little too acidic, and he is working on how to reduce the acidity of his own wines.

His very well-equipped 1995 winery, which has a tasting room for groups, is on the outskirts of Balatonfüred, overlooking the lake and the Tihany peninsula. From beginning to end, the must and wine are continuously under CO_2. Ottonel Muskotály, Sauvignon Blanc and Szürkebarát are briefly macerated, but Chardonnay and Olaszrizling are not. Selected yeasts are used and, when the pectin content of the grapes is high, enzymes are also added. Fermentations last from fourteen to twenty days, after which the wine is racked and goes either into stainless steel or into cask, where it remains on its lees for four months before being filtered and bottled (the latter being carried out by Hilltop). Figula will shortly build a new cellar with his own bottling facility.

Chardonnay is fermented after sedimentation in barriques – a mixture of French and Hungarian oak – for about six-and-a-half months, when it is put into stainless-steel tanks. Olaszrizling is treated similarly, but stays in barrique for five months only. Both undergo full malolactic fermentation, and are blended from barriques with different age usage (the maximum being four times). A small amount of cask-fermented, onion-skin-coloured Szürkebarát is also produced. Figula's equipment is not really suited to producing red wine, but in response to market demand, he makes a designedly light Merlot and a Kékfrankos, as well as a rozé.

Figula produces elegant and balanced wines with good varietal definition (as he wishes to do), and his barrique Chardonnay is one of the best I know of in Hungary. Even his unwooded Merlot, with its bracing raspberry bouquet and very good fruit, is more honestly typical of the variety than most in Hungary. None of his wines is less than very good, and they amply justify his nomination in 2000 as Winemaker of the Year. Figula sells in Hungary from his cellar (which is the only source of his museum wines), to high-class restaurants, and to Cora supermarket. He would like to export more.

JÁSDI PINCE KFT

H–8229 Csopak, Arany J. u. 2. Tel/fax: +36–87 446452. (a) István Jásdi, Péter Csiszár, János Ritecz. (b) 16.65ha (5.8ha not yet yielding): Sk 6.4ha; Or 4.7ha; CzF 1.5ha; Ch 1.35ha; Zen 0.8ha; F 0.3ha; Kf 0.9ha; CS 0.7ha. (c) 660hl. (d) János Ritecz. (e) Varietals. (f) 10% (Switzerland)

István Jásdi used to be a diplomat, which is how he got his taste for

French wine. He lives in an elegant house that once belonged to Bishop Ranolder and, later, to a Jewish wine merchant called Hüvös, whose winemaker's son was Károly Bakonyi, the propagator of Cserszegi Fűszeres. Buying and restoring the house in 1997 led Jásdi into winemaking, more for romantic than for rational or economic reasons. He decided to try to make wines that would restore the area's former reputation, so he installed a winery with absolutely *dernier cri* technology in the Bishop's old and capacious barrel-vaulted stone cellar.

Gravity based, the winery has been automated as much as possible. It is extremely impressive. Only half of its 2,000-hectolitre capacity is presently in use, and all the winemaking is reductive. Olaszrizling is matured in large casks, Szürkebarát in small casks, and barriques at the moment are used for half of the Chardonnay production. All the wine is bottled (using an Italian bottling line) and is sold through two Budapest agents.

Although the business is in family hands, there is a holding company with three partners, these being Jásdi, his winemaker, and his vineyard manager. There are about six hectares belonging to Jásdi around the house, and the other ten hectares belong to the vineyard manager. The old plantations, with wide rows and high cordons, are about twenty years old, having belonged to the local cooperative. New plantations, extending to 5.8 hectares, have a density of 4,000 vines per hectare, and are umbrella-trained.

The wines are of a distinctly vibrant kind, with no malolactic fermentation and slightly glaring acidity. This is particularly true of the very tropical-fruit-and-pineapple Chardonnay, despite its wood treatment. However, the Olaszrizling is very good, and the Sauvignon Blanc (made from grapes bought in from Balatonszőlős) is one of the best I have seen in Hungary. The surprise, however, is the Cserszegi Fűszeres, which has a Fumé Blanc depth to both its nose and palate, and is certainly the most serious Cserszegi Fűszeres I have ever encountered, appropriately enough, given Bakonyi's association with the property. A Merlot, made in a style intended to mirror the whites, is fresh, light, and fruity, getting its appeal from its wonderful Tihany fruit. Given that these are the first products of the winery, the achievement is remarkably high and promises much for the future.

HUDÁK BT (HUDÁK ZOLTÁN)

H–Balatonfüred, Köztársaság út 11/c. Tel: +36–87 341182. *(a)* Zoltán Hudák.
(b) 10ha: Sk 1ha; OR 6ha; Kf 2ha; M 1ha. *(c)* 1,000hl. *(d)* Zoltán Hudák.
(e) Varietals, rozé. *(f)* 10% (Switzerland)

Zoltán Hudák hails originally from Tokaj. After graduating in viniculture at the Horticultural University of Budapest, he did his practicals at the Badacsony State Farm. A short while later, after promotion and marriage, he decided to settle at Lake Balaton, and started his own business in 1998.

Hudák has vineyards – some of which were compensation for expropriated family vineyards – in Csopak (Olaszrizling), Balatonfüred (Sürkebarát) and Tihany (one hectare of Kékfrankos). The rest are in Balatonudvari. Half were already planted when he acquired them, and half he has planted himself, with a density of 5,000 vines per hectare and umbrella training.

His cellar, with the date 1846 over the door, has reasonable reductive fermentation technology and large oak casks. Previously tiny, it was extended in 2001 in order to receive tourists. Hudák also intends, eventually, to extend his vineyards to fifteen hectares. Above all, he wants to go for quality. He considers sixty-five hectolitres per hectare a reasonable yield. A third of his production is bottled for him by Dörgicse Bor. It is sold to Budapest restaurants and in supermarkets like Kaiser and Cora, while the unbottled wine goes in bulk to local restaurants.

I have been very impressed by Hudák's wines (apart from the rozé), and think they deserve a higher profile than they have at present. They are all stylish, well-crafted wines, clean and balanced, with good extract. A 1998 Spätlese Szürkebarát, for example, is very attractive, and his 2000 Tihany Kékfrankos is outstanding. Typically, his red wines have excellent colour, fruit, and flavour, even if they are a shade on the light side. A winemaker to watch.

BADACSONYI PINCEGAZDASÁG RT

H–8230 Balatonfüred, Zrínyi u. 11. Tel: +36–87 343 855. Tel/fax: +36–87 343 860. *(a)* Balatoni Borászati és Kereskedelmi Részvénytársaság. *(b)* 90ha. Badacsony 10ha: Sk 6ha; MO 4ha. Somló 60ha: Or 60ha. Tihany 20ha: Zw 7ha; Ko 5ha; M 4ha; CS 2ha; Kf 2ha. *(c)* 26,000hl. *(d)* János Fogl. *(e)* Varietals, rozé. *(f)* 10% (the Far East, Lithuania, Japan, and the US)

This company is the legal successor to the *Badacsonyvidéki Pincegazdság* (Badacsony Region Farm Cellar), a huge Transdanubian company founded in 1949, whose operations stretched from Balaton to Mór and Sopron. The new company was formed in December 1995, and the owners of the parent company are three Hungarians. The company presently operates in five places, with cellars in Balatonfüred, Badacsony, Tihany, and Zánka, and vineyards in Badacsony, Somló, and Tihany.

Winemaking is carried out only at Zánka, some fifteen kilometres (nine miles) west of Balatonfüred. The original 1965 winery, which in its heyday had a throughput of 5,000 tonnes a year, was replaced by a new one in 1997–9. The equipment is sophisticated, with a stainless-steel capacity of 15,000 hectolitres – somewhat larger than is presently required. A new bottling line is planned. There are three cask cellars, one of which is at Tihany in a lovely situation overlooking a small lake, and has a tasting room and restaurant.

The winemaker, János Fogel, is one of the less than a score of wine-makers in Hungary under the age of thirty-five. A graduate of the Horticultural University of Budapest, he worked with Gál at Ornellaia and did a vintage at Vega Sicilia before coming to Balatonfüred. He has a sophisticated attitude to what he is doing, and wants to improve quality – but that, he says, depends on the company acquiring more local vineyards and reducing its current range of wines. He is keen to introduce barrique treatment for red wine, with French rather than Hungarian casks.

The company has been making steady progress, and is only hampered in further modernization by lack of funds. The 1999 vintage wines were launched with new labels as part of an across-the-board effort to fashion a new, upmarket image. White wines are well-made and marked by strong fruit character, and those matured in cask gain in complexity without loss of character. The reds are more variable, but a 1999 Zweigelt that had been through a malolactic fermentation surprised me with its ripe Zinfandel aromas.

FEIND LAJOS

H–8164 Balatonfőkajár, Kossuth Lajos u. 13. Tel: +33 –88 483169. *(a)* Lajos Feind. *(b)* 54ha. Old: Or 18ha; Chas 5ha; Ch 4ha; CzF 3ha; Sk 2ha; Ez 2ha; Kir

1.5ha; PB 1.25ha; Kf 1.5ha; T 1.5ha; SB 0.75ha; ZV 0.5ha. New: CS 2.5ha; CF 2.5ha; M 2ha; Kf 2ha; PN 2ha. Rootstock: 1.5ha. *(c)* 5,000hl in 2000. *(d)* Péter Feind. *(e)* Varietals. *(f)* A little (Brazil)

Lajos Feind is an agricultural engineer. He farms 230 hectares of arable land, and owns fifty-five hectares of vineyards, partly in Balatonfüred, and partly at Balatonaliga at the eastern end of the lake. This area, including Balatonkenese and Balatonvilágos as well as Balatonfőkajár, is not strictly part of Balatonfüred-Csopak, but is a wine-producing area. The soil in this area is not volcanic, except minimally on some of the slopes, but has sand and medium clay. There is a lot of wind, so there are no mildew problems. Feind is the only large wine producer here, where most holdings are hobby vineyards of under 0.25 hectare. Many are currently for sale because they are hard to cultivate. Feind's old vineyards, between twelve and twenty years old, are widely spaced, with vines planted back to back and single-curtain training. The new plantations, made in 1998, preserve the wide spacing for the tractors presently in use, but are umbrella-trained. The yield is generally seventy hectolitres per hectare.

The winery is well-equipped with modern technology: an Austrian de-stemmer, a Swiss pneumatic press, and computerized, temperature-controlled stainless-steel fermentation and storage tanks. Fragrant white wines are stored in stainless steel, while the others go to wood. The reds are pumped over as they ferment and are left on their skins for three weeks after fermentation. Some are kept as reductive wines, other go into casks. Barriques are planned for Chardonnay and some red varieties.

Production changes from year to year as the situation develops. Bottled wines were first produced in 2000, when about seven per cent of output was filled. These are sold in Hungary, while the remaining wine is sold in bulk either to other wine-producers or to restaurants in the region.

Feind's son Péter is still in his twenties, and he makes the wine. After a year in Australia working a vintage in Western Australia and the Barossa Valley, he graduated in viniculture at the Horticultural University of Budapest. Péter says he was impressed by the Australian reds such as Shiraz, but thinks that Hungarian reductive wines are better. Confirmation of this view seemed to be apparent in tastings I made of the 2000 vintage in 2001. They proved to be a big surprise. A tank sample of a reductive Kékfrankos (Balatonaliga grapes, picked at 22° must sugar, with seven grams per litre acid, thirty-seven grams per litre dry extract and fourteen per cent alcohol) had a colour and intensity of flavour reminiscent of Australia but seldom met with in Hungary. This big, fresh, and balanced wine (not betraying any excess of alcohol) shows the potential of Kékfrankos when picked ripe and well-made. Two whites – a Királyleányka and a Zenit – had a late-harvest style, and were rich and impressive. Of three different samples of Olaszrizling, the last picked impressed most. Pinot Blanc was also rich, while the Szürkebarát was still closed. All in all, a stunning selection, and evidence that Péter is a talented young winemaker.

OTHER WINE PRODUCERS

Dörgicse Bor Kft (Pántlika Pincészet). H–8244 Dörgicse, Fö u. 42. Tel/fax: +36–87 444 379. *Fodorvin Családi Pincészet.* H–8241 Aszófő, Hunyadi u. 9. Tel/fax: +36–87 445027. (Cellar: H–8281 Szentbékálla, Dózsa G. u. 17.) *Koczor Pince.* H–8230 Balatonfüred, Bocsár dűlő 0118/12 hrsz. Tel/fax: +36–87 342873. *Salánki Családi Borpince.* H–8241 Aszófő, Tihanyi u. 2. Tel/fax: +36–87 445 436/437. *Vinarius, F zés R Kft.* H-8226 Alsóörs, Barátság u. 50. Tel/fax: +36–87 447292. *Zánka és Környe Pinceszövetkezet.* H–8272 Szentantalfa, Sósi u. 50. Tel: +36–87 479155/280; Fax: +36–87 479291

Salánki Családi Borpince is a family business in which father and son (both Sándor) work together. Having started as a hobby winemaker in 1971, while he was the winemaker for the Badacsony State Farm, Salánki in 1997 converted a nineteenth-century house next to the railway on the outskirts of Tihany into a winery and shop, and relaunched his business as a limited company. Although he has 22.5 hectares of vineyards on the peninsula (partly rented), eighty per cent of his production is of white wines made from grapes purchased locally from growers whose vineyards he manages, and from other Balaton regions. The winery has reasonable vinification equipment. Château Salánki is the top-quality range, followed by Nivegyvölgyi Selection. Standards are very variable. One or two of the Château Salánki whites have some personality, but the rest are disappointing, while most of the red wines are light, variously displaying sweetness, astringency or high acid levels.

Fodorvin Családi Pincészet was in transition in 2001, transferring from Aszófó to Szentbékálla, where the cellar and winery are being developed with a view to selling to tourists. With new stainless steel and climate-control, Gyula Fodor's production will become reductive. I hope that this will improve his wines, which at present strike me as too thin and light.

Koczor Pince is run by Kálmán Koczor, a consultant agricultural engineer. He and Zoltán Hudák launched a joint venture at the end of 2001, using a new winery that also incorporates a restaurant. I have high hopes for it. Zánka és Környe Pinceszövetkezet is a cooperative that is just managing to hang on, making sweetish wines mainly for the home market with technology close to dire. Vinarius, F and R – not to be confused with Vinárium (q.v.) – is a typical small-scale winery of the sort springing up along Lake Balaton. Its basic technology produces equally basic wines. Dörgicse Bor started in 1993 and has forty hectares of vineyards, mostly rented. Despite good reductive equipment, the wines lack freshness and are unimpressive. A semi-automatic bottling plant also caters for local producers.

BADACSONY

1,639 hectares: 1,559 white, eighty red
Fourteen wine communities, with 5,464 members

The area north of the west end of Lake Balaton is what remains of a volcanic landscape, scattered with periodic mounds and conical hills. Badacsonyhegy (437 metres/1,420 feet), the largest of the extinct volcanos, dominates everything, its sugar-loaf shape – best seen from across the water – making it unmistakeable. Pre-Second World War photographs of this view show a scene quite different from today's; previously, no trees were visible below the craggy rock escarpment that crowns the hill, whereas nowadays this area is quite well-wooded, and trees have taken over the old stone-walled terraces. Further down, where there used to be large areas of yet more terraced vineyards, the walls succumbed to the bulldozer in the early 1970s, and the vineyards that remain have been divided. Most poignantly of all, the old photographs show that there were hardly any houses on the hill – barely more than a century ago.

The number of vineyards began to go down in the 1960s when the comrades began to build summer residences for themselves. Until 1993, if you had 0.2 hectares, you could build on it. Latterly, so many plots were being bought by Germans (and Austrians, and Dutch . . .), who then ripped out the vines and built houses, that local building regulations had to be changed. Now you have to own 1.5 hectares if you wish to build a new cellar, and this land cannot be used for putting up a house. Badacsony has become part of a national park, and all building regulations have become very strict. Nevertheless, this tightening up cannot undo the damage that has accrued over the last forty years.

Badacsony is almost completely a region of white varieties and always has been. Besides the hill itself, the region includes the Tapolca and Kál basins and other volcanos, of which Szent Györgyhegy (415 metres/1,349 feet) and Gulácshegy (393 metres/1,278 feet) are the most significant. The vineyard terrains are mainly a mixture of clay and degraded basalt, with some areas of adobe and calcareous soil. The climate is moderate, but with many microclimates tucked in the folds of the hills.

The previous area of vineyards in the region was close to 6,000 hectares. However, in the 1960s, the vineyards on the hills, because they were more difficult to work, were largely abandoned in favour of level plantations on flat ground nearer to the lake. The area had both a state farm and cooperatives. The former was the *Badacsonyi Állami Gazdaság* (Badacsony State Farm) – not to be confused with the *Badacsonyvidéki Pincegazdaság* (Badacsony Region Farm Cellar), which existed from 1949 onwards, but had no vineyards of its own. The main cooperative was the *Badacsony Borászati Szövetkezet* (Badacsony Wine-Producing Cooperative), which still exists.

Badacsony wines were famous over many centuries. Described by Hungarians as "fiery", they are traditionally robust wines of substance, with a strong mineral character. Olaszrizling, Szürkebarát, and Tramini have long been established here, as has Kéknyelu˝ , a difficult variety not often encountered elsewhere in Hungary. Rizlingszilváni and Ottonel Muskotály Ottonel are also common varieties. Sweet wines were also part of the old tradition, and these are happily reappearing (in all the lakeside regions).

The last ten years have shown fewer outstanding producers than one might have hoped, although there is no shortage of hopeful small producers making wines to sell to tourists – here, as elsewhere round the lake, a major market. Sadly, most of these wines are rather feeble and uninteresting.

ELSŐ MAGYAR BORHÁZ SZENT ORBÁN PINCE KFT

H–8262 Badacsonylábdihegy, Romai út 93. Tel: +36–87 432 352; Fax: +36–87 432 532. *(a)* Huba Szeremley. *(b)* 105.4ha (101.7ha in Badacsony, of which 65 are old plantings, and 3.7ha Kf in Tihany). Or 13.5ha; RR 10ha; Sz 6.4ha; OM 5.4ha; Kn 4.4ha; IO 1.9ha; Z 1.4ha; Bz 1ha; PN 44.5ha; Kf 5.7ha; M 4.3ha; Ko 3.7ha; CS 1.5ha; CF 1.5ha. *(c)* 3,000hl. *(d)* Huba Szeremley and Béla Fölföldy. *(e)* Varietals, cuvées, late-harvest, botrytized wine. *(f)* 33% (France, the US, Japan, Sweden, Italy, Germany, Switzerland, Belgium, and the UK, both directly and through an agent)

Huba Szeremley is a character somewhat larger than life, doubtless the outcome of a varied and sometimes turbulent career. After a traumatic upbringing in the immediate post-war period, he fled with his wife and child to Austria in 1967, having been expelled from university (where he was studying plastics technology) for alleged political activity. His subsequent career took him to Iran and Nigeria, where he was involved in the construction business and where he still has business interests. These supply a significant part of his income, which in turn funds the development of his wine businesses.

A native of Lake Balaton, he often felt homesick during his exile, and it was therefore natural for him to return to Hungary in the changed political circumstances of the 1990s. He says he became a winemaker and producer by accident, "like everything else in my life". When he bought his present house in Lábdihegy, he purchased some land around it to enhance his privacy. This included vineyards, and that led to winemaking, releasing an interest which, he says, was in his genes.

Over the years, Szeremley has consolidated his land holdings, and he is now the largest proprietor on Badacsonyhegy. He takes elaborate care in his vineyards to end up with the best grapes possible, and he requires them to be very ripe. All possible tasks are mechanized. Vigour is reduced and roots are forced down by severe annual cutting round the vines, using a thirty-centimetre (twelve-inch) knife. The vines are trained with a double cordon on an umbrella system, with only four spurs left on each cane. No green pruning is necessary, and the canopy is not reduced except by the removal of old and dying leaves, so as to encourage maximum photosynthesis by the youngest leaves. Depending on the variety, and excluding late harvested wines, output ranges from twenty-eight to forty-two hectolitres per hectare. Szeremley is also an enthusiast for old

Hungarian varieties, and has rescued two from likely oblivion: Kéknyelű and Bakator. Of the latter, there is no wine as yet, but he is experimenting with micro-vinifications.

In 1999, he bought what had originally been built as a stable in about 1800 and was later the first Hungarian Pepsi Cola factory. This has already undergone considerable renovation (still in progress), and a second fermentation hall was built in 2001. A neighbouring building where he runs another business manufacturing chestnut paste will shortly become a second cask cellar. Much of the equipment of the winery, which is up-to-date and efficient, including a system of water-cooling with automatic electronic gauges, has been designed and constructed by Szeremley himself – a legacy of his engineering background – and he has trained a Romany as his own cooper.

There is no maceration of white grapes – not even for Ottonel Muskotály, which Szeremley prefers to make as a lightish wine – before they are whole bunch-pressed at very low pressure. Three-quarters of the juice is free-run, resulting from just filling the machine. Ordinary whites are cooled to around 0°C overnight to give a quick sedimentation before fermentation, which, using yeasts that Szeremley cultures himself from selected ripe grapes, takes place off the skins. Budaizöld and Muscat are bottled in November after sterile filtration, but without any wood treatment. Other wines, after earth filtration, go into large and small casks for varying periods of maturation before bottling.

Red wines – using his own Kékoportó, and Kékfrankos bought in from Sopron – are made fairly conventionally, but there is no malolactic fermentation because Szeremley considers that this is not part of the Hungarian winemaking tradition. Kékoportó is not given any wood treatment and is bottled in November, while Kékfrankos is cask-aged. Szeremley also produces, when conditions permit, a range of late-harvest and botrytis wines, some of which are stunningly good. They demonstrate clearly how suitable the Balaton region is for such wines. I wish he would make more, and that other people would also do so.

Szeremley's right-hand man is Béla Fölföldy, a local car mechanic whom Szeremley took on in 1994 when he was unemployed, only to find that, although Fölföldy has never read a technical wine book in his life and is not much of a drinker, he has a very sensitive palate. Consequently,

Szeremley, who is very modest about his own talents – "I am only a hobby winemaker" – has made Fölföldy his right-hand man. They make joint decisions about everything. "Two blind people have to hold each other's hands," Szeremley says.

Despite the modesty, there can be no doubting that Szeremley is one of the most talented winemakers in Hungary. He is wealthy enough to go straight for what he wants, and never cuts corners. He is also very down to earth. He scorns the exaggerated descriptions of wine by wine writers: "A wine only has to be a wine – not chocolate, or marmalade or coffee. If you want these characteristics, look elsewhere." Without being a rabid nationalist, Szeremley is keen on supporting the traditions of Hungary – or what's left of them – and has been instrumental in founding two important wine associations. The first is the local Badacsony wine-producers' guild, and the second is *A Pannon Bormíves Céh* (Guild of Pannonian Wines) (*q.v.*). A workaholic, he has many other business projects, including a new wine venture at Helvécia (*q.v.*). When not too wrapped up in such matters, he is a bridge fanatic.

In short, Szeremley is a rare talent who seldom fails to produce wines of great depth and character. For consistency and style, and his ability to demonstrate what Balaton wines are about, he can justly claim to be the entire area's leading producer.

A BIOVITIS PINCÉBEN BT

H–8300 Tapolca, Batsányi u. 27. Tel: +36–87 412 405. Tel/fax: +36–87 415 350. Winery: high on Szent Györgyhegy. *(a)* Zoltán Kovács and family. *(b)* 13.4ha: SM 2.6ha; Sk 4.5ha; Or 4ha; Kn 0.3ha; H 2ha. *(c)* 340hl in 1999. *(d)* Zoltán Kovács. *(e)* Varietals and cuvées. *(f)* Tiny amounts (France, Italy)

This is a small family business started in 1994. Kovács previously did biochemical research for a pharmaceutical company. However, disliking both his job and living in Budapest, he decided to extend the family vineyards and set up a winery. "I did not want to make a lot of money, but to be a man on my own." As a result, Hungary has one of its most idiosyncratic wine producers.

The vineyards, as mechanized as is possible, are on Szent Györghegy, and were chosen to suit each variety. Some 10.5 hectares are currently in production. Kovács uses only organic chemicals and fertilizers – his thesis was on organic farming – and rather than use pesticides he aims at utilizing the natural resources of the area's ecology. Compared to Badacsony, Szent Györgyhegy still has hedgerows and a generally more rural environment, so the ecology is balanced. The soil has a high, stony basalt content. The climate is Mediterranean, cooler and more equable than that of Badacsony. There are also various microclimates, providing marked temperature differences within his holding.

Kovács's policy is to harvest as late as possible. Some varieties are harvested twice to ensure maximum ripeness. Picking is done by hand. Yields on average are between fifty and fifty-five hectolitres per hectare; crop restriction is purely by means of winter pruning, with a maximum of fifteen to twenty buds per vine. Nor does Kovács believe in canopy management or defoliation. Birds are his main worry: in 1999 they took about 1.5 hectares of his crop.

His philosophy is straightforward, although some may consider it controversial. He looks for quality, and makes single-variety wines using traditional technology. "God protect me from producing cuvées," he says (because he considers them untraditional). He is astonished that the market prefers reductive wines, and he prefers to walk his own way. He realizes that he has chosen a more difficult commercial route, but believes that there are still enough people who like the style of wine he is trying to provide. "Hilltop flavours", he asserts, are achieved by harvesting a week before full ripeness. That is why, when a wine-maker wants to produce fruity wines with full aromas, it is best to harvest early – although, paradoxically, winemakers often talk about it being best to harvest as late as possible. Malolactic fermentation is used, he says, to make "popular" wines, but it is only possible (and necessary) to use it when the grapes are not fully ripe. He harvests his grapes so fully ripe that they have no malic acid. Nevertheless, he only makes dry wine. He sees botrytis (of which he does not get much) as a friend.

Kovács has his winery about halfway up the hill, facing east towards the village of Kisapáti, with Badacsonyhegy over to the right. It was built in 1996, although it does not actually have very modern equipment. Musts are spontaneously fermented in stainless steel with water temperature control at 18°C to 21°C. The wine is transferred to twenty- to fifty-hectolitre barrels without any fining or filtration, and remains in cask for anything from five to twelve months, or even a little longer. It is racked in December and again in the following year, and when mature, it is stored in stainless steel until bottled (in a striking and attractive livery). There is a distributor in Budapest, and there are some smaller outlets, but Kovács does not have enough wine to supply the demand, so he has both a need and a will to expand his production.

Not everyone likes Kovács's wine. I do. The deep, late-harvest colour, especially of the strawberry-wood cask-aged Szürkebarát, combined with a richly flavourful but dry palate, full of complexity, make these wines strikingly individual. They are about as close to bio-wines as you can get in Hungary, given the climate. Whether they are really in the traditional style that Kovács professes to seek, I rather doubt. What is certain is that, in quality terms, they are head and shoulders above a great deal of the local opposition.

BADACSONYVIN KERESKEDELMI KFT (VARGA KFT)

H–1222 Budapest, Hegyfok u. 2/C, Pf 114. Tel: +36–1 226 6766; Fax: +36–1 226 6300. Winery: H–8257 Badacsonyörs. Tel: +36–87 471211; Tel/fax: +36–87 471218. *(a)* Péter Varga. *(b)* 90ha in three areas: 30 in Badacsony; 30 in Balatonaliga; 30 in Eger. *(c)* 52,500 hl. *(d)* Gábor Csiszko. *(e)* Varietals, rozé, cuvées, sparkling wine. *(f)* 20+% (Czech Republic, Germany, Poland, Baltic States, and Austria)

Péter Varga, a former financial director of Hungarovin, started this winery in 1993 at Badacsonyörs. It is now the third largest producer in the country (after Egervin and Hungarovin). The winery was purchased from the Badacsony State Farm and has been the subject of massive investment. As its main priority, in 1998 the firm installed first-class vinification equipment with a processing capacity of 300 tonnes a day. In 1998–9 Defranceschi tank fermentation with a capability of producing 1 million bottles of sparkling wine a year was installed, and this is being expanded. Stainless-steel storage and chilling capacity are still being increased. (This means, for example, that red wines can be left on their skins for up to a month at the end of the vintage, when capacity is no longer under pressure, and they can also be given a malolactic fermentation.) Other developments, such as barrique fermentation and maturation, remain for the future. Now, however, the company can turn to its second priority, the renovation of its buildings.

In its first year, 1992, the company turned out 450,000 bottles; by

2000, this had risen to 7 million bottles. Half of the production is now red wine, and sixty per cent of the total production is Country Wine. This simply reflects the fact that supermarket quantities require the sourcing of grapes outside delimited regions, which means that the wine has to be classified as Country Wine, however good its quality. Comfortingly, research has shown that what counts most with consumers is the name of the company, then the type of wine, and then the region of origin, so this is not a big issue. Some 400,000 to 500,000 bottles of sparkling wine (dry white, *demi-sec* rozé and sweet white) are produced for export to Poland and Italy. There are sixty products in all, with an increasing proportion of cuvées. The winemaker is Gábor Csiszko, previously a cellarmaster of Egervin.

The firm wants to develop in two ways: (1) by producing wine from the Balaton area; (2) by establishing a wine-trading house to distribute wines from all over Hungary, and possibly to import wines as well. The present set-up does not fit either of these targets – it is too big for (1) and too small for (2). The company wishes to develop a total activity of up to 10 or 12 million bottles. So it is only halfway towards this figure, and future growth depends on being able to match vineyards and produce to markets. A start on planting the vineyards, belonging to family and friends, was made in the autumn of 2001, and this marks an important step in achieving the company's goals. The plantings have a density of between 4,000 and 5,000 vines per hectare, and are trained in a flat umbrella configuration suitable for eventual mechanical harvesting. Anticipated ideal yields are astonishingly high: for fragrant, low-price wines, 116 hectolitres per hectare, and for wines with depth, seventy hectolitres per hectare. Meanwhile, production comes totally from purchases of international variety grapes (ninety per cent bought under long-term contracts) and about 4,500 hectolitres of finished wine.

Although its export market is important, the firm believes that the domestic market must come first. The list of supermarkets through which it sells its products is impressive. Bulk wine is sold to Austria and Germany.

Péter Varga is still a comparatively young man. His son Bálint is presently studying economics, and hopes to join the firm soon. It is clear that the importance of this already large firm will increase. At present, its frankly commercial wines are of variable quality. The 1998s were made with inferior technology and, although clean, they tend to have faint bouquets and slightly variety-neutral tastes. Later vintages show some improvement, with a fruitier style, but the musts are still very dilute.

SIPOS TIHAMER

H–8257 Badacsonyörs, Szőlőu. 13. Tel: +36–30 9592744; Fax: +36–87 471153. (a) Tihamer Sipos. (b) 7ha: Sk 1ha; OM 1ha; Ch/Sk 1.5ha; Kn 1.75ha; Sk 1.75ha. (c) 1,000hl. (d) Tihamer Sipos. (e) Varietals, rozé, cuvée, Eiswein. (f) None

Sipos comes from Devecser and was cellar-master in the Badacsony State Farm until he lost his job in 1990. Construction of a new cellar started in 1998, and should be completed by the time this book is published. Besides spacious cellar accommodation and a bottling line, its design incorporates four flats for tourists.

The vineyards are mainly in Badacsony, on the hill, with a small part in Badacsonyörs, all planted by Sipos himself using umbrella training. The wines are reductively fermented. Only about ten per cent of the wine is bottled (by the family), all of the production being sold at the cellar to restaurants in the area and at local wine festivals.

The wines I have tried from the 2000 vintage seem to have suffered from the hot vintage and, except for the Kéknyelű, lack body. However, Sipos's 1999 Helikon Cuvée (Chardonnay, Szürkebarát, and Ottonel Muskotály, rounded out with a little Eiswein) is balanced and elegant. The 2000 (Tihany) Merlot Rozé, with a real *pelure d'oignon* colour, is one of the better rozés to be found in Hungary. Best of all, however, is a stunning 1999 Eiswein with a Germanic Beerenauslese character showing intense aroma and great depth of flavour – a good demonstration of the quality of sweet wines that can be achieved in the region.

SZENT-GYÖRGY PINCE

H–8265 Hegymagas, Szentgyörgyhegy 12. Tel: +36–60 334 444. (a) István Kiss. (b) 10ha: Or 4ha; Sk 3ha; OM 2ha; F 1ha. (c) Not disclosed: 20% of total production from bought-in grapes. (d) István Kiss. (e) Varietals, late-harvest, Eiswein. (f) None

István Kiss, a former wine salesman who studied agriculture later in life, has his cellar and restaurant on the lower southern slopes of Szent Györgyhegy. He started his enterprise in 1985. Although he has quite a large holding of vineyards to the west of his cellar, which he planted himself, he sometimes sells grapes. His production is small; this is, he says because his crop yield is minute: it never exceeds seven hectolitres per hectare, and for Eiswein is as low as 0.9 hectolitres per hectare. He only makes as much wine as he can sell. Half of it is bottled, and the rest is sold in bulk through the cellar and the sales point at his winery, four kilometres (two-and-a-half miles) away, at Gyulakeszi.

Kiss says that he tries to make wine "like the ancients did", and prefers single-variety wines to blends. He likes to harvest as late as possible so as to obtain maximum grape maturity. After crushing and maceration for up to eight hours, the grapes are basket-pressed – a system he had abandoned, but has returned to because he believes it gives better flavours to the wine. Fermentation takes place in wood, plastic or in stainless-steel tanks, depending on the degree of oxidation required. There is no cooling system, but fermentation temperatures do not exceed 16°C for early crops, while late-harvest grapes are fermented at between 12°C and 13°C. The wine – some for immediate consumption and some for keeping – is matured in wood, plastic, and stainless steel according to quality, the best lots being put into wood. Kiss uses small ten-hectolitre casks if possible, and ageing can be anything from eight months to three years. His wines have high acid levels, so they take ageing well. He does not like using barriques.

Kiss produces an astonishing range of more than a dozen white wines. They are of variable quality, the Szürkebarát being perhaps the most interesting of the dry wines. A 1982 Olaszrizling demonstrates that some of these wines do indeed age well. It has the toasty fragrance of an old Australian Riesling, and has weight and breadth without having lost any elegance. Much better, however, in my opinion, are Kiss's sweeter wines, which also benefit from ageing. A botrytized Olaszrizling, also 1982, has huge depth of colour, allied to great weight and intensity on the palate, and is, I think, quite sensational.

OTHER WINE PRODUCERS

Badacsony Borászati Szövetkezet. H–8284 Nemesgulács-Rizapuszta, Pf. 10. Tel:
+36–87 471 243/4; Fax: +36–87 471 922. *Békássy Péter.* H–8261 Badacsony,
Római út 140. Tel: +36–87 431271. *Borbély Családi Pincészet.* H–8300 Tapolca,
Najda J. u. 76. Tel/fax: +36–87/321833. *Németh István.* H–8261 Badacsony,
Római út 127. Tel: +36–87–431274

Borbély Családi Pincészet got going in 1993. With almost seven hectares,
it specializes in making white wines. Plastic tanks are used for reductive
fermentation, and the wine is sold to tourists and on the domestic market. István Németh has 1.5 hectares on Badacsonyhegy, half of it
Olaszrizling, but also some head-trained Budaizöld and some Kéknyelű.
This is traditional winemaking: a basket press, natural yeast, fermentation in cask, the wine twice racked, fined, and sold within the year. Best
are his late-harvest and botrytized wines, which are better balanced and
more intense than the others. Péter Békássy farms 9.5 hectares, of which
one is Kéknyelű. He produces 300 to 400 hectolitres a year, most of
which is sold to local wine bars.

The Badacsony Borászati Szövetkezet, founded in 1962, appears to be
keeping its head above water. In 1973, it was amalgamated with nine
other similar cooperatives, of which wine production was only a part.
With 300 members – down from 1,400 in 1992 – and access to between
300 and 400 hectares of vineyards, including (following fashion) some
new plantings of Cabernet Sauvignon, Kékfrankos, and Pinot Noir, it has
an annual production of around 25,000 hectolitres marketed under
around thirty labels.

A new cellar with French stainless steel, temperature-controlled fermentation tanks, and an Italian bottling line was inaugurated in 1995. A
quarter of the production is exported to the US, Germany, Denmark,
Poland, and Slovakia. There is now a restaurant associated with the
winery. Its terrace overlooks the lake (distantly) and has a lovely scenic
position. The cooperative also offers visitors during the vintage a hands-
on experience of picking, crushing, and filling traditional wooden
fermenting tubs. The wines are pretty much geared to their market – that
is to say, rather sweet and bland. The cooperative bottles for private local
producers under their own labels, but with the cooperative name,
although the bottles of these that I have sampled have never been better
than mediocre.

BALATONFELVIDÉK

1,351 hectares: 1,318 white, thirty-three red
Fifteen wine communities, with 5,440 members

This region consists of three parts. Two virtually enclose the Badacsony region. The first part, to the north, bordering the Balatonfüred-Csopak region, contains the villages of Köveskál, Szentbékkála, and Monostorapáti; the second part, to its west, contains Lesencetomaj, Balatongyörök and (north of Keszthely) Cserszegtomaj. The third surrounds Sümeg and, prior to 1999, was a wine-producing area. Before 1999, Balatonfelvidék was known as Balatonmellék, which is now the name of the region to the west, formerly called Zala – another confusing bureaucratic decision. Most of Balatonfelvidék consists of rolling country, the embodiment of pastoral tranquillity, with gently sloping hills but no volcanoes – hardly the "highlands" suggested by the region's new name.

The soil of Balatonfelvidék is quite varied. There is, indeed, some mineral-rich volcanic soil (magnesium and potassium) on the edges of the Tapolca Basin, and around Monostorapáti. It is lightly acidic. Westwards, however, around Lesencetomaj, the soil has a large limestone component, with basalt rock anything between one and three metres (around three to nine-and-a-half feet) below the surface. Further west still, at Cserszegtomaj, the limestone continues, but becomes more inter-mixed with loess and gravel as you near the Balatonmelléke region.

The wines of the region, consequently, have quite a lot of acidity and weight. With a few exceptions, this is a white-variety area, although the area was once famous for its red wines. Tapolca, although then only a small village, was an important trading centre for local wines in the eighteenth century, and has an astonishing network of cellars dating from that time. Trading was largely in Jewish hands, and several families, like the Lessners and the Ibozses, remained influential up until the twentieth century. It was they who organized the replanting of the area after phylloxera, the Lessners favouring Olaszrizling and the Ibozses Szürkebarát, now the classical varieties of the region.

HÉT KÁL-VIDÉKI SCHELLER BIRTOK

H–1165 Budapest, Sasvár út 103/B. Tel: +36–1 403 4388. Winery: at Monostorapáti. *(a)* Sándor Tóth. *(b)* 25ha: ZV 12.5ha; Or 4.2ha; Zen 4.2ha; Ch 4.1ha. *(c)* 1,000hl. *(d)* Sándor Tóth. *(e)* Varietals, cuvées. *(f)* 20–60% (Holland, Sweden)

Sándor Tóth, a graduate of the Horticultural University of Budapest, worked at the Balaton State Farm from 1968 until 1989. In 1990, the new government asked him to become head of its Department of Agricultural Structuring, responsible for the strategic modification of agricultural planning. His work became the basis of general agricultural policy and, two years later, he headed the Department of Agriculture. Between 1993 and 1994, Tóth bought twenty-five hectares of producing vineyards and a further nine hectares available for planting. Influenced by the fact that his mother's side of the family had had an involvement with wine going back to 1722, he gave up his job in 1995 to devote himself to wine-making.

The vineyards, with wide rows and a single cordon, face south and are unchanged from when he purchased them. Total replanting is required. His vineyard technology is guided by considerations of environmental protection. The crop is restricted by winter and green pruning. Birds are his main problem, made all the more difficult by the fact that his vineyards are situated in a protected national park where no guns are allowed. Last year, he lost five out of ten hectares of Chardonnay and Zenit.

Tóth's house is built on top of a 1739 cellar, which is used for cask age-ing, and alongside it there is a modern (1994) winery. The equipment is modern and very good – pneumatic press and stainless-steel tanks with a chilling unit. As he harvests as late as possible, the weather is already cold. Fermentations, using commercial yeasts, take place at between 12°C and 15°C. After a bentonite fining, the wine is put into casks with a capacity of up to thirty hectolitres for anything from three weeks to twelve months. In general, Tóth prefers short periods in wood for his wines. He uses casks for eight years, having them scraped every three years. The wine is racked twice, and then kept in stainless steel for any-thing up to four years before bottling (done in the cellar by a mobile bottler, or by Szent Orbán Pince at Badacsony). Some wines, notably Chardonnay, have no wood treatment at all. The long period of storage is said by Tóth to be his interpretation of the Roman technique of storing wine in amphorae. Tóth says he believes there is little to choose between stainless steel and bottle storage as methods of maturation, but I suspect he chooses the former mainly because it is a much cheaper alternative. Tóth's Hungarian market is the top sector of the restaurant trade and specialized wine shops. Exports vary from year to year. His wines are consistently excellent: complex and sophisticated, with charm and finesse rather than power, and purity of fruit combined with fine, rounded acidity. He is, in the last analysis, dedicated to producing the highest quality he can, and thinks he is lucky to own some of the best plots in the Kál Basin. Wine-producing, he says, is either a passion or a business, and for him it is definitely a passion.

NÉMETH BORHÁZ KFT

H–8360 Keszthely, Kertváros, Tomaji sor 40. Tel: +36–83 318723. *(a)* Members of the Németh family. *(b)* 22ha. Own land 17ha: Ch 15ha; Sk 2ha. Rented land 5ha: ZV 3ha; Ch 2ha. *(c)* 1,400hl. *(d)* Gabriella Virág and Csaba Németh. *(e)* Varietals, rozé. *(f)* Sporadic (Canada, Germany)

This is a family business. Csaba Németh's father worked in the Balatonvidéki Pincegazdaság until he retired in 1990. He soon began to buy land with compensation vouchers and his savings, and a cluster of family businesses began to develop. Németh's father developed the wine firm and built the present winery, which was opened in 1996. In the same year, Németh, who had previously been working in the oil business and then in the grocery trade, returned to Keszthely and joined his father. Two years later, unfortunately, his father died, and Csaba Németh has effectively been running the firm since then. His sister and brother-in-law (Csaba Bezerics) run the Bacchus hotel and wine museum in Keszthely, and Bezerics is not just involved in, but is very much one of the motivating forces behind the new wine firm. Although Bezerics has a degree in agriculture, Németh runs the vineyards. Gabriella Virág, a qualified chemist as well as a qualified winemaker, is regarded by Németh as his second in command.

Both the Németh family's own vineyards in Badacsony and those rented in Zalaszentgrót were planted by the family using Guyot training. Unfortunately, there is a preponderance of Chardonnay (between thirteen and fifteen years old) at Cserszegtomaj, so some is sold to buy other varieties from other regions (Pannonhalma, Sopron, Ászár-Neszmély, and Szekszárd).

The cellar is bright and well-designed, and is equipped with excellent modern reductive vinification technology. Apart from a barrique Chardonnay, none of the white wines is put into wood, but reds mature in a 150–year-old cellar that once belonged to Gróf Széchenyi, where there are 300 hectolitres of cask storage. Since 2000, the firm has also made experimental micro-vinifications of twenty-two grape varieties (some of them crosses) grown on ten hectares on behalf of the Keszthely Georgikon Faculty of Agriculture. All the wine is bottled by the company, and is sold to supermarkets like Julius Meinl (its biggest customer) and Tesco.

The company philosophy, guided by Bezerics, is to go for ever-increasing quality. It depends on Julius Meinl at the moment, but the ultimate goal is to get out of supermarket supply (and the image that goes with it), and aim for really high quality. The company is well on the way to doing this. Even making allowance for the rich musts obtained in 2000, all the wines I have tasted have been serious, with style and quality. Only a Sauvignon Blanc, which suffered a stuck fermentation, failed to please. Time will tell.

LESENCE SZŐLŐ, GYÜMÖLCS ÉS SZESZIPARI RT

H–1022 Budapest, Endrődi Sándor u. 8. Tel: +36–1 326 5676, Fax: +36–1 326 5677. Winery: H–8318 Lesencetomaj-külterület hrsz 0405. Tel/fax: +36–87 436 102. *(a)* János Kázsmér and a Swiss national, Kázsmér having the controlling interest. *(b)* 60ha: PN 25ha; Sk 25ha; Ch 6ha; SB 4ha. *(c)* 15,000hl. *(d)* László Kamrás. *(e)* Varietals, cuvée, botrytized wine. *(f)* 99% (the UK, Italy, and Japan)

Lesence's winery is about five kilometres (three miles) north of Lake Balaton, just outside the village of Lesencetomaj – one of several small villages incorporating the name of the little Lesence River, which flows through the broad Tapolca basin. Woodlands on a rise behind the winery look down towards Badacsonyhegy and protect the surrounding vineyards, which rise to a height of 255 metres (829 feet). The older plantations are of Chardonnay and Sauvignon Blanc, but those of Pinot Noir (the first in the region in recent times) and Szürkebarát, on a green-field site, date from 1996.

Kázsmér, one of the firm's two proprietors, decided to go for a high proportion of Pinot Noir because he remembered that it was grown here when he was a child. "We cannot compete with Chile and Australia with Merlot and other red varieties," he believes, "but perhaps we can with Pinot Noir." Using metal posts, the new plantations have high densities to control vigour and avoid the necessity of green pruning. The target crop will be a maximum of two kilograms of grapes per vine. The vineyards are also designed for maximum mechanization, and some picking is done by machine, although where quality is important, it is done by hand.

The winery took six months to construct in 1997, and was ready for the company's first harvest. Highly automated and designed for an efficient work-flow, it has some of the best French and Italian vinification technology to be found in Hungary, including such "high-tech" assistance to the winemaker as a reverse-osmosis filter, not to be found anywhere else in Hungary (as far as I am aware). Kázsmér strongly believes that "high-tech" will be the future of winemaking, and that it will enable winemakers to equalize the differences between good and bad vintages. The winery is also equipped with pressure tanks for sparkling-wine production.

At the moment, the winery functions purely for white-wine production, but the company plans to build a new red winery on a symmetrical plan in the near future. With such modern technology, the company has to produce at least 15,000 hectolitres of wine to make it a profitable venture, so eighty per cent of the company's grape requirements are bought in, sometimes as must, from Mátraalja and Balatonboglár as well as from Balatonfelvidék. Winemaking follows predictable reductive lines, "interfering as little as possible with the character of the wine.

Lesence produces a wide range of mainly white wines, and uses a wide range of techniques for making them. For example, besides cask-matured wines, there are barrique versions not just of Chardonnay but also of other white varieties. I think the Barrique Szürkebarát is, in fact, the company's best wine. Some Chardonnay is fermented *sur lie* in barrique and the rest kept on its lees until the end of February, when it is put into barriques. Ageing of top-quality wines is done in the company's cellar in Tapolca, the construction of which started in 1780 and finished in 1820.

The company aims at a quality equal to medium-rank wines available in supermarkets in England, using the crop of its old plantations for the best quality. At the moment, almost one hundred per cent of the company's wine is exported, but because, for the time being, Lesence does not trade under its own name, ninety-five per cent of it leaves the winery as bulk. Kázsmér is happy with that for the present; the Hungarian market, in his judgement, cannot pay for quality wine, so export has to be the company's main aim. In a few years, however, it is anticipated that all the wine will be bottled under the company's own label. There appears to be no lack of money here, and the potential for development must be high.

KÁL-VIN PINCÉSZET KFT
H–8253 Révfülöp, Tavasz u. 16. Tel/fax: +36–87 464 754. *(a)* The Varga family and a Dutch national, the former having a controlling interest. *(b)* 10ha: Or 5.5ha; Sk/Ch 3.7ha; Sk 0.8ha. *(c)* 860hl. *(d)* György Varga. *(e)* Varietals. *(f)* 35% (Germany, Austria)

Kál-Vin was established in 1993 by a husband-and-wife team of viticulturists. György Varga makes the wine. The spacious, medium-sized winery, in an attractive building completed in 2001, also houses a tasting room with a terraced tourist area giving views of the lake, a shop and catering facilities for groups of up to eighty. Underneath there is a century-old cellar. The production capacity is 2,700 hectolitres, which Varga reckons is the maximum possible for the family still to be able to retain full control of the operation, and this should be reached by 2004. The equipment is very modern from start to finish, and a bottling line is planned. Previously all the wines were oxidative (fermented in cask and then kept under pressure in the casks, thereby reducing oxidation), but the new equipment will offer the possibility of making both oxidative and reductive wines, including ageworthy wines, in the future.

Some of the Vargas' vineyards are about twelve kilometres (seven miles) distant in the Kál Basin, which is in Balatonfelvidék, but the rest are at Balatonrendes, which is in Badacsony. The Vargas would in the end prefer to expand their own vineyards and so reduce dependency on bought-in grapes, but they cannot afford to do so just yet. However, they have integration contracts with their growers and, by giving help in the vineyards, they can effectively control them.

The wine is marketed in Hungary, half through chain stores such as

Metro, and half through restaurants, small stores, and (using plastic containers) cellar-door sales. The exports are of bottled wine. I have only had the opportunity to taste wines made before the new winery was commissioned. Most impressive were a couple of 1999 late-harvest wines, one (a Szürkebarát) made from the first crop taken from new plantings. Their quality suggested that Kál-Vin, with its new vinification facilities, may be just about to take off.

OTHER WINE PRODUCERS

Inhoff Malom-Borház. H–8296 Hegyesd, Zrinyi u. 56. Tel: +36–87 412383/435284. *Ódon Pince.* H–1073 Budapest, Dob u. 98. Tel: +36–1 3225 959/352 4456. Winery at H–8274 Köveskál. *Szakálvin Kft Pincéje.* H–8254 Kővágóörs, Krisztina Major, 0210/7 Hrsz. Tel: +34–87 464106; Fax: +36–87 464054. *Szakcsoporti Kistermelök Szövetkezet.* H–8314 Vonyarcashegy, Major köz 1–3. Tel/fax: +36–83 349 598

Ódon Pince belongs to István Tombor, a third-generation textile dyer with a dry sense of humour. Tombor got into wine by accident in 1987. His cellar, open to tourists, is on 4.5 hectares at Köveskál. The wine – 200 hectolitres a year – is made for him professionally (currently by György Pásti). He continues the tradition of oxidative winemaking, because he believes reductive wine is just a fashion. Apart from cellar sales, bottled wine goes to wholesalers, wine shops, and restaurants. I find his 2000 white varietals flat and lacking acidity. Older vintages are better, and late-harvest wines seem to be his real forte.

Szakcsoporti Kistermelök Szövetkezet is a cooperative with 270 members who jealously guard their autonomy by producing their own traditionally-made wine, which the cooperative guarantees to buy and which it sells through its restaurant, six wine bars, and a local distribution network. Seventy per cent of its trade is through foreign-owned outlets. The cooperative therefore acts as a safety net for its members, who have no marketing worries, and profits are ploughed back into cooperative development.

Szakálvin Kft Pincéje is a Révfülöp family firm consisting of Tivadar Bákos and his daughter and son-in-law, Viktória and Míklos Juhász. The firm started in 1996. Vineyards (twenty-one hectares at Köveskál, eleven of them yielding) and the winery building – a renovated former cooperative stable – are rented. Basic plastic-tank fermentation with a heat exchanger turns out reductive wines, while a Chardonnay and a Merlot are cask-aged. Just over a quarter is bottled for restaurants, wine bars, and supermarkets, while the rest is sold at the cellar or in bulk to another company. The wines are of average quality, somewhat lacking aroma or depth.

Inhoff Malom-Borház operates in an evocative and charming old mill, producing about 200 hectolitres a year. New fermentation equipment introduced for the 2001 vintage will, one hopes, raise the quality of the wine, until now made using a neighbour's facilities.

BALATONMELLÉKE

921 hectares: 878 white, forty-three red
Sixteen wine communities, with 10,050 members

A scenically attractive area with rolling, well-wooded hills, this is the latest Hungarian wine region to have been recognized – in 1997. It was then called Zala, but in 1999 its name was changed (confusingly) to its present Balatonmelléke. It is the wettest of all the regions within Hungary.

Its vineyards are grouped into five areas. One main area stretches from Bérbaltavár southwards, on both sides of the River Zala valley, as far as Zalaszántó in the east, and includes the village of Csáford. The second, to the west of Lake Balaton, takes in Szentgyörgyvár and Sármellék. The third, west of Lake Kis-Balaton, includes Zalaszabar, Orosztony, Nagyrada, Garabonc, and Zalakaros. The fourth centres on Homok-komárom, while the fifth, on the Croatian border, is north of Letenye and contains Csörnyeföld.

The terrain of the region is composed mainly of sandy clay overlaid by loess, and brown forest soil. The region formerly had several cooperatives and a state farm, and white varieties were grown to provide base wine for Pannonvin. Almost ten per cent of the plantings are now red: not of high quality, but easy to sell. Locals expect the vineyard area to decline further.

Alsóhegy, part of Csáfordhegy, is an idyllic little valley nestling in the hills south of Zalaszentgrót. It could be the Cotswolds, which may be why a certain English knight in the entourage of Henry II called Stafford – of which *Csáford* is apparently a corruption – settled here when returning from a crusade. The valley has its own special microclimate, and the wine never suffers from low acids; if anything, the opposite is true. Before phylloxera this was mainly a red-wine area, and afterwards it was extensively planted with direct-producing varieties. Until 1940, every slope was covered with vines, and it was regarded as a first-class area. Under the cooperative, established in the 1960s, it declined. Over the course of the 1990s, the area of vineyards shrank still further by about a third, and now accounts for only about ten per cent of those in the region.

Szelemihegy is a hill south of Nagyrada, more or less due west of Lake Kis-Balaton, with about sixty hectares of private vineyards on clay and brown forest soil. Zalaszentgrót had some 500 hectares of vineyards before the Second World War. Those high up were abandoned by the cooperative, and you can see the inevitable acacia trees where they used to be. There is a big cooperative plantation just south and west of the village.

Before the Second World War, Csörnyeföld was equal to Badacsony in celebrity. Seventy per cent of its wineries belonged to Croatians, who used to come across the border to tend them, and within a two-kilometre (one-mile) radius of Csörnyeföld, there were about 600 hectares of vines; now there are only fifty hectares, with perhaps one hundred hectares within the thirty-kilometre (nineteen-mile) stretch between Letenye and Lenti. People say that before the war there was no untended area larger than a tablecloth to be found anywhere, and to see what it used to be like one should go across the border to nearby Lendava, in Slovenia. After the war, the whole area fell into decay because the Hungarian government did not want any important developments close to the Yugoslav border. The area is slowly being regenerated, and even some Croatians are beginning to return. However, although Balatonelléke is just beginning to raise its profile, it has a long way to go before it will be really interesting to serious wine buffs.

BUSSAY PINCE

H–8872 Muraszemenye, Béke u. 8. Tel: +36–93 379005; Fax: +36–93 379252. *(a)* László Bussay. *(b)* 2.7ha, with 0.25ha rented: Sk/T 0.7ha; Sk/Or 1ha (planted 1999); Sem 0.25ha; Or/Kv/SM 1ha (planted 2000). *(c)* 40hl. *(d)* László Bussay. *(e)* Varietals, cuvée, late-harvest. *(f)* None

László Bussay is the local doctor at Muraszemenye, close to the Croatian border. His aim is not just to prove that this region is ideal for quality winemaking, but that the grape varieties traditionally grown here still make the best wine. In pursuit of his first goal he began by seeking out a vineyard site with a superb microclimate. As for the second, it is typical that, having been told that Kövérszőlő used to be a very successful variety here before the war, he has now planted some. Having started to make wine as a hobby, he finds that it now takes more and more of his time.

Bussay's vineyard and cellar are close to Csörnyeföld, on the southern slopes of a range of hills that stretches in a horseshoe from Lendava in Slovenia to Letenye. These slopes offer excellent exposure to the sun, and from them there is a very extensive panorama over the Mura-köz, the vast plain between the River Mura (which forms the border about seven kilometres/four miles away) and the River Dráva in Croatia. This spectacular view is best enjoyed from the little veranda in front of the winery, sipping a glass of Dr Bussay's excellent wine.

Bussay started winemaking "from zero" in 1988, carving his vineyard out of a jungle. Since then he has built up his holding to 2.7 hectares, and he wants to expand as and when he can find more premium-quality sites. He chose Lenz Moser training to begin with, but now prefers Guyot's lower yield of about 1.5 litres of must per vine. He does all the work himself, and bought a small tractor in 2000. Bussay has had no formal wine training, but has learned from other professionals and from reading books. He has a very laid-back attitude and refuses, despite the success of his wines, to see them as more than a hobby. "If I wanted to make money, I wouldn't be fooling round with making wine." He seems to make no effort to market his wine, and people have to buy it at the cellar. That cellar is at the end of a very rutted and, in summer, very dusty track, which twists and turns as it climbs the hill to the vineyard – so the people who seek out Bussay's wines must be very motivated indeed.

His aim, he says, is to make dry white wines from very ripe grapes with a high sugar content, and this he normally achieves by simply letting the musts ferment out. The harvest usually starts on October 15, by which time the acid and sugar of his grapes are in balance. However, in 1999, he picked in November and the sugar did not ferment completely, so he unintentionally made a late-harvest wine. This suggests a slightly hit-or-miss winemaking technique.

The cellar, which is a deep one, was specially dug. It normally has a temperature of 9°C. The wines are fermented in large casks made from Slavonian oak, which Bussay claims is the equal of French Oak, and are specially made for him. They range in size from fifty to 1,200 litres, and his total storage capacity of one hundred hectolitres enables him to keep wines in cask for more than a year if he wishes to. There follow two rackings, with a bentonite fining, and there is a sterile membrane filtration before bottling, which he carries out himself. He likes to keep his wine in bottle for some time before releasing it to the public.

Some of his wines strike me as understated – perhaps because they have been made from young vines – and there may be a lack of adequate acidity, making them unlikely to be long-lasting. Perhaps, in fact, he should deliberately aim at sweeter wines, for the late-harvest Tramini made in 1999 is extremely good. It has huge extract and alcohol, and is in every way the equal of a really good Alsace *vendange tardive*.

OTHER WINE PRODUCERS

Diogenes Kft. H–8800 Nagykanizsa, Pf 167. Tel: +36–93 310305. Winery: H–8746 Nagyrada, Szelemenhegy. Tel: +36–93/389351. *Kovács Ottó* H–8746 Nagyrada, Petőfi u. 3. Tel: +36–93 389250. *Sebestyén Pincészet.* H–8790 Zalaszentgrót, Szentpéteri u. 51. Tel: +36–30 2047753. *Vinum Veress – Családi Borpince.* H–8900 Zalaegerszeg, Harangvirág u. 14. Tel/fax: +36–92 320547. Winery: H-8790 Zalaszentgrót, Csáfordhegy. Tel/fax: +36–83 362415

Vinum Veress, run by János Veress, whose main business is steel construction, is (with 15.5 hectares) the largest producer in Csáford. He sells to large producers. Veress, almost uniquely it seems, has a variety called Pintes, once thought to be extinct. He hopes it may have a commercial future, though I am not fully convinced. His wines have a tight, acidic style. Both Veress, who has just invested in a small bottling plant, and Sebestyén, at Zalaszentgrót, have seen clearly that tourism will play a big part in the wine development of the region, and have designed their cellars to take advantage of their attractive locations.

BALATONBOGLÁR

2,663 hectares: 2,030 white, 633 red
Eighteen wine communities, with 4,782 members

Despite its favourable climate, and although vines (red varieties) have been grown south of the lake since the departure of the Turkish invaders in the seventeenth century, Balatonboglár has never been considered part of the classical Balaton wine-producing area. Its soil is quite different from that on the other side of the lake, and is basically loess. The region, which until 2001 was known as Dél-Balaton, consists of five separate parts. The first two lie south of Balatonkeresztúr on either side of Route 68, while the others stretch east from Balatonboglár through Balatonlelle as far as Siófok, the holiday playground of south Balaton.

Balatonlelle and Balatonboglár used to be one town, but they separated in 1990 and are, in fact, 3.5 kilometres (two miles) apart. The region's change of name from Dél-Balaton – which was geographically apt – is doubly unfortunate: the easterly part of the region has no connection with the town of Balatonboglár; and the new name directs attention not just to the town, but to the firm of the same name, putting other interesting firms in the region at a disadvantage.

While the north side of the lake has managed to retain a certain amount of poise despite the onslaught of tourists, much of the south side is highly commercialized in a rather unattractive way. However, if you avoid the run-down hotels and go a short distance inland, you reach undulating hills scattered with clumps of woodland and punctuated by occasional vineyards. Precipitation reaches an annual average of 623 millimetres (about twenty-four inches), with an average temperature of 10.6°C. Here, close to Kéthely, the lake does not have so much influence, and the area is not as hot as Badacsony, for example, which has more hours of sunshine and is two weeks ahead of Balatonboglár in terms of vine growth. In this region, Rizlingszilváni leads the harvest at the beginning of September, with Cabernet Sauvignon ripening in mid-October.

The proportion of red to white varieties in the region is changing as more and more of the former are planted. This can be quite a windy area, and precipitation is higher than the national average. Fungal problems arise, and botrytis can cause difficulties. Hail has also been a problem in recent years. Tourism affects the labour market in Balatonboglár, as elsewhere on the lakeside and, although unemployment is two per cent above the national average, some of the larger producers have to rely on bussing in their workers, making mechanization more and more desirable.

BALATONBOGLÁRI BORGAZDASÁGI RT

H–8630 Balatonboglár, Zrinyi u. 93. Tel: +36–85 500400; Fax: +36–85 500444. *(a)* Henkell & Söhnlein Hungária. *(b)* 358.24ha: RR 56.24ha; Chas 44.1ha; Kir 41.27ha; Ch 33.61ha; ZV 21.54ha; SB 19.39ha; L 17.66ha; Zg 17.65ha; IO 11.83ha; VF 10.48ha; Zen 5.85ha; Rs 5.53ha; Fav 2.69ha; SM 1.11ha; PB 2.23ha; Mus 4.53ha; Sem 3.42ha; P 1.04ha; Ker 1.81ha; H 0.57ha; Car 0.3ha; Zw 25.25ha; Kf 20.19ha; CS 4.57ha; Cin 2.66ha; PN 2.42ha. *(c)* In 2000, 76,000hl of still wine and 58,000hl of sparkling wine. *(d)* Dénes Gádor *(e)* Varietals, rozé, cuvée, sparkling wine. *(f)* 31% of still wine; 2% of sparkling wine (Germany, the UK, Sweden, Finland, Poland, and Russia)

This enterprise – known in Hungary as "BB" – is descended from the Lengyeltóti State Farm, which started in 1949 and continued until 1956 when, after a series of mergers, the Balatonboglár State Farm was formed. It encompassed fourteen villages and covered 3,500 hectares, of which 1,500 hectares of vineyards were its largest interest. This company continued until partial privatization in 1992–3, when it lost major parts of its vineyards. In 1995, Hungarovin (*q.v.*) became the majority owner of its shares, and took over the remainder the following year. There are one hundred to 120 employees, and the company is one of the biggest in Hungary, with unusual amenities such as a nineteenth-century country house at nearby Szőlőskislak, with conference and hospitality facilities and a wine museum.

BB hires the land for its vineyards from the state. They have wide rows, the old plantations being high-cordon Lenz Moser-trained, while those planted by the company are umbrella-trained. Richard Smart, the Australian viticulturalist, has acted as a consultant since 1999, and new vineyards are planted under his direction. Three-quarters of the company's wine is made from grapes purchased under integration contracts with growers owning about 1,300 hectares.

The winery is an immense industrial complex built in 1970. Henkell

& Söhnlein have made huge investments, and both the building and its equipment are still undergoing progressive modernization; some of the technology is very up-to-date, while the rest is just adequate. The white-winemaking facilities are better than those for red, which are now being upgraded. Between 400 and 500 tonnes of fruit can be processed each day. The central cellar, four storeys high, has a 400,000-hectolitre storage capacity. More than half is in steel or stainless steel, and part is in 300 tile-lined tanks, which are being progressively re-cemented and lined with fibreglass.

BB was the first in Hungary to use nitrogen flotation for must cleaning, and nitrogen is added at each movement of the wine in order to preserve the fruit quality. Fermentation lasts for fourteen days at 14°C, and ends at 18°C as a result of the cooling equipment being turned off. The wine is cleaned and moved to containers, and fined only if necessary. After stabilization and sterile filtering, it is bottled. Bottling was done at BB until the end of 1998, since when it has all been done at Hungarovin in Budafok – a move justified in terms of the better utilization of plant.

Sparkling-wine production, started in 1982, is still a major activity, and there is a capacity of 40,000 hectolitres. The wine is tank-fermented. Three styles, fermented for a minimum of six months, are sold under the BB brand to the Hungarian market, and a Chardonnay and a Pinot Noir/Chardonnay, fermented for a year, are sold under the Chapel Hill label exclusively to the UK market.

At Rádpuszta, a short distance east, is the company's wood-maturation cellar. Built in 1850, it belonged to the Festetics family, and has a 6,000-hectolitre capacity in large wooden casks and a 1,300-hectolitre capacity in Hungarian and French oak barriques. Some high-quality wines are also fermented here in open wooden tubs. Each barrique is used a maximum of five times. Barrique-fermented Chardonnay is taken out of wood in May; barrique-matured Chardonnay is taken out of wood in September; and Cabernet Sauvignon remains in cask for a year.

Even before the advent of Henkell & Söhnlein, the company took steps to break into the UK market. The UK importer insisted on an Australian winemaker being employed, so Kym Milne was invited to become a technical adviser. He has maintained his association with the company, and currently Clive Hartnell, a New Zealand winemaker, works under Milne's direction and in conjunction with the company's chief winemaker, Dénes Gádor, who has been at Balatonboglár since 1971. Gádor sees the next step in the company's development as a move towards even better quality, and this will be primarily in the viticultural sector, where an improvement programme has been in progress since 1997. While BB would like to break into the top-class wine market, its main aim at present is to serve its larger group of customers.

BB was developed as a brand name in Hungary in the 1980s, and market research shows that it is basically the only brand known to most Hungarians today. The BB range comprises Premium (Quality Wine), Traditional (Country Wine), and Classic (Table Wine). A third of the company's production is exported, that to the UK and Sweden under the Chapel Hill label range comprising a Single Vineyard Selection, Winemaker's Selection, and Varietal Selection. The general standard of the Chapel Hill wines is considerably higher than most wines produced by Hungarovin. The care taken in the vineyards and the skill shown in vinification are beginning to show, putting the white wines in the top category of good commercial wines. The reds are less impressive, being on the whole too light in weight.

SZENT DONATUS PINCÉSZET KFT (VINÁRIUM RT)

H–1222 Budapest, Sörház u. 20. Tel: +36–1 227 4060/4061. Fax: +36–1 227 4062. Winery: H–8638 Balatonlelle, Kishegyi u. 42. Tel: +36–85 354701; Fax: +36–85 354903. *(a)* Vencel Garamvári and János Konyári. *(b)* 81ha. Old plantings 60.5ha: Rs 12ha; Ch 9ha; Kir 6.5ha; Sk 5ha; RR 5ha; T 3ha; SB/Sem 3ha; OM/IO 2ha; M 13ha; CS 2ha. New plantings 21ha: CS 8ha; CF 1.5ha; PN 1ha; SB 5.5ha; Ch 5ha. *(c)* 6,500–7,500 hl. *(d)* János Konyári. *(e)* Varietals. *(f)* 50% (the UK, Sweden, the US, Finland, Germany, Switzerland, and Holland)

Szent Donatus is close to Kishegy, a small hill with tourist facilities about two kilometres (one mile) south of Balatonlelle. Vencel Garamvári and János Konyári, formerly a winemaker at BB from 1974 until 1991, had known each other for about ten years when they decided to benefit from privatization by establishing Szent Donatus. It was started in 1993 as a consortium of Konyári, six other growers and Vinárium (*q.v.*), a company mainly owned by Garamvári. The compact winery was built in 1993–4 and has a cellar capacity of 12,000 hectolitres, with very up-to-the-minute equipment. The winery, with its red-tiled roof and flanking twin towers, is architecturally striking.

The company's view is that good wines are made from good grapes, so a major effort has been put into the vineyards, replanting those that had varieties unsuitable for their sites or were of an inferior sort. It has also planted twenty hectares in the last four years at a density of 5,000 vines per hectare. Crop yields are on the low side. Additionally, the aim is to reverse the present proportion of red to white varieties to give seven to three, partly because of market demand, but also because of the acquisition of 7.5 hectares (with another three hectares available for planting) on the best part of Sínaihegy. Konyári and Garamvári believe that their new vineyards there will in time yield red grape quality to rival the best of Villány, and will enable them to make premium wine.

Wines are made reductively. In the case of red wines, the must is pumped over the cap, and vinification can last for five weeks, including malolactic fermentation. The filtering and ageing cellar is below ground. Another ageing cellar on Kishegy is under a restaurant run by Konyári. From here there are unequalled panoramic views of Lake Balaton – Badacsonyhegy is directly opposite – and a peacefulness interrupted only by the hum of bees.

A basic stock is held for the local market, otherwise bottling is done to meet orders. Fifty per cent goes to export, and the rest to Hungarian hotels and restaurants, and to supermarkets. The company is very successful and wants to expand, because only half of its production capacity is currently used. It presently produces good, and sometimes very good wines.

ÖREGBAGLAS BORÁSZATI ÉS KERESKEDELMI KFT

H–8713 Kéthely, Baglashegyi Pince, 062 hrsz. Tel/fax: +36–85 339 168. *(a)* Hans-Ulrich and Thomas Burkhalter. *(b)* 96.6ha. Family land 17.3 ha including new plantations: Ch 3.5ha; CS 6ha; Or 3ha; CF 1.3ha; Zw 0.5ha; N 0.5ha; M 0.5ha; Kf 1ha; and propagation stock 1ha. Rented land: Sem 17ha; Or 14ha; Rs 11ha; T 11ha; IO 9ha; Ch 6ha; Chas 3ha; Kir 2.3ha; M 0.5ha; SM 0.5ha. Other: PN 5ha. *(c)* 5,000hl. *(d)* Thomas Burkhalter. *(e)* Varietals, rozé, cuvées, late-harvest. *(f)* 80% (Holland, Germany, Switzerland, Canada, and Scandinavia) Öregbaglas, started in 1993, is run by Hans-Ulrich and Thomas Burkhalter (father and son), who are Swiss. Asked how they come to be in Hungary, they replied, "Ask God, not us." In fact, Thomas wanted to be a winemaker, but thought he did not have good prospects in Switzerland.

Then his father, in Hungary on business, happened to hear not only that Öregbaglas was for sale, but that Ludovico Antinori was rumoured to be interested in it. Believing that the price was very reasonable compared to that of western European vineyards, but spurred on also by the rumour, the Burkhalters decided to buy.

The cellar was founded by Gróf Hunyadi in 1773. Its wines were always well-known in Hungary, and sold to the rest of Europe from the 1850s onwards. In 1956, the state confiscated it, although it remained as a winery for another twenty years before being incorporated into the local cooperative, from which the Burkhalters purchased it in two stages. During this time, the Hunyadi family went to Tuscany – it is related to the Antinori family – but the young Gróf has now returned, and is planting vineyards in conjunction with Öregbaglas.

The Burkhalters' own vineyards are planted on a one hundred-hectare green-field site, which they plan to develop at the rate of five to seven hectares a year. They have a density of 4,000 to 4,500 vines per hectare and rows 2.5 metres (eight feet) wide, but are not yet giving proper quality. The yield is forty-nine to eighty-four hectolitres per hectare. The Burkhalters also hire a further one hundred hectares of vineyards, twenty-three of which have already been lifted because they were in such bad condition. The rest need replanting, but this project has been postponed for a few years. These old vineyards yield thirty-five to forty-two hectolitres per hectare, but as many as a fifth of the vines in them have died off. Another five hectares of Pinot Noir, planted in conjunction with Gróf Hunyadi, yielded its first crop in 1999. Finally, there is a vine nursery started in 1999 which provided between 100,000 and 120,000 vine shoots for sale in 2000, many of them western varieties sourced from Bordeaux. Bench grafts are available. The target is to produce 1 to 2 million grafts a year, with a view to selling on the European market.

Thomas is the chief winemaker and Lájos Huszár is the cellar-master. In practice they make joint decisions. The winery is an old building, still showing signs of its previous run-down state, but everything is clean. The German and Italian vinification technology is modern, and the techniques used are sophisticated and current. However, somewhat unusually, the Burkhalters use ordinary steel tanks with enamelled interiors. Large reconditioned casks and Hungarian barriques are used to mature the wines.

Eighty per cent of the production, including some Country Wine, is exported to Dutch supermarkets as own-label wine. This, in many ways, constrains what the Burkhalters do. Thus, the supermarkets' requirement for a full range of wines means that they have to make a significant amount of red wine (from grapes sourced from Balatonkeresztúr, Balatonberény and Kéthely), despite their view that local Lenz Moser-trained vines cannot produce red wines of depth and character. (They cannot wait for their own vineyards to begin producing.) There is also a requirement for easy-drinking wines, made from neutral varieties like Rizlingszilváni. Supermarkets need it, so the Burkhalters have to produce it. On the domestic market, they sell to wine shops in Budapest, and to hotels and restaurants. Trade with Hungarian supermarkets is also on the increase.

Despite the supermarket sales context, the Burkhalters produce reliable wines that are always agreeable and drinkable, and at their best very good indeed. But what marks them out, in my opinion, are the dessert wines they produce, which vary from excellent to quite stunning. Sémillon, Olaszrizling, and Tramini are the varieties used, and botrytized grapes are utilized where possible. A 1997 Olaszrizling shows wonderful potential, with an almond-paste bouquet, and a palate combining apricots and dried fruits with refreshing acidity. Best of all, perhaps, is a 1997 Tramini, weighing in with fourteen per cent alcohol, 120.5 grams per litre sugar, and 8.7 grams per litre acid. The Burkhalters do not wish to undersell these wines, however, knowing what their equivalents get in Germany. Fortunately, the cash-flow of the winery is such that they can afford to age them. In this way they hope to build up special wine stocks and use them as part of their image.

LÉGLI SZŐLŐ ÉS BORTERMELŐ GAZDASÁG

H–8630 Balatonboglár, Kilátó u. 7. Tel: +36–85 350975. Tel/fax: +36–85 353719. (a) Ottó Légli. (b) 17.5ha: Ch 6ha; SB 4.9ha; Or 1.7ha; Kir 1.4ha; RR 1.2ha; PB 1ha; IO 0.3ha; M 1ha. (c) 700–1,000hl. (d) Ottó Légli. (e) Varietals, rozé, cuvées. (f) 5% (the US, Switzerland, Germany, and Belgium)

Ottó Légli worked at Balatonboglár, but he did not like the low-acid style of wines produced there. He felt there was a new market for wines in accordance with his tastes. Strongly motivated by a wish to be independent, in 1989 Légli decided to work alone. In 1992, he joined forces with

József Eifert and they founded a joint firm – Eifert és Légli Borház – but things did not work out, and they separated in 1997. At the same time, Légli had continued to produce wines under his own name, and he regards his present company as the one he originally founded in 1989 under a new name. He bought his present 200-year-old cellar at Öreglak, unused since the Second World War, in 1995.

His aim is to make wines that combine acidity with elegance and lightness. He started experimentally (without focusing on market demand), and now thinks he has too many varieties. Ideally, he would like to confine himself to Chardonnay, Sauvignon Blanc, and Olaszrizling. His vineyards are on ten plots, near Balatonboglár and on the Somogy hills, just south of the villages of Szőlőskislak and Szőlősgyörök. The latter is an elevated situation with a wonderful exposure and rocky, calcium carbonate-rich soil. The work on his vineyards is carried out under contract with some local families. He counts himself fortunate to have some very good Chardonnay planted in 1966, which he got cheaply because the owners were going to grub it up. His next project is to plant some Sauvignon Blanc with a density of 4,600 plants per hectare, using single-Guyot training.

All his white wines are reductive except for Chardonnay, which is fermented in new 350-litre Hungarian oak casks made specially for him (Hungarian Oak is normally sourced from the Zemplén forest in the Tokaj-Hegyalia region). He believes that they produce better flavours than commercial barrels. The casks are used three times, and each vintage is made from a blend of wine matured in casks of differing ages for around five months. He has his wine bottled at Szent Orbán, and happily finds that it sells easily to top restaurants, hotels, and wine shops.

Légli is a perfectionist, and is clearly hampered by a lack of money. His equipment is not high-tech, but it is adequate. Despite this, he does not cut corners, and he is managing to produce just the kind of wine he wants. The wines are complete, with firm, fruity flavours, evident but rounded acids, and while not having any world-shaking complexity or special qualities, are eminently and satisfyingly drinkable.

OTHER WINE PRODUCERS

Biokultúra Egyesület. H–8630 Balatonboglár, Török B. u. 24. Tel: +36–85 350755. *Bujdosó Pince (Bujdosó Szőlőbirtok és Pincészet).* H–8636 Balatonszemes, Gárdonyi G. u. 2. Tel: +36–84 361188. *Czakó Sándor.* H–8638

Balatonlelle, Arany J. u. 112. Tel: +36–85 353770. *Eifert Borház Kft.* H–8630 Balatonboglár, Szabadság u.19–23. Tel: +36–85 550052. Tel/fax: +36–85 550053. *Kalász Pincészet.* H–8630 Balatonboglár, Zrinyi Miklós út. 10. Tel: +36–85 350345. *Katona Borház.* H–8691 Balatonboglár-Szőlőskislak, Expres u. 10. Tel/fax: +36–85 353461. Cellar: H–8630 Balatonboglár, Hétház u. 8. *Koltai Pincészet.* H–8692 Szőlősgyörök, Malom u. 6. Tel: +36–85 330586. *Opperheim József (Opperheim Családi Pincésjoböl).* H–8627 Kötcse, Petöfi S. u. 32. Tel: +36–84 367589; Fax: +36–84 367911. *Országh Pince.* H–8638 Balatonlelle, Vasúti sétány 15. Tel: +36–85 351034. Cellar: H–8691 Balatonboglár-Szőlő skislak, Boglári u. 15. Tel: +36–85 353602. *Pócz Pincészet.* H–8638 Balatonlelle, Petöfi S. u. 16. Tel: +36–30 9298854. Tel/fax: +36–85 350935. *Szent Anna Borház.* H–8692 Szőlősgyörök, Akácfa u. 4. Tel/fax: +36–85 330581. Winery: H-8692 Szőlősgyörök, Rekeszdűlő. Tel: +36–85 433092. *Szentpály Pincészet.* H–8630 Balatonboglár, Török B. u. 1. Tel: +36–30 3414334. *Trunkó Bor.* H–8692 Szőlősgyörök, Köztársaság u. 18. Tel: +36–85 330128.

Kalász Pincészet is a partnership between two employees of Balatonboglár: László Kalász and Denes Gádor, its chief winemaker. With ten hectares between them, they produce decent, well-made wines for immediate consumption – no faults, but nothing exciting. Bulk distribution is local (to restaurants and hotels), with some wine being bottled.

Eifert, who worked with Légli until 1997, has five hectares, and produces 360 hectolitres of reductive white wines each year from a cellar formerly in the possession of the Rothschilds. He bottles at the cellar to order. Germany imports twenty per cent, and domestic sales are to restaurants and bottle shops. Tank samples of wines three and four years old, his current offering, appeared faded to me.

Pócz Pincészet is a family-run business started in 1991, making generally underpowered wines, as does Koltai Pincészet. Bujdosó Pince, run by Zsigmond Bujdosó, started in 1991 and has sixty-five hectares in Szőlőskislak, Balatonlelle, and Hollád. There is a modern winery and a bottling line. Production is 4,000 hectolitres a year, mostly sold in bulk to other producers around Lake Balaton, including a Királyleányka made as a base wine for BB, which it also bottles and sells under its own label. I find the wines underpowered and without varietal differentiation.

Országh Pince makes good, clean, above-average wines. Czakó Sándor produces decent and interesting white wines, and a quaffing red. Trunkó Bor's wines are rather a mixed bag, but his Sauvignon Blanc is excellent, and his barrique Chardonnay, Zöld Veltelini, and Rizlingszilváni are all sound. The white wines made by Szentpály Pincészet eclipse its characterless reds. József Opperheim runs a family company with four hectares making wines of average quality. Szent Anna Borház makes rather dim wines, apart from a good Tramini. Biokultúra Egyesület, as the name suggests, make organic wines from Látrány, but I find them singularly unimpressive.

7

Budapest and Surroundings

BUDAPEST AND BUDAFOK

The capital city of Budapest is naturally where you will find the head offices of some of the larger Hungarian producers and distributors. However, Buda (the part of the city north of the Danube) was for centuries quite a famous wine-growing area until, in the late nineteenth century, housing development – initially of large, smart villas – began to push out the city boundaries. During the twentieth century, this urban sprawl gradually swallowed up most of the vineyards, and you now have to go about ten kilometres (six miles) from the centre to find anything bigger than the occasional little plot. Pilisborosjenő, Budakeszi, Tök, and Budajenő are the most important areas, and these were joined with Etyek in 1997 to form the Etyek-Buda region.

Apart from having the pleasure of being in Budapest, one of the world's most attractive capital cities, the wine-lover will find restaurants – such as Gundel's and those of the big international chain hotels – with extensive lists of top Hungarian wines, as well as the best-stocked wine shops in the country. The *Magyar Borok Háza* (House of Hungarian Wine), situated opposite the Hilton Hotel on Buda Hill, stocks 700 wines for purchase. This is an ideal place for newcomers to introduce themselves to Hungarian wines, although only a selection of the cheapest (and, sadly, the least impressive) is normally available for tasting. Wine bars can also serve this purpose, including the atmospheric subterranean bar in the Hilton Hotel, where, on my first visit to the country, I started my own Hungarian wine education.

From the point of view of wine production, however, the most important part of Budapest is Budafok, an upstream suburb on the northern bank of the Danube. Thanks to its strategic location for shipping, from the 1830s on this became the main trading centre for Hungarian wine. Estimates of the combined length of its cellars range from thirty to forty kilometres (nineteen to twenty-five miles); nobody knows for certain. Many ran down to the river, for ease of loading. Some of these cellars are very famous. For example, that owned by Vinárium was originally built between 1750 and 1760 and belonged to Magyar Borkivitel, a firm founded by a man called Palugyay (born in 1842) that had branches in Vienna and Bratislava and was the largest wine merchant in Hungary until 1949.

During the Communist period, Budafok, naturally, was home to some of the largest and most influential state companies. Within the last ten years these have all been privatized, but most of them have maintained a certain identity through their cellars. The following are among the most notable, but, without exception, I have never been able to get enthusiastic about their wines.

Promontobor, a family business, occupies extensive cellars (sold to the state by the Neugebauer family in 1901) which housed the *Magyar Állami Pincegazdaság* (Hungarian State Farm Cellar), later called the *Budafoki Pincegazdaság* (Budafok State Farm Cellar). It produces between 50,000 and 60,000 hectolitres a year of wine from various regions, forty-five per cent of which is bottled and the rest of which is exported in bulk.

Lics Pincészet is another family business, started in 1990 and owned by a former director of production at Hungarovin. It handles about 6,000 hectolitres a year, the Budafok cellars being only for storage and ageing. Twenty-five per cent of the wine is bottled, and most of the rest is sold in bulk in Hungary. The wines are more or less sweet to accord with Hungarian taste.

Budafokvin Borászati és Kereskedelmi, with three kilometres (approximately two miles) of cellars previously used by the *Agker Állami Pincészet* (Agker State Cellars), is a wine-trading and distribution company with an annual turnover of 25,000 hectolitres.

HUNGAROVIN

H–1222 Budapest, Háros u. 2–6. Tel: +36–1 226 5511; Fax: +36–1 226 0551. *(a)* Henkell & Söhnlein Hungária. *(b)* 1,062ha: Etyek 785ha; Pázmánd 225ha; Bodrogkeresztúr 52ha. Varieties unspecified. *(c)* In 2000: 62,000hl of still wine;

108,000hl of sparkling wine. (d) László Kemendy, László Romsics. (e) Varietals, rozé, sparkling and Aszú. (f) 60% of still wine; 5% of sparkling wine (Germany, the UK, Sweden, Poland, Canada, Finland, Estonia, Japan, and many more)

Hungarovin is owned by Henkell & Söhnlein Hungária, founded in 1997, which in turn belongs to Henkell & Söhnlein Sektkellereien KG, a Wiesbaden-based sparkling-wine company owned by the German Oetker family. The Oetkers have a large variety of interests, including shipping and hotel chains, with a five-billion euro turnover, of which Henkell & Söhnlein represents only ten per cent. It controls satellites in Austria, the Czech Republic, Poland, Slovakia, and Hungary. Hungarovin and Balatonboglári Borgazdasági are the two largest wine companies in Hungary. The former was bought by the German company in 1992 while by 1996 it had become the majority owner (99.9 per cent) of Balatonboglár.

The very size of Henkell & Söhnlein Hungária, and the complexity of its operations, makes it quite impossible to do it full justice in the space available here. Some facts and figures for the entire company operation (including both firms) will make this clear. The company's net annual turnover in 2000 was HUF10.97 billion (US$37.44 million). Investments between 1996 and 2000 totalled HUF3.25 billion (over US$15 million). Production figures for 2000 were 21.1 million bottles of sparkling wine and 18.4 million bottles of still wine. The company's share of the domestic market for sparkling wine is 72.3 per cent, and for still wine eleven per cent. Exports are to more than fifty countries worldwide.

Hungarovin was founded in 1971 as the Budafok Export Wine Cellar. It incorporates three sparkling-wine firms, two of them with interesting histories. Törley was founded in 1882 by a Hungarian who had worked in Reims. His product achieved worldwide renown (even in Paris), and he had warehouses in Berlin, Hamburg, and Copenhagen. Production ceased in 1944, when a bomb wrecked his architecturally interesting factory (now restored). Two brothers called François, employees of Törley's, deserted him to found a rival company in 1886, and this also succumbed to bombing during the war.

Hungária was founded in 1955. Törley and Hungária merged in 1960, and were incorporated in Hungarovin in 1973, while François was relaunched by Hungarovin in 1982. In its heyday during the Communist period, Hungarovin's annual production was 50 million bottles of sparkling wine and 30 million bottles of still wine, destined for export mainly to Comecon countries. The quality is reputed to have been pretty dire.

Among the company's main assets are its cellars in Budafok. Leander Cellar has a total length of six kilometres (approximately four miles), and is the largest of the individual cellars in Budafok, with storage for 100,000 hectolitres. Before nationalization, it belonged to a family with an association with Lajos Kossuth, the revolutionary patriot of the nineteenth century. It has an important marketing function and is open to visitors, who can inspect the largest fillable barrel in Europe (1,022 hectolitres), made in 1974 to celebrate the twenty-fifth anniversary of nationalization. It weighs eighteen tons when empty, and the steel bands alone weigh four tons.

Apart from those at Tokaj, the company's vineyards are at Pázmánd and Etyek. They are from ten to fifteen years old. Sauvignon Blanc is umbrella-trained, but the rest is high-cordon, back-to-back single-curtain. The normal density of the vineyards is between 3,100 and 3,200 vines per hectare. Apart from white varieties, there are forty hectares of new plantations of red varieties in Pázmánd, between one and five years old. In Etyek and Pázmánd there are between 700 and 800 millimetres (twenty-seven to thirty-one inches) of rain a year, which is relatively high, but Pázmánd has more sunshine hours and is warmer than Etyek. The reason for growing red varieties here is frankly commercial, but Hungarovin is still monitoring them to see whether or not they will provide acceptable quality. The density of the new vineyards is higher than previously, but they are also planted to single-curtain.

The number of buds left after pruning depends on whether the vines have two or three canes. If two canes, seventeen or eighteen buds are left per cane; if three, then fourteen buds are left. In the new vineyards, where there are two canes only, twelve to fourteen buds are left on each. In mid-June, the lateral shoots are removed to open up the canopy, and in mid-August the leaves shading the grapes are removed. Some of the vineyards are green-pruned. In vineyards with a density of 3,200 vines per hectare, the normal yield of Chardonnay is eighty-four to ninety-eight hectolitres per hectare, and for selected wines, fifty-six to seventy hectolitres.

Etyek has a processing plant to provide chilled must, which is delivered to Budafok mainly for use in making sparkling wine. The better-quality grapes from Etyek are sent to Pázmánd, where there is a very modern and well-equipped processing plant, installed in 1995, with a capacity to deal with 3,000 tonnes. Enzymes, ascorbic acid, and SO_2 are added to the grapes, which are then destemmed and fed to Defranceschi pneumatic presses. After pressing, the must is chilled and settled for twenty-four hours. (Aromatic varieties are given four to six hours of maceration if the grapes are healthy.) Clear juice is separated from the pressed must and fermented at 14°C to 16°C. After fermentation, the wine is resettled and chilled, and treated with SO_2 and nitrogen. It is then delivered to Budafok. The wine is fined with bentonite, which is sometimes used during fermentation (on laboratory advice) to help stabilize the wine. The aim is to use minimum quantities of chemicals.

For the red wines, the fermentation lasts about five days and then the wine is left on the skins for two weeks. The best of the pressings go into the wine, and the best wines are given malolactic fermentation. There are plans to increase tank capacity so as to be able to increase the amount of skin contact.

The greater part of Hungarovin's production continues to be sparkling wine. The grapes are sourced from the company's vineyards in Etyek, fermented in the huge plant at Budafok built by the pre-Henkell & Söhnlein company, and matured in the company's extensive Budafok cellars. Traditional-method (formerly *méthode champenoise*) wines are sold as Törley Chardonnay Brut and François President Brut. Transfer method wines are sold in a variety of styles under the Törley and Hungária labels, while Charmat (tank-fermented) wine is sold only under the Törley label. The standard is somewhat commercial, and even the *brut* wines have a perceptible sweetness (as the Hungarian market requires). The Törley Chardonnay Brut is streets ahead of the others, with a defined Chardonnay aroma and a yeasty taste, although, in my opinion, excessively fizzy.

Hungarovin's still wines encompass various regions. There are company wineries in Etyek (acquired with the company), Pázmánd (inaugurated in 1993), Sopron (acquired in 1990), Szekszárd (acquired in 2000), and Tokaj (acquired in 1993), but some regional wine (for example, that from Eger) is sourced from other producers. The Budafok plant does not vinify still wines; it makes the base wines for sparkling wine, and is used for blending and maturing wines. The chief winemaker at Hungarovin until April 2001 was László Kemendy, a 1989 graduate of the Horticultural University of Budapest, who is now general manager. He was succeeded by László Romsics, a 1990 graduate from the same university, who has been with the company since then, but has also had experience of making wine in Breisach (near Freiburg, southwest Germany) and Chile, at Errázuriz and Montes. He has responsibility for all Hungarovin still and sparkling wines, and for the company's operations at Tokaj, Sopron, and Szekszárd. His department is the biggest in the company, with one hundred workers, including three assistant winemakers (one each for white, red, and sparkling wine) and six cellar-masters.

Hungarovin's bread-and-butter exports are two branded wines: Balaton (a red wine that goes to Germany, Poland, and Sweden) and Csárdás (which exists in both white and red versions that go to Germany, Poland, Finland, and Lithuania). Balaton, the first branded Hungarian wine on the German market, was launched in August 1996, and was designed on the basis of extensive market research to have maximum consumer appeal. The initial goal of half a million bottles a year was achieved within the first four months; since then, 15 million bottles have been sold, 5 million of them in 1999 alone. Orders now outstrip the possibility of supply.

The success of Balaton led to the introduction of Csárdás, both red and white, and a change in strategy. Previously a Country Wine, the quality and price of Balaton has increased. It is now a blend of Kékfrankos, Kékoportó, Zweigelt, and Pinot Noir, with twelve per cent alcohol and seven grams per litre of residual sugar. Previously made from grapes sourced from southern Transdanubia and the Great Plain, it is now made from grapes from the Balatonboglár region. Csárdás (white and red), introduced in June 2000, is a Country Wine priced slightly below Balaton. The red is a blend of Kékfrankos and Zweigelt, with 7.3 grams per litre of residual sugar; the white is a blend of Olaszrizling and Szürkebarát with nine grams of residual sugar: a level determined, again, after extensive customer research in three German cities. A new company, Csárdás Bor, has been created to look after the new brand.

Varietal wines, cuvées, and Aszú are sold in a series of ranges. The

Hungarovin brand range includes Top Selection, Barrique, Varietal Selection, and Wine Region Selection. The György Villa range is designed for top restaurants; the Saint Stephen's Crown range consists of the Tokaji and four international varieties varietals.

Hungarovin, by its very size, is necessarily a straightforwardly commercial winemaking operation. As one might expect, the white wines at all levels tend to show better than the reds, which, pre-1999, have usually struck me as too light and easy-drinking in style. In general, the whites from the 2000 vintage show lots of ripe fruit flavours, and enough acidity to be pleasant to drink. Some are a bit better than that. Tank and cask samples of red wines did not show very well when I tasted them in the summer of 2001, many of them having been made from just-yielding young vines. However, one should bear in mind that, since they were made, Romsics has been appointed chief winemaker, so everything may now change. I hope it does, because frankly, there seems to be a lot of room for improvement.

VINÁRIUM BORGAZDASÁGI RT

H–1222 Budapest, Sörház u. 20. Tel: +36–1 226 5133; Fax: +36–1 227 4062. *(a)* Vencel Garamvári, Zsuzsa Fülöp, Gáspár Miklós. *(b)* None. *(c)* 6,600hl of still wine, 1,050hl of sparkling wine. *(d)* Vencel Garamvári. *(e)* Varietals. *(f)*. 42% (the UK, the US, Sweden, Canada, Finland, Poland, Germany, and Switzerland)

Vinárium is a small company established in 1990 by Vencel Garamvári, his wife, and sales manager Gáspár Miklós. Garamvári, educated first at the Soós School in Budafok, then as an oenologist at the Horticultural University of Budapest, started to work for Törley in 1966. He became sparkling-wine production manager in 1969, and a director in 1970. At that time, Törley produced 15 million bottles of sparkling wine annually. Then, when Hungarovin took over responsibility for Törley in 1973, Garamvári found himself a deputy director of Hungarovin, still in charge of its sparkling-wine production. When there were management discussions regarding the sell-off of Hungarovin, Garamvári unsuccessfully opposed its sale to Henkell & Söhnlein and lost his job in June 1990. "It was the biggest bit of luck I ever had in my life," he says.

By August 1990, Vinárium, a company aiming to find and market the best emerging small producers, was up and going, and by 1993, the decision was made to invest in wine production. Thus, in conjunction with

János Konyári, a new company closely allied to Vinárium – Szent Donatus Pincészet – was started in Balatonboglár. Since then, the aim has been to produce good-quality wine while retaining the connection previously established with existing producers. In 1997, Vinárium was able to purchase its present 30,000-hectolitre capacity Budafok cellar from Hungarovin (Garamvári sold his house to raise capital to do so) and, ever since, the firm has been working to renovate the buildings and the cellar.

Vinárium's current activities are fourfold. First, it still acts as agent for small producers from eight wine regions, with (often exclusive) selling agreements in Hungary and exports to the United Kingdom and other countries. These include, for example, Szent Orbán Pince, Nyakas Pince, and Aranyfürt in Szekszárd; Weninger in Sopron; Tiffán, Tamás Gere, and Jekl in Villány-Siklós; GIA and Thummerer in Eger; and Bene and Bodrog-Várhegy in Tokaj. Secondly, it has its own still-wine production, buying grapes, must or wine, fermenting them (elsewhere), and then age-ing and bottling the wine in Budafok. Thirdly, it administers Szent Donatus, and lastly it produces – as one might expect from Garamvári's background – its own sparkling wine, Château Vincent.

This has been a runaway success: production reached 140,000 bottles in 2000, and is set to double. Château Vincent exploits a niche market by combining traditional Champagne technology with competitive pricing. At the moment, only Hungarovin offers any competition. In my opinion, Château Vincent – available as *extra-brut*, *brut*, and *demi-sec* – is without question the best sparkling wine currently produced in Hungary. The *extra-brut* (sixty per cent Chardonnay, twenty per cent Rajnai Rizling, twenty per cent Szürkebarát) has a tight, persistent mousse, a yeasty nose, and considerable breeding. Garamvári now intends to make a Chardonnay and Pinot Noir base wine, and to move towards a truer, more elegant Champagne style.

The firm expands every year by a minimum of twenty-five per cent, partly because its agency partners are also expanding, and it has the capacity to become three times its present size. All this has been achieved through total dedication: Garamvári and his wife have had only eight days' holiday in the past ten years.

CORVINUM KFT
H–1223 Budapest, Dézsmaház u. 19/A. Tel: +36–1 226 9599; Fax: +36–1 226 9600

CorVinum was established in the early 1990s by a group of young producers to introduce the best Hungarian wines to home and foreign markets. The company represents twenty-nine producers, most of them well-known in Hungary, and exports to Singapore, Hong Kong, Holland, and Brazil. It also provides courses on wine and participates in international wine exhibitions.

MONARCHIA BORÁSZATI KFT
H–1092 Budapest, Kinizsi u. 30–36. Tel: +36–1 456 9800; Fax: +36–1 456 2726

This company, backed by a consortium of Hungarian and foreign investors, burst onto the wine scene in 2000. As a distributor, its first aim was to market (domestically, and eventually abroad) the best wines made in Hungary. To this end, it set up agreements with top producers – currently about twenty of them – whereby it commissions them to make special wines to be sold under the Monarchia label, giving valuable support to smaller producers by financing the wine while it matures, and in some cases by offering their own-label wines a wider distribution. Monarchia's portfolio is already spectacular, and it is set to expand. It looks as if its activities will give a much-needed boost to the reputation of Hungarian wine. From its initial aim, it has now moved on to producing wines for itself, and has acquired land and a cellar in Eger (*q.v.*).

OTHER WINE PRODUCERS
Budafokvin Borászati és Kereskedelmi Kft. H–1222 Budapest, Sörház u. 17. Tel/fax: +36–1 226 0160. *König Pince.* H–1222 Budapest, Sörház u. 37. Tel: +36–1 226 4144. *Lics Pincészet.* H–1221 Budapest, Kossuth L. u. 44. Tel: +36–1 229 382;. Fax: +36–1 206 0128. *Promontorbor Rt.* H–1221 Budapest, Kossuth L. u. 82–94. Tel: +36–1 229 3448/3426; Fax: +36–1 229 3449

ETYEK-BUDA

1,868 hectares: 1,737 white and 131 red
Six wine communities, with 2,640 members

The Etyek-Buda region stretches over two counties between Pilisborosjenó and Budakeszi, on the outskirts of Budapest in the north, through Etyek, to Lake Velence in the south. The region is constantly growing, and presently consists of seven separate sub-areas: Pilisborosjenó, Budakeszi, Budajenő (with Telki and Tök), Etyek and Csabdi, Kajászó, Pázmánd, and the Alsútdobozcarea (the most recent addition to the region). Although making wine for everyday needs has gone on here for hundreds of years, this region was not seen until very recently as having viticultural importance. Now it has been "discovered" as a source of fresh, fruity wines.

The Etyek area enjoys special climatic conditions, being at the interface of cold winds coming down from the north and the Danube through a gap between the Vértes and the Gerecse Hills, meeting with heat from the flatlands of the Southern Danube and the eastern regions. The number of sun-hours is relatively small, with grape-sugar levels normally around 16° to 17°. However, the area in the south, at Pázmánd, is warmer than Etyek, and it has plantations of red varieties. Otherwise, this is a white-wine region. The soil at Etyek is limestone and gravelly clay, while at Pázmánd it is loess. There is not much more suitable land left for planting in the region, and very little indeed at Etyek, the very heart of the region.

Etyek is a village with around 8,000 inhabitants. Ninety-five per cent of the local wine community's plantations are owned by Hungarovin, so although many of the villagers own a cellar and make some wine for themselves, independent wine production is a small part of local employment. The village, twenty kilometres (twelve miles) northwest of the capital, has become a dormitory for Budapest, and there is a local industrial park. Originally an eighteenth-century Swabian settlement with a continuous tradition of white wine-growing, it was part of the Törley empire up until the Second World War. However, after the expulsion of the Germans in 1946, when virtually all the 3,600 people of the village had to leave within twenty-four hours, the region was more or less abandoned; only in the 1960s did people remember the previous wine prosperity of the village and return to put the vineyards and houses back in order. This continued during the 1970s and early 1980s. However, as these were seen as "peasant" plots, they were never nationalized.

Hungarovin, to which Törley belonged under the Communist regime, began to develop the area again in the 1980s, planting several hundreds of hectares of Chardonnay for sparkling wine base material, and this development has been continued under the ownership of Henkell & Söhnlein, which now has 785 hectares in the Etyek part of the region, and 225 hectares at Pázmánd. In 1990–1, a group of oenologists started Hungary's first modern technological reductive plant here, and as tastes have veered towards fresh, fruity wines, the area has grown in importance. In Hungary, although some other regions have climbed on the bandwagon with varying success, Chardonnay is now synonymous with Etyek.

The traditional vineyard area of Etyek, however, is on a small hill called Öreghegy – (Old Hill). It is about one kilometre (half a mile) long, running east–west, and is situated just to the north of the village. It was divided into five sectors by the Swabian settlers, whose charming traditional press-houses and cellars border a track through the middle of the vineyards. The division appears to have been purely for administrative convenience rather than because of any soil or other differences, and there was no systematic planting. Each villager had a section between eighty and one hundred metres (260 and 325 feet) long, sufficient for five rows. North of Öreghegy there are extensive state plantings.

The village contains four groups of old, typically German, cellars. The oldest, the Körpince, is possibly unique, and is a circular hollow with the cellar doors around its circumference facing inwards.

There are a few small independent producers in Pázmánd, Székesfehérvár, Tök, and other parts of the region, but the largest concentration – about a dozen – is in Etyek. It is to be hoped that they will benefit from a small bottling cooperative, laboratory, and administrative centre that is being set up.

ETYEKI KÚRIA.

H–2091 Etyek, Öreghegy Pf. 7. Tel: +36–22 223930; Fax: +36–223929.
(a) István and Ágnes Ottrubay, with an expatriate Hungarian partner. *(b)* 5ha: Ch
3ha; Kir 1ha; SB 0.5ha; Sk 0.5ha. *(c)* 45,000hl. *(d)* Rudolf Krizan and Daniel
Szerafin. *(e)* Varietals, cuvée. *(f)* Minute quantities

István Ottrubay is a lawyer who works full-time as a financial manager, so
the task of running this winery falls to his wife Ágnes. This venture, on
Öreghegy, started in 1995. The five hectares of vineyards presently producing will eventually become twenty-seven hectares; meanwhile, grapes
are sourced from a further fifteen hectares under integration contracts.
All the wine is white, but Pinot Noir will be planted shortly. Production –
60,000 bottles in 2000 – will soon rise to meet the winery's 150,000–
bottle capacity.

Etyek Kúria has state-of-the-art reductive equipment. The striking
wooden press-house, rather like a Scandinavian barn, was based on
Austrian models of ergonomic design, and is very compact. The must
runs under gravitational flow to the immense 1925 fermentation cellar
underneath the bottling line, which also provides potential storage
capacity of up to 2,000 hectolitres. Fermentation temperatures are from
13°C to 14°C. The barrique cellar is beneath a renovated press-house,
now a tasting room, and barrels made by Kádár, a prominent Hungarian
cooperage, are used.

In the absence of a suitably experienced local winemaker, the
Ottrubays employ a recently graduated Hungarian winemaker in tandem
with an Austrian wine consultant, and this works well. Quite a bit of
experimentation is still taking place, especially with barrique technique,
and the owners and winemakers accept that there is room for improvement. Wines from the 1999 vintage were marked by excessively high
acidity, so the 2000 vintage had some malolactic fermentation. There is
also a lot of CO_2 in the wines, but this is deliberate: István Ottrubay even
refers to their tank Chardonnay as "almost sparkling". It is believed that
this style appeals to the younger generation, but I confess that it does not
appeal to me.

The wines have had enormous success. The 1998 Barrique
Chardonnay, which spent over twelve months in new oak, was *Borbarát's*
choice as best Hungarian Chardonnay of the year, while their cuvée
Borbála (equal parts of Chardonnay, Királyleányka, and Sauvignon

Blanc) has been chosen as its official wine by the Women's Association of Friends of Wine. There is no doubt that this winery, already with considerable achievement to its credit, has great potential – although one hopes that the Ottrubays will not get too carried away by their CO_2 philosophy.

NYAKAS PINCE KFT

H–2073 Tök, Központi Major. Tel/fax: +36–23 341023. *(a)* Nyakashegy (a holding company with eleven Hungarian owners). *(b)* 162ha (owned by the directors): Ch 58ha; Rs 37.5ha; IO 27.5ha; SB 19ha; Sk 16ha; RR 4.5ha. *(c)* From 6,000 to 7,000hl. *(d)* Ernő Malya. *(e)* Varietals. *(f)* None directly

The Tök area consists of small hills, with a cool climate and a high mineral content in the soil giving elegant, fresh wines. Its vineyards (some 230 hectares) belonged to the Tök Cooperative, which sold its grapes to Hungarovin until it was privatized in 1990. In 1991, a company called Nyakashegy, resulting from a management buy-out of the cooperative, started a number of enterprises. Nyakas Pince, formed in 1997, was one of these. It immediately built a new, beautifully equipped winery, with the fermentation hall (having a total capacity of 2,500 hectolitres) and the cellar totally underground. Its first vintage was 1998. The company sources grapes from its directors' vineyards, all of them old cooperative plantations dating from 1984, with wide rows and high cordon training. Yields are of fifty-six hectolitres per hectare, apart from Irsai Olivér and Rizlingszilváni, which are from sixty-three to seventy hectolitres per hectare.

The winemaker is Ernő Malya, formerly a teacher of winemaking at the Horticultural University of Budapest. The wines are made in an uncompromisingly reductive style, with slightly garish acids but high levels of extract. There have been problems, however. In 1999, every wine had so much acidity that calcium tartrate (0.5–1 gram per litre) was used to reduce it. All the wines have clear driven fruit, with some complexity, coupled with fairly vibrant, clean acidity, and are good examples of this style, if it appeals to you.

The wines are sent away from the winery when ready (there being no storage space), and are distributed through Vinárium, CorVinum, Julius Meinl, and Rothschild, to reach the market each year before Christmas.

ETYEKI BORUDVAR KFT

H–2091 Etyek, Kecskegödör Pincesor. Tel: +36–22 708008. *(a)* Tibor Bíró, Ármin Nádpor, László Hernyák. *(b)* 3.5ha: Sk 2ha; SB 0.6ha; ZV 0.5ha; Kir 0.4ha. *(c)* 120 hl. *(d)* László Hernyák. *(e)* Varietals. *(f)* None

This is a family concern, and the story of how this winery was founded, and of the sheer grit and determination that have enabled one man and his wife to achieve so much, is remarkable. Hernyák, a Hungarian from Csantavér in Serbia who was displaced by the political situation in 1991, came to Etyek with his wife and son, but little else. An economist by education, he found no jobs open to him in Hungary, so decided to make a livelihood from distilling spirits – a common hobby in Csantavér. Although he was remarkably successful, an eightfold increase in mandatory duty deposits between 1993 and 1998 gradually drove him out of business.

Anticipating this, Harnyák had to rethink his whole life and how to invest the small profits he had made since 1991. While his wife took an administrative job, he started to produce wine, educating himself in how to do so by reading, talking to other winemakers, and by trial and (remarkably little) error. He began selling wine under his own name in 1997, and, from an original 3,000 bottles (hand-bottled by the family), by 2000 had already increased this fivefold to 15,000 bottles (bottled now by Etyeki Kúria).

At present, Hernyák has five cellars; three of these he has fully renovated with his own hands in architecturally striking styles. (He may have missed his vocation as an architect.) One cellar is for receiving tourist groups; one, small but compact, is where he makes his wine; and one is for bottle storage. Hernyák has 3.5 hectares of producing vines, with more awaiting replanting.

One might expect a man in Hernyák's position to go after quick profits, turning out wine of minimal quality and maximum quantity to get a small but easy profit. But not a bit of it. Hernyák goes for low cropping and makes his wine, without pressing, from free-run juice. The yield averages about fifty per cent of normal pressed juice. This technique certainly make wines with more depth and interest than are usually found in Hungary.

All varieties (except, normally, Sauvignon Blanc and Szürkebarát) are placed in a tub, treated with enzymes (which soften the skins and assist the juice to flow), and left to macerate for from four to eight hours. They are placed in a drainer to collect the juice, which, after selected yeasts have been added, is fermented at (October) cellar temperature, mainly reductively in ten-hectolitre stainless-steel tanks, but occasionally in barriques. The reductive wine is then settled and put in Slavonian oak barriques to mature.

Hernyák likes to pick overripe, is not afraid of high-alcohol wines if the balance is right, and is not afraid to experiment. He blends two batches of Sauvignon Blanc – his primary variety – composed twenty per cent of early-picked grapes to get high acidity and fresh, green flavours, and the rest of a late-picked batch with high sugar and tropical fruit flavours. In 2000, he used a similar technique for Szürkebarát, with late and early picking, some or no maceration, and stainless-steel and barrique maturation as variables. In the same year, he added a barrique-fermented Zöld Veltelini.

Hernyák's wines have, for Hungary, an unusual generosity on the palate; they are uncompromisingly dry, with unusually high levels of extract that give them an uncommon seriousness. The Sauvignon Blanc is quite out-standing, with good fruit rounded out by a little wood. The Szürkebarát is highly promising, with enormous fruit depth, while a 1999 Királyleányka, picked with 20° sugar, provided a big, rich, and complex mouthful after only a year. In short, all are wines to capture attention.

Until 2001, the wines were sold only from the cellar by tasting, or as part of tourist programmes. However, as a result of another happy development on the now-revived spirit side of Hernyák's business, that is due to change. In 1999, a group of five financial backers enabled him to restart spirit production under the auspices of a new company, Spirits-68. The pressed juice, made after he has taken the free-run juice for his wine, finds its way into Hernyak's brandies, which are on sale in the village at the Etyek Párlatház, a sort of bar, with coffee, cigars, books, and periodicals, that is intended to appeal to both Budapestians and tourists. There is also an agreement with some distinguished producers (Szepsy, Tiffán, Pók, Légli, Figula, and Molnár) for Hernyák to make distillations from lightly pressed *marc* which they provide, and these will be matured for up to six years. Monarchia has contracted with Hernyák to sell his spirits, and for advertising purposes, he has agreed to let them have a limited selection of bottles of wine to sell. In this way, his wines are destined to reach a wider and – I have not the slightest doubt – very appreciative market.

OTHER WINE PRODUCERS

Bormester Pincészet. H–2091 Etyek, Mester u. 32. Tel: +36–22 353613. *Gombai Nagy Tibor.* H–2091 Etyek, Mester u. 72. Tel: +36–22 353612. *Kovács Ferenc (Kovács Pince–Tök).* H–2072 Zsámbék, Gagarin u. 3. Tel: +36–30 494498; Tel/fax: +36–23 342103. Winery: H–2073 Tök, Pincesor 1334 Hrsz. *Tátrai Pincészet.* H–2091 Etyek, Sánci Borház, Kossuth L. út. Tel: +36–22 223307. *Wine City Kft.* (Báthori Tibor) H–2091 Etyek, Kossuth L. út 35. Tel: +36–22 223372

MÓR

868 hectares: 843 white, twenty-five red
Four wine communities, with 2,471 members

Mór is essentially an exclusively white-wine region southwest of Budapest. Its vineyards surround the town of Mór and five other villages: Csókakő, Csákberény, Pusztvám, Söréd, and Zámoly. Only the first two of these are of importance, the others consisting of small private plots.

This is yet another part of Hungary where, from 1697 onwards, Swabians put down their roots, and they have always been the backbone of winemaking here. From 1752 until the end of the nineteenth century, when phylloxera devastated a third of the vineyard area, wine production was largely in the hands of two landowners: the Berényi and Lamberg families. The repatriation of the Germans at the end of the Second World War had a major impact, slightly mitigated by the fact that some vineyards were taken over by Slovaks and Hungarians from other parts of the country.

In 1975, at the height of development during the Communist period, some 2,500 hectares of vineyards were under cultivation in the region, and there were cooperatives in Mór (the Kossuth MGTSZ), Csákberény and Pusztavám, and a state farm (Móri Állami Gazdaság). The latter had a cellar with a 100,000-hectolitre capacity, and farmed 685 hectares of vineyards during the 1980s. A hundred hectares of these were taken up in 2000, ten hectares have been replanted, and some were privatized. Of the original vineyards, 300 hectares survive, rented out on thirty-year leases from the state to about twenty growers. Some do not take adequate care of them. The state farm's winery was sold off to a man from Belarus who dismantled much of it and took it off to Minsk.

The vineyards on the southern slopes of the Vértes mountains between Mór and Csókakő give high-quality grapes. The soil is a light clay with seashell residues. West of this is Pohárhegy (Cup Hill), while three lesser hills run parallel with, and south of, the Vértes slopes: Vénhegy (Old Hill), Kecskehegy (Goat Hill) and Dávidhegy (David Hill). The south-western slopes of these three hills have private plots, but there are state plantings on the northwestern slopes of Dávidhegy. Vénhegy and the southern slopes of Pohárhegy are also among the best vineyard areas, but Csókakő is considered by many as giving the best quality in the region. Part of this area has loess, and part is brown forest soil. Csákberény is said to be the least-favoured area. It has poor soil, with a lot of chalk, and gives wines with even higher levels of acidity than the rest of the region.

Only a score of growers in the region produce wine for the market, of which the largest are Bozóky and Varga Béla. There are about fifteen serious growers in Csókakő, and they sell to Hilltop and Danubiana. The remaining growers are hobby growers, making wine only for the family. Stake-training was traditional here, but not much can be seen now. The old state plantings (inevitably) have wide rows, and are either single-curtain or Lenz Moser-trained. A few recent plantings are umbrella-trained.

The signature wine of the region has always been Ezerjó, intro-duced by the Swabians. In the nineteenth century, it was as famous and as expensive as Tokaji, because, with high levels of extract and alcohol, it travelled and matured well. The other varieties to be found here are Tramini, Leányka, Rajnai Rizling, and Ottonel Muskotály. Chardonnay was introduced in 1964. High acid levels of 8.5 grams per litre or more are characteristic of the region. Malolactic fermentations are not used, and malic acid levels of between two and three grams per litre are typical. There is normally no need to adjust sugar. In 1999, for example, Csákberény grapes had levels of sugar from

18° to 19°, while in 2000 they were a degree or so higher. Over-cropping is a major problem. Raisined grapes can be obtained every year, and botrytis wines can be made, on average, in two years out of every ten.

Mór has very traditional press-houses, many with their old screw and beam presses still in use. At 30 Pince út, for example, there are two such presses dated 1834 and 1853. On the back of the door, looking like the scores of bump races at Oxford, the total of each year's pressing is chalked up in groups of five strokes, each stroke representing a *puttony* or *putt* for short, a traditional wooden harvesting hod that holds between twenty and twenty-five kilograms (forty-four to fifty-five pounds) of must. In 1993, only fifty-three were pressed, but in 1979, the total was 108. Fermentation is traditionally in oak barrels, and the wine is matured in oak casks of various sizes.

The producers are fiercely proud of their Ezerjó, but I have never found any wine of sufficient quality to justify its local reputation. In its first year it is bland and uninteresting, and needs several years to develop any real character. However, when the wines are made from dilute musts, ageing adds little to them. In general, virtually all the region's wines suffer from being made from musts so dilute and flabby that they hardly have the strength to get out of the bottle. They are a consistent dis-appointment.

Since the demise of the cooperatives and state farm, the major problem in Mór is that there is no longer a large firm to represent the region either at home or abroad. A few of the smaller producers are keen to see a new cooperative in which everyone would cultivate his or her own grapes but which would produce wine under a single label. One grower, Béla Vécsei, is trying to organize such an arrangement between some eight or ten producers. A wine route with fifteen mem-ber cellars was launched in autumn 2001. A St George's Day festival takes place at the end of April, and a wine festival in the first week of October. Despite these initiatives, however, Mór strikes me as a rather sleepy (and even rather complacent) wine region, at the moment very much on the fringes of the Hungarian wine scene. Only two of the commercial producers, István Bozóky and Endre Bognár, merit serious attention, although some individual wines made by József Frey, Károly Friedl, and István Biró rise above the mediocrity of the rest. The wines of István Biró, however – although none are bottled, and they can only be bought in Csákberény – are fermented traditionally with natural yeasts, and are clean, crisp, and full-flavoured, with excellent balance.

BOZÓKY BT (BOZÓKY CSALÁDI PINCE)

H–8060 Mór, Pince u. 22. Tel/fax: +36–22 407 797. *(a)* István Bozóky. *(b)* 15ha: Ch 5ha; T 3ha; OM 2ha; E 1.5ha; SB 1.5ha; various 2ha. Access to a further 35ha (lease or contract): mainly E, some T. *(c)* 5,250hl. *(d)* Péter and Zoltán Bozóky. *(e)* Varietals and Aszú. *(f)* Very little (Germany, Finland)

István Bozóky's business was founded in 1991. Previously a director of the Mór State Farm, he started to make wine for himself in a small way in 1989, with a half-hectare family vineyard. When the state farm failed he quickly decided that his future lay in aiming at the top end of the wine market. His business is carried out from an attractive 300–year-old cellar (originally part of the town's Franciscan church), housing a small museum of wine artifacts, a bottle-ageing store, and a museum collection of wines going back to 1959. The recently extended cellar, where the wine is made and cask-aged, is elsewhere in Mór. His two sons act as winemakers; Péter studied at Budafok, and Zoltán spent two years in Burgenland, Austria.

Bozóky crops an average of twenty-one hectolitres per hectare, and sells half his grape production to Hilltop. He makes only a limited number of wines, in both dry and sweet styles. These are made in a generally conservative style, although methods of vinification are being altered slightly from year to year. Bozóky says his aim is to have very good grapes to start with, to conserve colour and taste, and to have a weighty, strong style. There is no need to chill the must, because the vintage begins on November 15, and normally fermentation is between 15°C and 18°C. The wines are mainly matured in barrels of from two to 200 hectolitres in capacity. Racking is kept to a minimum, and altering and fining take place prior to bottling, which is done in the cellar.

Bozóky's wines, especially those with some age, give a good idea of what the region's wines can be about, but seldom are. After eight years or so, their bouquet develops overtones of petrol, and the palate broadens, although the high acidity keeps them fresh. Especially noteworthy are Bozóky's Aszú wines, some of which reach sugar levels of 190 grams per litre. His Trockenbeerenauslese Ezerjó 1997 is particularly impressive.

BOGNÁR ENDRE PINCÉSZETE
H–8064 Csókakő, Nagysalló u. 8. Tel: +36–22 422030. *(a)* Endre Bognár. *(b)* 27ha: E 10ha; Ch 9ha; Or 5ha; L 3ha; Zen 0.5ha. *(c)* 1,000hl. *(d)* Endre Bognár. *(e)* Varietals. *(f)* Occasional (Kenya)

Having gone to the Soós School in Budafok, and then to the Horticultural University in Budapest, where he studied winemaking, Bognár worked first at the Mór State Farm, where he became cellar-master, and then (until 1978) at the Mezőfalva State Farm. Thereafter, until 1993, he worked in the field of insurance, latterly as an adjuster.

Bognár had a hobby plot as far back as the 1970s. He now has twenty-seven hectares, of which fourteen are over thirty years old, two are fifteen years old, and eleven (planted by Bognár) are between two and six years old. Vine training is a mixture of high-cordon, middle-cordon, and umbrella. At present, he sells fifty-five per cent of his grape production, but his new plantations, when mature, will increase his annual production from 1,000 hectolitres to 3,500.

Winemaking is carried out below his house, where there is storage space for 200 hectolitres. A fifth of the wines are fermented in stainless-steel tanks without temperature control, and the rest in barrels. At present, twenty per cent of Bognár's wine is bottled (by a mobile bottler) and sold to hotels, restaurants, and tourists. The rest is sold in bulk to pubs. Bognár plans eventually to bottle all his wine (400,000 bottles a year). In 1994, he purchased another brick-vaulted, crypt-like cellar, once the property of Gróf Zichy and then of the Bishop of Esztergom, with the aim (as yet unrealized) of developing a tourist trade.

Bognár is the largest producer in Csókakő. His wines, on the whole, show much better than most. All my tasting notes are positive, and he and Bozóky must count as the best and most consistent producers in the region.

OTHER WINE PRODUCERS

Biró István. H–8073 Csákberény, Dózsa u. 36. Tel: +36–22 424106. *Frey József.* H–8060 Mór, Ezerjó u. 9. Tel: +36–22 406124. *Friedl Károly.* H–8060 Mór, Pincesor u. 39. Tel: +36–22 407570. *Geszler József.* H–8060 Mór, Zrinyi u. 25. Tel: +36–22 407721. *Király Imre.* H–8074 Csókakő, Vár u. 12. Tel: +36–22 422015. *Manner Márton.* H–8060 Mór, Hársfa u. 2. Tel/fax: +36–22 407677. *Molnár József.* H–8060 Mór, Pince u. 42. Tel: 407166

8

Alföld (The Great Plain)

The Great Plain wine region of Central Hungary occupies the area between the Danube and Tisza rivers. Previously one region, since 1990 it has been divided into three regions: Kunság, Hajós-Baja and Csongrád. There are some soil differences, but this is mainly a region of white sand. In the parts of Hajós-Baja and Kunság close to the Danube there is quite a lot of fluvial mud (a relic of the flooding that took place between 200 and 300 years ago, before the adjustments to the course of the river). Hajós Baja is also a hillier region than the other two, with only a thin layer of sand on top of loess. The soil and climate of Csongrád are basically the same as those of Kunság, and the two were separated (it is said) purely on the grounds of the county border. Part of the Csongrád region also benefits from fluvial soil originating from the River Tisza. The climate ranges from hot in summer to harshly cold in winter (35.5°C to −16.6°C, giving a mean of 10.6°C), with 2,042 sunshine hours and 515 millimetres (twenty-one inches) of precipitation.

There has always been a certain amount of wine production here. Under Turkish occupation the Great Plain became depopulated, and large parts reverted to near-desert conditions. Resettled by foreign settlers, and by refugees returning from Transylvania after the departure of the Turks, these areas were reclaimed, with the encouragement of Maria Theresa, through the planting of vines and orchards. A further boost to development occurred at the end of the nineteenth century, when it was discovered that the phylloxera louse cannot survive in sand. Ungrafted vines are still not unusual in the region.

Under the Communist system the Great Plain became regarded as an important wine region. In the 1960s and 1970s, there were more than

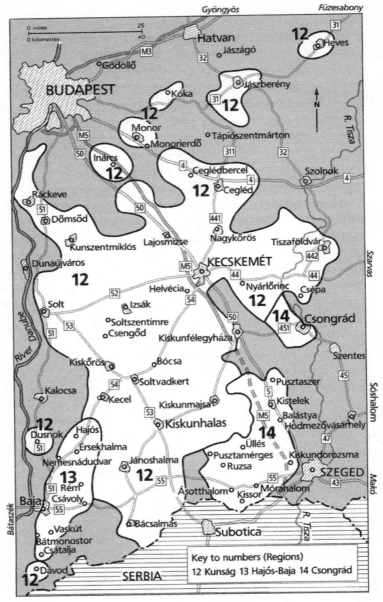

Alföld (The Great Plain)

The reader is referred to the note in Appendix I.

100,000 hectares of vineyards controlled by eleven state farms and approximately fifty cooperatives, of which twenty had wineries. Production was directed towards export to the USSR and its satellites, and remained reasonably efficient until the mid-1980s, when extremely severe frosts during three consecutive winters between 1984 and 1987 caused widespread vineyard damage. In the winter of 1986–87, the temperature fell as low as −26.9°C (although a record −38°C was recorded in Baja in 1942). These disasters were swiftly followed by the effects of the economic factors recounted in Chapter One.

High-cordon cultivation became fairly general in the mid-1970s, even before the severe frosts of the mid-1980s necessitated the covering of traditionally trained low-cordon vines. In Hajós-Baja, this is confined to the lowest-lying areas. In Kunság and Csongrád, a tractor is generally used to cover the cane with soil to a height of thirty centimetres (twelve inches) in winter, and this is removed in the spring using compressed air. Only some small farmers, doing the work themselves, are still able to carry out low-cordon training. However, some varieties such as Kadarka, which is still traditionally cultivated on a single stake, cannot be trained on a high cordon, and so will always have to be covered.

The ratio of white to red varieties is about four to one. Until about 1960, Kadarka was widely cultivated in the region, and red varieties predominated. Subsequently, white varieties were favoured for export markets and, in Kunság, for making base wines for sparkling wine (discussed in more detail below), so post-1960 plantations followed suit. Since the end of the Communist period, however, market sentiment has turned back towards red wines, and the present trend is for plantings of red varieties (slowly) to increase. Because it is relatively resistant to the conditions on the plain, Kékfrankos is very popular, and the proportion of Merlot is also increasing.

The general standard of wine produced is depressingly low, and it is really difficult to find any wine in the Great Plain to become enthusiastic about. Over-cropping is rife, but in any case the sand does not permit the making of sophisticated wines, the reds in particular lacking backbone and complexity. The current vineyard area is now only a third of what it was previously, and production is very fragmented and small-scale. The state farms have disappeared or no longer make wine, and the number of cooperatives – ten in 2001 – gets smaller year by year as adverse market conditions make them progressively less viable. Most have had their local trade quite seriously undermined by fake wines, not just because they cannot compete with the selling price, but because public knowledge of fake wines has damaged the reputation of all the Great Plain's wines. Ask a local cooperative director "How do you see the future?" and a despairing silence is often the eloquent reply. More than half the growers on the plain are part time and cultivate less than half a hectare. They, too, are finding it an uneconomic pursuit, because they have lost their traditional *in situ* purchasers, and national producers are not usually interested in buying their grapes, because the varieties available are not the ones they want, and they correctly regard the quality as too low. The prices on offer are, therefore, derisory.

There is a voluntary organization, founded in 1989, called the Union of Grape Growers and Winemakers of the Hungarian Great Plain, whose role is to lobby on behalf of its members' interests. When it started, its membership included state farms and cooperatives, but at present, out of the 160 wine producers who have a cellar capacity of more than 1,000 hectolitres, only sixty-five are members. Run on a shoestring, it does not appear to be very effective, and it does little to help the 5,000 to 6,000 people who make between ten and twenty hectolitres of wine for selling. The sad truth is that there is no future for most of these growers, and a painful rationalization is in store for them.

The choice of producers to profile in this section has been difficult. Some of the larger companies have been omitted because the wine they make is at best mediocre (and usually worse), or because it is exported in bulk immediately after fermentation. Some producers, both privatized and not privatized, have badly maintained wineries dating from the 1970s which are among the most primitive survivals of their kind to be seen anywhere in Hungary, and it is a miracle that any drinkable wine at all can be made in them. Some are on the verge of financial collapse, and I would not bet on their surviving until this book gets published.

KUNSÁG

25,935 hectares: 20,273 white, 5,662 red
Sixty-seven wine communities, with 32,419 members

This is the biggest region in terms both of area and of production, and it is split into eight districts (stretching from close to Budapest down to the southern border of the country). These, from north to south, are Cegléd-Monor-Jászság, Dunamente, Izsák, Kecskemét-Kiskunfélegyháza, Tiszamente, Kiskőrös, Kiskunhalas-Kiskunmajsa, and Bácska. In the mid-1980s, the region had between 55,000 and 62,000 hectares of vineyards. Of the total area registered as being under vines at the moment, over 4,000 hectares are derelict and waiting to be grubbed up. The eight districts are contained within sixteen discrete land areas.

Two-thirds of the region is given over to varieties previously regarded as suitable for mass-production wines. They were, and for some growers remain, popular because they cost less to produce; for example, their resistance to fungal disease requires less spray protection. Zalagyöngye, Bianca, and Kunleány are the three main varieties, followed by Kövidinka and Ezerjó. Aranysárfehér (still commonly called Izsáki in spite of an official ban on associating the names of varieties with place names) is a high-yielding and medium-quality variety suitable for sparkling wine, the product for which much of the region's crops was previously destined.

Towards the end of the Communist era, the trend was towards planting quality varieties such as Olaszrizling, Rajnai Rizling, and Chardonnay among the whites and, among the reds, Kékfrankos, of which there are now about 3,000 hectares. Almost all new planting (150 to 200 hectares a year) is of red varieties. The proportions of Cabernet Franc, Cabernet Sauvignon, and Zweigelt are increasing, while those of Kékoportó and Kadarka – of which there were at one time 2,500 hectares, now reduced to something over 600 hectares – are dwindling. More than seventy varieties are recorded as being planted in Kunság, but two-thirds of production comes from only ten varieties.

Of the total membership of wine communities, only about 4,000 are both growers and wine producers. Nevertheless, the region has, apart from that of Eger, the two largest wine communities in the country: Kiskőrös and Soldvadkert. Soldvadkert, for example, has 3,164 hectares of vineyards and 1,600 wine community members, including two cooperatives. It produces more than a fifth of Hungary's entire wine output, but only eight Soldvadkert producers bottle their own wine. The greater part of Kunság wine is still exported in bulk to the east.

The region is beset by problems. Previously one of the most prosperous areas in Hungary, Kunság is now, because of the reduction in vineyards and wine production during the 1990s, relatively poor. The local market is, therefore, only for the cheapest wine – sold here at about the same price as mineral water – and this diminishes incentives for improvement. There is very little tourism, the saving grace of small wine producers in many other regions, and eastern export markets not only pay rock-bottom prices but are undependable. Because Kunság is the biggest producer in terms of volume, and has a reputation for poor quality even by Hungarian standards, an unfortunate and unwished-for element of hostility has arisen between it and other regions. Producers here believe that other regions support the introduction of regulations that are against their interests, and are always trying to push Kunság down. No wonder they feel beleaguered. They may well do so for, with an ailing agricultural economy and little by way of industry in the region, what, apart from wine, do they have to turn to?

ARANYHEGYI PINCESZÖVETKEZET

H–2737 Ceglédbercel, Cserő-major. Tel/fax: +36–53 378840. (a) Cooperative with fifteen members. (b) 135ha: 65ha producing, and 70ha beginning to produce: Ch/H/L/RR/CzF/B/Zg/Kf/Zw. (c) 10,000–15,000hl. (d) László Farkas. (e) Varietals. (f) None

This is a rare thing in Hungary: a small, voluntary, post-privatization cooperative, quite unrelated in any way to state-owned cooperatives and based on French and German models. It is situated northwest of Cegléd, in the southern part of the Gödöllő Hills. When nationalization of land took place, the vineyards in Ceglédbercel, already state-owned but administered by the local Roman Catholic church to provide it with maintenance funds, became part of the local state cooperative. When the vineyards were privatized in the early 1990s, their new owners found themselves without any support or practical help in running them. Fifteen growers out of the 200 in the area (then working one hundred hectares of vineyards) therefore decided, in 1993, to establish their own small cooperative. Now it is not so small, because by 2001, these fifteen men owned sixty-five of the original one hundred hectares, while the number of farmers owning the remaining thirty-five hectares had halved. Moreover, since 1997, the fifteen members have established a further seventy hectares that are just beginning to be productive.

Vine cultivation, with advice from an expert in plant protection György Klément, and the running of the cellar are treated as separate operations. The soil is basically loam. Vine-training is mainly single-curtain, although some of the older plantations have mid-height cordons. Mechanized services, soil management and plant protection are sold to local growers from whom the cooperative buys grapes. Because of limited storage space, however, only the best grapes are retained and up to fifty per cent of grape production is sold to another cooperative. The winery, previously a stable, has a pneumatic press from which the must is taken gravitationally to stainless-steel tanks cooled by computer-controlled water circulation. When I visited, the whole set-up was in an impressively clean state, despite being in full-steam-ahead use. Even the workers' toilet was impeccably clean – a sure sign of firm direction and a preoccupation with hygiene which are not all that common in Hungary.

The cooperative is managed by Béla Arany. White grapes make up all but ten per cent of production and, as storage is limited to 8,000 hectolitres, excess production is sold as must. Only ten per cent of the wine is bottled for sale through members, the rest being sold in bulk. I was shown some white wines, all clean but made from rather dilute musts. It is not for the quality of its wine, however, that I have written about this venture. It is because I applaud the vision of its owners, because I believe it shows one way of combating the problems that face small growers, and because it should be an example to others.

The cooperative has been financially successful and wishes to expand further through stockholder investment rather than by incorporating new members. Although profits are re-invested, these are not enough for the development that will be required when new plantings come on stream. One hopes that they will find suitable sponsors, because if enterprise deserves success, this is certainly a prime case.

BORANAL BORÁSZATI KFT

H–6200 Kiskőrös, Középcebe 1. Tel: +36–78 312264; Fax: +36–78 311792.
(a) László Pecznyik, Mihály Suhajda, László Vaszary. *(b)* 220ha. 66ha red: Kf
16.5ha; CF 19.8ha; M 19.8ha; CS 9.5ha. 154ha white: OM 77ha; Ch 30.8ha; ZV
15.4ha; Or 15.4ha, L 15.4ha. *(c)* 3.5–4m bottles. *(d)* Gizella Reile. *(e)* Varietals
(a wide range), rozé, cuvées. *(f)* 98% (Baltic, Czech Republic, Poland, Malaysia,
Denmark, the UK, Slovakia, Russia, and the US)

An important and reasonably buoyant company, Boranal is run by its
three director-founders, all of them with degrees in oenology and horticulture. When it started in 1989, it was (the owners claim) the first
private small-scale wine enterprise in the country. Even at this early date,
they grasped that the moment was propitious for private initiative, and
decided right from the start to produce and bottle quality wine solely for
export – an aim that persuaded the banks to lend the company money at
low interest rates, and thus enabled it to get off the ground. The site for
the winery was chosen because it had nearby vineyards, offered on-site
services, and has good logistical connections. *Boranal* means "wine
analysis". A public limited company of that name has existed since 1983,
giving advice to growers and analysing wine, and this continues to be run
as a parallel enterprise.

The winery was built in 1992, and the company acquired all its vineyards (planted twenty to twenty-five years previously) in 1995. They
supply half the production requirements. Boranal is fortunate that most
of the red varieties in its vineyards are international ones, and that
Ottonel Muskotály, its most popular wine, constitutes half of its white
varieties. Replacement of the older vines is now a priority.

The winemaker, Gizella Reile, is a graduate of the Horticultural
University of Budapest, and previously worked for a state farm. All the
wine is reductively made, using pneumatic presses for white grapes and a
screw press for the red. Cooling of the fermentation is by water curtain.
Until 2001 the wine was stored only in stainless steel, but barriques have
just entered the picture. The wine is piped to an adjacent bottling line,
where bottling is done to order.

Although the company realizes that the continual upgrading of its
technology will be necessary for it to continue to compete successfully on
the export market, unfortunately it has insufficient capital to carry out all
its plans at the moment. However, the wine is already of a consistently

decent, exportable, supermarket standard – perhaps the best in Kunság – and the company appears to be basically in a strong position.

HELVÉCIA RT

H–6034 Gazdasági dűlő 11. Tel: +36–76 579032; Fax: +36–76 579 033. *(a)* Huba Szeremley. *(b)* 195ha. About 120ha of white varieties, including Kun 70ha; Sk 10ha; Ez 10ha. About 60ha of red varieties, including CF 17ha; Kad 12ha; Kf 3ha. *(c)* 35,000hl. *(d)* András Weller. *(e)* Varietals, cuvées. *(f)* None

Helvécia, close to the town of Kecskemét, has an interesting history. The soil here is rather different from that of most of the rest of the region, with between eight and one hundred centimetres (three and thirty-nine inches) of sand on top of a layer of clay fluvial deposits with good water retention. Where there are undulations of the terrain, the substratum is nearer the surface on the higher land. Normally the water table is about 1.5 to 2.5 metres (five to eight feet) below the surface. However, recent flooding of the Tisza, some forty-eight kilometres (thirty miles) distant – anticipated to become a regular phenomenon – has resulted in the appearance of surface water in small indented areas of scrub. There is an appreciable quartz content in the soil, and this warms up and retains summer heat, with beneficial ripening effects on the grapes. Despite the tradition of white varieties here, the proportions of the components of the soil are considered good for producing red wine, more and more of which is being made. The red wines of Helvécia matured in tank have a reputation for tasting like cask-aged wines, a result (it is surmised) of some component of the soil. Acidity is high. In 2000, Kékfrankos was processed with 10.5 grams per litre, which was reduced by malolactic fermentation to seven grams per litre, while Szürkebarát had one gram per litre higher acidity than at Badacsony.

Helvécia is, in a sense, the successor to the Helvécia State Farm, itself formed round the nucleus of a company founded in 1892 by a Swiss called Ede Weber. Weber realized that phylloxera would not survive in sand and decided to use Helvécia (so named in his honour) to preserve native *Vitis vinifera*. He farmed 550 hectares of vineyards and 500 hectares of other crops. Moreover, he gave sanctuary and hope to 105 families[1] from north Balaton, whose vineyards had been wiped out, by

---

[1] Hulej and Kovács, pp. 99–105. Halász (2), p. 79, wrongly gives the number as 150.

offering them plots at Helvécia and financing them until they found their own feet. Weber even built himself a small turreted castle, which stands, incongruously and somewhat the worse for wear, next to the ugly old state farm installations. Its new owner intends to restore it.

The state farm having failed, its wine-processing plant was bought by Huba Szeremley in 1999, and his new company, Helvécia, made its first vintage in 2000. The company owns 550 hectares. Of this, 180 have old state plantings, fifteen hectares were planted in 2001 with Kékfrankos clone K1 (an improved clone developed in Kecskemét, with stems and berries bigger than normal), and the rest is uncultivated, awaiting development at an intended rate of thirty hectares a year.

The old installations are the subject of a complete programme of renewal scheduled to finish in 2005. The chief winemaker is András Weller, who hails from Badacsony. The year 2000 was the first trial vintage, with fifty per cent of the grapes bought in. A high-quality Cabernet Franc which, having had almost three months' skin contact, has a huge depth of colour, is being matured in Hungarian oak casks, and will not appear for some time. However, apart from a really fine Kékfrankos, I have to say that I found the first release wine from Helvécia unimpressive. Huba Szeremley has high hopes of Helvécia, and has even said that he believes it could become the Médoc of Hungary! Only time will tell.

HUNGASEKT RT

H–6070 Izsák. Tel: +36–76 374222; Fax: +36–76 374555. *(a)* István Kiss, János Szaniszló, Jenó Molnár and József Makkos. *(b)* None. *(c)* 8m bottles in 1999 (all products). *(d)* Ferenc Szabó. *(e)* Sparkling wine, vermouth, non-alcoholic drinks. *(f)* 6% (Poland, Baltic states, Finland, Brazil, Mongolia, and Vietnam)

Since the early nineteenth century, sparkling-wine production has been a big part of the Hungarian wine culture, and remained so during the Communist period, when the Izsák State Farm became an important production centre. In the late 1980s, it produced about 14.5 million bottles a year, solely for export to the USSR. The present company, led by the state farm's former financial director, was started in 1992. Export to Russia continued until 1996, when it completely stopped, just as the company, after a period of lower production, had managed to rebuild its output. Now the firm has to concentrate on the domestic market, dominated as it is by Törley. However, its share of this market has been growing over the past few years, and reached twenty per cent in 2000. Hungasekt handles its own distribution to wholesalers and supermarkets.

The company sources its grapes mainly from within the region, but also from Mátraalja and Tokaj. The main variety used is Aranysárfehér, which gives the acidic character to the sparkling wines; Rizlingszilvani, Rajnai Rizling, Zalagyöngye, Irsai Olivér, and Cserszegi Fűszeres are sourced from Kunság, while Chardonnay and Muskotály are sourced from Gyöngyös. The company also purchases must and wine (after first racking) from other wineries, but tries to limit this to less than ten per cent of its needs. There has been continuous investment in the technology of the winery since 1998, and the facilities are, for the most part, extremely modern. Cleanliness, especially of the cellar, is impressive. All the sparkling wines are tank-fermented in an entirely closed system. After their second fermentation, the wines are matured for one year, given a second filtration, and then bottled. The winemaker is Ferenc Szabó, a graduate of the Horticultural University of Budapest.

The product range is extensive. The premium sparkling wines are Chardonnay Brut, Grand Brut (using a base wine blend of Olaszrizling and Rajnai Rizling) and Blanc Sec (based on Aranysárfehér). Then follows "Claudius Caesar" (based on a blend of Olaszrizling, Rajnai Rizling, Aranysárfehér, and Chardonnay), a quality wine in three styles (*sec, demi-sec,* and *doux*). After these come Walton and Pompadour, both in various forms. The company also produces a sparkling wine for the Russian Champagne Factory (RISP, now a privatized company with fifty per cent Irish ownership), as well as a dry white wine from Aranysárfehér and a vermouth for export.

Hungasekt aims at niche domestic markets, but would like to increase exports and break into the UK market. With their new fermentation equipment, they are well-placed to compete on quality. The best wines are from the premium range: the Blanc Sec appeals most to me, being elegant, with a shade more flavour than the Chardonnay but less than the Grand Brut, and just about the right balance of fruit and acidity. It is marginally better in my opinion than the top-range Törley wines, but not as good as Château Vincent Brut or the BB Chardonnay/ Pinot Noir cuvée supplied to the UK market.

OTHER WINE PRODUCERS

Bor-Ászok Kft. H–6222 Csengőd, Kiscsengőd 186. Tel: +36–78 441095; Tel/fax: +36–78 341095. *Eszesvin (Eszes Befektető Kft).* H–6200 Kiskőrös, Kossuth L. u. 5. Tel: +36–78 311373/312933. Winery: H–6222 Csengőd. Tel: +36–78 441111/441650. *Frittmann Testvérek Kft.* H–6230 Soltvadkert, Eötvös u. 5. Tel: +36–78 381513. *Halasi Borászati Kft.* H–6400 Kiskunhalas, Batthyány u. 54. Tel: +36–77 422228. *Kastély-Bor Kft.* H–6230 Soltvadkert, Kertész u. 29. Tel/fax: +36–60 381358. *Kecel-Borker Kft.* H–6237 Kecel, I. Körzet, 59. Tel: +36–78 321023; Fax: +36–78 321596. *Kecskemétvin 2000 Rt.* H–6000 Kecskemét, Kiskőrösi út 18–20. Tel: +36–76 482199/324380; Fax: +36–76 324380. *Kerbor Kft.* H–2213 Monorierdő, Szárazhegy. Tel/fax: +36–29 619206. *Kiss Pince (Kiss Vállalkozás).* H–2711 Tápiószentmárton, Segi út 41. Tel: +36–29 424 007; Fax: +36–29 424 338. *Kute-Vin Rt.* Budapest office: H–1194 Budapest, Hofherr Albert u. 20–22. Tel/fax: +36–1 280 8754. Registered Office: H–6223 Soltszentimre, Dózsa Gy. u. 79. Tel: +36–78 445 260. *Pohan-Vin Kft.* H–6200 Kiskőrös, Petőfi u. 106. Tel/fax: +36–78 511050/060. *Schiszler Péter.* H–6230 Soltvadkert, Ifjúság u. 29. Tel: +36–78 581200; Fax: +36–78 581201. *Szent Donát Borok.* H–2243 Kóka, Pesti út 36. Tel/fax: +36–29 428157. *Szikrai Borászati Kft.* H–6032 Nyárlőrinc, II. Ker. 105. Tel: +36–76 343020/177/133; Fax: +36–76 343003. *Szőlőskert Pinceszövetkezet.* H–6230 Soltvadkert, Szentháromság u. 96/1. Tel: +36–78 381439; Tel/fax: +36–78 381211. *Weinhaus Kft.* H–6235 Bócsa III, körzet 14. Tel: +36–78 353011/353103; Fax: +36–78 353100

Bor-Ászok, started in 1990, is a holding company, with four separate wineries and its own marketing company. In addition to its 328 hectares, it has access through integration contracts to a further 2,000 hectares, and has a total production capacity of 100,000 hectolitres. All its wine is sold in bulk: sixty per cent on the home market, forty per cent abroad. Kecel-Borker, a family firm founded in 1991, operates from a former winery of the Kecskemét State Farm Cellar and makes 50,000 hectolitres of wine (mostly what they call "big-quantity sellers") from bought-in grapes with adequate new equipment. Bottling is only done to order; thirty per cent of production is exported in bulk (mainly to Germany), and the rest finds its way on to the home market.

Eszesvin is a company of potential interest rather than present achievement. Output reaches about 90,000 hectolitres per year, including wine which is bought in, but the eighty per cent presently exported is of Table Wine quality, with better-quality wine going to Hungarian supermarkets. However, there has been considerable investment in up-to-date technology, and the company's future direction will be towards higher quality, tilted towards increased domestic sales. The dominant impression is of a well-managed, go-ahead winery which, if it turns itself round, could do well.

Pohan-Vin dates from 1992. Run in conjunction with the best hotel in the area by János Pohánkovic, whose family (from Dalmatia) has been in the wine trade since 1718, it makes bulk wine, fifty per cent of which is exported. A new bottling line came into use in 2001. Kute-Vin, which started in 1994, is a large company turning out 120,000 hectolitres a year. It has three well-equipped wineries making reductive wine almost entirely for the home market. It needs to achieve a big improvement in quality if its export ambitions are to be realized.

Kecskemétvin 2000 is the privatized Közép-Magyarországi Pincegazdaság (Mid-Hungarian Cellar), and has wineries in Kecskemét and Kiskunfélegyháza. Inability or unwillingness on the part of the owners to upgrade or replace the existing vinification facilities hampers the talented winemaker, Berta Polyákné, who does well in adverse conditions. Weinhaus, successor to the Kiskőrös State Farm, produces mainly Table and Country Wines, but hopes soon to upgrade its equipment and quality. Szent Donát Borok is in Kóka, a little village east of Budapest that was added to the Kunság region in 2000. Miklós Haris leads the many small-scale producers in the village. His wines are of uneven quality (a one-off blend of Chardonnay and Cserszegi Fűszeres was rather unexpectedly successful), but mostly above the regional average in quality.

HAJÓS-BAJA

1,940 hectares: 1,141 white, 799 red
Seven wine communities, with 2,901 members

Although not exactly hilly, this part of the Great Plain is by no means boringly flat. The land undulates gently, and trees break up the landscape. Apart from wine, the region is also a large producer of apples for juice. The soil is sand to a depth of about forty centimetres (sixteen inches), with loess underneath, which makes for good drainage. Average rainfall is 467 millimetres (eighteen inches) a year. Winters are severe, and this is another region where low-trained vines have to be covered to protect them against frost. Half the vineyards have now disappeared, having been largely abandoned or made into tree plantations. Sixty per cent of the wine produced in the region is white, with low levels of acidity. There are between twenty-five and thirty wine-producing firms in the region.

The region has two noteworthy wine villages: Nemesnádudvar and Hajós. The former has 800 wine cellars and not a single house for living in: a totally silent village. Hajós is the largest wine village in Hungary, but with an admixture of houses. Both date from 1742, and each cellar has, on average, about fifty to sixty hectolitres of storage capacity. Cellars are sometimes built under or over other cellars, starting in one street and coming out at a slightly higher level in the street behind. Most belong to people with a hectare or less of vineyards, and they sell from their cellars. Those in Hajós are (haphazardly) open daily between May and October. In Nemesnádudvar, they open to groups by appointment, and at weekends.

BRILLIANT HOLDING LTD

H–1026 Budapest, Bimbó u. 212. Tel/fax: +36–1 275 9456/0070. Winery: Nemesnádudvar. Tel/fax: +36–79 378177. *(a)* Magdalena Kőfalvi and East-West Trading (an English finance company). *(b)* 80ha. Old plantings (10–20 years) 65ha: CS 35ha; Kf 10ha; M 10ha; Zw 6–7ha; PN 3ha. New plantings 15ha: CS 15ha. *(c)* 5,500hl. *(d)* Kálmán Szabó. *(e)* Varietals, rozé. *(f)* 90% (in bulk to the UK, Japan; in bottle to Switzerland, Germany, Japan, Estonia, and the US)

This was one of the first joint-venture companies set up in Hungary, and dates from 1989, when it was simply called Brilliant. It started as a firm to manufacture a Pepsi-like drink and other soft drink concentrates, and this remains part of the company's business, both domestically and abroad. The wine business started in 1992, when the name was changed to Brilliant Holding.

The winery previously belonged to the Baja State Farm, and was offered for sale with 430 hectares of vineyards (which the company, to its regret, turned down). The building, last used by the state farm in 1989, has now been completely reconditioned, with a new (1994) underground bottle cellar. The firm produces only red wine. All the equipment is stainless steel and temperature-controlled, the heating capacity being more relevant when, as once happened, the vintage is carried out at −10°C. Yields are held to a maximum of fifty-six hectolitres per hectare. Fermentations are natural, and there is minimal chemical treatment of the wine. Bottling is done on demand.

The company does not wish to expand. It exports almost everything, but also sells in Hungary to hotels, restaurants and wine shops. The wines vary considerably in quality. Older (pre-1998) vintages often display green, harsh tannins and a jammy character; more recent vintages show more consistency and better balance.

SÜMEGI BORÁSZAT KFT

H–1025 Budapest, Búzavirág u. 3. Tel/fax: +36–1 325 5871. Winery: H–6500 Baja, Pf. 250 (51–es főút 154 km). Tel/fax: +36–79 325 766. *(a)* József Sümegi and family. *(b)* 80ha: RR 21ha; Ch 11ha; L/Kir 21ha; ZV 5ha; Kf 16ha; Kad/CS 6ha. *(c)* 5,000–6,000hl. *(d)* József Sümegi. *(e)* Varietals. *(f)* 60–65% (Czech Republic, Poland, and China)

This is a family firm, started in 1993. Sümegi, a product of the Soós School in Budafok, worked from 1965 until 1993 in the Baja State Farm, starting as a winemaker, then becoming director of winemaking and, finally, general manager. Sümegi bought his present vineyards from the state farm when it was privatized. Some replanting of them will take place shortly.

His winery was built in 1996 and commissioned in 1997. There are three bright, well-designed buildings: a fermentation hall with good, modern equipment, overlooked by an office area and tasting room; a bottle store; and a bottling plant (dating from 1998). These are conveniently situated in a thirty-two-hectare vineyard beside the main road north from Baja. A barrique cellar is planned.

The wines are made reductively. Red wines are fermented in tanks with pump-over facilities and then matured in casks or barriques in a cellar in Nemesnádudvar. Dating from 1850 and twice extended, this is one of the largest and most atmospheric cellars in the village. Apart from casks and barriques, it houses a stock of over 4,000 bottles of museum wines dating from 1976, and a personal collection of wines representing each of the forty-four countries Sümegi visited while working at the state farm.

Exports are mainly in bulk, but some bottled wine is sold in Hungary to supermarkets, to restaurants, and at the cellar door. The style is clean, light, and simple.

PIEROTH HUNGÁRIA PINCÉSZET

H–6344 Hajós. Tel/fax: +36–78 404429. *(a)* Ferdinand Pieroth, D-6531 Burg Layen, Mainz, Germany. *(b)* None. *(c)* 15,000hl. *(d)* Jürgen Hofmann. *(e)* Varietals. *(f)* 100% (Germany)

Pieroth, based in Germany, is well-known worldwide for its wine-marketing technique; personable young salesmen knock at the door, offering a free wine-tasting in the hope of making a sale. The purchase of Hungarian wine had already been a big part of Pieroth's business for a quarter of a century when, to meet growing consumer demand for red wine, it decided to set up its own winemaking plant here in 1998. The aim of the company is to make *Ausbruch* red wines (*Ausbruch* is a German term for sweet wine made from overripe, sometimes shrivelled, and even botrytized grapes; the name is more usually applied to white wines). Only Cabernet Sauvignon is made in a dry style; the rest, of which eighty per cent is Kékfrankos, is sweet.

Hajós was chosen in preference to other regions because of its soil and above-average hours of sunshine. The disadvantage of the area, which Pieroth frankly admits it underestimated, is the difficulty of persuading growers that quality is more important than quantity, and that harvesting should be delayed. The company is trying to combat this by entering into integration contracts with its growers.

Pieroth built a 15,000-hectolitre-capacity winery, completed in six months at a cost of DM8 million (around four million euros), in time for the 1999 vintage. It is the most impressive state-of-the-art winery in the region, with many refinements not often met with in Hungary, such as a fully automatic, self-cleaning Sartorius cross-flow filter. (There is a dedicated emergency telephone link to the manufacturers in Germany, who can even control and readjust the machine over the link.) The vinification techniques, involving pasteurization of grapes at 85°C prior to pressing, are, frankly, those required for making mass-market wines. Pieroth also buys dry, finished wine from other producers, and uses fifteen per cent of its own production to make concentrated must for sweetening them. The wine is rested until March, and is then taken by tanker to Germany. The winemaker is Jürgen Hofmann, a 1997 graduate of Geisenheim, and Petra Bernhardt, the parent company's oenologist, supervises.

OTHER WINE PRODUCERS

Anna Borház. H–6348 Érsekhalma, Fő u. 35. Tel: +36–78 448156; Fax: +36–78 448100. *Gilián Borászati és Kereskedelmi Rt.* H–6520 Bátmonostor, Petőfi S. u. 30. Tel: +36–79 361222; Fax: +36–79 361455. Winery: at Giliánkastély, Route 51, south of Bátmonostor. *Kovács Borház.* H–6344 Hajós, Jókai M. u. 23/A. Tel: +36–78 409947; Fax: +36–78 404551. *Stadler Ferenc.* H–6344 Hajós, Wesselényi u. 47. Tel: +36–78 404452

Ferenc Stadler is primarily a squash and soft drinks manufacturer, but came out with his own label in 2001. Presently producing red wine from one hectare, but with four hectares of Cabernet Franc planted in 1998, he vinifies traditionally. His Zweigelt impresses most at the moment, and suggests that Stadler is a winemaker to watch.

József Gilián, with interests in twenty-seven different sectors of commercial activity, must be one of the richest men in Hungary. He runs a two-pronged wine operation producing 64,000 hectolitres a year, partly in Bátmonostor, where he operates a run-down 1960s winery originally belonging to the Baja State Farm, and partly in Gyöngyös (*q.v.*). Made from the produce of his own 112.5 hectares in Szekszárd and forty hectares in Csátalja-Vaskút, supplemented by bought-in grapes, little of the Hajós production is bottled, and much of it has recently been purchased by Hungarovin.

Kovács Borház is a family enterprise owning sixty hectares that started in 1993. The construction of a very well-equipped winery between 1998 and 2000 brought a temporary halt to production; because older vintages are unimpressive, it is difficult to assess this firm's future potential. Anna Borház is owned by the Gonda family, and was started in 1992. Production of 150 hectolitres is a mixture of reductive and oxidative wine, some being matured in barriques, and most of it is sold locally.

CSONGRÁD

2,683 hectares: 1,681 white, 1,002 red
Ten wine communities, with 2,8251 members

The first reference to winemaking in the region, concerning vineyards near Alpár and Csongrád, can be found in the foundation deed of the monastery of Garamszentbenedek, signed by Géza I (1074–7). However, although there was some viticulture in Pusztamérges from the eighteenth century onwards, Csongrád never became a classical Hungarian wine region, and only started to be notable for winemaking during the Communist period. This is still mainly an arable and farming area, producing wheat, corn, sunflowers, alfalfa, lettuce, tomatoes, and other vegetables, and breeding sheep, cattle and pigs.

The region has four districts: Csongrád (which is self-contained), Kistelek, Pustamérges, and Mórahalom. All were within the compass of the Szeged State Farm (later called the Southern Great Plain Cellar), which had six wineries within the region. Three of them are now used by post-privatization companies: that in Csongrád by Csongrádbor, that in Ásotthalom (in the Mórhalom district) by Somodi Borgazdasági, and that in Pusztamérges by Berla. Those in Mórahalom and Balotasállás no longer exist, while that in Kistelek still exists, but has become very small because of a ninety per cent diminution in the local vineyard area.

In 1975, the state farm was at its peak, making 220,000 hectolitres a year, but from 1980 it went into decline, and finally collapsed in 1994. There were also a number of cooperatives, but these, too, have either been transformed or have disappeared. Since 1980, the region's vineyard area has been reduced from 5,700 hectares to its present 2,683 hectares. It was once famous for red wines, but white grapes now have the edge. The best varieties in the region are considered to be Cserszegi Fűszeres, and Olaszrizling, while Kékfrankos and Cabernet Franc do "as well as can be expected", to quote one realistic local winemaker.

With the exception of Ásotthalom, where the sand is dark (and thought to be better for growing red varieties), the region has white, sandy soil. Temperatures are not so extreme as further north, but can reach 37°C in summer, and sugar levels range from 17° to 22°, depending on variety. Acidity tends to be low and, as was the case in 2000, is often adjusted.

The size of Öregszőlők, Csongrád's vineyard area close to the River Tisza on the town's northwestern side, has recently diminished by half. Very little new planting is being done, but slowly there is some progress, notably by Pál Gémes, previous president of the Bokros-Kossuth Cooperative. At least two vineyards have drip irrigation, an unusual sight in Hungary. There are also some domestic plots with quite a lot of horn-pruned and staked vines, and this is the only place in the world where I have seen vineyards carpeted with such a riot of vividly coloured wild flowers.

Mórahalom does not have a long history of winemaking, In the 1870s there were around one hundred hectares planted with table grape varieties. During the Communist era, all the vines were planted by state organizations. The state farm had 626 hectares, planted in 1976 and 1989, of which 180 hectares survive. The Ásotthalom Cooperative owned 480 hectares, but in the 1980s it could not afford to continue cultivating them; by the time they were privatized, they were in such an appalling state that people walked away from them. Meanwhile, three small companies have been formed to exploit the remaining vineyards, which are situated between Kissor and Mórahalom. There has been hardly any planting in the last ten years.

The vineyards of Pusztamérges have dwindled to about half their extent since 1980. One can see hectare upon hectare of abandoned vineyards on the road between Üllés and Ruzsa. Around 500 hectares were planted between 1976 and 1984, but now there are only 276 hectares, shared between the ninety-nine members of the wine community, some of whom sell their grapes.

There is little to interest the serious wine-drinker in Csongrád. Many wines show high levels of malic acid, and many are oxidized. The makers appear not to notice this (or were hoping, perhaps, that I would not).

Hódmezővásárhely, to the east of Szeged, is not within the region proper, but counts as a wine-producing area. The vines at Aranyhág, the traditional fruit- and grape-growing area in the town, survived the phylloxera louse, but not the Communists. Phylloxera, however, brought the planting of vines to Sóshalom, where Gróf Károlyi was the landowner before the Second World War. Sóshalom was taken over by the Rákóczi Cooperative, formed in 1960. After privatization in 1992, when all the land reverted to its members, the winemaking part of the cooperative was converted into a limited company by its remaining 172 members.

CSONGRÁD BOR KFT
H–6640 Csongrád, Aradi út 14. Tel/fax: +36–63 483055. *(a)* Árpád Agrar AG. *(b)* None. *(c)* 20,000hl. *(d)* György Pálfi. *(e)* Varietals. *(c)* None

This firm was originally part of the Southern Great Plain Cellar, which went bankrupt in 1994. Through a series of transactions, it now belongs to Árpád Agrar, thus named since 1999, but formerly the Árpád Zöldségtermelő Szövetkezet (founded in 1960). The processing line has been modernized, but still lacks proper temperature control. On the other hand, there is a modern German bottling line. The company buys grapes from local producers, and its entire production is red, apart from some white wine it buys in to provide restaurant customers with a wider range. Seventy per cent is made with natural yeasts, and is given a malolactic fermentation. In order to get a good cash-flow, some wine used to be sold immediately after fermentation, and the rest (after fining and filtration) in bulk, but now some 4,500 hectolitres are matured in traditional forty-hectolitre casks and bottled for sale locally and through a supermarket. Barrique wine production of Cabernet Franc started in 2000. The wines are, on the whole, well-enough made: light, balanced, and generally the better for a bit of ageing.

TAKÁCS FERENC
H–6800 Hódmezővásárhely, Hakói út 25/c. Tel: +36–62 246694. *(a)* Ferenc Takács. *(b)* 7ha: Kf 2ha; Zw 1ha; Bl 0.5ha; Or 2ha; CzF 1ha; ZV 0.5ha. *(c)* 180–200hl. *(d)* Ferenc Takács. *(e)* Varietals, cuvée. *(f)* None

Takács worked at the Southern Great Plain Cellar from 1953 until 1980, eventually as its winemaker. Now he is the deputy manager of Vásárhely Róna in the Hódmezővásárhely wine-growing area. He favours umbrella-training for his vines, and grows the bunches at the end of the canes. Some of his production is sold as grapes. He gets this entry purely on the strength of his traditionally made 2000 Cuvée (Kékfrankos, Zweigelt, and Blauburger). It is not only better than any wine I encountered in the Csongrád region, but is actually quite impressive. Weighing in with thirty-five grams per litre of dry extract, it has a very deep colour, soft tannins, considerable depth of flavour, and no aggressive acidity.

OTHER WINE PRODUCERS

Berla Kft. H–6785 Pusztamérges, III ker. 53. Tel: +36–62 286730. *Bokros Borászati Kft.* H–6640 Csongrád-Bokros, Tanya 1523. Tel: +36–63 479189. *Farkas Testvérek.* H–6785 Pusztamérges, Petöfi u. 65. Tel: +36–62 286866. *Gulyás Ferenc.* H–6640 Csongrád-Bokros, Hóvirág u. 31. Tel: +36–63 479065. *Somodi Borgazdasági Kft.* H–6783 Ásotthalom, VI ker. 916. Tel: +36–62 291322. *Triovin 2000 Kft.* H–6783 Ásotthalom, Béke u. 39. Tel: +36–62 291533. *Vásárhely Róna Kft (Sóshalmi Borászat).* H–6800 Hódmezővásárhely, Tanya 1633. Tel/fax: +36–62 2444875. *Vitifarm Kft.* H–6783 Ásotthalom, I ker. 5. Tel: +36–62 291501

Triovin 2000 makes drinkable, light, and fruity wines without much character, using very basic, old technology. Vitifarm, a family firm, is the largest company in Ásotthalom, making wine from its own seventy hectares of vineyards, and selling it in bulk to national producers. Berla, with access to its five owners' 103 hectares of vineyards, is the largest producer in Pusztamérges with around 10,000 hectolitres a year, mostly in sweet styles, which it sells in bulk to the Czech Republic. Its technology is badly in need of upgrading. Bokros Borázati, a firm deriving from the Bokros-Kossuth Cooperative, sells only in bulk.

9

The South I

MECSEKALJA

773 hectares: 658 white, 115 red
Seven wine communities, with 2,860 members

This is the third-smallest region in Hungary. In 1943, Villány and Pécs, which had hitherto been considered one region, were separated. In 1977, Pécs and Versend were combined, and in 1992, Szigetvár was added to them. The name *Mecsekalja* is derived from the range of Mecsek Hills north of Pécs. The region sprawls eastwards as far as Mohács and the Danube, and comprises the areas described below.

Pécs, as a wine-producing area, is only a shadow of its former self. As recently as 1980 there were 1,000 hectares of vineyards on the southern slopes of Mecsekhegy behind Pécs, but gradually, housing development has replaced all but a couple of hundred hectares. Cirfandli is the traditional grape here, and is surprisingly hard to find in either the town or the district. It is another of the Hungaricum varieties that appears to need some ageing to make it remotely interesting. After five years it develops peachy, apricot flavours which are arresting enough, but rather an acquired taste. Pannonvin, now privatized and split up, was one of the largest state wine cellars during the Communist period. Its headquarters were in Pécs. A big cooperative planting, now privatized, straddles Route 6, just north of the town.

Szigetvár is on the western extremity of the region. This fairly flat area north of Route 6 (from Szentlőrinc to Mozsgó) consists mainly of family plots. One hundred years ago it was entirely planted with Kékfrankos, and local growers reckon that its brown forest soil is ideal for growing red

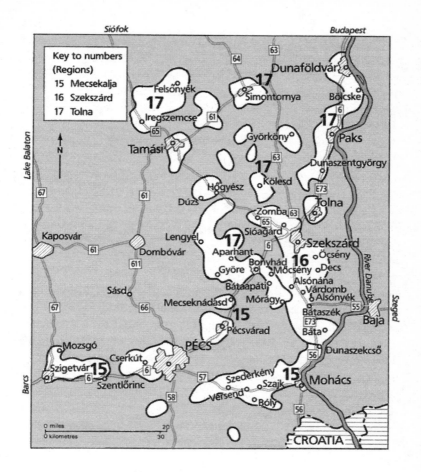

Key to numbers
(Regions)
15 Mecsekalja
16 Szekszárd
17 Tolna

Mecsekalja, Szekszárd and Tolna

varieties, although these now make up only one-fifth of the area. In fact, the climate here is not as warm as in Mohács or Pécs, and the acid content of the grapes is appreciably higher than elsewhere in the region. Only four or five cellars in Szigetvár bottle their wine and sell it beyond the immediate area. Trust Hungary, one of Hungary's principal coopers, is also located here.

Midway between Pécs and the Danube there are two wine areas – Szederkény and Bóly (north and south of Route 57, respectively), with the less important Versend and Szajk (both north of Route 57). They are both on gently rolling, almost flat land. Szederkény has some 104 hectares planted by the local cooperative in 1975. The growers here are too poor to plant new vineyards, and too conservative to want to diversify their production of almost entirely white varieties. The traditional variety in the area, as at Bóly, is Juhfark – grown for over a century for sparkling-wine production and, until the Second World War, planted on some 1,500 hectares. Nowadays, other varieties such as Chardonnay, Olaszrizling, and Cserszegi Fűszeres are bought mainly by Hilltop.

Bóly, with a population of German origin, has a long tradition of winemaking. Most growers belonged to cooperatives until 1995, and until then the configuration was mainly one of small plots, producing thirty to fifty hectolitres a year. Only recently has any relatively large-scale farming started. At the moment, there are 1,100 families in the village, and around 400 wine cellars. Year by year, some twenty hectares of new vineyards are being planted, and traditional varieties are being jettisoned in favour of international ones. Sauvignon Blanc is on the increase, and Szürkebarát – not traditional in the area, as are Királyleányka and Juhfark – has made an appearance, as have some red varieties.

Around a dozen producers make over 1,000 hectolitres a year, bottle their wine, and sell it in Hungary, as well as exporting some to Germany; another dozen make between 300 and 500 hectolitres, a little of which is bottled; and the rest weigh in with between thirty and forty hectolitres a year, all of it sold locally. Across the board, between fifteen and twenty per cent of all wine is sold in bottles. The largest producer in the area is a former cooperative, Belvárdgyula MGSZ. It makes wine from about sixty hectares, but does not bottle any of the wine, which is sold to Budafok.

Mohács is mainly an area of small plots (visible on Szőlőhegy north of Route 57), as is Dunaszekcső further north, and little commercial wine is made here. With brown forest soil over loess (about one metre/three feet deep), and a humus content of under two per cent, the soil is very suitable for red varieties, which were grown exclusively in both areas before the war but presently make up a tenth of production. Mecseknádasd, on the northern limit of the region bordering Tolna, is set in a picturesque little valley, visible from Route 6. It was never a cooperative area, and has little commercial winemaking.

From the point of view of sales, the whole region – especially Bóly – is very much oriented towards tourism. With its Swabian connections, the area attracts mainly German tourists. A Mohács-Bóly White Wine Route covering eleven villages and towns, with thirty-one places to visit, is being developed.

MÉSZÁROS-PÓLYA PINCE (EUVITIS KFT)

H–7754 Bóly, Bánki D. u. 28. Tel: +36–69 368629/369126; Fax: +36–69 368437. *(a)* Diána and Kálmán Mészáros. *(b)* 5.8ha. Villány: Kékoportó 2ha; CS/M 1ha. Nagyharsány: Or 1ha. Versend and Szederkény: Ch 1ha; SB 0.5ha; T 0.3ha. *(c)* 500hl. *(d)* Diána and Kálmán Mészáros; *(e)* Varietals, rozé, cuvée. *(e)* None

The cellar was founded in 1991 by a married couple who started their first vineyard in 1986 when they were both still students in Budapest. The name commemorates Diána's father, who inspired her love of wine. Their (former cooperative) central cellar in Bóly has been partially remodelled, but fermentation is also carried out in a separate cellar in Villány – an inconvenience to which the Mészároses appear to be reconciled. Kékoportó is made in a nouveau style, and kept in barrels for only three months, while Cabernet Sauvignon is covered after fermentation and left in skin contact for three weeks. White wines are fermented in stainless steel without temperature control, and the wines are stored in twenty-hectolitre barrels. Barrique Cabernet Sauvignon was first made in 1999, and barrel-fermented Chardonnay in 2000.

All the wine is bottled in the Bóly cellar, and is sold either to Budapest distributors or, with a different label, independently to Budapest restaurants. The wines, particularly the whites (despite lack of temperature-control), are in the main very competently made. Olaszrizling and Juhfark, with good extract, are clean and pleasing. The Sauvignon Blanc (from Versend grapes) is one of the best in Hungary: balanced, without any overblown or exaggerated features, it exhibits a lovely varietal nose and fresh taste. The red wines are on the light side, but well-balanced.

NÁDASDI BORHÁZ KFT

H–7695 Mecseknádasd, Rékavölgyi u. 17. Tel: +36–72 463295; Fax: +36–72 563004. *(a)* József Hauck and János Hetényi. *(b)* 29.5ha: Kf 24ha; BK/BI/CS 4.5ha; Ch/Sk/CzF 0.8ha. *(c)* Not known. *(d)* József Hauck. *(e)* Kf. *(f)* Occasional (Finland, Seychelles)

József Hauck and János Hetényi are both from wine families. They jointly own a building firm, and decided to branch out into wine. The firm was started in 1993, when the cellar was built, and is the largest in the north of Mecsekalja. The main winemaker is Hauck, who learned first from his grandfather and is now learning, as he puts it, "from the wine". Production at the moment is entirely of Kékfrankos, because other varieties, planted in 1999, are not yet yielding. The partners have forty hectares in Alsonána and in Mecseknádasd for future planting.

Part of the production is made in concrete tanks with pump-over facilities and no temperature-control, and part is reductively made in stainless-steel pump-over tanks, with a water curtain. As the wine is immediately taken off its skins, its colour "comes from God". There is no malolactic fermentation. Wine is aged in large casks for one year, and ten per cent of it (all completely oxidative) is bottled and sold via a distributor to hotels, restaurants, and wine shops. The rest is sold in bulk to other producers, or at the cellar. Although not hugely exciting, the wines are well above the regional average.

NEUPERGER BALÁZS

H–7754 Bóly, Park u. 74. Tel: +36–69 368 870; Fax: +36–69 368 850.
(a) Balázs Neuperger. *(b)* 8ha: Kf 3.5ha; PN/CS 2.8ha; M 1ha; Or 0.7ha.
(c) 350–400 hl. *(d)* Balázs Neuperger. *(e)* Varietals, rozé. *(f)* 15% (Germany)

Neuperger, descended from eighteenth-century Swabian settlers, graduated in 1989 as an agricultural technician. Preferring an active, open-air sort of life, he took up a number of jobs, including soldiering and footballing, until 1992, when, after spending a month in Germany, he earned enough money to purchase a 0.33-hectare vineyard on his return to Hungary. "In this way," he says, "I found my vocation." Since the success with his first wine in 1994, he has built up a holding of vineyards in Villány, Nagyharsány, and Bóly. He started to bottle his wine in 1997 and, in 1999, he bought an 1881 cellar from the Bóly Cooperative, which he is slowly renovating.

Neuperger's methods are very traditional. Whites are fermented in wooden vessels and reds in new concrete fermenting tanks. There is no malolactic fermentation except for Pinot Noir. All wines are stored in wooden casks, and there is no racking. The wines are fined just before bottling, which Neuperger does himself. He sells about 15,000 bottles a year, a little to wine merchants in Budapest, and the rest he sells in bulk to high-profile producers in Villány who, I am almost certain, sell it at a huge profit under their own labels. This alone indicates the high quality that Neuperger achieves. He is a typical case, I fear, of a talented wine-maker limited both technically and commercially by a lack of funds. He wants to stop making white wine, which he does simply to make money, and needs to buy more vineyards. Eventually he would like to sell all his wine under his own label. I wish him luck.

PANNONIA CÉZAR PEZSGŐGYÁRTÓ ÉS BORKERESKEDELMI

H–7621 Pécs, Szent István tér 12. Tel: +36–72 224839; Fax: +36–72 214438.
(a) The Cézar Group (Stefán Császár and two Swedish investors). *(b)* None. *(c)* See text. *(d)* Ágnes Fischer. *(e)* Sparkling wine, varietals. *(f)* 50% (Sweden)

Stefán Császár, the prime mover in this enterprise, is a Hungarian emigré who runs a hotel, catering, and wine-distribution business in Sweden. In 1996, he bought this historic winery, complete with stocks, from Pannonvin. Situated in the historic centre of Pécs, the winery is a hand-some classical building with a 2.5-kilometre (one-and-a-half-mile), cata-comb-like network of cellars on five levels, parts of which date back to Roman times. It originally belonged to Lőrinc Littke, who founded the first Hungarian sparkling-wine company in 1859. The building has now been completely and sympathetically refurbished: Littke's flat and guest rooms in an elegant way, and the bottling line (on display to the public) in a bright and modern way.

The sparkling wine, made in twelve styles grouped in four label fami-lies (Club, Pannonia, Fünfkirchen and DSR), is produced by the transfer method (fermented in magnums – of which five per cent explode!) from base wines made from Chardonnay, Rajnai Rizling, Olaszrizling, Zöld Veltelini, Hárslevelű, and Királyleányka. The cuvées are matured for between three and four years. In addition to sparkling wine, the firm sells still white wines (made from grapes bought in Siklós), and ready-made red wines from Szekszárd. Both white and base wines have, in the past, been supplied by Pannonvin, but in 2001, nothing had been bought from them or any other supplier since 1997.

The house style emphasizes lightness and freshness, these being Császár's personal taste and also the preference of the Swedish market. However, there has been a growing realization that many customers prefer more weight, and there will be a move in this direction in the future. I find the wines clean but characterless, the *demi-sec* wines being more attractive than the dry, because their slight sweetness makes up for lack of weight and gives a better mouth-feel. Sadly, the firm cannot exploit the Littke name and label, because the right to use the label lapsed as a consequence of a gap in production between 1949 and 1966. The company appears to be marking time at the moment, and will, in a sense, relaunch itself with a rather different product when it has moved some more of its first production.

OTHER WINE PRODUCERS

Eberhardt György. H–7700 Mohács, József A. u. 4/a. Tel: +36–69 311854. *Hárs József.* H–7754 Bóly, Rákóczi u. 3. Tel/fax: +36–69 368900. *Hauk István.* H–7712 Dunaszekcső, Rőzsa u. 1. Tel: +36–6 2098 07316. *Lutz Tibor.* H–7754 Bóly, Széchenyi tér 9. Tel: +36–69 368307. *Novák Pince.* H–7900 Szigetvárszőlőhegy 3712 hrsz. Tel: +36–73 413491/312072. *Pannonvin Rt.* H–7621 Pécs, Szent István tér 12. Tel: +36–72 427022; Fax: +36–72 411801. *Rothné Mészáros Ágnes.* H–7754 Bóly, Rákóczi u. 23. Tel: +36–69 368933.

Pannonvin is the descendant of the Villány-Mecsekaljai Borgazdasági Kombinát (later the Mecsekvidéki Borgazdaság) formed in 1950. In 1977, it took over the grape-growing part of the Villány-Siklós State Farm, and in 1984, was renamed the Pannonvin Borgazdaság Kombinát. In 1986, Pannonvin was at the height of its success. It made 180,000 hectolitres of wine a year, of which 56,000 hectolitres (two million bottles) were sparkling. Of this, almost three-quarters were exported to Eastern bloc countries. In 1990, it took its present name, and in 1992 was split into four units: Szőlő-bor, now Villány Borászat; Pécsi-Pezsgő, sold in 1993 to a Moldavian, bought back in 1997, and currently used as a warehouse; the historical Littke cellar, sold in 1996 to Pannonia Cézar; and Siklós Gönter Szőlészet-Borászat. The last of these belongs to Pannonvin, and produces grapes and wine from 112 hectares in Siklós – what remains of Pannonvin's original 1,000 hectares in Siklós and Villány. The company is planning a resurrection, starting with still wine from the 2002 vintage.

István Hauk is a cattle farmer and self-taught winemaker, who in 1993 changed his hobby to winemaking when he became too old for football. He has equal amounts of Chardonnay and Olaszrizling in his 1.2-hectare vineyard, and buys in Királyleányka and Rajnai Rizling. He sells his wine easily to local restaurants and pubs, and has no time to bottle it – which is a pity, because his Olaszrizling and a Chardonny-Királyleányka cuvée are among the best wines to be found in the region.

Ágnes Rothné runs her winery with her son, a professional winemaker in Villány, since her husband László died tragically in 1997 from fermenting gas. She owns twelve hectares of white vineyards in the area, and rents a further ten hectares of red vineyards in Villány. Her cellar is 200 years old, and is the largest in Bóly. It used to produce must for Littke. Rather average wines, some of which are exported to Austria and Germany.

SZEKSZÁRD

2,149 hectares: 495 white, 1,654 red
Six wine communities, with 3,140 members

Until 1997, the Szekszárd region was larger than it is now and consisted of two parts: a central core (the region as it is now, then planted predominantly with red varieties), and to its west, Völgység (now part of the Tolna region, and then regarded as a white-variety area). The Szekszárd part of the region had two main reasons for wanting to ditch Völgység and become an independent wine region. First of all, to help it to become more competitive with Villány (of whose success Szekszárd is openly jealous), it wanted recognition of what it regarded as the superior quality of the wine from its part of the old region. Secondly, because Paks – a town with a nuclear power station – wanted to become part of the old region, Szekszárd was apprehensive that, should this occur, it would generate adverse publicity. When the division occurred and Tolna was created, therefore, the new region included not only Völgségy but Tolna, Paks, and other areas north of Szekszárd. At the same time, the new, smaller region of Szekszárd was divided into six subregions: Báta, Bátaszék (which itself includes Alsónyék, Várdomb, and Alsónána), Szekszárd (town), Decs, Zomba, and Sióagárd.

Szekszárd (town) subregion is as big as the rest of the region, and most of its vineyards are to the east and south of Szekszárdhegy. This is really more of a range of small, low hills about eight kilometres (five miles) long from north to south, with lots of re-entrants and little valleys, each with its own microclimate. This varied topology gives Szekszárd wine a multi-faceted character, characterized overall by its spiciness – often described as "paprika-like". Sadly, as in Villány and Somló, there was considerable building of holiday cottages on the slopes during the Communist era, and larger vineyards were divided into small plots, each with its house. The southern aspect of the hill is dotted with small houses from this period, and woodland scrub with tell-tale acacia trees has overgrown the upper slopes.

The soil, several metres deep, is very rich, being loess with an abundance of minerals, below which there is terra rossa. After some years, when the vine roots get down to the terra rossa, the plant becomes greener, grows more intensively, and survives drought more readily. Musts with very high extract levels – from twenty-four grams per litre up to twenty-seven grams per litre, and sometimes higher – are obtainable. Sunshine averages 2,100 hours a year (as in Villány, further south). Many, therefore, consider the conditions for grape-growing to be optimal, and it is perhaps no wonder that Szekszárd is the largest red grape-growing region in Hungary.

Up until the Second World War, there was a tradition of quite large vineyard ownership by professional people such as lawyers and doctors, who would employ their own cellar-master and sell their surplus wine for export through the Szekszárd Cellar Cooperative, itself the successor to the Szekszárd Wine Sellers' Company, founded in 1856. In the nineteenth and early twentieth centuries, the vineyards in Bakta, now a suburb on the south side of Szekszárd, were regarded as the best vineyards on the hill – considered so valuable, it is said, that they could only be inherited, never purchased. Bakta is now the site of the town's hospital, and continuing creeping suburbanization has reduced the vineyard area to something between eight and ten hectares, mostly in plots of from 300 to 800 square metres (3,228 to 8,608 square feet). Elsewhere it is much the same story: the average size of a vineyard is 0.3 to 0.4 hectares, and there are very few indeed that are larger than ten hectares. Trying to consolidate tiny plots in the best areas at the moment is nearly a lost cause, and almost everyone is bedevilled by it. The general view seems to be that as the plots become less and less viable for wine production, their owners will be forced to sell to the bigger producers. Unlike Villány, however, where there is virtually no new potential vineyard land to be had, estimates of untouched land suitable for plantation in the region as a whole are placed as high as 1,600 hectares.

Kadarka used to be the traditional variety in Szekszárd, but it has become scarce because, being tender and difficult to grow, it fell out of favour during the Communist regime. Nevertheless, some pre-war plantings survive. Kékfrankos was introduced to the region in 1972, and French varieties at the end of the 1970s. Kékfrankos, it is generally agreed, is better adapted to conditions in Szekszárd than in Villány, as is Zweigelt. Kékoportó, on the other hand, seems to do better in Villány. Apart from Kadarka, Szekszárdian producers are fiercely proud of their Merlot, which is frequently claimed to be the best made in Hungary. I can say with confidence that this is wrong; the best now comes from Villány.

Like Eger, Szekszárd has traditionally produced a Bikavér, or "Bull's Blood", but it is nowhere near as popular here as in Eger. This may be because, under Communism, the making of Bikavér was confined to Eger, and the right to make it has only recently been re-established by Szekszárd. Nevertheless, although Eger has its own account of how the wine got its name – Turkish soldiers saw the wine-stained uniforms of the troops of István Dobo and concluded they had obtained their strength and courage by drinking bulls' blood – it was apparently the nineteenth-century Szekszárdian poet János Garay, who, in 1851, baptized the local wine with this name:

> Pour it into the glass, a wonder to behold,
> Red is its colour, like the blood of bulls . . .

As in Eger, the basis of Bikavér used to be Kadarka, but is now universally Kékfrankos, and the only legal requirement regarding the varieties used in the blend is that there should be at least three. Theoretically, therefore, a Bordeaux blend of Cabernet Sauvignon, Cabernet Franc, and Merlot could qualify as a Bikavér, in practice, many of the cuvées made in Villány and other parts of the country are not essentially different from the Bikavérs produced here and in Eger.

Intriguingly, mud was traditionally used in Szekszárd and Villány in the making of red wines – and it still is. The method involved placing wooden containers with a capacity of between sixty and one hundred hectolitres in the press-house. After they had been filled with crushed grapes, fermentation begun by natural yeasts would occur, eventually producing wine on the surface of which the cap of skins would float. The cap would then be covered with walnut or vine leaves, on top of which would be spread a layer of clay-textured mud – frequently taken from the cellar (if it was burrowed into earth rather than rock), and occasionally mixed with a little lime to help it to set. This would be about 1.5 centimetres (three quarters of an inch) thick, and pressed to the sides of the fermenting vessel to make an airtight seal. The family could then get back to work in the fields, and the oldest member of the family would return each day to moisten the mud with a brush. After a month, a malolactic fermentation having taken place, the mud would have curled away from the sides of the container, and crystal-clear wine could be racked off from the bottom of the container. This method of making red wine was usual in the south of Hungary until the late 1980s and early 1990s, and small producers still use it, though the fermenting vessel is more often made of concrete or plastic, and brown paper bags are used in place of vine leaves. Another modern variation is the use of a plastic blanket over the container, weighed down by sand to provide the seal.

There are several wine rows (streets consisting of cellars) to be found in the town, of which the most extensive is Kadarka utca, running north from the town centre. There are Rizling and Ezerjó streets as well, but not, as yet, any named after European varieties. To find the largest concentration of Szekszárd cellars, however, one has to go about five kilometres (three miles) north of the town to Leányvár, in the angle of Route 65 to Siófok and the road to Sióagárd. Here, around 200 cellars are built into a small hill, of which some fifty are in use.

Despite the rivalry with Villány, I detect a certain air of self-satisfaction in Szekszárd. Its wines have a large following in Hungary, and forty per cent of all the wine produced in Szekszárd is now exported, mainly to Germany. Nevertheless, I have to reveal that I find most of Szekszárd's red wines wholly unimpressive. Partly it is because there is a tradition of making light blush wines, almost devoid of tannins, that rely on their acidity for whatever ageing capacity they have – although, admittedly, they take on more colour if matured in wood for three years. At their best, they are clean and refreshing, and they often reveal an impressive fruitiness, but fundamentally (with some exceptions noted below) they are simple wines, without complexity or depth. Perhaps, in the end, it is just a matter of taste. Perhaps, as I suspect, the soil is too rich to make really good wine. It is characteristic of the region also that, unlike Villány, most of its wine is sold in bulk rather than in bottle.

ALISCAVIN BORÁSZATI RT (SZENT GAÁL KASTÉLY)

H–7100 Szekszárd, Epreskert u. 8, Pf. 135; Tel: +36–74 416955. Fax: +36–74 411564. Sales office: Garay János tér, 19. *(a)* József Kovács. *(b)* 30ha. 23ha producing: Kf 8ha; Zw/M 7ha; Kad 6ha; CF 2ha. 7ha planted in 2000: CS 4ha; Zw 3ha. *(c)* 3,500hl. *(d)* Ernő Módos. *(e)* Varietals, rozé, Bikavér. *(f)* Variable amount (Finland, Canada, Belgium, Thailand, the US, and New Zealand)

"Joe" Kovács left Hungary in 1956, and spent his working life as an architect in Canada and Africa. A present of the *Larousse de Vin* from his daughter in 1994 fired his imagination and made him decide to invest his retirement funds in Hungarian wine production. Aliscavin, owned by a giant grape-growing cooperative, went bankrupt in 1995, and Kovács was able to buy it for a song. It soon became obvious, however, that this was not the trouble-free investment he had intended. The plant required renovation and he soon found that, far from yielding a profit, it was costing him $1.5 million (approximately £1 million) a year to keep it going. This forced him to come and live in Hungary to keep a close eye on things. Up to ninety-five per cent of his grapes are bought in, and between ninety and ninety-five per cent of his wine is sold in bulk, largely to Hungarovin.

In August 2000, he was fortunately able to sell the winery to Hungarovin, which increasingly needs red table wines for the German market. At present, he is marking time, rethinking how he wishes to position himself in the market, whether by constructing a new, purpose-built winery, or by finding a trading partner. In the meantime, he maintains a cellar that originally belonged to the Benedictines when they first came to Szekszárd in 1062, and he has developed a single-storey French-style *château*, dating from the nineteenth century – Château Szent Gaál – as a small country hotel. A picture of it on the Aliscavin labels gives an image to the product. Kovács would also like to extend his vineyard holding to one hundred hectares in the next few years.

Kovács says that he aims at low yields – although cropping forty-two to fifty-six hectolitres from vineyards with a density of from

2,000 to 3,000 vines per hectare (giving about three to four kilograms per vine) strikes me as a high yield. His Bikavér is made up of sixty per cent Kékfrankos, thirty per cent Merlot, and ten per cent Kadarka.

DÚZSI TAMÁS – SZEGZÁRDI SCALÁDI VÁLLALKOZÁS

H–1700 Szekszárd, Vadz u. 2. Tel: +36–74 319025. *(a)* Tamás Dúzsi. *(b)* 7.2ha: Kf 3.3ha; Zw 0.4ha; M/Kf/CS 0.3ha; Ez 3.2ha. *(c)* 350hl. *(d)* Tamás Dúzsi. *(e)* Kf, rozé, cuvée. *(f)* Not known

Dúzsi is, in my opinion, a very talented winemaker – perhaps the best in Szekszárd. However, as a producer he fights a constant battle against under-capitalization, and it is tragic that one of the great talents of the country is held back in this way.

Dúzsi, just past his half-century, did a horticultural and winemaking course at Gyöngyös. There followed a varied career. He worked first in the Liszt Pincészet (while it was still a state farm), then as a teacher in the agricultural school at Lengyel, and still later as a bottling technician, first in a soft drinks firm and then, from 1984, for Aliscavin. Dúzsi finally started up his own business in 1995, having been able to acquire 3.3 hectares of Kékfrankos, seventeen years old and not in good condition, with compensation vouchers. None of this was easy with five children (the eldest born in 1991), because with high interest rates, he found it impossible to obtain credit. Consolidation of his business has, therefore, been very slow and painful. For example, in his first year his vineyard was severely affected by fungal disease, but he could not even afford to buy the necessary spray treatments, and in consequence lost three-quarters of the crop. But, whatever difficulties he had in the early years, he has always managed to save a little of his best-quality wine – between five and twenty hectolitres – to sell under his own name, and to build up an image of quality.

Dúzsi's cellar is a renovated press-house in Leányvár, where he uses stainless-steel tanks for most of his winemaking, and open fermenters – one a forty-two-hectolitre stainless-steel container with a cover – when he runs out of closed tank capacity. The grapes are destalked but are not mechanically crushed, and there is not much maceration. Fermentation takes place at 28°C for one week; sometimes the must has to be heated, when it is late in the harvest, to get the fermentation started. During this period, Dúzsi lives with the wine. "When it is being born is the moment that a new child needs maximum attention," he says.

The Kékfrankos is harvested in two stages – normally between October 5 and 15, and 15 and 20. The first harvest (from Leányvár) has better colour, and is light and fruity. It is used for a varietal wine, which he bottles in the summer, ten months after the harvest. The second harvest has more concentration of flavour; by leaving it on the lees for a month after fermentation, its complexity is further increased. This is reserved for Dúzsi's cuvée. Tastings confirm that the second-harvest Kékfrankos is a serious wine, with considerable depth and structure – arguably the best in the region.

Dúzsi's rozé is made from Kékfrankos, and is deservedly very famous, because it is quite simply the best one made in Hungary. Dúzsi can sell as much of it as he can make. Having a spring market, his rozé helps his cash flow and finances the keeping of reserve wine. It is made by taking between twenty per cent and thirty per cent of first-pressed must, the rest being fermented as red wine. In a good year he harvests as late as possible, and is sometimes the last to harvest with as much as fifty per cent of his crop. He believes that rozés should be made from the same material that is used for red wine, and that Kékfrankos is particularly good for rozé because it has a viable acid content; when made from ripe grapes it matures with an enjoyable acidity not obtainable from early harvesting.

Finally, his cuvée is made up of seventy per cent Kékfrankos, fifteen per cent Merlot, and fifteen per cent Cabernet (itself one-third Cabernet Sauvignon and two-thirds Cabernet Franc). The malolactic fermentation takes place without air, and the wine is racked in December. The cuvée wine goes into a mixture of large casks and barriques (both old and new), while the Cabernet component of the cuvée is kept in barriques for one year. Dúzsi tries to avoid giving the wine any obvious barrique character and finds that, even after four or five years' use, the wine extracts enough wood character from his barriques to provide the balance he wants. After *assemblage*, the cuvée is matured in cask for only a few months, and is bottled three years after the vintage.

Pressings are blended with Zweigelt and sold off to other suppliers of bulk wine. (This is his only reason for growing Zweigelt.) It gets a reasonable price, and is not bad business.

The wines are bottled partly by Dúzsi himself, with a small hand-bottling machine, and the rest is done by Aliscavin. He is just preparing a new facility of his own. The wine is sold through the Budapest Wine Society and a few other outlets. Despite all the difficulties, in two years (1998 and 1999) he managed to expand his output to the level he had planned to reach over five years. He does not want his firm to be bigger than he can control, but has not yet decided how big that is. Dúzsi also experiments: he has tried a barrique Merlot and a barrique Kadarka, both of which he would like to develop further.

Here is a winemaker who knows what he wants to produce, and shows that he has the knowledge and skill to get the right result. He also shows wisdom, I think, in concentrating on a limited range, and notably does not produce a Bikavér. If he were freed from financial contraints, what great wines might we not see? The "Szegzárd" in his logo is a registered mark, and is the old spelling of the town's name.

TAKLER PINCE

H–7100 Szekszárd, Bem u. 13. Tel/fax: +36–74 315187. *(a)* Ferenc Takler.

(b) 11.6ha: Kad 3ha; Zw 2.5ha; M 2ha; Kf 2ha; CF 1.5ha; various 0.6ha.

(c) 1,200hl. *(d)* András and Ferenc Takler. *(e)* Varietals, rozé, Bikavér, cuvée.

(f) Irregular

The Taklers have been a wine-producing family in the region since the eighteenth century. The present head of the family is Ferenc, who is assisted as manager and as winemaker by his son András, who studied winemaking at the Horticultural University of Budapest, and as cellar-master by his other son Ferenc. Takler began producing wine in bulk in 1987, but started the present phase of the family business in 1996.

Takler's vineyards are mainly in Decsihegy, but are also at Görögszó, Hidaspetre, Faluhely, and Felső-Cinka. The yielding vineyards, with the exception of 1.5 hectares planted by Takler, are state plantings with a density of 2,350 vines per hectare. All the vines are umbrella-trained except the Kadarka, which is staked.

The present cellar, south of Szekszárd, was built in 1998 in a Soane-like vaulted style. It is already too small, and will be extended to provide space to store wine in cask for two or three years. The press-house has open fermenters as well as temperature-controlled stainless-steel tanks.

However, Takler's operation is under-capitalized, and he has to use plastic holding tanks. He has refused offers of foreign partnership, and prefers to remain independent.

Takler makes three types of wine. Firstly, there is Kékfrankos, his bread-and-butter wine, which, with bulk white wines, finances his better-quality wines. Then there are the quality varietal wines that he produces every year, including Kadarka. And, finally, there are the top-quality wines produced only in selected years. These are his Bikavér and his cuvées: Takler, a Bordeaux blend, and Trio, which appears to be a Bikavér by another name. For the Takler cuvée, although the varieties are separately vinified, the two Cabernets are initially aged together in large oak casks while the Merlot is aged separately. The blend is made in March and then put in Hungarian barriques for twelve months. Barriques are used twice, scraped, then used twice more.

Takler's Bikavér combines Kékfrankos, Kadarka, Merlot, Cabernet Sauvignon, and Cabernet Franc, all of which are held separately for one year, blended, then matured for six months. The percentage of each variety differs according to the year, the aim being to get a harmonious blend in which no individual variety is identifiable – as big a challenge, in Takler's view, as organizing a race with five horses so that they all pass the finishing line simultaneously. Most of his Bikavérs need a minimum of five years to reach full maturity.

Sales are mainly in Hungary, to restaurants, hotels, and wine shops. The wines strike me as rather variable, with the 1999 Takler cuvée on the light side. Best of all are a 1999 Cabernet Sauvignon (sixty per cent) and Cabernet Franc (forty per cent) cuvée made for export, and a 1999 barrique Kékfrankos sold under the Monarchia label. The former has impressive depth of colour and flavour, with abundant soft tannins, while the latter shows just how good Kékfrankos can be. Otherwise, the wines tend to be of a very acceptable standard, although unlikely to set the world on fire.

V & V BORÁSZATI BT (VESZTERGOMBI PINCE)

H–7100 Szekszárd, Munkácsy u. 41. Tel/fax: +36–74 316059. *(a)* Ferenc Vesztergombi. *(b)* 11.5ha. 10ha producing: Kf 4ha; CS 2ha; CF 2ha; M 1ha; Kad 0.5ha. 1.5ha planted in 2000: M 1.5ha. *(c)* 1,000hl. *(d)* Ferenc and Czaba Vesztergombi. *(e)* Varietals, Bikavér, cuvée. *(f)* 15% (Switzerland, Germany)

There has been a Vesztergombi tradition of winemaking for 200 years, and Ferenc worked in various state-owned wineries for thirty years. With the fall of Communism, Ferenc and his brother József founded a firm to produce quality wine in 1992. Ferenc's son Csaba joined the firm in 1993, having graduated in agricultural engineering and marketing at the University of Gödöllő. József's decision to withdraw from the firm in 1999 led to a division of the vineyards, and this has left Vesztergombi with a larger proportion of white grapes than he needs. However, he has a prized half-hectare of centennial, individually staked Kadarka. Most of the vineyards are between twenty and thirty years old, and their renewal will provide an opportunity not only to change the balance of the varieties, but to introduce new working methods into the vineyards. Optimum yields per vine at present are: Kadarka 1.5 kilograms; Kékfrankos 2.5–3 kilograms; Merlot and Cabernet Sauvignon two kilograms.

The company trades from an attractive, old-fashioned building opposite the baroque church in the middle of town, but the main cellar is in Kadarka utca, one of the several old wine rows in Szekszárd. Vesztergombi aims to preserve the Szekszárd character of his wine while preparing it with modern technology. Red wines are reductively made in stainless-steel tanks, in which the must is pumped over the cap three times a day with a simultaneous small amount of deliberate aeration. The wine is left on its skins for eight to ten days (although Csaba disagrees with this), then is transferred to stainless-steel storage until its first racking in December or January, when it is put into large ten- to forty-hectolitre barrels, or into barriques.

Vesztergombi's Bikavér has Kékfrankos as its base, with Kadarka, Merlot, and Cabernet Sauvignon as the other components. Kékfrankos and Kadarka are normally matured for eight months in Hungarian barriques, and put on the market as fruity wines, while Merlot and Cabernet Sauvignon are given fifteen months. The wines are fined by earth and bentonite and bottled in the cellar.

Vesztergombi's wines enjoy a considerable reputation (he was Winemaker of the Year in 1993), but I find them problematic. They are clearly serious, with more extraction and weight than most in Szekszárd, but too often disfigured by harsh, green tannins suggestive of unripe grapes – which is strange, because Veszergombi is usually the last to harvest in Szekszárd. Cask samples tasted in 2000 showed a slight barrique woodiness, the 1998 Cabernet Sauvignon being green and tannic in the usual way. On the other hand, a 1997 cuvée made by Csaba – his first trial – was neither green nor woody.

VIDA PÉTER

H–7100 Szekszárd, Alkotmány u. 9. Tel: +36–74 317753. *(a)* Péter Vida.
(b) 5.2ha Bakta: M/Kad/Ch 1ha Baranyadűlő: CF 3ha Hidaspetre: Kf 1.2ha.
(c) 170hl. *(d)* Péter Vida. *(e)* Varietals, cuvées. *(f)* Undisclosed

Péter Vida is a wine zealot. His is a complex character, and his ideas about wine are tied up with philosophical and religious ideas. He is almost a wine mystic. "Wine is a matter of feeling"; "Wine is unique – the result of a complicated biological process – and people have only one way to behave towards it: humbly, simply and with respect"; "My wines will be valuable only if my soul can be felt in them". His cellar, in the shape of a Roman cross with a domed intersection and small, blank windows surmounted by raised brick crosses closing each "transept", is irresistibly like a small Saxon church. When I said as much, Vida's response was, "Not by chance."

Vida turned away from the family tradition of teaching, and worked in the Aranyfürt Cooperative between 1975 and 1995, first as a winemaker and then in an office job. Before 1990, he could not have believed that anything so exciting as setting up his own winery could ever be possible. When he did so in 1995, it was a very difficult decision, and he continues to have severe problems arising from a lack of capital. However, he refuses offers of help because, even if progress is slower, his aim has not altered. It is to make wine as honestly as possible and to preserve its integrity without making compromises.

Right from the start Vida aimed at the international market, and he still wants to make wines which have a place there. He is lucky enough to have a hectare in the famous Bakta vineyard, purchased by his father in 1966. The musts it produces are never below 21°, and the wines justify Bakta's reputation. He also has a vineyard in Baranyadűlő, facing south and southeast. It is a superb site for a vineyard, apart from also being a tranquil and beautiful spot. Here the vines are twenty-nine-year-old Cabernet Sauvignon, low-cordon-trained with a narrow canopy, and they yield two kilograms per vine, with 22° musts, in mid-October. His

Kékfrankos, on the other hand, is trained with a high canopy, and yields 1.5 kilograms per vine.

Vida ferments his wines in temperature-controlled stainless-steel fermenters for a week, pumping the must over the cap for less than two hours a day, at between 24°C and 27°C. The fermented wine is then left on its lees for two or three weeks while it undergoes a malolactic fermentation. Vida first began experimenting with barriques in 1994, but almost all his wines are matured in traditional large casks. When I visited him in the summer of 2000 he was experimenting with a four-variety cuvée, but could not decide which were the best proportions. His regular cuvée is not a barrique wine, but in 2000 I was shown a 1996 Cabernet Franc still in Kádár barriques (which I thought rather woody), and a 1999 Cabernet Franc in Trust Hungary barriques (which was not woody).

Although Vida's wines are all essentially in the Szekszárd mould, and none has great weight, they all have a striking purity of fruit, breeding, and finesse. In Vida's case, making wine with feeling clearly pays off.

OTHER WINE PRODUCERS

Aranyfürt Mezőgazdasági Szövetkezet. H–7101 Szekszárd, Béri Balogh Ádám u. 70, Pf 128. Tel: +36–74 15438; Fax: +36–74 315311. *Bátaszék Térségi Agrár Kft.* H–7140 Bátaszék, József A. u. 25. Tel: +36–74 491226. *Grünfelder Károly.* H–7100 Szekszárd, Kandó Kálmán u. 8. Tel: +36–74 314886. *Halmosi Pincészet.* H–7100 Szekszárd, Béri Balogh Á. U. 60. Tel/fax: +36–74 319899. *Heimann és Fiai Pincéje Bt.* H–7100 Szekszárd, Szabó D. u. 1. Tel: +36–74 315740. *Mészi Bt (Mészáros Pál Pincészete).* H–7100 Szekszárd, Mérey u. 10. Tel/fax: +36–74 417962; Tel: +36–74 419165. *Nagy Sándor.* H–7100 Szekszárd, Remete u. 7. Tel: +36–74 318357. *Rosavin Bortermelő és Kereskedő Kft.* H–7100 Szekszárd, Harmat u. 2, Pf 21. Tel/fax: +36–74 488406. *Sárosdi Pince.* H–1700 Szekszárd, Préshaz u. 48. Tel/fax: +36–74 419879. *Szekszárdi Mező-gazdasági Rt (Liszt Pincészet).* H–7100 Szekszárd, Rákóczi F. u 132, Pf 2. Tel/fax: +36–74 410119; Tel: +36–74 412332; Fax: +36–74 416438

Bátaszék Térségi Agrár is the largest producer in Szekszárd, wholly owned by István Nagy, the president of the Bátaszéki Búzakalász Mezőgazdasági Szövetkezet, a non-wine-producing agricultural cooperative. Nagy, who also has other private agricultural interests, currently owns 145 hectares of vineyards in the south of the region – just under twenty-five per cent of the total vineyard area. His winery in Bátaszék, previously the property of Villány Borászat, does not have any facilities for maturing wine, so he sells his 22,000 hectolitres after its first racking to Danubiana, Hungarovin, Hilltop, and Villány Borászat. He plans to bottle his wine under his own name in the near future.

Szekszárdi Mezőgazdasági – better known as the Liszt Pincészet – was a state farm until 1992, when it was bought by Clemens Freiherr von Twickel. The present company has wide-ranging agricultural interests, including fruit and animal-feed production, and winemaking is a small part of the business. The cellars have no connection at all with the composer Liszt but, as he often came to Szekszárd and was particularly fond of its wine, his portrait appears appropriately on the Liszt Pincészet label.

The company rents 230 hectares of vineyards from the state, and these are constantly being regrafted or replaced. Von Twickel has invested more than HUF400 million (£960,000) in the company, with very visible results. The winery has very sophisticated vinification equipment, and a barrique programme was recently started. József Gál, the winemaker, was appointed in 1999, but the company employs both national and foreign consultants. The wines come in four ranges: Liszt Pincészet Selection (top-quality), Liszt Pincészet, Astor Range, and regional wines. Three-quarters of the 6,375-hectolitre production is exported, mainly to the UK. Until József Gál's appointment as winemaker, the Liszt wines were dull and disappointing. He is capable of making first-class wines – his 1999 Rajnai Rizling is one of the very best I have found in Hungary – so one hopes that quality will now improve.

Aranyfürt was founded in 1960, and swallowed up two other cooperatives in 1978. It makes wines largely from grapes bought from its 360 members, who also supply wines for blending. Cropping levels are between fifty-six and eighty-four hectolitres per hectare. Stainless-steel tanks are cooled by water curtain but, despite this, fermentation temperatures can reach 36°C to 40°C. Wines are matured for from six to eight months in large wooden casks, and sixty to seventy per cent of the wine is sold in bulk. The cooperative encourages new small-grower members.

Ferenc Heimann, eighth generation of a family originally from Stuttgart, was president of the Aranyfürt Cooperative until 1988, and since 1990 has been making wine in the family name. Bikavér with variable proportions of Kékfrankos, Kékoportó, Kadarka, Merlot, and Cabernet Franc, is open-fermented in the traditional way, and has its malolactic fermentation in large casks. It is blended in July into large oak casks, and bottled ten weeks later. To be at its best, it needs up to four years of bottle maturity. A barrique cuvée, Cervus, is a blend of Cabernet Franc, Kékfrankos, Merlot, and Kékoportó made both traditionally and reductively. It has port-like overtones on the nose and, in my view, is rather over-extracted.

Károly Grünfelder is a small, traditional producer who uses the mud-seal technique with his red wines. He is notable only because he sometimes produces a real rarity: a Kadarka without skin contact. "It used to be a favourite with our grandfathers," he says, but it is so unusual that it was unknown to OBI the first time he submitted it for approval.

Rosavin, a joint venture between László and Rose Mérey and Hermann Junger, was established in 1996 when eighteen hectares at Strázhegy were bulldozed into broad terraces and replanted with red varieties. A new winery with basic but good vinification equipment (without cooling facilities) was put up in 1997. Decent wines from first crops in 1999 and 2000 seem to augur well for future success. Ferenc Sárosdi aims at combining local tradition with new technology, and commissioned his new winery in 2001. Previous wines have been light, fruity and disappointing, but his new vinification equipment may herald wines of more substance. Halmosi Pincészet is a family enterprise going back for four generations, but registered in its present form in 1998. It is very wedded to traditional ways, and older vintages show attractive bottle maturity, but are very light.

TOLNA

2,739 hectares: 1,579 white, 1,160 red
Twenty wine communities, with 3,127 members

This region divides into four main clusters: Tamási, Simontornya, Tolna (Paks), and Völgység (Bonyhád). The north is predominantly a white-grape area, giving fruity wines with balanced acidity; the area bordering the Danube has varying admixtures of sand in its soil over a clay base, and produces light wines, lacking in acidity. As you go south, the proportion of red wines increases, as does their complexity. Much of the area (Lengyel, Bátaapáti, Kölesd, and Simontornya) formerly belonged to the Apponyi family. During the Communist period there were several cooperatives. The one at Bonyhád has just closed its wine operations, while those at Paks (now a private company) and at Mőcsény struggle on. The region is dominated by two large producers, Danubiana and Eurobor, whose size rather stifles competition.

Tamási and the area to its north are a law unto themselves, and do not have much to do with the rest of the region (even at the wine community level). There are no active cooperatives here, and growers sell to large national producers. It is rumoured that a lot of fake wine emanates from this part of the region. Simontornya, nearby, has larger vineyards than Tamási, and the bottling of wine is more common. Bölcske, further east and on the Danube, incorporates a village of 500 cellars in eight rows, intermixed with hobby plots and houses. The soil (a heavy mix of clay and sand) and climate conditions are good, and the area once prospered because its situation on the Danube made commerce easy.

Paks is mainly an agricultural area, with a long tradition of wine production started by eighteenth-century Rhenish and Austrian settlers. The soil is black sand over clay, and acid levels are high. The nuclear power station dominates the area; it is the biggest employer, the largest sponsor of small local enterprises, and probably the area's main tourist attraction. A square in the town centre, the Sárgödör, consists of fifty cellars, of which fourteen are protected heritage properties. Most are just hobby producers. Practically everyone here grows grapes as a supplementary source of income, and almost nobody does so as their main source of income. The main vineyard area is a former cooperative plantation at Hidegvölgy, on the west of the town, where there are 360 hectares. There has been no new planting.

Györköny, to the west of Paks, is famous for its independent wine village – the Pincehegy – situated across a small valley from the town. The cellars in the front row are jokingly said to be the least desirable, because wives looking across the valley can see what their menfolk are up to. Before the war, there were 450 cellars in the village, but many fell into ruin after the repatriation of half the German population, and only 310 have survived. An interesting development has been the formation by about one hundred members and eighteen pensioners of the now-defunct state cooperative of their own new small cooperative, called the Györkönyi Gazdaság Szövetkezet. While the members have their own press-houses and make their own wine, they share machinery and invest in commonly held buildings, such as the press-house in the Pincehegy that has been fitted out to receive tourists. There is a similar new small cooperative at Dúzs.

Tolna is not a region to get one excited. There are signs of a wine market developing in conjunction with tourism, and a wine route got started in 2000. I also know of one or two young winemakers with up-to-date ideas just at the point of their first production, but it would be premature to consider them here. The small producers who have come to my notice, however, are making very modest wines – to put it as kindly as possible – and the region will have to buck its ideas up very considerably before it starts to be of interest to the world at large.

DANUBIANA

H–7150 Bonyhád, Széchenyi tér 14. Tel/fax: +36–74 450424/451212. *(a)* Herold Binderer, München. *(b)* 48ha: L/Sk/Ch/OM. *(c)* 200,000–250,000hl. *(d)* Vióla Ritter. *(e)* Varietals. *(f)* 95% (Germany, the UK, and Scandinavia)

The parent company of Danubiana also owns St Ursula Weinkellerei in Bingen am Rhein, which it bought from Nestlé in 1985. Binderer was originally an importer-bottler whose strength lay in its connection with eastern European wine countries – with a link to Hungary going back almost thirty years. Currently, it imports wine from all over the world, but mostly from Hungary, Romania, and Macedonia, and it is the largest importer of Hungarian wine into Germany. It also maintains a significant presence in Britain and Scandinavia.

Danubiana was started in 1990. The change in the Hungarian political scene gave the company an opportunity to invest in its own wine making facilities, and in 1994–5 it purchased a former state farm at Gyöngyös (*q.v.*). Later, Danubiana realized that its operation in the north of Hungary needed to be complemented with a similar one in the south, so construction work started on a green-field site at Bonyhád in 1997. Now Gyöngyös only makes white wine, while Bonyhád makes both white and red.

The company leases forty-eight hectares of state land previously used for grain crops, which was planted in 1998 with stock from France at a density of 4,300 vines per hectare. Yield reduction will be done by canopy management, with anticipated yields of between forty-two and fifty-six hectolitres per hectare. Currently, the entire Hungarian operation crushes between 15,000 and 20,000 tonnes, with about 10,000 tonnes at Bonyhád (this being less than the winery's capacity). Some finished wine is bought in.

The winery equipment is state-of-the-art: German de-stalking and variable-strength crushers, and a German pneumatic press; French autovinifiers and 175-hectolitre capacity tanks with pump-over facilities; 7,000 hectolitres of insulated stainless-steel tanks with precision temperature-control; fittings for gas – both sulphur dioxide (SO_2) and nitrogen are used – and fixed overhead piping to move the wine around; a separate refrigeration plant; and an insulated, air-conditioned cellar. There is also a cellar with 500 Hungarian and American barriques – some Chardonnay, Merlot, and Cabernet Sauvignon are barrel-fermented. All bottling is done in Gyöngyös, whence most wine is depatched abroad. Sales through supermarkets in Hungary were started in 2001, and in the same year a premium range, Graf Károly, was launched in Germany.

There is a sophisticated quality-control team, led by an Australian, Con Simos, a Roseworthy graduate working from Germany. Winemakers are exposed in a variety of ways to worldwide wine styles, and are given opportunities to work vintages abroad. Run entirely by Hungarians, Danubiana is now self-financing. This is a mass-market winery aiming at an acceptable commercial standard. In my opinion, the white wines show much better than the reds, which still have considerable room for improvement.

EURÓPAI BORTERMELŐK KFT (EUROPEAN WINE PRODUCERS LTD – EUROBOR)

H-7164 Bátaapáti, Hővösvölgy u. 4. Tel/fax: +36–74 409327/409222. *(a)* Piero Antinori, Michael Böhmers, Interloan (an investment company), Jacopo Mazzei, Miklós Sikabonyi, Peter Zwack. *(b)* 149ha. 109ha in production: Ch 22.9ha; ZV 14.4ha; T 10ha; IO 7.5ha; Kf 22.5ha; Zw 11ha; CS/CF 9ha; BK 5.7ha; Ko 3.2ha; M 0.5ha; various 2.3ha. 40.4ha planted 1997–2000: SB 17.2ha; M 12.5ha; PN 7.5ha; T 3.2ha. *(c)* 5,600hl. *(d)* Erzsébet Tóth. *(e)* Varietals, rozé, cuvées. *(f)* Over 70%

Eurobor started on July 4, 1991. How the diverse group of owners came together is too long a story to tell here. Suffice it to say that they were impressed by the potential of the area, and set about buying components of the Mőcsény Cooperative, which became the nucleus of the firm. The cooperative, incorporating five villages, had been a producer of grapes, but had no vinification facilities. Nevertheless, it had a 250-year-old cellar at Bátaapáti, originally belonging to Gróf Apponyi, which was then (and probably still is) the biggest in the Tolna region.

Bátaapáti is a tiny and somewhat remote village in a beautiful setting at the juncture of three valleys. The picturesque old cellar building (now used for offices) is not far from the small but beautiful old church, and close by is Eurobor's new (1991–3) winery, housed in two parallel buildings. The first is a compact and well-designed fermentation hall, and the other houses a bottling-line, laboratory, and a carton store. The fermentation area has good, standard stainless-steel equipment with a capacity of 5,000 hectolitres – sufficient only for the next three years. Since 1999, Tibor Gál has been the director in charge of technology and winemaking.

Eurobor owns 250 hectares of land, of which just over a fifth is in pro- duction, and the intention is to bring the vineyard total up to 200 hectares. The firm buys Sauvignon Blanc and Tramini, and sells Zöld Veltelini, surplus Chardonnay, Kékfrankos, and Zweigelt because the present plantings do not give them the varieties they need for production. They do not, however, purchase finished wines.

The vineyards, mainly on hilltops, are in three different places – Bátaapáti, Mócsény, and Morágy – at altitudes varying between 220 and 250 metres (715 and 813 feet), and the soil is loess. Hot days and cool nights promote good evolution of the grapes. All the new planting material comes from France, except for the Tramini and Sauvignon Blanc, which are from Northern Italy. The new vineyards have a density of 5,000 vines per hectare, and the training method is low-cordon, sometimes Guyot.

The company produces three ranges of wines under its Bátaapáti Estate, Mőcsény Kastélybor, and Peters' [sic] Hill Estate labels, of which the first represents its top-quality. Ten per cent of the Chardonnay is barrel-fermented, and Gál is experimenting with open fermentation of Pinot Noir. No large casks are used, and Gál favours barriques made by European Coopers, a joint-venture cooperage linked with the Italian coopers Antinori e Gamba. Chardonnay, Cabernet Franc, Merlot, and Kékfrankos are all aged in wood.

Gál joined the firm in time for the 1999 vintage. Previously there had been an Italian flying winemaker – replaced, Gál says ruefully, by a Hungarian motoring one. His remit is to sort out problems that the company ran into in the late 1990s, and it will take time for Eurobor to show its true potential. Rain up until August 9 resulted in a poor 1999 harvest at Bátaapáti, and the wines, especially the reds, generally reflected this. Bright spots are the company's Tramini, among the best in Hungary, and the oaked Chardonnay shows Gál's sure touch. His influence will doubtless soon be felt in the reds as well.

STEITZ JÁNOS

H–7052 Kölesd, Szekszárdi u. 4. Tel: +36–74 436027. *(a)* János Steitz. *(b)* 0.5ha: Ch/Or/Kf/CS. *(c)* 50hl. *(d)* János Steitz. *(e)* Varietals, rozé. *(f)* None

Kölesd is, in many ways, the centre of the Tolna region, and Steitz has been and still is influential in its development. A financial consultant, accountant and auditor by trade, he has had a hobby vineyard since 1978. When Tolna became a separate region, he and the local mayor organized the new wine communities, and he became president of the regional committee. He appears to be at the heart of most local initiatives. Having got the wine route off the ground, he is now trying to establish a small cooperative.

Steitz has a very large and impressive cellar, and he is slowly improving his equipment. He has set up a very small bottling plant for the community, and is also thinking in terms of building a model winery – an insurance against the failure of the cooperative to get started. The intention would be that other farmers could hire its facilities. He does not produce a commercially significant quantity, but his best wines (Olaszrizling and rozé) are a class above the regional average.

OTHER WINE PRODUCERS

Beck Tibor. H–7081 Simontornya, Mózsé–hegy. Tel: +36–74 486647. *Főglein János.* H–7130 Tolna, Ybl M. u. 3. Tel/fax: +36–74 440175. *Hanák Pincék.* H–7025 Bölcske, Havasi pincesor 2–3. Tel/fax: +36–75 335514. *Konnáth Ferencné.* H–7030 Paks, Virág u. 16. Tel: +36–312167. *Lehmann és Fia Borház.* H–7191 Högyész, Ady E. u. 7. Tel: +36–74 488087. *Szabó Gábor.* H–7150

Bonyhád, Liget u. 9/A. Tel: +36–74 451263. *Szőlőtermesztő és Borászati Kft.*
H–7030 Paks, Pf. 116. Tel: +36–75 314288. *Varga Sándor.* H–7052 Kölesd,
Zsámbék u. 14. Tel: +36–74 436054.

Gábor Szabó is a big producer of grapes and wine, with ninety-two hectares under cultivation, forty of them planted in 1999–2000. Sixty per cent of his production is of red wine, made with fairly up-to-date equipment. The best of it is purchased by Hilltop and Danubiana. Szabó wants to bottle more of his own wine, but to succeed, needs to improve its quality. Szőlőtermesztő és Borászati is a grape-growing company with 126 hectares. It sells to large producers in Szekszárd and Kecskemét, and to Danubiana.

10

The South II

VILLÁNY-SIKLÓS

1,801 hectares: 651 white, 1,150 red
Six wine communities, with 2,797 members

Villány-Siklós has a high profile. After Tokaj, it is the area well-informed wine-lovers outside Hungary identify with quality, and rightly so. From complete obscurity ten years ago, it is now a well-organized, go-ahead place, with more and more aspiring producers appearing every year. They recognize a success story when they see one. In 1997 there were forty-two entries on the wine route guide; in 2001, there were eighty-two. Each year, along the main road through Villány, lots of new cellars open to the public. Everyone wants to climb on the bandwagon but, sadly, being from Villány is not an automatic guarantee of quality. A handful of top producers make exceptional wines, but no more than half a dozen of them; another half-dozen produce reliable quality, but are never likely to set the world on fire. And then there are the rest.

The region, close to the Croatian border, lies mainly to the south of a range of lowish slopes known as Villányhegy, and is a union of Siklós on the west and Villány on the east. Siklós, more noted for its white wine, comprises areas surrounding the town of Siklós and the villages west of Máriagyűd as far as Hegyszentmárton. Villány is mainly a red-wine area, with a more complex geography. Part of it, between the towns of Siklós and Villány, lies to the south of Villányhegy and north of the villages of Nagytótfalu, Kisharsány, and Nagyharsány. A less important part of it runs northwest of Villány, on the north of Villányhegy, and takes in the villages of Villánykövesd and Palkonya. Villánykövesd has a

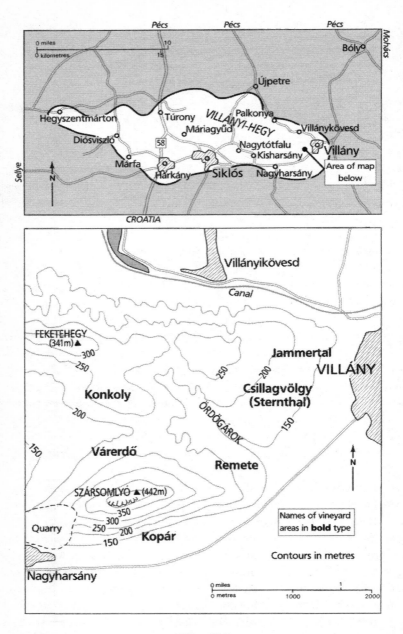

Villány-Siklós

much-photographed cellar row on two levels, and is a pleasant spot to have lunch. Palkonya, a short drive through gently rolling hills punctuated by large reed-lined ponds, has an even more notable wine village, but evidence of vine-growing seems confined to some new, well-tended vineyards to the southwest of the village.

The most famous of Villány's vineyards are on the southern slopes of a distinctive, almost pyramidal, rocky mound called Szársomlyó (442 metres/1,437 feet), which is behind and to the east of Nagyharsány, and on the southern and eastern slopes of the tail end of Villányhegy, which connects Szársomlyó to the town of Villány. This latter area is famous as the battleground where the Catholic Alliance headed by Austria won a decisive victory against the Turks in 1687.

Starting to the east, on the slopes behind Villány, is the Jammertal vineyard – thought by many to be the best vineyard area in the region, although others favour the Kopár vineyard. Working westwards, separated from the Jammertal by an irregular line of trees, there is the Csillagvölgy (Sternthal) vineyard, which goes as far as a small valley called the Ördögárok. On the eastern slopes of Szársomlyó, below the woodland on its upper slopes, is the Remete vineyard. Round the corner, on the southern slope of Szársomlyó, is the Kopár vineyard, where the upper slopes of the hill are exposed rock (with scrubby trees). This rock absorbs heat and makes the Kopár the hottest vineyard in the whole of Hungary, comparable with the Côtes du Rhône in summer. The Kopár stretches from the town of Villány as far as the village of Nagyharsány, and at the ridge on the hill which separates the southern slope from the western slope there is a massive and unsightly limestone quarry, from which stone is transported to a nearby cement factory. North of Szársomlyó, Konkoly is on a re-entrant between it and Feketehegy, a lower hill to its north, while further south is the Várerdő vineyard, reckoned the least satisfactory of all.

There are stories, part historical and part legendary, from which these vineyard areas get their names – names that have been used for centuries to indicate places, but which have only recently been applied to vineyards. The Jammertal was the slope on which the Turkish army was routed in 1687, a *jammer* being a cry of pain. After the battle there was no cultivation in this area and it became densely forested. The Csillagvölgy, or in German, *Sternthal*, allegedly gets its name from the fact that the trees were so thick that the only way you could guide yourself was by the stars, *Stern* being the German word for star. Kopár means "barren", and having been used for growing peas during the Communist period, this was effectively a green-field site when it was replanted with vines in 1994.

The soils are all basically loess over limestone and red clay, with some variations between the vineyards. Thus Kopár has a high magnesium and calcium content in its soil, imparting a mineral character to the wine. Csillagvölgy, on the other hand, has deeper loess with a topping of twenty to thirty centimetres (eight to twelve inches) of humus, giving fuller-bodied wines. Villány-Siklós is the warmest of all the Hungarian wine regions, with the largest number of sunshine hours (2,314) and temperatures ranging from –12°C to 35°C, averaging 11.5°C per annum, and 17.5°C during the vegetative period. Spring comes early, summers and autumns are long (with a summer monsoon towards the end of May), and winters are cool. Precipitation averages 689 millimetres (twenty-seven inches) a year, of which between 400 and 450 millimetres (sixteen and eighteen inches) falls during the growing season. Downy mildew occurs in one or two years out of every five; powdery mildew caused by nocturnal dew and autumnal botrytis are more frequent problems.

After the expulsion of the Turks, the Austrian emperor rewarded with grants of land allies who had provided military and material help. Two notable estates survived until they were nationalized in 1945. The Bélye Domain, of which Villány was a part, was granted to Eugene of Savoy in 1699, and later became a crown property administered by a succession of archdukes. Count Ádám II Batthyány (the family that owned Siklós Castle after 1728) was given the Domain of Bóly, together with Villánykövesd, in 1700, and this passed through marriage to the Montenuovo family.

After 1723, German emigrants began to settle, and by 1883, their community numbered 1,809, many of them prominent among the eighty or so wine merchants in Villány in the nineteenth century, and many of them successfully exporting to countries like the United States and Brazil, as well as all over Europe. The phylloxera crisis that brought Teleki to prominence changed all this, and it was not until 1914 that the vineyard area regained its former size, and estate and smallholder winemaking again became the norm.

After nationalization, a cooperative was formed, as well as two state farms which merged in 1961 to form the Villány-Siklós State Farm, itself swallowed up in 1984 by the Pannonvin Borgazdaság Kombinát. Before phylloxera, traditional varieties grown in Villány had included Juhfark, Furmint, and Kéknyelű among whites, and the inescapable Kadarka, as well as Kékoportó and Kékfrankos, among the reds. The last two remain popular, with Kékoportó more prominent here (unlike in other regions) than Kékfrankos, and generally made with more panache. Both compete, even now, with the omnipresent western varieties.

GERE ATTILA PINCÉSZET

H–7773 Villány, Diófás u. 4. Tel: +36–72 492839; Tel/fax: +36–72 492195.
(a) Attila Gere. *(b)* 23ha: M 10ha; CS 6ha; CF 6ha; Ko 1ha. *(c)* 1,500 hl. *(d)* Attila Gere. *(e)* Varietals, cuvée. *(f)* 25% (Austria, Holland, Switzerland, Poland, Germany, Denmark, and Finland)

Attila Gere is living proof that you can be a winemaker without any formal training and still reach the top of your profession. Originally a forester in the Újpetre MGTSZ, Gere moved to Villány in 1978 after marrying a local girl. Learning originally from his father-in-law, who had a hobby plot, Gere soon acquired his own vineyard and began to make wine. Until 1986, when he started to bottle his wine, he sold in bulk to four restaurants in Szeged. About the same time he began to travel to Italy, Austria, Switzerland, and France (often with Tiffán, Bock, and Tamás Gere) to find out more about wine. The visits that influenced him most were to Bolgheri (where Gál was making wine), the Clos des Jacobins in Pommerol, and Château Haut-Marbuzet, where he saw green pruning for the first time.

After 1989, many foreign visitors came to Hungary in search of wine. Their view that very high-quality wines could be made in Villány, allied to what he had learned abroad, convinced Gere he should aim high. In 1990, when he began to buy in grapes (including Cabernet Sauvignon), he soon discovered that if you made better wine, you made more profit, so he gave up being a forester in 1991, and at the same time opened a *panzió* (guest house) in the middle of Villány. In 1992, a new market opened for him when restaurants were privatized, and since then he has never looked back. Since 1991, he has been able to bottle all his wine, and since 1992, he has doubled his production.

Gere bought his first vineyard in 1991, and now has seven hectares in Kopár, five in Csillagvölgy, and eleven in Konkoly – where Teleki's press-house is situated. All his vineyards are mechanized, including mechanical canopy management, with defoliation in June and July. He started to plant Cabernet Sauvignon and Merlot in 1994, and got his first crop from Kopár in 1997. The first crop from Konkoly, which Gere suspects may turn out to be his best vineyard, was in 2001.

Gere is interested only in increasing his quality, and not in further expansion. This commitment to quality is shown by the rigorous control of his vineyards. He prefers Guyot-type vine training, and prunes each vine to twelve to fourteen buds, reducing them later to six. There is a further cull of the least promising (least coloured) bunches later in the summer, with twenty per cent of them being discarded. Thus, production is limited to one to 1.5 kilograms per vine, with typical yields of thirty hectolitres per hectare for Cabernet Franc and forty hectolitres per hectare for Cabernet Sauvignon. All new plantations will have a density of 5,500 vines per hectare, with the aim of having one vine producing the must for one bottle of wine, and even less in the case of Cabernet Sauvignon. This will mean restricting each vine to twelve buds and six bunches.

Gere has benefited from the well-equipped winery jointly owned with his sister company, Weninger & Gere. However, in June 2001, he began to build a separate winery for his own firm, scheduled to be ready for the 2002 vintage. Production is devoted to red wine, apart from white wine made exclusively for sale at Gere's *panzió*. The red grapes are destemmed but not crushed before going into a pneumatic press, of which only the first two pressings are used (to avoid over-tannic wines). Fermentation, in stainless-steel, temperature-controlled tanks, is within the range of 26°C to 30°C. After fermentation, the wines are given ten days' additional skin contact. The malolactic fermentation starts in the tank, but after the maceration period, the wine is racked into barrels, where the malolactic is completed. Gere does not rack often; he tastes the wine, and only racks when he thinks the wine needs it. Fining is done subsequently. The bar-riques are ninety-five per cent Hungarian (from Kádár), and five per cent French and Austrian. After they have had sufficient wood-ageing, the wines go to stainless-steel holding tanks. Bottling is done on demand, as there is no bottle storage space.

Gere produces a dazzling array of wines, each one better than the last, and most needing from three to ten years to reach their peak. The Gere Cuvée (a barrique Cabernet Sauvignon and Kékfrankos) is a big but stylish wine, complex and ageworthy. Unblended Cabernet Sauvignon comes in three forms: traditionally matured in large casks, matured in barrique, and as a single-vineyard (Kopár) barrique-matured wine. The last two are in a class apart, both notable for their depth and concentration, their approachable but firm tannins, and their great potential for ageing. Finally, there is a barrique-matured Merlot, more impressive for its evidence of *terroir* than its varietal character. It comes from an unknown clone; however, four hectares using French grafts, not yet productive, were planted in 2000. Both 1999 and 2000 were good years for Gere's wines. While the latter yielded wines that are richer and have more body, the former is perhaps preferable for being more elegant and aromatic.

In April 2001, Alain Rousse, an oenologist from southwestern France who trained in Toulouse, joined Gere's team – though this does not herald a change towards a more French style of wine. In fact, a Gere style already exists: full-bodied with considerable depth of colour, and (coincidentally) quite close to that of Rousse's native Madiran wines. The explanation has more to do with the increasing time Gere has to spend in travel, and the necessity of having constant, qualified control over the cellar. Another significant addition to the team will shortly be Gere's son – another Attila – who recently finished high school and is now studying winemaking.

Three-quarters of Gere's wine is sold in Hungary: fifteen per cent in direct sales to the public in Villány, and the rest through Vinárium. In 2001, Gere reached agreement with Victor Lanson, of the Champagne family, to import his wines into the UK.

WENINGER ÉS GERE KFT

H–17773 Villány, Diófás u. 4. Tel/fax: +36–72 492195/492839. *(a)* Franz Weninger & Attila Gere. *(b)* None yet planted. *(c)* 700–750hl. *(d)* Attila Gere. *(e)* Varietals, rozé, cuvée. *(f)* 30% (Austria, Holland, Switzerland, Germany, Denmark, and Finland)

Weninger & Gere is a fifty-fifty joint venture started in July 1992. Impressed by Villány ever since his first visit in 1986, Franz Weninger offered Attila Gere financial backing in February 1992. Gere had hesitations, and the outcome of the negotiation was the foundation of this separate joint company, initially financed by Weninger. A purpose-built winery (jointly owned by the two companies) was immediately constructed, providing an immense benefit to Gere, who was able to use it for his own wine production. Apart from this, the two companies are independently run. Seven hectares were planted in 2002, half with Cabernet Sauvignon and half with Cabernet Franc.

Gere makes the company's wine, with quality standards as rigorously high as those of his own company – Weninger & Gere is by no means a second label. Cuvée Phoenix (Cabernet Sauvignon, Cabernet Franc, Merlot and Kékoportó) may be less complex than the Gere Cuvée, but the 1997 Cabernet Franc Selection is, in my opinion, a demonstration wine, showing the level of excellence achievable in this region. The wine is sold through the same outlets as Gere's wines.

VYLYAN SZŐLŐ BIRTOK ÉS PINCÉSZET RT

H–7821 Kisharsány, Fekete-hegy. Tel: +36–72 579701; Fax: +36–72 579702. *(a)* Pál Debreczeni. *(b)* 55.7ha: CS 15.8ha; Ko 8ha; Zw 4.8ha; PN 4.3ha; M 3.6ha; CF 3.3ha; Kf 1.1ha; Ch 4.7ha; Or 4.6ha; RR 4.6ha; Ci 0.9ha. *(c)* 2,000hl. *(d)* István Ipacs Szabó. *(e)* Varietals, cuvées. *(f)* 63% (Finland, Germany, France, Sweden, and Japan).

Vylyan (an early medieval spelling of Villány) is the name of a very special relative newcomer to the region, owned and financed by Pál Debreczeni, who has set his sights on becoming the leading producer of top-quality wine in Hungary. Vylyan's latest wine releases show very clearly that this is not an absurd ambition. Debreczeni, now in his early fifties, hails from Szeged and has become one of the country's leading industrialists. As he puts it: "I earn my money from manufacturing domestic appliances, and I spend it here at Vylyan." When pressed, he admits to being an idealist. Quality, without counting the cost, is his unswerving goal.

Having become convinced that Villány is one of the very best areas for red wine, Debreczeni travelled in France, Italy, South Africa, and California to find out how the best wineries in these countries functioned. In 1988, with considerable foresight, when land values were still cheap, he also purchased three plots totalling 130 hectares just north of Kisharsány. Since then he has built up a team of well-qualified colleagues to make his dream a reality. Interestingly, and almost uniquely in Hungary, these are all very forward-looking young men, completely open to new ideas and influences. And to clinch the matter, since 1998 he has employed Jean-Pierre Confuron, the young oenologist from Vosne-Romanée, as a consultant. There is also a connection with the Hétszőlő vineyard in Tokaj, started in 1999, whereby Vylyan puts its trading system at Hétszőlő's disposal in return for viticultural advice.

Apart from twenty-five hectares of Kékoportó planted in 1962 (with a density of 3,300 vines per hectare), the land at Kisharsány was a green-field site. A planting scheme carried out between 1992 and 1996 has brought the vineyard area up to fifty-five hectares. A new planting pro-gramme began in 2000, since when a further fifty hectares have been planted, and around twenty-five hectares will be planted each year until the full 160 hectares have been exploited. Until 1996, vines were umbrella-trained, but Guyot Royal Cordon is now preferred (with the cordon at a height of forty to fifty centimetres/sixteen to twenty inches) because this provides the grapes with more earth-reflected heat and gives better canopy management. The density of vines is 7,000 per hectare. The current Siklós cuvée (made from Rajnai Rizling and Olaszrizling) will disappear and the vines will be regrafted to red varieties. The amount of Cirfandli will be increased.

Debreczeni has built one of the three or four most impressive wineries in Hungary. Started in 1994, the year of Vylyan's first harvest, it was sub-stantially completed by the winter of 1998–9, and is designed on the gravity system. The equipment is state-of-the-art. Grapes are selected first in the vineyards, then on inspection trays at the winery. For white wines – except Chardonnay – the grapes are pneumatically whole bunch-pressed. The model for Vylyan's Chardonnay is Pouilly-Fuissé. The grapes are destemmed and pressed, and the must is chilled. The juice is then racked from the sediment, inoculated, and fermented in tanks, after which it is put in barriques. *Bâtonnage*, or stirring the lees, is carried out twice a week.

Red grapes are normally destemmed and crushed, but only two-thirds of the Pinot Noir and the Zweigelt are crushed, the remaining third being bunch-fermented. The fermentation tanks are as high as they are wide, giving ideal skin contact, and have temperature control and CO_2 facilities. Lighter wines are made like Beaujolais (that is, whole bunch-pressed in closed conditions under gas), and in 2000 this technique was also used with Pinot Noir. For Pinot Noir, Zweigelt, and Kékoportó, the temperature is reduced to between 8°C and 10°C and the must is kept for a week. After that, the temperature is allowed to rise and yeast is added at 18°C. The temperature is then brought to 28°C to 30°C. Cabernet Sauvignon, Cabernet Franc, and Merlot are made along Bordeaux lines. The wine is kept on its skins for three or four weeks, and the cap is pressed. The wine is then transferred to large casks for a malolactic fermentation, after which it is put in barriques of Hungarian oak. Pinot Noir and Zweigelt are matured for eight to ten months, and Cabernets and Merlot for twelve to eighteen. Vylyan shares my reservations about Hungarian oak – indeed, mid-1990s bottlings show all too familiar woodiness and aggressive tannins – so it is planning to build its own cooperage. As things are, it already purchases and seasons its own barrel staves.

In size and aesthetic grandeur, the cask hall is reminiscent of a top Bordeaux *château*. It is automatically ventilated by an overnight air-exchange system. A further air-conditioned cellar, with humidity controlled by water sprinkling, is to be built. All wine is bottled at the same time on the sophisticated bottling line, and is not released until it is considered mature.

The young winemaker is István Ipacs Szabó, who took over the winery for the 1999 harvest. He first studied as an agricultural engineer, progressing to winemaking and vineyard management. Having worked in Austria for a while, he then worked in California before coming to Vylyan. Tasting his wines out of cask during 2000 and 2001 was an exciting experience, for they are on the very highest level of quality and surely indicate that Debreczeni made an extremely wise choice in entrusting his winery to him.

Vylyan manages to do impressively what few other Hungarian wineries would even think of trying. The firm continues to make an arresting barrique Kékoportó, even though there remain residual doubts about whether or not this variety can ever make a great wine. The old vines, planted in 1962, are better than those now available, and Vylyan is taking cuttings from the best specimen vines for further plantings. Zweigelt is also made as a serious wine, aged in new oak, the reserve version being cooled for five days and made in the Burgundian way (like Pinot Noir). The Pinot Noir – thanks, no doubt, to Confuron – is already impressive, the 1999 vintage having been hailed by the French internet guide *Magnum Vinum* as "the best non-Burgundian Pinot Noir of the last five years".

Apart from these, there is an impressive Cabernet Sauvignon, and two cuvées: Montenuovo (a blend of varying composition), named after Gróf Montenuovo, who was killed in the 1950s by the Communists, and whose vineyard belongs to Vylyan; and what is presently their flagship wine, Duennium (a blend of Cabernet Sauvignon, Merlot, Zweigelt, and Cabernet Franc). The 1998 and 1999 vintages of the latter show elegance allied to weight in a beautiful balance, but still await full maturity. Another cuvée of Cabernet Sauvignon, Cabernet Franc, and Merlot, to be called Evolution Cuvée, will appear under the Monarchia label. In 2002, a second mid-price label, Montevino, was launched under a separate company.

Whatever the merits of earlier Vylyan vintages, I think that, in future years, it is the 1999 vintage that will be seen as a turning point in the company's history. The 1999 Merlot, from vines planted in 1992–3, is quite simply the best Merlot I have encountered in Hungary, and cask samples of the 2000 vintage confirm that quality has moved up to a new level. One's dominant impression at Vylyan is of dedicated professionalism backed by more than adequate capital resources – an uncommon combination in Hungary, but one that looks set to achieve Debreczeni's ambition.

MALATINSZKY KÚRIA

H–7773 Villány, Batthyány u. 23. Tel/fax: +36–72 493042. *(a)* Csaba Malatinszky. *(b)* 15ha: Or 6ha; Ch 2ha; CS 2ha; M 2ha; Kf 2ha. *(c)* 700–800hl. *(d)* Csaba Malatinszky. *(e)* Varietals, cuvées. *(f)* None

Malatinszky is a remarkable young man who, all his life, has been fascinated by wine. Now in his early forties, he has already had a varied career that has encompassed managing a restaurant, being Hungary's first modern sommelier (at Gundel's Restaurant), and opening La Boutique de Vin in Budapest in 1992: the first top-quality wine shop in Hungary. In 1997, he opened his winery in Villány, which some people (including me) think may become a front runner in the Villány top-quality wine stakes. The winery displays no name, but this is indicative, perhaps, not so much of Matatinszky's modesty as of his determination to keep a low profile until he knows he is achieving perfection. He is very much the cat that walks by itself.

Malatinszky's wine studies have been eclectic. In 1991, he began to work with several producers in Villány, like Bock, Vinolund Plus, and Neuperger, selling wine under his own label and trademark, "Le Sommelier" – though often with their name on the label. Between 1994 and 1997, he sold wine wholesale while managing to visit France several times to study winemaking. This made him very critical of Hungarian wines (for their dilute musts and lack of complexity), and gave him the idea of creating a new winery with French technology to make Bordeaux-inspired wines in Hungary. Thus, Malatinszky Kúria came into being – Kúria being a mansion or country house.

His extremely well-designed, business-like winery works on the gravity principle from grape reception until the wine reaches the cask cellar. White must is chilled for two days, sedimented, and fermented with selected yeasts. The making of the serious red wines is modelled on "Bordeaux technology and my inventions", but Malatinszky seems reluctant to reveal quite what the latter are. This much is clear: there is no maceration, fermentation is slow (between three and four weeks) with temperatures never above 20°C, and the must is pumped over the cap.

Light wines like Olaszrizling and Kékoportó are racked, covered with nitrogen, and moved to stainless-steel tanks, but Chardonnay is put into barriques with some sediment, given some *bâtonnage*, or lees stirring, and allowed to age. French and Hungarian (Zemplén) barriques are extensively used. However, because Malatinszky wants "just a touch of oak" in his wines, he seasons his own Hungarian oak to avoid rough tannins, and has his barriques made by a local cooper. White wines are aged in lightly toasted barriques, while to eliminate oaky aromas, Kékfrankos is aged in old barriques. Other reds are aged in a mixture of first, second, and third fillings of light- and medium-toasted barriques. Malatinszky has his own bottling plant, and markets his wine through his own shop in Budapest. He is not yet exporting, but would like to do so.

Malatinszky agrees that, at first sight, "Cabernoir" – a blend of

Cabernet Sauvignon and Pinot Noir – seems a crazy idea. Most people, especially Frenchmen, think so until they taste the blend. However, because most Pinot Noir in Villány is a clone with a darker colour, more skin tannin, a higher glycerine content, and less acidity than in Burgundy, it does in fact marry quite well with Cabernet Sauvignon.

His flagship wine is called Kúria, and 1997 was the first vintage. The wine is unfiltered, and spends seventeen-and-a-half months in French barriques, and two-and-a-half months in Hungarian barriques – both first fillings. The wine (an unblended Cabernet Sauvignon) has quite a high acidity level, because it had only a partial malolactic fermentation – to keep it from being boring after the tannins have softened out, according to Malatinszky. It has dense fruit and great complexity, and is sophisticated and impressive. Other wines – barrique Chardonnay, Merlot, and Cabernet Sauvignon – show a similarly serious character, all of them structured wines with concentrated fruit and a capacity for considerable ageing.

"My goal is to make wine comparable to the best in the world. For me it is an idea – not a business – and I am working to produce something prestigious rather than just to maximize profit." So runs Malatinszky's credo and, having refused foreign backing, he is content to work slowly towards this goal. He is doing so with considerable success.

BOCK PINCE

H–7773 Villány, Batthyány u. 15. Tel: +36–72 492919; Tel/fax: +36–72 492388.
(a) József Bock. *(b)* 7ha: CS/CF/M 4.5ha; Sy 1.5ha; Ko 1ha. *(c)* 1,200hl.
(d) József Bock. *(e)* Varietals, rozé, cuvées. *(f)* Variable (Holland, Switzerland, France, Germany, Japan, Denmark, and Finland)

Bock is descended from eighteenth-century German settlers, and his family were grape and wine producers until their vineyards were nationalized after the Second World War. Having worked as a mechanical engineer, he gave up his job in 1992. Starting with a family cellar in the Jammertal (now used for storage), Bock began to build a new cellar in 1994, incorporating a *panzió* that opened in October 1996.

Red wine makes up ninety-two per cent of his production. His vineyards are scattered over twenty-three plots (although chances of consolidation do exist). They are mechanized, with a density of between 5,600 and 5,800 vines per hectare, yielding between forty-nine and sixty-three hectolitres per hectare. Bock uses Guyot training, with a single sixty-five-centimetre-high (twenty-five-inch high) cordon, and prunes to four buds per cane, with six to eight bunches per vine. Although he has no integration contracts, he supervises the vineyards from which he purchases grapes. Bock's philosophy is that "clean grapes make clean wine".

Bock brought the equipment of his winery fully up-to-date in 2000, when the cellar was also extended, with the purchase of a pneumatic press. He has his own bottling line, and probably the most extensive bottle store in Villány, apart from that of Vylyan. He makes his wine using modern technology, but in the spirit of the traditions he was taught by his father. Bock claims he was the first Villány winemaker to offer a blend – his first Bock Cuvée (Cabernet Sauvignon and Cabernet Franc) was produced in 1991, to sell in 1992. That was the year he started making barrique wines, now a quarter of his production. The cellar holds 500 barriques, and each barrique is used only three times. Having the familiar doubts about Hungarian oak, Bock buys Mecsek and Zemplén oak and matures it himself for three years before having it made into barriques by his own cooper.

Bock's wines are always dependable, and sometimes exciting. He was Winemaker of the Year in 1997. The family is actively involved in the business: his son-in-law works for him, and his son is presently training in Budapest.

TIFFÁN'S BT
H–7773 Villány, Teleki Zs. u. 9. Tel: + 36 72 492417. Winery: H–7773 Villány, Erkel F. u. 10. Tel/fax: +36–72 492500. *(a)* Ede Tiffán. *(b)* 13ha: CS 4.2ha; CF 4.2ha; PN 2ha; Kf 1.2ha; M 0.6ha; Ko 0.6ha; Kad tiny amount. *(c)* 750hl. *(d)* Ede Tiffán. *(e)* Varietals, rozé, cuvées. *(f)* 33% (Holland, Japan, France, Germany, Switzerland, Austria, and the UK [through Vinárium])

The Tiffáns settled in Villány in 1746, and Ede belongs to the ninth generation. Having graduated in Budapest as a horticultural engineer in 1965, he worked for a state farm for seventeen years, and then for ten years in a cooperative. In 1988, he acquired the cellar that had belonged to a famous merchant, Jákó Gyimóthy, earlier in the century. Although he started to bottle wine and sell it in 1989–90, his own firm began officially only in 1991. He was among the makers who exported to England through Interconsult, and in 1993, he began building his present modern and well-appointed cellar. He is also involved in a joint venture company called Mondivin, which started in 1993 with two partners: Jan van Lissum, a Dutch wine journalist, and Erik Sauter, a Belgian wine merchant. Mondivin's wine, from five hectares, is made in Tiffán's cellar, but a separate cellar is planned. Tiffán has been much helped by Sauter, who has had twenty-five years' experience in Bordeaux as a wine consultant, and he is now assisted by his son Zsolt, who joined the firm in 1995, was trained by his father, and acts as cellar-master.

Tiffán takes enormous care in his vineyards, the best of which are in Jammertal and Kopár. His new plantations have 6,000 vines per hectare, and are Guyot-trained. He prunes down to six to eight buds on each vine, and takes away the shoots. He aims for a yield of thirty to forty hectolitres per hectare.

Tiffán's wines are fermented reductively, using temperature-controlled, stainless-steel tanks. After fermentation the lees are pressed and added to the wine. "Traditional" reds are matured in large oak casks for from six to twelve months, and the highest-quality wines are matured in barriques made from Hungarian oak, which are used for three years, scraped, and then used for a further three years. In the first two years they hold either Cabernet Sauvignon or Cabernet Franc; in the third they are used for Tiffán's Cuvée (Cabernet Sauvignon and Kékfrankos), made from bought-in grapes and matured for two years, one in barriques and one in large (110-hectolitre) oak casks. The wines are covered with CO_2 when being blended and when being bottled. Tiffán has his own bottling line, but has to bottle on demand because of lack of storage space.

Tiffán produces Kékoportó, Cabernet Sauvignon, and a Jammertal Cuvée (Kékfrankos and Kékoportó) in addition to Tiffán's Cuvée. His premier wine, however, is his Grand Selection (sixty per cent Cabernet Franc, forty per cent Cabernet Sauvignon), made only in especially good vintages from the best casks of each wine. The 1995 Grand Selection is justly celebrated – a wine that shows all the strengths of Villány wine at its best – and 1997 looks set to follow in its footsteps. Tiffán was Winemaker of the Year in 1991 – the first-ever nominee.

OTHER WINE PRODUCERS

Bajor Családi Pincészet. H–7800 Siklós-Máriagyűd, Tenkes u. 14. Tel/fax: +36–72 351143. *Blum–Bor Bt (Blum Pince).* H–7772 Villánykövesd, Rákóci u. 15. Tel: +36–72 493088; Fax: +36–72 492133. *Daka Zsolt.* H–7800 Siklós, Váralja u. 69. Tel/fax: +36–72 351857. *Gere Tamás.* H–7773 Villány, Fáy A. u. 7. Tel/fax: +36–72 492400. Winery: H–7822 Nagyharsány, Kolónia 106. Tel: +36–72 468338. *Günzer Tamás Pince-Borozó.* H–7773 Villány, Baross G. u. 79. Tel: +36–72 493163. *Günzer Zoltán (Günzer Pince).* H–7773 Villány, Oportó u. 13. Tel/fax: +36–72 492414. *Kecskés Pince Kft.* H–7773 Villány, Dózsa Gy. u. 29. Tel/fax: +36–72 493 055. *Kürti István.* H–7773 Villány, Hunyadi J. u. 27. Tel: +36–72 492057. *Magonyi & Maurer Pince-Borozó.* H–7773 Villány, Baross G. u. 84. Tel: +36–72 492641. *Mayer Márton Pince (KDM Űdítőkészítő, Palackozó).* H–7773 Villány, Batthyány. 13. Tel: +36–72 492410. *Molnár Tamás (Tamás Bátya Pincéje).* H–7773 Villány, Batthyány I. u. 42. Tel: +36–72 492596. *Ősi Mihály.* H–7822 Nagyharsány, Kossuth u. 75. Tel: +36–72 468834. Fax: +36–72 493091. *Polgár Pince.* H–7773 Villány, Rákóczi u. 32. Tel: +36–72 492053/860/574; Tel/fax: +36–72 492194. *Preisendorf János.* H–7773 Villány, Baross u. 101. *Schuth Kft (Schuth Pince).* H–7773 Villány, Deák út, 24. Tel/fax: +36–72 492524. *Solt Pince Panzío.* H–7773 Villány, Batthyány u. 3/a. Tel/fax: +36–72 492483. *Szemes József Szeszfőzde.* H–7773 Villány, Baross G. u. 2/a. Tel: +36–72 492479/492350. *Szende Pince-Borozó.* H–7773 Villány, Baross G. u. 87. Tel: +36–72 492396; Fax: +36–72 493014. *Tiffán Imre Borászati és Borkereskedő Egyéni Ceg (Tiffán Imre Pince).* H–7772 Villánykövesd, Kossuth u. 11. Tel/fax: +36–72 492446. Winery: H–7772 Villánykövesd, Pincesor u. 14–15. Tel: +36–72 493085. *Tóth Pince.* H–7815 Harkány, Diászó Dűlő 2/b. Tel: +36–72 429024. *Villányi Borászat Rt (Château Teleki Pincészet).* H–7773 Villány, Ady fasor 2. Tel: +36–72 492141/492923; Fax: +36–72 492009. *Villány "Új Alkotmány" MGTSZ.* H–7773 Villány, Batthyány u. 24. Tel/fax: +36–72 492156/8/9. *Vinoland Plus Kft.* H–7775 Villány, Petőfi S. u. 46. Tel/fax: +36–72 492729. *Wunderlich Alajos.* H–7773 Villány, Szőlő u. 7. Tel/fax: +36–72 492468 Wineries making good and interesting wine, if not quite in the very top flight, certainly include those of Gere Tamás and Polgár Pince.

Tamás Gere (not a blood relation of Attila Gere, but his brother-in-law) was a metalworker until he became an independent winemaker in 1989, sharing for a while with Attila the cellar he still has in Nagyharsány. Since then, his business has expanded, and his son Zsolt has become the wine-maker. Vinification equipment is adequate rather than modern, but all wine is reductively fermented in stainless-steel tanks. Whites do not undergo malolactic fermentation (to maintain acidity), nor do Kékoportó and Kékfrankos, which are matured in large oak casks. The Cabernets and Merlot, however, have their malolactic fermentation in tank, and then go into small casks and barriques. Zsolt describes the Tamás Gere style as drier and more tannic than is usual in Villány: to me they seem a little homespun and rustic. However, as Zsolt gets into his stride, I would expect to see the quality improving. The wine is distributed and exported by Vinárium.

Zoltán Polgár was Winemaker of the Year in 1996. He and his wife Katalin are both qualified horticultural engineers, and had hobby vineyards of over eight hectares (in various family names) as far back as 1974. The present enterprise started officially in 1990, and now has thirty hectares (twenty red, ten white). The efficiently designed and very well-equipped winery was built in 1993 and extended in 2000, and wine is made along modern reductive lines, with reds being matured in large wooden casks and around 200 barriques. Cuvées blending French with Hungarian varieties are a house specialty. Sixty per cent of the production is sold in Budapest, thirty per cent in the cellar and adjoining panzió, and the rest is exported. Recent vintages do not, in my opinion, quite match the achievement of the mid-1990s.

Villányi Borászat is descended from a firm established in 1949, and incorporates the vinestock firm that belonged to the Teleki family. In 1961, it became part of the Villány-Siklós State Farm, which became, in 1984, the Pannonvin Borgazdaság Kombinát (dealt with in Chapter Nine). This was the largest of its twenty-one wineries and, when Pannonvin was dismantled in 1989, it was taken over by a bank and privatized in 1992, known first as Szőlő-Bor, then as Villányi Borászat. It owns 297 hectares of vineyards, of which one hundred, all planted since 1985, are in production, and sixty-seven are newly planted. The firm produces between 15,000 and 18,000 hectolitres each year, requiring the purchase of forty-five per cent of its grape requirements. In 2001, a major reconstruction programme was started, involving the replacement of the original winery and its equipment. The winemaker is Antal Bakonyi. The Borászat owns Teleki's cellar in the centre of Villány, which is organized as a museum and holds museum stocks dating back to 1987. The firm's range of products is a pyramid: under the museum wines come the

Château Teleki range, then the "V" range, then the "Mediterranean" range, and finally Country Wines made to a Quality Wine standard. All are exported, and the last three are distributed through supermarkets in Hungary.

Bajor Családi Pincészet is the largest and most important of Siklós producers. Péter Bajor has fifteen hectares, and an atmospheric cellar at the foot of the steps leading up to the large baroque church that dominates the village of Máriagyűd. His production places an understandable emphasis on the white wines of the region. They are sound if unexciting, those matured in barriques being the best.

The Villányi Új Alkotmány ("New Constitution") Cooperative was the first to be founded in the area, in 1948, and owns the original Batthyány cellar, built in 1754, at Villánykövesd. With 500 members, it covers ten villages and over one hundred hectares of vineyards. Many members sell their grapes, but bottled wines of a rather average standard are obtainable in the cooperative's shops in Villány and Harkány.

Among the small- to medium-sized producers who make their red wines by the traditional method, using mud to seal the fermentation vessel, are Günzer Tamás, Günzer Zoltán, Kecskés Pince, Kürti István, Preisendorf János, Schuth Pince, Solt Pince, Szende Pince, Tiffán Imre, Vinoland Plus, and Wunderlich Alajos. Molnár Tamás, Magonyi & Maurer Pince, Mayer Márton Pince, and Ősi Mihály do not use mud, but have made their own adaptations of traditional methods. Standards are uneven, but most make wines of a good average quality, representative of the traditions of the region, with the occasional outstanding bottle. The following deserve special attention.

Alajos Wunderlich, who has his vineyards and cellar in the Jammertal, and who says that his aim is "to combine elegance with strength, while keeping the fruit character in the wine", can make impressive, ageworthy wines. Ferenc Schuth's cellar is a rare survival from the past, as the ambience created by old photographs and posters, framed certificates of competition awards from the nineteenth century, and wine antiques makes abundantly clear. The family business in the Rauenthal in Germany was founded in 1701, but the Schuths did not arrive in Villány until 1866, when Ferenc's great-great-grandfather, Wilhelm, became cellar-master at the archducal estate. I find his wines a little light and austere.

Tamás Molnár – or *Tamás Bátya* ("Uncle Tom") – has only one hectare of his own vineyards, but supervises a further four from which he buys grapes. From modest vinification equipment at home he turns out wines with a dense, fruity character – his Kékoportó is outstanding – and he has started using barriques. Occasionally, however, I detect a tendency to over-extraction. Handsome labels using the names of the Alliance generals at the Battle of Nagyharsány are designed by Maczák János, an artist working in Pécs, and have a mesmerizing similarity to Dürer etchings. Some bottles, of which the brass labels appear to be the plates from which the etchings were made, are surely collectors' items. He has recently made an agreement with Monarchia.

József Kecskés became a full-time winemaker in 1990, but the company was registered only in 1998 when it became a family enterprise (incorporating his daughter). Fifteen hectares of vineyards comprise fourteen plots stretching across twenty miles from Harkány to Versend (in Tolna). Wine has been bottled since 1992, and exported since 1995. Barriques made in Harkány have been used since 1997. Quality is improving, with Kékoportó and Kékfrankos becoming specialities. Kecskés is another producer who appears in Monarchia's list.

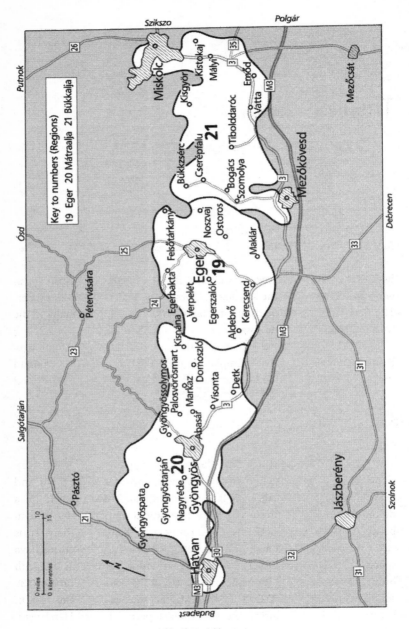

Northeast Hungary

11

The Northeast

EGER

5,080 hectares: 2,197 white, 2,883 red
Fourteen wine communities, with 7,731 members

Eger is the largest and most important of three regions that form a vast wine-growing area on the southern slopes of the Mátra and Bükk ranges. The Eger district occupies the middle of the range, with Mátraalja to the west and Bükkalja to the east.

Eger is on the move. Since 1995, approximately half of all new Hungarian vineyards have been planted here. Pushed by market demand for red wine, these new plantings have brought the regional total of red vineyards to over fifty per cent. The main producing areas are to the west and east of Eger town. Traditionally, the western side was predominantly a white-wine area, although the best locations were always reserved for red varieties, while the eastern side was mainly for red wines. The best wine areas are considered to be the southern, higher, and very steep slopes of Egedhegy (also known as Nagyeged), northeast of the town, and nearby Síkhegy. Here, the soil is a shale and sandstone mixture on a dolomitic rock base, producing good ripening conditions. The land in between, according to some, is also a prime area. Pajdos, to the west, is also considered a good area, the soil being loess and clay. All three have special microclimates. Other notable areas are Almagyartető, an area with brown forest soil noted for white wine north of Eger, and Kőporos, to the south, with tufa soil. Debrő, in the extreme southwest of the region, became well-known during the Communist period for its Hárslevelű. Previously considered part of the Mátra region, it was transferred to Eger in the 1980s. Here, the volcanic subsoil is overlaid by alluvial sand from the river which runs through the valley connecting the three main villages in the region. Sadly, I have never found any current Debrői Hárslevelű worthy of special note.

Unfortunately, the best vineyards on many of these sites (particularly Egedhegy and Pajdos) were abandoned during the Communist period because they were too difficult to cultivate, and by late 2001 only forty out of almost 120 hectares of prime land on Egedhegy had been privatized, mainly because they were mortgaged by their previous owners and the tangle has still not yet been finally sorted out. Local producers are angry at this scandal, and believe, probably rightly, that vested interests have prolonged the delay. Land on Pajdos only started to be replanted in 1995.

Before the Second World War, Kadarka was the predominant red variety in the region, making up (according to differing estimates) between forty per cent and sixty per cent of all red plantations. Discarded by the Communists, its place has been taken by Kékfrankos, now accounting for forty per cent of all red-grape production. After Kékfrankos come Kékoportó and Zweigelt. However, some Kadarka is being replanted, as well as other previously popular varieties like Kékmedoc (which, although it may be related to Mornen Noir, is thought by many experts to be indigenous, despite its French name). It is also said that Blauburger does better in Eger than anywhere else in Hungary.

Pinot Noir was grown in the area before the war. Enthusiasts point out climatic similarities with Burgundy. If they are right (but the case has yet to be proved), Pinot Noir could, in time, become the principal non-indigenous variety in the region. On the other hand, most authorities (such as the local research institute), do not believe that Cabernet Sauvignon is suited to the Eger climate, although Cabernet Franc appears to do quite well. Among the white varieties, Leányka is the most widespread, followed by Olaszrizling, Ottonel Muskotály, Tramini, and Királyleányka, while Chardonnay is popular in new plantations. The climate is Continental, with annual precipitation of 523 millimetres (twenty inches).

In many people's minds, Eger is synonymous with Bull's Blood (Bikavér). In fact, as was explained in the previous chapter, Eger does not have a monopoly on Bikavér. Nevertheless, it regards the name as its most marketable asset, and quite naturally wants to exploit it. This, however, is not without its problems, and my own view is that at the moment Egri Bikavér might be described as a wine with a well-known name still in search of a style.

Over a period of some two centuries, the varieties composing the wine – up to as many as eight at any one time, but always including Kadarka – have varied. Before the Second World War, it had protection-of-origin status. I suspect, though I cannot prove, that at this time the wine was a natural blend rather than one contrived by the winemaker, because it was vinified from varieties which were promiscuously rather than block-planted in the vineyards. During the late 1970s, however, whatever uniqueness or quality it might have had previously were debased. There was a state directive that most of the local red wines should be sold as Bikavér, and Egervin sourced wines from other regions to augment what rapidly became a successful marketing venture. The quality exported to the west was appallingly low, and the reason that the name is so well-known in Britain is that many generations of students drank it as a cheap-and-cheerful quaffer.

Some progress has been made in recovering from this situation, but it has been and remains rather slow. The reality is that a new Bikavér tradition is being established, not an old one recreated. The rules that currently govern the making of Bikavér are: (1) the wine must come from the region; (2) the blend must be of at least three varieties; (3) the average yield is limited to eighty-four hectolitres per hectare (12 tonnes per hectare) for vineyards with densities of from 3,500 to 5,000 vines per hectare (as opposed to the local limit of ninety-eight hectolitres or 14 tonnes per hectare); (4) the varieties must be harvested at 2° sugar above the minimum in other Hungarian regions, making the minimum for most varieties 17°, and for Cabernet and Merlot 19°; (5) the wine must be made by fermentation on the skins, and has to spend at least twelve months in any type of oak barrel; (6) the wine can only be marketed fourteen months after the vintage – a limit to be extended by one month, year by year, until it reaches eighteen months in 2005. In addition, the wine has to be passed by a regional wine qualification committee that, currently, rejects thirty per cent of all wine submitted.

This may sound rigorous, but it is not. As in Szekszárd, there is no legal requirement for even one of the varieties used in the blend to be a native one. The yield and must-sugar minimum rules seem, to a western observer, inadequate to produce really top-quality wine, and although all Bikavér that passes the qualification board is entitled to have – indeed, *must* have – a special quality neck label, much of the Bikavér that reaches the market does not merit this distinction. Some producers in other regions believe (correctly) that this poor-quality Bikavér devalues the significance of the special quality label. The biggest criticism of all, perhaps, is that there is no semblance of a unifying style to Bikavér. This is not a matter of quality – many Bikavérs are extremely good – but, one might say, of customer expectation. Someone buying a bottle ought to have some idea of what sort of wine is being purchased.

A league of nine producers dedicated to promoting Bikavér as a top-quality wine – the *Egri Bormíves Céh* – is trying to influence progress in the direction of voluntary acceptance of a stricter set of rules. They are faced with opposition from the big (and cheap) producers, and in 2001, the point was reached at which the Céh members were threatening to stop producing Bikavér if the goal of controlled, genuinely high-quality status could not be established.

Eger is one of the regions where efforts are being made to extend the control-of-origin status at present enjoyed by Bikavér, Debrői Hárslevelű, and Leányka. The wine community selects the best vineyard areas, coupled with selection of varieties, limitation of yield and quality-control rules. Arising from this, individually named vineyards are assuming greater and greater significance.

There are noticeably few foreign investors in Eger, despite an optimistic official calculation that the region has 21,000 hectares of potential vineyard land. Although this is an exaggeration, clearly Eger has unrealized potential for quality development. Unofficially, I have been told that foreigners are actively discouraged from involving themselves in wine in the region because of fears of an invasion similar to that in Tokaj. Facilities for wine tourism are also rather limited, apart from the atmospheric Szépasszony-völgy cellar row just outside the city. This is certainly geared to tourists, with gypsy fiddlers and opportunities to taste and buy wine. Opportunities to find good wine, however, are another matter.

Despite some of the big-structured wines that were made in 1999 and 2000, Eger generally cannot, and should not try to, compete with Villány in the production of such wines, but should find its own style. There is ample evidence that it can offer very complete wines, intense but elegant, for which there should certainly be a place not just in the market, but in every serious wine-lover's cellar.

EGERVIN BORGAZDASÁG RT

H–3300 Eger, Széchenyi u. 3, Pf 27. Tel: +36–511222; Tel/fax: +36–511226. *(a)* Timesco (an investment consortium). *(b)* 300ha. No new plantations: planting details withheld by the firm. *(c)* Péter Román, with György Lörincz, and flying winemakers. *(d)* 90,000–110,000hl. *(e)* Varietals, rozé, cuvées, Bikavér. *(f)* 25% (the UK, Germany, Scandinavia, Canada, Japan, the US, and 24 other countries) Egervin was founded in 1949, with headquarters in Gyöngyös, but the centre of operations was moved to Eger at the beginning of the 1960s. During the 1970s, there was a rapid growth both in production and sales, culminating, at its peak, with a production of 350,000 hectolitres a year. Egervin was among the first Hungarian companies to export to the west. However, the eventual collapse of its main export markets saddled the company with debt, and by the end of 1991, Egervin was in receivership. Eventually, a Hungarian investment group (with interests in the meat and agricultural industries) bought it, and ninety-seven per cent of the shares are still in the hands of this group today. The privatized company started up in 1993.

There have been many changes since 1993, and a big programme of modernization and reorganization is still in progress, changing the image of the company and its range of products. Sales have doubled in the last seven years, and Egervin is now a leading company on the domestic market, with fifteen per cent of all bottled wine sales. There are three categories of wine in Egervin's portfolio: (1) big-volume, commercial wines, of which seventy per cent is Quality Wine, and thirty per cent is Table Wine; (2) a hotel and general catering sector, with eight premium wines (the Gróber range) introduced in 2000; (3) museum stocks of half-a-million bottle-aged wines of vintages as far back as 1964. These wines are available in Eger, and some are exported.

Egervin furnishes just twenty per cent of its requirements from vineyards temporarily under its control – including the yet-to-be-privatized vineyards on Egedhegy, which are such a sensitive issue that Egervin declined to give me any details of them. A further sixty per cent of the firm's grape requirements are bought (half under integrated contracts) in Eger and other regions, and twenty per cent are secured in the form of bought-in wine and must. The company has two winemaking plants: one in Eger, and the other in Verpelét. The Eger winery makes both white (twenty per cent) and red (eighty per cent) wine. Most reds are fermented on their skins, and all the white wines are reductive. The Verpelét winery makes only white wine, both reductively and traditionally, to satisfy the company's big domestic demand. Both plants have a capacity for temperature-controlled fermentation, although the Eger winery has rather dated technology and some fermentation tanks have no cooling facilities. The introduction of pneumatic presses and smaller tanks is eagerly awaited by the winemakers. A flying winemaker scheme started in 1996, intended primarily to raise the commercial winemaking to a higher level. Since 1999, Stephen Hall, an Australian, has been in charge. The company makes wines from both international and indigenous varieties, and has introduced cuvées combining both sorts to familiarize customers not just with new tastes, but with new varietal names.

Egervin receives tourist groups at its cellars, which are on three levels and total four kilometres (two-and-a-half miles) in length, having been made into one cellar from many smaller private cellars after nationalization. The total capacity for wood ageing is 200,000 hectolitres. Egervin's two big export markets are the UK and Germany, the latter for bulk wine. A concise assessment of Egervin's wines is difficult. Many are of a fairly basic, mass-market quality, and many of the white wines show excessive levels of CO_2. However, at the top of the commercial range, the beneficial influence of Australian vinification is plain, and some wines are of excellent quality. The museum wines offer a fascinating insight into the wines of the old Communist world. My notes contain phrases like "exotic but compelling", and even "completely outside any kind of wine-taste tradition known to me". Some are quite wonderful: for example, a 1988 Debrő Hárslevelű offers a deliciously rich and complex mouthful, showing just why "honey" is brought to mind by Hárslevelű.

GIA KFT

H–3300 Eger, Verőszala u. 22–24. Tel/fax: +36–36 429800. *(a)* Tibor Gál, Niccoló Incisa della Rocchetta, Burkhard Bovensiepen (Alpina BMW). *(b)* 35ha belonging to Tibor Gál: PN 16ha; Kf 4ha; Sy 3ha; Ch 3ha; Ko 1ha; M 1ha; Sk 1ha;

PB 1ha; Mo 1ha; V 1ha; Kad 2ha; T 0.5ha; SB 0.5ha. *(c)* 1,125hl. *(d)* Tibor Gál, with cellar-master Tamás Gromon. *(e)* Varietals, Bikavér. *(f)* 60% (Switzerland, Germany, Italy, the US and, through Vinárium, the UK)

GIA – an acronym of its owners' names – started in 1993. Incisa is the proprietor of Sassicaia (in Tuscany) and Bovensiepen's Alpina, besides being a manufacturer of personalized cars, is also a German wine importer. The company came about as a result of Gál's time in Italy as winemaker for Lodovico Antinori at Ornellaia, when he made contact with his two partners. The first vintage was made in 1993. Antinori was at one time a partner, but later relinquished his shares.

Gál has west- and south-facing vineyards mainly at Síkhegy and at Pajdos. Only a third of them, started in 1997, are as yet producing. Almost half his plantations are of Pinot Noir, showing considerable faith in the future of this variety in the region. They have a density of 5,200 vines per hectare, the distance between the rows being relatively wide to avoid shading by neighbouring rows. They are Guyot-trained, with a seventy-centimetre (twenty-seven-inch) cordon, and a total height of 1.80 metres (almost six feet). The aim is to harvest about 1.5 kilograms (around three pounds) per vine, with a maximum of two kilograms (around five pounds); that is, approximately sixty to eighty hectolitres per hectare.

Until recently, only two clones of Pinot Noir were available in Hungary, one of which was suitable only for making sparkling wine. Gál decided to import bench grafts from France, with a preference for the rootstock *berlandieri* SO4, chosen because it suits Eger's calcium-rich soil. He has also planted other varieties, not yet yielding, that are rarely seen in Hungary: Syrah, Mondeuse, and Viognier. Gál planted 1.5 hectares of traditionally stake-trained Kadarka in 2001.

GIA operates in five extensive cellars more than 200 years old (one has the inscription "Renewed in 1786") in Eger's cellar row. They contain first-class fermentation equipment, a bottling line (available to other firms), cask and barrique storage, and a bottle-ageing store. Ninety per cent of grapes are purchased, and there are integration contracts with thirty farmers.

The winemaking is straightforward. Most of it is reductive, but Gál likes to experiment with open fermentation as well, and is trying to see how fermentation in wood changes the flavour of the wine. Gál's Bikavér contains fifty per cent Kékfrankos, thirty per cent Cabernet Franc, and twenty per cent Cabernet Sauvignon. Each variety from each vineyard is vinified and matured separately before blending, and gets from sixteen to eighteen months of wood maturation. The firm ages its own wood (with a three years' stock) and has its barrels made in Putnok. They are used for a maximum of three years.

The company deals with its own exports except those to the UK. These are handled by Vinárium, as are domestic sales. The wines appear mainly in supermarkets. Gál believes there is room for the company to grow a bit, with up to fifty hectares of vineyards, but does not want it to get too big. He was Winemaker of the Year in 1998, and was undoubtedly one of the most influential winemakers during the 1990s. He still makes very good wine, but I hope that he will turn his attention to making one or two premium wines to rise above what is already a high standard, and to rival the very best that is appearing elsewhere in the country.

KŐPOROS BORÁSZAT

H–3300 Eger, Nagykőporos út 11. Tel/fax: +36–36 321103. *(a)* The Simkó family and relations. *(b)* 17ha: Kf 4ha; CF 3.6ha; Bl 1.7ha; PN 1.7ha; CS 0.8ha; Zw 0.2ha; Ch 1.9ha; Or 1.2ha; L 1.1ha; Zgő 0.8ha. *(c)* 1,500–2,000hl. *(d)* László Katona. *(e)* Varietals, cuvée. *(f)* 10% (China, France, Germany, Colombia, and Canada)

Managed by Zoltán Simkó, an architect and construction engineer, this is very much a family firm, employing no fewer than seven of its members. The firm was founded twenty-six years ago by Simko's father-in-law, and refounded in its present form in 1995 with a big investment in new technology. The winemaker (and Simkó's right-hand man) is László Katona, who once worked as a technologist for Egervin, and subsequently taught in a secondary school for winemaking.

The aim is to combine tradition with up-to-date technology. With 24.5 hectares of vineyards due to become productive in 2002, the firm will become self-sufficient. Vinification equipment is fairly modern, although a water curtain is used to cool white wine ferments. Natural yeasts are used for red wine fermentation, which makes up eighty per cent of total production, with skin contact continuing for thirty days. The cellar can age 1,200 hectolitres in wood, of which 140 hectolitres are in Zemplén oak barriques, and there are 2,700 hectolitres of stainless-steel storage.

Bikavér is made first by blending the wine and then ageing it in wood. The base is seventy per cent Kékfrankos, and other varieties are Cabernet, Zweigelt, Kékoportó, and Merlot. The style is less robust than some, showing richness and complexity on the palate with a complementary backbone of soft tannins. The firm also produces an interesting barrique Olaszrizling.

PÓK-POLÓNYI PINCE

H–3300 Eger, Verőszala u. 66. Tel: +36–36 436021. *(a)* Monarchia Borászati and Tamás Pók. *(b)* 3ha: L/Zgő/Kf/CS/CF/M. *(c)* 300–330hl. *(d)* Tamás Pók. *(e)* Varietals, Bikavér, cuvées. *(f)* Small amount (Belgium)

Founded in 1995, this winery originally had two owners, Polónyi being a sleeping partner. In 2001, however, his share was purchased by Monarchia, of which Pók is winemaking director, and Polónyi has now dropped out of the picture. While the winery will be used to make Monarchia's wines, Pók will continue to make his own wines under the Pók-Polónyi label.

Pók's background includes working at the Eger and Kecskemét research institutes, a two-year spell in Napa Valley, and finally a job with Eurobor at Bátaapáti from 1990 until 1997. The 200–year-old cellar has a bright, white-tiled press-house, using grapes from his own (medium-cordon and well-established) vineyards. Stainless-steel tanks lack temperature-control, so water cooling is used for the white wine. The red wines are given a maceration period of between three and four weeks. All the oak is Hungarian, being either 600-litre barrels, or barriques. Both white and red wines are aged for one or two years, although shortage of wood storage means, for example, that Pók's Kékfrankos may go into stainless steel before going into cask. During maturation the wines are left undisturbed, then they are given a gentle filtering and bottled. After six months they are released, and are sold through Budapest distributors and Monarchia.

A third of Pók's production is Bikavér. The blend has Kékfrankos (from Egedhegy and Nagygalagonyás), Cabernet Sauvignon, Cabernet Franc, and Medina. He also produces an interesting Zengő, but is still experimenting to find the best way of making it. Pók is fond of making blends, and there are two cuvées: Rhapsody in Red (Cabernet Franc, Cabernet Sauvignon, Kékfrankos, and Merlot), which was first produced in 1997; and Bazilika (Cabernet Franc, Cabernet Sauvignon, and Kékfrankos).

These are aged in different-sized barrels, because Pók believes this makes a considerable difference to the wine.

Pók, to my mind, is the most exciting and innovative winemaker in the region. His wines are stylish, elegant but serious, and uncompromisingly well-made. An already risen and still ascendant star.

THUMMERER VILMOS SZŐLŐ-ÉS BORGAZDASÁGA (THUMMERER PINCE)

H–3304 Eger, Alvégi u. 32. Tel: +36–36 463269. Winery: H–3325 Noszvaj, Pf 1. *(a)* Vilmos Thummerer. *(b)* 50ha (25 ha yielding): Ch 2.3ha; Kir 2.3ha; Sk 2.3ha; Or 2.3ha; L 1.2ha; OM/Ker/IO 1.1ha; Kf 12ha; Bl 6ha; M 6ha; CS 5ha; PN 4ha; CF 2ha; Ko 2ha; Kad 1ha; Zw 0.5ha. *(c)* 1,050hl. *(d)* Vilmos Thummerer. *(e)* Varietals, Bikavér, cuvée. *(f)* 40% (Finland, Belgium, Switzerland, and Germany)

Vilmos Thummerer worked for Nagyréde Cooperative from 1965 until 1972, then deserted wine to start a private flower business. That lasted until 1985. In 1982, however, he rented seven hectares from the state and planted them, with the object of making high-quality wine. Today, he has fifty hectares, and moved to his present cellar in 1992, having bought it from a cooperative. In 2001, his development plans reached completion, providing a separate office building with a flat that he and his wife were glad to move into after eight years of trogloditic existence in a small cave dwelling hollowed out of the same tufa (volcanic rock) as the cellar. This is the sort of sacrifice you have to make if you apply your funds uncompromisingly to improving the quality of your wine.

It is said that east of Eger and south of Egedhegy, where there are brown forest soil and tuff, is the best area for quality wine. This is where Thummerer is lucky enough to have his vineyards, all except two hectares of which he planted himself. Guyot training with a single or double fifty-centimetre-high (twenty-inch) cordon is favoured. Cropping varies between thirty-five and seventy hectolitres per hectare, depending on the desired quality.

Thummerer makes young, fruity, and fresh reductive white wines. However, the Swiss market likes gentler, less acidic wines, and for this reason Királyleányka and Leányka have been given some malolactic fermentation since 2000. He has a well-equipped winery, and in 2000 tried barrique fermentation and maturation for the first time. He also plans a cuvée of Zenit and Sauvignon Blanc, blended after separate barrique fermentation – "to have something quite different from everyone else". The red wines ferment on their skins from eight to thirty days (depending on the product), and are aged in oak for a minimum of one and a half, but normally for two years. The basic wines for Bikavér are Merlot, Kékfrankos, Kékoportó, and Blauburger. Bottling is carried out in the cellar, with up to a year's bottle maturation before the release of the red wines. Thummerer's wines are mainly seen in restaurants and hotels, but he also produces Kaptárkő Cuvée (Pinot Noir, Merlot, and Cabernet Sauvignon) for Monarchia.

Thummerer was Winemaker of the Year in 1995, and is among the top two or three in Eger. His wines are complex, balanced, and elegant, without being blockbusters. They set a standard for the region.

TÓTH ISTVÁN–TRADICIONÁLIS PINCÉSZETE
H–3300 Eger, Kisvölgy út 52. Tel/fax: +36–36 313546. *(a)* István Tóth. *(b)* 3ha: Bl 0.9ha; Kf 0.9ha; CS 0.6ha; L 0.6ha. *(c)* 400hl. *(d)* István Tóth. *(e)* Varietals, Bikavér. *(f)* None directly

Tóth is the latest Eger producer to emerge into the limelight. He calls his winery "traditional" to emphasize a five-generation family wine connection. Largely self-taught, his professional background was in agricultural planning and insurance. Motivated by a love of grapes and wine, he became a full-time producer in 2000, when he found that his wine business, dating back to 1980, had become economically self-sufficient.

Tóth buys a third of the grapes he requires from good vineyards with the quality he wants, and he sells off his Leányka. From his own vines he takes no more than 1.2 kilograms (two-and-a-half pounds) per vine. Winemaking is as reductive as possible, using pump-over tanks, with skin contact for four weeks. The wines are matured mostly in large casks.

For the moment he produces Merlot, Cabernet Sauvignon, and Bikavér, although Kékfrankos is planned for the future. Bikavér is the most important of his wines, and the blend includes Kékfrankos, Merlot, Cabernet Sauvignon, and Blauburger, the proportions of each varying with the vintage. The aim is "to have refined, silky acids; to keep the fruit; and not to have too much pushy tannin" – an aim the wines amply achieve. Wines are kept separate according to variety, vineyard, and slope. They spend one year in large casks, one year in small (hundred-litre) casks, and then a further year back in large casks. The wines are blended three months before bottling. Some barriques were used experimentally for the 1999 vintage.

The wines are bottled partly under his own label (by GIA) and partly under that of Monarchia, which bought up his entire 1998 vintage. Asked what the future holds, he says that what he hopes for are more vineyards, larger storage capacity, and that both his sons will follow in his footsteps. Krisztián, the elder, already does.

VINCZE BÉLA

H–3300 Eger, Baktai úti ipartelep, Váci M. út 65. Tel/fax: +36–36 427515.
(a) Béla Vincze. (b) 32.5ha. 13ha yielding: Ch 3ha; Or 5.5ha; Rs 3.5ha; T 1ha.
19.5ha planted 1999–2000: CS 8.5ha; CF 6ha; PN 5ha. (c) 1,500+ hl (d) Béla Vincze. (e) Varietals, Bikavér. (f) 20% (Japan, Canada, Netherlands, and Germany)
Educated at the Horticultural University of Budapest, Vincze spent his rookie days at the Egri Csillagok Cooperative from 1985 until 1995, making small quantities of interesting wines besides the obligatory bulk wine. He started his own company in 1994, raising money from a government subsidy, by selling his house, and by borrowing from his family in order to build a winery that he planned entirely himself. He made the 1994 vintage in a medley of plastic containers in a building without doors or windows! No yeast was added to the musts, simply because he had no money to buy it. Nevertheless, the Cabernet Franc he made that year won him a gold medal in Bordeaux in 1997 – making him the first Hungarian winemaker to get one – and this put him on the map.

The winery, in an industrial estate on the outskirts of Eger, is built on the principle of a two-storey French *chai* (a building for storing and maturing wine) and is now very well-equipped. Until 1999, Vincze sold off all of his white grapes, but now he makes reductive Chardonnay and Tramini. He has to buy in ninety per cent of his red varieties, which are fermented in stainless-steel tanks on their skins for from seven to ten days. His Bikavér is a blend of sixty per cent Kékfrankos and forty per cent Cabernet Franc and Cabernet Sauvignon. At the moment, the weakest part of his winemaking is that he cannot put all the red wines of any one vintage into barrels at the same time. They are, therefore, shuffled between stainless steel and wood so that they all get the same amount of wood maturation in the end. Except for the Cabernet Sauvignon, which is completely matured in barriques, each variety is then blended to eliminate differences between the lots.

I have to say that after the miraculous 1994 vintage, Vincze's wines appear to me to have taken a dip. The 1997 Bikavér and Cabernet Franc were tart and acidic, the latter with green tannins (the problem of bought-in fruit). Happily, the 1999 vintage brought him back on form with a stunning Cabernet Franc, showing rich fruit and depth.

OTHER WINE PRODUCERS

Bakondi Endre (Bakondi Pincészet). H–3300 Eger, Verőszala u. 18. Tel: +36–36 429197. *Egri Csillagok Szövetkezet.* H–3300 Eger Verőszala u. 21. Tel/fax: +36–36–471559. *Ker-Coop Borászati Kft.* H–3351 Verpelét, Dózsa Gy. út 3/1. Tel: +36–36 494037; Tel/fax: +36–36 359053. *Lauder-Láng Pincészet.* H–3300 Eger, Verőszala u. 80. Tel: +36–36428796. *Lörincz Pince.* H–3394 Egerszalók, Jókai út 28. E-mail: lgyorgy@agria.hu. *Monarchia Borászati Kft.* H–1092 Budapest, Kinizsi u. 30–36. Tel: +36–1 456 9800. Fax: +36–1 456 2726. *Ostoros-Bor Borászati Szövetkezet.* H–3326 Ostoros, Nagyvölgy u. 2. Tel: +36–36 356044. Tel/fax: +36–36 356178. *Simon József (Simon Pincészet-Síkhegy Kft).* H–3300 Eger, Nagykőporos 80. Mobile: +36–209 412948. Fax: +36–36 356028. *Tóth Ferenc.* H–3300 Eger, Dr Nagy J. u. 20. Tel: +36–314973. *Vitavin Kft (Szőlőtermelő Feldolgozó és Kereskedelmi).* H–3324 Felsőtárkány Pf. 8. Tel/fax: +36–36 434221

Endre Bakondi, until 1998 the director of the city's agricultural department, began making wine in 1978 and started to sell it privately in 1985. He has six hectares and a simply equipped cellar. Until 2000, he produced only Bikavér, but in 2001 he also made a white, Cuvée Regina (Leányka and Királyleányka), sold under the Monarchia label. The components of Bakondi's Bikavér are Kékfrankos (largest), Cabernet (Sauvignon and Franc vinified together in an open vat), Bibor Kadarka, Merlot, and Blauburger. Unlike other producers, Bakondi assembles his blend after clarification, but before putting it into wood. There are no barriques. It is matured for one year in 125-litre barrels made by his father; in new 800-litre oak casks for another year or, exceptionally, two; and finally for a year after bottling. The result is an elegant and harmonious Bikavér, with well-knit wood and fruit, but a shade lighter than is usual.

Simon Pincészet is a family company that started in 2000. Production relies largely on bought-in grapes, although yields are limited to fifty-six hectolitres per hectare. Vinification equipment is a mixture of stainless steel, plastic, and open fermenters. Red wines are left with skin contact for up to forty days, and are matured in wood. Barriques are used only once (and thereafter for storage). Bikavér, made from two differing blends (correlated with the source of the fruit), is matured in one hundred- and 120-hectolitre casks. The first blend is Kékfrankos (fifty per cent), Cabernet Franc (ten per cent), Kékoportó (thirty per cent), and Cabernet Sauvignon (ten per cent). The second is Kékfrankos (forty-five per cent), Cabernet Franc (thirty per cent), Kékoportó (ten per cent), and Merlot (fifteen per cent). The components are aged together for a minimum of one year in wood and six months in bottle. Sixty per cent of production is sold in bulk – to Promontobor – and forty per cent is bottled for sale to restaurants and supermarkets. The wines I have tasted have strikingly attractive fruit appeal.

Vitavin, a partnership between Károly Juhász (an ex-Egervin wine-maker) and Gábor Kis, was started in 1990. A winery and separate bottling plant were built in 1999. The company rents thirty hectares of vineyards, controls a further one hundred through five sub-companies, and also buys must. Fermentation equipment is neither elaborate nor modern, but clearly adequate. The firm has a market for just over 1 million bottles, and it has the capacity to process and bottle this amount (although storage capacity is at the moment insufficient). The entire production is bottled, and sixty-five per cent is exported. There are two ranges: the first consists of medium-quality commercial wines; the second consists of premium wines, such as the 1997 fruit-driven, New World-style Bikavér, which can be impressive.

Despite the misleading implication of the name, Ker-Coop Borászati is not a cooperative but a private company founded in 1991. Its very well-equipped winery – with specially designed cylindrical red fermenters, as deep as they are broad – was built in 1993, and expanded in 2000. This is the biggest wine producer in the Debrő district, traditionally famous for its Hárslevelű, and it is participating in a research programme on this variety. Three-fifths of the production, partly from its directors' forty hectares of producing vineyards, is of white wine. Top wines, intended for restaurants, are the Gál Lajos Selection, and others are distributed through supermarkets. Half is exported. With its new technical equipment and the advice of its consultant, Gál Lajos, there is surely considerable potential here.

György Lőrincz, a young oenologist and cellar-master at Egervin, runs his own company, which he started in 1999. With 1.3 hectares planted, he is beginning to build up his vineyard holding. Like the wines he makes for Egervin, he favours quite a big style and makes impressive open-fermented wines partly matured in new oak, with good colour and structure, and a rich berry character.

GIA makes the wines (under contract in its own cellar) that Lauder-Láng uses in its Budapest restaurant Gundel's, including a Bikavér, Cabernet Sauvignon, and a Chardonnay. There are two ranges: Black Quality, and Gold Premium. I find them over-light and rather commercial.

The Egri Csillagok Cooperative suffers from lack of capacity, necessitating short fermentations at 24°C for white wines, and 40°C for reds. The firm is the largest Hungarian bulk exporter to Poland. ("Poland will buy any wine so long as it is semi-sweet.") Not one of Eger's glories, nor ever likely to be.

Formed from the combination of two local cooperatives in 1974, Ostoros-Bor Cooperative buys grapes from the 500 hectares of its 300 members. Two-thirds of production (15,000 hectolitres) are of Table and Country Wine, which are sold in bulk to national producers, the remainder (Quality Wine) being bottled and sold to supermarkets. Diminishing profitability makes life difficult, but there is a ten-year improvement plan, and the cooperative is converting itself into a closed shareholder company. The wines are above the general average, but unremarkable.

Monarchia Borászati (q.v.), diversifying its activities, has acquired the Pók-Polónyi cellar and twenty hectares at Eger (ten on Tekenőhát, ten on Egedhegy), to be planted with local varieties in 2002. It will come to the market initially with the 2000 vintage, made from bought-in grapes by Pók, its winemaking director.

MÁTRAALJA

6,844 hectares: 5,869 white, 975 red
Twenty-five wine communities, with 15,308 members

Mátraalja, surpassed in size only by Kunság and larger than Tokaj-Hegyalja, is the second-largest of Hungary's wine regions. It is also, in terms of quality, one of the most disappointing. Only a handful of producers make really interesting wines, and a few manage to make the worst wines I have come across in Hungary: concoctions to which any connection with the grape seems totally alien. In between, the majority produce pleasant enough wines, undemanding and perfectly drinkable, but of a rather low average standard. Their natural home is where they are often found – on the lower shelves of Hungarian supermarkets.

It is also the region in which, even more than Kunság perhaps, outworn, dated, and badly maintained vinification plant is still widely in use. One cooperative I have visited, which I shall not embarrass by naming, inspired the following note:

> *"Its 1960s technology (although the machines are not that old) remains as an example of how appalling fermentation facilities can still be in Hungary. When I suggested to its staff that it should be kept as a museum, there was amused agreement. I have to add that this was perhaps the dirtiest cooperative I have ever seen. Only a camera, not words, could adequately portray the crumbling concrete, the rusting metal, the flaking paintwork, the caked dirt in crevices and corners, the begrimed old rubber hoses used to move the wine around, the general corrosion and the air of utter decay; and only a camera could record the state of this machinery. Given that the harvest had ended several weeks earlier, it had still not been given even the most elementary cleaning. It is simply amazing that anything remotely potable can be made in such conditions, and I was continually reminding myself as I went over the building that alcohol is a powerful antiseptic."*

Gyöngyös, at the heart of the region, is a pleasant, small town, although it lacks the immediate appeal of some of the more picturesquely baroque towns in Hungary. To its west are vineyards surrounding various villages incorporating the town's name; to the east, the wine villages stretch as far as the Eger region, in a landscape dominated by the ugly electricity generating station at Vécs. All are on the gentle southern slopes (300 to 600 metres/975 to 1,950 feet) that form the foothills of the Mátra range (the highest point of which is Kékeshegy at 1,014 metres/3,296 feet), and receive protection from northern winds. There are extensive state plantings on a series of ridges on Öreghegy, stretching southwest from Nagyréde.

Little summer residences have replaced vineyards on the Gyöngyössolymos side of the Sárhegy, which stretches north from Gyöngyös, but the southwestern slopes of the Sárhegy, overlooking Abasár and Markaz, are still reckoned the best for vines in the area, although their upper parts were abandoned in 1960 and have still to be reclaimed. Some areas have vineyards with remarkable micro-climates, like the Cserepes vineyard in Gyöngyöspata, recognized as one of the best in the region. A few others have microclimates resembling conditions in Tokaj, so late-harvest wines are possible, though not common. These do not, however, justify a general increase in the proportion of red varieties being planted in the region. In Markaz, for example, Zweigelt and Kékfrankos musts do not usually reach sugar levels of more than 16.5°, and invariably have to be chaptalized (the term for having sugar added). I cannot, therefore, accept that this is really red-wine country. The soil is a mixture of clay, sandy loess, and volcanic tufa, giving a wide range of mineral elements very suitable for the production of good white wines.

There are still six old-style wine-producing cooperatives in Mátraalja, one of which was recently privatized. They were formed in 1959–60. In the mid-1980s, the cooperatives began to plant new vineyards with wide rows, although until then, narrow traditional rows of vines were still standard. Varieties that most people now wish to be rid of, such as Zalagyöngye and Rizlingszilváni, were then widespread. However, Olaszrizling is now becoming quite widely grown, and Ottonel Muskotály and Tramini provide fast-selling popular wines, while a certain amount of Chardonnay has made its appearance. Most cooperatives export must from their least-desirable varieties to eastern markets for the thinnest of profits, and save their better varieties for their own wine.

The region has interesting cellars. The Haller Pince was created by a Habsburg general called Samuel Haller, and it was built between 1736 and 1746 by 130 French prisoners of war. It continued to belong to the

Haller family until the Second World War, and is the longest straight cellar in middle Europe, having a length of 542 metres (1,762 feet). Along this cellar there are 170 one-hundred-hectolitre wooden barrels (now, alas, filled with water).

Abasár is a typical old village, founded in 1042 by Aba Samuel, the third king of Hungary, who is credited with first planting grapes in the region. Cellars in the village row have small, almost undetectable, inter-communicating holes made during the Second World War to enable people hiding in the cellars to make contact with each other. Most remarkable of all, however, is the 3,000 square-metre (32,280 square feet) complex of twenty-six mainly interconnecting cellars just outside Gyöngyös, partly used by Farkasmályi Bor. Originally fashioned by hand out of tufa and granite in 1783, they sheltered hundreds of families from local fighting in 1944.

Unlike its high-profile neighbouring Eger, Mátraalja is only beginning to awaken to modern realities. Its wine route covering thirteen villages is still rather undeveloped, but encouragingly, mutually supportive group-ings of growers and producers are starting up. Apart from the one organized by Sándor Koncsos, which is described below, I can report another initiative by István Kovács, a local vinicultural consultant, who is trying to form an association of Gyöngyöspata winemakers to promote exports. Slowly, things are beginning to look up.

SZŐKE MÁTYÁS

H–3036 Gyöngyöstarján, Jókai tér 28. Tel: +36–37 372008. *(a)* Mátyás Szőke. *(b)* 30ha: Ch 6ha; OM 5ha; Sk 4ha; Kir 2.5ha; Or 1.5ha; T 1.5ha; Kf 6ha; CS 4ha. *(c)* 4,000hl. *(d)* Zoltán Szőke. *(e)* Varietals. *(f)* 35% (Switzerland, Germany, Netherlands, and Brazil)

Szőke's parents were once the biggest wine producers in the Gyöng-yöstarján area, but he himself trained as a mechanical engineer. After his son Zoltán graduated in both viticulture and viniculture at Budapest, they decided in 1990 to restart the family business. The family cellar was much extended in 2000, by which time their original two hectares had grown to thirty. These are south-facing and productive, nineteen hectares having been planted by Szőke himself with a density of 3,330 vines per hectare and an eighty-centimetre-high (thirty-one-inch-high) cordon. The old plantations are being changed from Lenz Moser to umbrella training. Nonethless, Szőke does have to buy in a quarter of his grape requirements, and he has integration contracts with four large producers. The winery has extremely up-to-date equipment. The fermentation hall, with German equipment, is underground, the stainless-steel tanks doubling as holding tanks for the big bottling line installed in 1999. All wines are fermented reductively under computer control. Adjacent to the fermentation hall is a barrique store. Wines spend one year in barrel, and each (Kádár) barrique is used only once to treat the wine, after which it is used purely as a storage cask. This is an almost uniquely luxurious approach to barrique technology – and not just in Hungary.

At the moment, Szőke produces eleven kinds of varietal – including Cabernet Sauvignon, which he regards as a technological challenge – but thinks that he should reduce the range to those wines he finds easiest to sell. A cuvée made an appearance in 2001 – a concession to the market, because Szőke dislikes them. "I like to taste the character of the grape," he says. Szőke's wines are well-known in Hungary, and are distributed through two Budapest agents and to hotels, restaurants, and wine shops. They show considerable consistency of quality, with rich, deep flavours and (in 2000, certainly) excellent rounded acids. They are undoubtedly the best in the area, rivalled only by the best from Szőlőskert.

SZŐLŐSKERT RT

H–3214 Nagyréde, Gyöngyösi út 1. Tel/fax: +36–37 373162, 373399.
(a) Undisclosed number of shareholders. (b) None. (c) 80,000–90,000hl.
(d) Benjámin Bárdos. (e) Varietals, rozé, cuvées. (f) 70% (Germany, the UK, Sweden, Finland, Japan, the US, Benelux, Switzerland, and Greece)
Wine records in Nagyréde, a village in the southwest of the region from which the first prince of Transylvania originally came, go back as far as 1275. Phylloxera was particularly severe here, and between the world wars a local grafting industry was so successful that former day-labourers became wealthy farmers. A cooperative, the predecessor of Szőlőskert, was formed in 1959. At its peak, it had between 800 and 1,000 members with 3,000 hectares, of which 1,000 were vineyards. In 1990, the cooperative sold about 90,000 hectolitres of wine, and graft production reached four million a year. In 1999, the firm stopped being a co-operative and became a limited share company, the shareholders being its

former members. This alone indicates that, against the trend of the 1990s, Nagyréde turned itself into a success story. Various factors contributed to this: the cohesive, industrious character of the villagers themselves; the intelligent and innovative leadership of the management; and diversification of activities, such as its deep-frozen fruit (raspberries) and vegetables division, and the provision of vineyard services. The production of rootstocks and grafts, however, has been discontinued.

Szőlőskert purchases all of its grapes – ninety per cent of them white – from an area of approximately 800 hectares within a radius of four to five kilometres (three to four miles). There are five-year integration contracts with 500 growers in the neighbourhood of the winery, regarded by the company as the foundation of stable, quality-oriented grape production. The winery is adapted to regional conditions, and sixty per cent of production is from Chardonnay, Szürkebarát (from the largest single block in Hungary), Ottonel Muskotály, Rizlingszilváni, and Tramini. Hungarian varieties such as Leányka, Zenit, and Hárslevelű are largely sold on the domestic market, only because they are difficult to sell abroad.

The company makes both reductive styles, directed towards the UK market, and wines using overripened grapes for Germany. Since 1993, there has been a consultancy agreement with Kym Milne, who visits and instructs the local winemakers, and from time to time the company has employed other flying winemakers. Szőlőskert values direct contact with its customers and tries to meet their changing requirements; by the time of the harvest, it knows seventy per cent of the final buyers of the vintage.

The winery has excellent modern technology, equalling the best to be found in other large-scale Hungarian wineries. As at Balatonboglár, one hundred per cent clear white musts are obtained by means of flotation separation (instead of sedimentation), and the must undergoes computer-controlled fermentation for ten days at from 14°C to 20°C, depending on variety. New wines are immediately cleaned, but to the minimal degree possible to maintain aromas and fruitiness. Nitrogen or CO_2 is used for all treatments. Two technologies are used for making the red wine. The first, used for Cabernet Sauvignon and Cabernet Franc, is standard tank fermentation, allowing skin contact for ten to fourteen days. There is only a small capacity for doing this kind of fermentation. The other involves flash heating of the grapes and "cooking" them at 40°C prior to pressing, as described in Chapter Four. Only five per cent of the 100,000-hectolitre storage capacity is in wood, the rest being in stainless steel in a climatized storage hall. Some Chardonnay and Cabernet Sauvignon are matured in barriques – half French, half Hungarian.

The bottling line minimizes oxgyen contact with the wine, and the ISO 9000 quality system is used. Seventy per cent of all production is exported; that to English-speaking markets goes through an export company, Montrade, which is partly owned by Szőlőskert, but in which Hungarovin and Balatonboglár also have shares. On the domestic market, sixty per cent is sold through supermarkets, while forty per cent goes to restaurants and wine shops. Top of the range is the Selected Wines label, made from grapes purchased from one grower, or from a particular slope producing the highest quality.

The future aim of the company is to develop its technology to increase volume without sacrificing quality. The company will probably not go public, because it would prefer to remain one hundred per cent Hungarian-owned. The wines are all of a good supermarket standard, and sometimes a lot better than that. I particularly like a barrel-aged Szürkebarát-Zenit blend made for Tesco.

DANUBIANA BT

H–3200 Gyöngyös, Karácsondi u. 11. Tel: +36–37 313096; Fax: +36–37 313098. Manager: Sándor Keresztes. For further details, see under this firm's main entry in Chapter Nine (Tolna)

Danubiana runs two wineries in Hungary. This one, in Gyöngyös, is solely for making white wine. The site was purchased from the Gyöngyös-Domoszló State Farm in 1994, and a newly equipped winery was constructed in 1995. This has resulted in a very modern set-up, the only problem being that it is already too small for the company's needs. Its fermentation capacity is 28,000 hectolitres, and there is a total storage capacity of 105,000 hectolitres. However, in 2000 the winery crushed 11,000 tonnes, and so really requires a total capacity of 150,000 hectolitres. The company, which has no vineyards of its own, buys the produce of 300 hectares in Mátra (as grapes, not must).

Vinification procedures are fairly standard. Some varieties are macerated, and some not. Must is protected by CO_2 in snow form, settled for up to forty hours, then fermented at computer-controlled temperatures of from 16°C to 18°C. Must concentrates are also made to supply sweet wine to the German market. The old cellar, directly below the bottling line, has extensive stainless-steel storage, and a new air-conditioned cellar can be used to induce malolactic fermentation. A barrel store, with a capacity of 1,000 hectolitres, is used to mature red wines brought from the firm's other winery at Bonyhád. Experiments in maturing Chardonnay and Szürkebarát in Hungarian, French, and American barriques are in progress. Wines from Gyöngyös are bottled first in order to make room for wines from Bonyhád, which are also bottled here.

GILIÁN JÓZSEF
H–3200 Gyöngyös, Kohári út 1–3. Manager: János Rákóczi. For further details, see under this firm's main entry in Chapter Eight (Hajós-Baja)

In 2000, Gilián rented a winery in Gyöngyös, formerly operated by a now-bankrupt company called Vinimax. Dating from 1906, the winery, with its fine, classical French façade, originally belonged to a stock company, the Gyöngyös-Visontai Szövetkezet, set up in 1897 in the wake of phylloxera. It rejoiced in the name of "First Hungarian Wine Palace". Between the wars, the firm produced 40,000 hectolitres a year, all exported to Europe, but went bankrupt in 1939. In 1949, it became part of the Gyöngyös-Mátra Region Farm Cellar.

A previous deputy director of Szőlőskert and part owner of Vinimax, János Rákóczi now manages exclusively white-wine production for Gilián. Vinimax operated at about the same level as Szőlőskert and Danubiana, and the plant is typical of an old cooperative, but has been fairly well-maintained. It has a fermentation capacity of 20,000 hectolitres.

The wines made in 2000 for Gilián were all very marketable, and considerably above the quality level of those he makes at Hajós Baja. Gilián has plans to buy the winery, and is, in my opinion, fortunate to have found Rákóczi as his winemaker.

KONCSOS BT (KONCSOS SÁNDOR)
H–3264 Kisnána. Tel: +36–37 324018. (a) Sándor Koncsos. (b) 2.2ha: Kf/CF/Or/Rs/OM. (c) 50hl. (d) Sándor Koncsos. (e) Varietal, cuvées (in 2000). (f) None

Kisnána, a little village between Domoszló and Verpelét with a picturesque ruined castle, nestles in a dip at the foot of the Mátra range. Here the mayor, Sándor Koncsos, has drawn the three other commercial producers in the village into a loose alliance. They are Ferenc Borsos, Jenő Lizák, and József Gyetvai. They avoid duplication in their combined range of wines so as to offer the public as wide a selection as possible, and all four market their wines under a uniform label. Oddly, however, they do not all use the same distributor, thereby lessening, one would think, the potential impact of the shared label. I only know Koncsos's wines, which are light and sound, if not hugely exciting. The point is, however, that this sort of cooperation is all too rare in Hungary, but might, if copied, be the salvation of many small and worthy producers.

OTHER WINE PRODUCERS

Abasári Borászati Szövetkezet. H–3261 Abasár, Fő u. 179. Tel: +36–37 360016; Fax: +36–37 360080. *Barátság Mezőgazdasági Szövetkezet Detk–Gyöngyöstarjáni Borászati Üzeme (Haller Pince).* H–3036 Gyöngyöstarján, Petőfi S. u. 2. Tel: +36—37 372010; Fax: +36—37 375022. *Béres-Deák Ferencné Pincéje.* H–3035 Gyöngyöspata, Arany út 10. Tel/fax: +36–37 364012. *Dér István és Fia (Dér Pince).* H–3261 Abasár, Fő u. 79. Tel+36–37 360691. *Farkasmályi Bor Kft (Orczy Pince).* H–3200 Gyöngyös, Farkasmály. Tel: +36–37 311148/309194. *Kiss Család Borászata (Kiss Sándor).* H–3261 Palosvörösmart, Rákóczi u. 15. Tel: +36–373 360211. *Kovács Ferenc (Kovács Pince).* H–3262 Markaz, József Attila u. 6. Tel/fax: +36–37 363657. *Ludányi József Pincéje.* H–3036 Gyöngyöstarján, Rákóczi u. 56. Tel: +36–37 372303. *Mátra Kincse Szövetkezet.* H–3200 Gyöngyös, Szurdokpart u. 9. Tel: +36–37 312441; Fax: +36–37 311678. *Mátragyöngye Mezőgazdasági Szövetkezet.* H–3263 Domoszló, Deák tér 12. Tel: +36–37 365220; Fax: +36–37 365236. *Mátravölgye Szövetkezet Markaz.* H–3262 Markaz, Mikes út 5–7. Tel/fax: +36–37 328133/131. *Navin Bt (Németh Pince).* H–3036 Gyöngyöstarján, Damjanich u. 4. Tel/fax: +36–37 372027. *Solybor Kft.* H–3231 Gyöngyössolymos, Szabadság u.118. Tel: +36–37 370007. *Vinum 93 Kft.* H–3035 Gyöngyöspata, Rákóczi Major. Tel/fax: +36–37 364501/564002. *Visontai Mezőgazdasági Szövetkezet.* H–3271 Visonta, Sport u. 2. Tel: +36–37 360010/621; Fax: +36–37 360081

The fifteen-hectare rootstock nursery of the Abasári Borászati Szövetkezet is now the largest in Hungary and produces 1.5 million grafts a year. The Mátragyöngye MGTSZ just manages to keep its head above water; despite paying dividends, it finances improvements by making charges for its services. The Visontai MGTSZ sells fifteen per cent of its seventy members' grapes to a large producer, and from the rest, using middling equipment, it makes must and very light but clean wine for sale in bulk at home and abroad.

Mátravölgye Szövetkezet in Markaz was formed in 1960, and became one of the five most successful Hungarian cooperatives by the end of the 1980s. Damaged by competition from fake wine after 1993, it embarked on a loan-based improvement programme, but came close to bankruptcy in 1999 when wine sales became insufficient to service the loan. At the eleventh hour, in 2000, it was salvaged when it found three Hungarian investors to take eighty per cent of its shares.

The Barátság MGTSZ Detk–Gyöngyöstarjáni Borászati Üzeme, more briefly the Haller Pince, was formerly part of the Mátraaljai Egyesült MGTSZ, Gyöngyöstarján. Its purchase by the Detk Cooperative, made possible by the disposal of surplus buildings to an open-cast mining company, makes this a rare but not unique example of one cooperative acquiring another. Having had a HUF200 million (£480,000) facelift to its technology, it produces reductive white wine, all of which is sold in bulk. The profit from export sales is a mere HUF3 to HUF5 (about a British penny) a litre, despite this being fresh, well-made wine, far above the local average.

Navin is a family firm run by András and Attila Németh (father and son). András, once director of Mátraaljai Egyesült MGTSZ, favours open fermentation of red grapes with their stalks to give the wine structure. Attila, with experience of winemaking in California, also wants to recreate the heavier style of red wine he remembers from youthful experience of the cooperative's museum stocks. In my opinion, their musts do not have the weight, concentration or full ripeness to benefit from this technique. Much better are their reductively made, cask-matured white wines, a barrel-fermented Chardonnay with an almost Burgundian style being specially impressive.

Solybor is an enterprising, and apparently financially secure, company with 130 hectares of vineyards. A very sophisticated new winery built in 1998 produces light and elegant reductive wines geared to domestic market demand. Future plans are directed at the post-EU entry era when, having secured its home market, the company intends to improve quality for export sales.

Vinum 93 is an undercapitalized company with poor facilities that got started in a hand-to-mouth sort of way. Large-scale exports of must generate sufficient cash flow to purchase enough grapes for the business to be viable, and to enable Istvánné Marozsán, its talented but frustrated winemaker, to make some quite decent white. Farkasmályi Bor buys grapes for vinification by other wineries, and then matures the wine in its amazing cellars.

BÜKKALJA

1,504 hectares: 1,072 white, 432 red
Fifteen wine communities, with 3,566 members

Bükkalja is one of the least-known wine regions of Hungary. It adjoins the Eger region, and runs eastwards as far as Miskolc. However, although Bükkalja is adjacent to Eger, both its soil and its climate are different. The soil is adobe and loess with an appreciable tufa and lime content. The Bükk Mountains protect the area from north winds, and their southern slopes are the most suitable for grape-growing. The best part of the region is said to be the valley running north from Bogács. However, even here climatic conditions are far from ideal. Must sugar levels in Tibolddaróc, for example, rarely exceed 17° (even in 2000), so chaptalization is usual. When there is rain (the annual average being 523 millimetres/twenty inches), the red varieties tend to have high acidity and are very prone to botrytis, which is a considerable problem in the region. It is one of the reasons why growers harvest too early.

Little wine here gets bottled, and most of the growers either make hobby wine, or sell grapes to big producers. Two thirds of the wine in the region is white. Bogács has a cellar row in a picturesque setting, with some cellars decked out like bars or cafés, because for the last ten years, the village has held an international wine festival – the Bükinvest – attended in 2000 by upwards of 20,000 people.

I would be less than honest not to admit that I have never found a single wine I unreservedly liked here. Bükkalja, for me, is the natural habitat of crawling wines. The extraordinary levels of rasping, aggressive, mouth-wrenching acidity would be hard to imagine by anyone who has never experienced them. When I have commented on this, I have been told that rhyolite and tufa give high acidity. So, I was tempted to add, do unripe grapes. Wines like this are difficult to drink, even out of politeness; I often had to compose my face muscles in order not to flinch visibly.

MEZEI PINCÉSZET

H–3421 Tibolddaróc, Széchenyi u. 3–5. Tel: +36–49 337035; Tel/fax: +36–76 360121. *(a)* Mihály Mezei. *(b)* 32ha of which 12ha are new: Ch/Or/CF/PN/Sz. *(c)* 300hl. *(d)* Mihály Mezei. *(e)* Varietials and rozé. *(f)* None

Mihály Mezei, one of the owners of Darócvin and a former director of wine production in the state winery at Izsák, came to Tibolddaróc in 1992. He bought a ruined cellar – a plaque above the door announces that it belonged to Josef Schmitt in 1861 – and seventy hectares of vineyards. Of these, twenty-six have been grubbed up, twelve had been replanted by spring 2001, and thirty-two are yielding. The cellar has been meticulously restored and houses very adequate, quite modern fermentation equipment. Wines are made reductively in stainless-steel tanks with temperature-control and pump-over facilities. Four nearby cellars house a total wood capacity of 6,000 hectolitres, and a new bottling line was installed in 2000. The white wine and Kékoportó are matured in wooden casks for one year, while Kékfrankos and Zweigelt get two years. Despite his sophisticated equipment (the best I know of in the region), all of Mezei's wines that I have tasted suffer from the extreme tartness characteristic of the region.

OTHER WINE PRODUCERS

Darócvin Kft. H–3423 Tibolddaróc, Széchenyi u. 5. Tel: +36–49 337400. *Fekete Rudolf–Fekete Családi Pincészet.* H–3412 Bogács, Ady Endre u. 13. Tel: +36–49 334315. *Hórvölgye MG Szövetkezet.* H–3412 Bogács, Alkotmány út 45. Tel: +36–49 334111. Tel/fax: +36–49 334039. *Prokai László.* H–3412 Bogács, Felszabadítók u. 46. Tel: +36–49 334004

Prokai works in the construction industry. He started with one hectare in 1993, making wine for friends, and now has four hectares. White wines are fermented in closed plastic tanks, without temperature-control, after having spent twenty-four hours in open fermenters. Red wine is fermented in open containers for from eight to ten days, reaching a temperature of 30°C. Prokai's biggest success was with a 1999 Czerszegi

Fűszeres, which won him a national gold medal, and none of his other wines comes close in quality.

The Hórvölgye MG Szövetkezet was formed by the amalgamation in 1970 of four separate cooperatives started in 1961. It has 348 members in the villages of Bogács, Bükkzsérc, Cserépfalu, and Szomolya, and is the only cooperative making wine in Bükkalja. All of the 15,000 hectolitres production is sold in bulk, over half of it to Hungarovin for sparkling wine. The rest is sold either in Hungary, or to countries like the Czech Republic and Canada. Profits are reinvested in much-needed technological improvement.

The Fekete family have made wine for themselves for hundreds of years. Currently they have four hectares, one of which is in Olaszliszka in Tokaj. Rudolf Fekete, who makes the wine by traditional methods, is keen to expand their production by targeting the unexploited tourist market. The amount produced (ninety hectolitres) is limited by cellar capacity, and none of the wine is bottled.

Darócvin is a service company that makes wine for clients, in addition to other activities like plant-protection services. There are three owners, all of whom also make wine on their own account. The company acquired a cellar belonging to the Rákóczi Agricultural Cooperative when it was privatized in 1992. One client takes forty per cent (5,000 hectolitres) of its entire production.

Bertalan Dusza, one of the owners of Darócvin, is keen to create a local cellar cooperative, because it is easier to sell wine than grapes. His cellar has a production capacity of 5,000 hectolitres, and will be at the disposal of a projected cooperative with fifty members.

12

Tokaj-Hegyalja

THE REGION

5,662 hectares: 5,659 white, three red
Twenty-one wine communities, with 15,137 members

Hegyalja is a word meaning "foothills", and Tokaj-Hegyalja is, as the name suggests, an area of gently rolling hills in the northeast of the country. It is a long, narrow strip of land with a southwest to northeast orientation, strung out for about sixty kilometres (thirty-seven miles) on either side of Route 37, connecting Szerencs in the south with Sátoraljaújhely on the Slovakian border in the north. It is effectively bounded to the northwest by the well-wooded Zempléni Hegység (the source of so much oak for barrels), and to the southwest by the line of the River Bodrog. On June 27, 2002, the World Heritage Committee meeting in Budapest declared the Tokaj region cultural landscape a world heritage site of outstanding universal value. Before the Treaty of Trianon reduced the size of Hungary, the Tokaj region extended a little further north to Szőlőske (Viničky) and Kistoronya (Malá Tŕňa), now part of Slovakia. To the dismay of Hungarian producers, a very inferior "Tokaji" which they consider detrimental to the reputation of their own wine is still produced there, but they have found themselves powerless to prevent it.

Tokaj is a small and charming town from which both the region and the wine get their name. Its previously important strategic position at the confluence of the River Bodrog with the larger River Tisza, and its situation at the foot of the large and vineyard-clad Kopaszhegy (512 metres/1,664 feet) – sometimes referred to as Tokaj Hill – doubtless brought it to prominence. There are, however, three other towns and twenty-three villages in the region – twenty-seven communities in all – of which the most important are Tarcal, Bodrogkeresztúr, Mád, Tállya, Tolcsva, Sárospatak, and Sátoraljaújhely.

It is not until the middle of the fifteenth century that we find references to Tokaji wine, but at this time it was quite certainly not the same kind of wine for which the region later became famous – that is, what the Hungarians call *Aszú* wine. This is wine made from aszú grapes, so called because not only have they overripened and shrivelled to become raisins, but they have in the process been attacked by a fungal disease called *Botrytis cinerea*, or botrytis for short. This fungus, an enemy to the maker of dry table wines, is a friend to the maker of sweet dessert wines. Botrytis is nurtured by damp conditions and accelerated by heat, and finds ideal circumstances for its develop-ment in the Hegyalja, where frequent autumnal morning mists and dew, to which the local rivers benignly contribute, are gradually dispelled by the midday warmth of the sun. As the fungus takes hold, the skin of the grapes in tight clusters frequently bursts, then the moisture evaporates and, as the grape shrivels, its sugar content becomes concentrated.

The Hegyalja has a climate of extremes: dry, hot summers; long, dry autumns; cold, snowy winters; late, relatively short springtimes. Annual precipitation averages 516 millimetres (twenty inches); the average number of sunshine hours is 2,007 per year, with around nine-and-a-half hours a day in the growing season. The annual average temperature is 9.7°C, ranging from 33.8°C down to −15°C.

The soil in the region is divided between loess, primarily on the slopes of Kopaszhegy at Tarcal, Tokaj, and Bodrogkeresztúr, and volcanic clay elsewhere. The top of Kopaszhegy remained unplanted after phylloxera, and the soil there has now been lost to erosion. The best vineyards in the region are on slopes of up to 200 metres (650 feet) above sea level with good exposure to the sun. As might be expected, the soil differences lead to wines of contrasting character. Grapes grown on vol-canic soil produce wines with higher acidity and more robust flavours than those made from grapes grown on loess, which tend to be more refined and elegant.

This is entirely a white-grape area. Until phylloxera struck, four

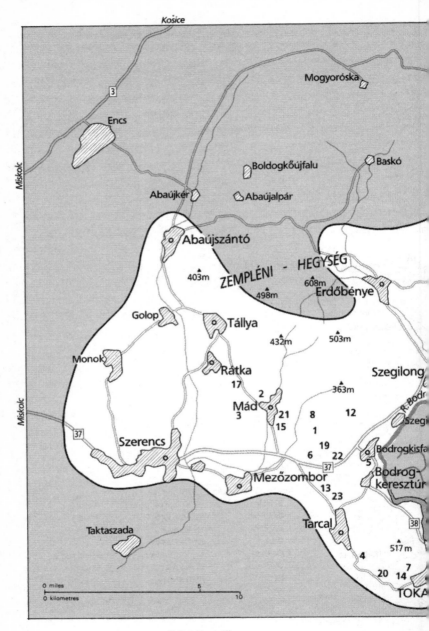

Tokaj-Hegyalja

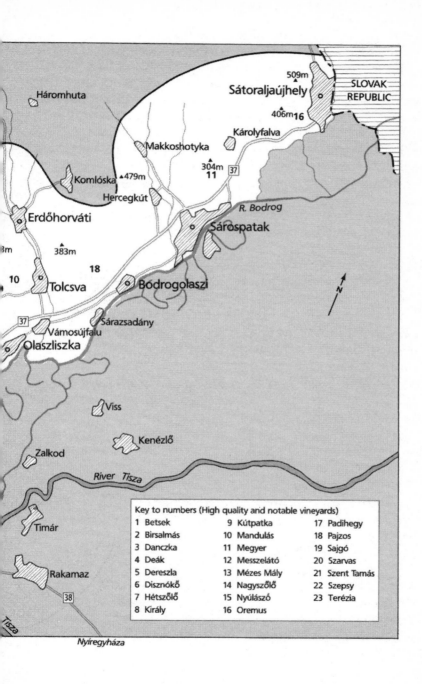

Háromhuta

509m
Sátoraljaújhely
SLOVAK
REPUBLIC
406m 16

Károlyfalva

Makkoshotyka

Komlóska ▲479m

304m
11   37

Hercegkút

Erdőhorváti

R. Bodrog

Sárospatak

383m

3m

18

10   Tolcsva   Bodrogolaszi

N

37   Sárazsadány

Vámosújfalu

Olaszliszka

Viss

Kenézlő

Zalkod

River Tisza

Tisza

Timár

Rakamaz

38

Tisza

Nyíregyháza

Key to numbers (High quality and notable vineyards)

1	Betsek	9	Kútpatka	17	Padihegy
2	Birsalmás	10	Mandulás	18	Pajzos
3	Danczka	11	Megyer	19	Sajgó
4	Deák	12	Messzelátó	20	Szarvas
5	Dereszla	13	Mézes Mály	21	Szent Tamás
6	Disznókő	14	Nagyszőlő	22	Szepsy
7	Hétszőlő	15	Nyúlászó	23	Terézia
8	Király	16	Oremus		

varieties were common: Furmint, Kövérszőlő, Hárslevelű, and Gohér. Today the recommended varieties are Furmint (the dominant variety), Hárslevelű (the next dominant), and Sárga Muskotály (which appeared in the area only in the twentieth century). Authorized varieties are Zéta, formerly called Oremus, and Kövérszőlő. Zéta became authorized in 1990, but has not become particularly popular with growers; Kövérszőlő has been authorized since 1998, but only a little has been planted, and it is not clear whether it will make much of a comeback. Gohér has also been arousing some curious interest recently, but has not yet been authorized, although it surely will be.

Furmint is the variety that gives Aszú its structure and its main character. It requires good drainage and is, therefore, grown mainly on upper slopes. Owing to the very tight clusters and skin contact between the grapes, botrytis spreads quicker on Furmint than on Hárslevelű, which has long and loose clusters. Hárslevelű requires moisture (otherwise it does not produce decent-sized berries), so it does best on middle or lower slopes, as does Sárga Muskotály. Sárga Muskotály tends to get botrytis earlier than the other varieties, when acid levels are still high and must sugar is not yet at its peak. In general, the region does not yet have enough Sárga Muskotály, although it is on the increase. Zéta is an early ripener and generally gives more aszú berries than Furmint, but makes a dull still wine. However, in conjunction with Furmint, it enhances the sweetness of the Aszú and gives it a creamier structure. In the older, widely spaced plantations, Lenz Moser and single-curtain are the most usual forms of trellising. In new plantations, Guyot (often in an adapted form) is popular.

The region is notable for its cellars, many of them carved out of tufa, the earliest examples of which date from the thirteenth century. Private cellars often consist of a single gallery varying in length between five and fifty metres (sixteen and 163 feet), and wide enough to have a row of casks along one or both sides. Coarse sand or gravel is commonly strewn on the floor and kept well-raked to detect intruders rather than for aesthetic reasons. Unlike other regions of Hungary, where cellars are characteristically built into a hillside, the cellars here are subterranean, with elaborate doors at ground level, beyond which a flight of stairs gives access. These doorways are often dotted rather irregularly along pathways and have a sepulchral quality, like the entrances to so many mausoleums. On a misty morning it is all too easy to imagine Dracula emerging from one of them.

Many small cellars were linked up during the second half of the twentieth century to make larger units, but the region also has many designedly large cellars. Notable among these is the fifteenth-century Rákóczi Cellar in the centre of Tokaj, which belongs to Hétszőlő and has a twenty-eight-metre (ninety-one-foot) long room where the Hungarian Diet met in 1526 and elected János Szapolyai as king. Tokaj Kereskedőház, on the other hand, has an immense modern cellar, largely constructed between 1968 and 1978 by a team of from twenty to eighty labourers working without tunnelling equipment. They used pneumatic drills, and finished off the last ten centimetres of the roof and walls by hand chiselling. There are five metres (sixteen feet) between the two levels of the cellar, thirty-six lateral passages, and the cellar has a total length of 4.5 kilometres (2.8 miles).

These cellars play an important part in the maturation of Aszú. What strikes the visitor most forcefully is the thick black fungus (white when young) that covers the walls and eventually, in a decorative way, the bottles. This is *Cladosporium cellare,* a wholly benign fungus that performs several useful functions such as cleaning the atmosphere and maintaining humidity, as well as killing potentially harmful airborne bacteria. (One French company, not understanding this, at first made the mistake of cleaning one of its cellars entirely of mould.) Most cellars have a humidity in excess of ninety per cent, which is one of the main reasons why bottles of Aszú can be stored standing up. It is, conversely, the reason why you should not keep bottles standing up in the under-stair cupboard of your centrally heated flat. Even in the humid conditions of these cellars, corks have to be changed periodically, and at least every twenty-five years.

A SHORT HISTORY

Tokaji Aszú is the crowning glory of Hungarian wine. Its worldwide fame, stretching back for centuries, has more than a hint of the exotic about it, due, no doubt, to the remoteness of the region it comes from, its former popularity with some of the most famous crowned heads of Europe, its almost superstitiously venerated reputation as a near-corpse reviver, and – not least – its awesome cost.

Nobody knows for certain when Aszú as we now know it became general in Tokaj. In the fifteenth century it was apparently a dry wine, but the records of vintage dates starting in the early sixteenth century suggest that picking took place late enough for the berries to have been shrivelled, if not botrytized. Tradition credits Laczkó Máté Szepsi with the discovery of Aszú (as a botrytized wine) in 1630 – some say 1633 – when, as the domestic priest of Zsuzsanna Lorántffy, wife of György Rákóczi, Prince of Transylvania, he postponed the vintage on Oremushegy at Sátoraljaújhely from fear of a Turkish attack. By the time the grapes were eventually picked, they had turned into aszú berries and, so the story goes, were made into the first Aszú wine. What is clear is that Aszú antedates 1630, although Szepsi appears to be the first person to have written about the method of producing it. What is far from clear is when the wine began to be made from botrytized rather than from merely shrivelled grapes.

The word *aszú* (meaning "desiccated") appears during the previous century in Balázs Fabricius Szikszay's *Nomenclatura*, published in 1590, but apparently written before 1576, and there is an even earlier reference to "fifty-two casks of Aszú grape wine" in a deed by Máté Garay in favour of his brother János, dated May 15, 1571, recently discovered by the historian István Zelenák.[1]

Records of bottles of alleged seventeenth-century Aszús abound. Fukier, a Polish company that had imported Tokaji since the sixteenth century, is said to have had 328 bottles of 1606 Aszú and several thousands of 1668, 1682, and other old vintages just before the Second World War. A bottle purporting to be 1646 Tokaji was auctioned by Sotheby's in 1984; another, from the Royal Saxon Cellar, thought to be the 1649 vintage, was auctioned by Christie's in 1968; and a bottle of the 1670 vintage is presently in the possession of Tokaj Kereskedőház. It certainly appears that Aszú was well-established by the seventeenth century.

What is also certain is that various enactments in 1641, 1655, and 1660 regulated the selection and maintenance of vineyards, the harvesting of aszú berries, and their exemption from taxation. By the end of the seventeenth century, a system of Aszú wine production had developed

[1] See Borbarát, Vol. 5, No. 4, Winter 2000, pp. 97–9.

that was so sophisticated it had given rise to a delimited classification of vineyards – arguably the first in the world. According to Antal Szirmay, in his book *Notitia topographica, politica, inclyti Comitatus Zempleniensis*, the classification was ordered by Ferenc Rákóczi II (the local landowner) in 1700. Whatever the truth of this – according to László Alkonyi, the classification was made by Mátyás Bél in 1730 – it gained legal status only through the national censuses of 1765 and 1772.[2]

The classification suffers substantially from the same drawback as the Pombaline Douro demarcations in eighteenth-century Portugal: namely, the impossibility of determining in many cases the precise geographical boundaries of the vineyards after the changes that have taken place over nearly two-and-a-half centuries (and more particularly since 1945). However, the classification was repeated in Szabó and Török's *Album of the Tokaj-Hegyalja* in 1867, and in many cases there is no problem in identifying vineyards associated with great estates, such as Szarvas, Hétszőlő, and Disznókő. It has recently been adopted by Tokaji Renaissance, a group of Tokaji producers, and is being used by an increasing number of them to identify the origin of their Aszú. The classification identifies two great first growths: Mézes Mály (north of Tarcal) and Szarvas (the imperial vineyard, belonging to the Austrian crown). The rest are divided into first, second, and third growths, of which some of the most important in the first category (in no particular order) are Disznókő, Hétszőlő, Nyúlászó, Nagyszőlő, Szent Tamás, Király, Betsek, Messzelátó, and Pajzos.

The success of Tokaji abroad was helped by special duty concessions not enjoyed by other Hungarian wines, and was doubtless stimulated also by its popularity with crowned heads as diverse as Peter the Great, Louis XIV, Frederick the Great, Maria Theresa, Catherine the Great, Emperor Franz Joseph, and Queen Victoria. From 1733 until 1800, the Russian court kept an agent in Bodrogkeresztúr to purchase Tokaji, supervised from St Petersburg by a Commission for Hungarian Wines, which maintained a troop of cossacks to guard its reserves.

Poland was traditionally the best market for Aszú, but at the end of the eighteenth century, political changes in that country, coupled with protectionist duties imposed by Austria on Hungarian pro-

[2] See Alkonyi, p. 172.

duce, especially after 1848, slowly undermined trade to the point that in 1853, a society called *A Tokaj-Hegyaljai Bormivelő Egyesület* (Viticultural Union of Tokaj-Hegyalja), was formed to promote the cause of Tokaji. Its efforts were themselves soon to be undermined by the onset of phylloxera in 1885, and just as recovery began to seem possible in the twentieth century, by the outbreak of hostilities in 1914.

Despite that, Tokaji continued to have a certain appeal on some markets. In England it was sold by Berry Bros & Rudd, who in 1933 published an unintentionally funny book to publicize the miraculous, death-cheating medical aspects of Esszencia, purporting to be letters from satisfied customers. Two examples will suffice to give a flavour of its delights:

Dear Mr Berry

Your Tokay has given me good nights . . . I have a wine glass nearly full . . . then the Masseuse Sister comes and rubs my back with a special liniment and I curl round like a contented pussy and go to sleep.

. . . Send immediately one case of the wine that removes the screws from the coffin lid.

Appended to the book is a list of the vintages of Esszencia then available, ranging from 1811 down to 1914, at from £3.60 down to £1.05 per half-litre.

The story of the Hegyalja under Communism follows a now-familiar pattern. State farms – those of Tokaj-Hegyalja, Tolcsva, and Abaújszántó – were consolidated through amalgamations in 1967 and 1974 into one huge organization called the *Tokajhegyaljai Állami Gazdaság Borkombinát* (Tokaj-Hegyalja State Farm Wine Combine). In addition, there were at one stage twenty-two cooperatives, but this was latterly reduced to six. The area the vineyards covered was around 7,400 hectares.

During the period of the Borkombinát, the quality of the Aszú was, to say the least, questionable. One of the winemakers of the period summed the matter up thus:

"To begin with, 'classical' winemaking continued to be practised, but in the 1970s and 1980s the big priority was to supply the Russian market. It was an 'easy' market – that is, uncritical and accepting – and what it

needed was vast quantities of sweet and semi-sweet wine. So, what nature did not supply to the winemakers, they had to achieve by technical means in order to create the requisite style. For example, when must sugar was below 19°, then must with sugar of 15° was concentrated until it got up to 19°. The trouble was that this concentrated the bad things as well, so the winemaker had to try to emphasize the good qualities. There were several levels of winemaking. The worst was the wine for the eastern market. The best was the wine that was exported to the west. But when small growers brought in good musts, these were selected to make the best quality on a serious level."

Privatization began seriously in 1991. The inclination of the government was to sell half of the entire Borkombinát to Unterberg, the Swiss-German consortium. András Bacsó, now manager of Oremus, fought this proposal, and was able to defeat it by a very narrow margin. He was immediately elected head of the Borkombinát by his fellow workers – an unofficial appointment that was later endorsed by the government, which told him to get on with privatization. Bacsó had, he says, no instructions on how to set about this task. In the end, he decided to reconstitute the old historical proprietary structure, creating estates of from forty to one hundred hectares, as well as small plots for small producers, which had also been a tradition of the region. Except for Bodrog-Várhegy and the Royal Tokaji Wine Company, this was the moment the first big international companies were founded, like Disznókő, Pajzos, and Oremus, to which the Borkombinát sold off plant, vineyards, cellars and wine stocks. This created a completely new situation. Suddenly, there were new companies, each with its own philosophy and no direct experience of Tokaji and its traditions – a veritable (and, it must be admitted, rather speculative) invasion of foreign investors attracted by the combination of the cheapness of land and the erstwhile fame of Tokaji. And with the new companies came new views about how Aszú should be made; the only thing on which they appeared to be agreed was that something had gone wrong during the period of the Borkombinát, and that the best way to make Aszú had to be rediscovered.

It may seem strange to the reader to learn that there could be doubts about how to make one of the classical wines of the world, but even now, ten years later, reputable winemakers will tell you: "We are still experimenting and trying to find out." Indeed, I have never heard the word "experiment" used quite as much as it is used in Tokaj.

THE WINES

Tokaji wines comprise four groups: (1) still table wine; (2) Szamorodni, which may be dry or sweet, and is made from a mixture of ordinary and aszú grapes; (3) wines made using aszú grapes called Esszencia and Aszú (which come in various degrees of sweetness), as well as two derivative wines, Fordítás and Máslás; (4) late-harvest and noble late-harvest wines, similar to those made elsewhere in the world. In this section, however, we deal with the first two and the fourth, leaving consideration of the third until the next section.

Still table wine. By far the greatest amount of wine made in the region is table wine, known locally as "dry wine" (to distinguish it from Aszú), even if it is on occasion only semi-dry. For convenience, the same convention is adopted in this chapter. Aszú berries always form a minuscule part of the vintage, leaving a vast amount of ordinary grapes to be made into dry wine. Although 2000 produced an abundant harvest of 1,458 tonnes of aszú berries, it also gave 33,156 tonnes of almost unsaleable ordinary berries. The trouble is that Tokaji dry Furmint, to be honest, does not at the best of times make a very attractive table wine. It is often made from unripe grapes, and is thin and acidic. Tokaji dry Furmint is, therefore, notoriously difficult to sell, and companies that do not have their own vineyards fight shy of it, apart from making a base wine for their Aszú. What to do with this surplus of grapes poses a tremendous problem – the more so, because the region needs the aszú and therefore has to accept the ordinary berries as the *quid pro quo*. A spokeman for Tokaji Renaissance, an organization of the main producers that promotes Tokaji and lobbies on their behalf, once remarked to me that "we have to consider dry wines, quite frankly, as a by-product of the Aszú wines". If dry wines were all that there were in Tokaj, no one would be remotely interested in making them.

In this situation, the state-owned company, Tokaj Kereskedőház, is constrained by the government to act as a buyer of last resort. In 1999 it received a special grant of HUF1,500 million (£3.6 million) to buy up surplus grapes. In 2000, the grant was even higher, at HUF2,500 million (£6 million). The Kereskedőház therefore purchased 11,700 tonnes, that is, thirty-five per cent of the 33,156 tonnes produced, giving it the headache of having to make and sell what is an almost unsaleable product.

Szamorodni. This wine, whose name is derived from Polish that means "as it comes", is something of a specialty. It is made from bunches of grapes with a variable percentage (up to about forty per cent) of over-ripened, shrivelled, and aszú berries in them, as they happen to come – what is left, in fact, after the main selections of aszú berries have been made. The bunches are pressed and allowed to macerate before being pressed again. The must is then fermented. According to the amount of sugar in the must, which in good vintages may be quite high, the must will either ferment out, providing a dry Szamorodni or, when enough residual sugar is left, a sweet Szamorodni.

Dry Szamorodni is treated differently from sweet Szamorodni. One maker (Szabó) racks it after it has stopped fermenting. After three months it is given a second racking, but the cask is left one-third empty. After another three months it is again racked, but this time the cask is completely filled again. This procedure is repeated until the wine reaches its optimum taste. Another maker (Bodnár) leaves the cask up to fifteen per cent empty for three months each year. Because the pH of the wine is very low, it can never become over-oxidized. While the barrel is partially empty, a very thin and incomplete film of *flor* (a floating yeast similar to that which forms on fino sherry) may appear on the surface of the wine – a phenomenon confined to dry Szamorodni. The resulting wine, which often has both a high dry extract and a high percentage of alcohol, has some of the nutty, sherry-like character of the *Vin Jaune* of Arbois, and a more or less oxidized taste. If not too oxidized, it can be a delicious aperitif.

Late-harvest wines. Late-harvest wines are not part of the Tokaji tradition – the first one appeared in 1995 – but the number of producers making them is on the increase. The custom used to be to pick grapes to make dry wines before aszú berries started to form. Among several companies, however, the tendency now is to leave grapes to overripen, and even to make the base wine for Aszú from the grapes that, after the aszú crop has been picked, were traditionally used for making Szamorodni.

This has encouraged the production of late-harvest and noble late-harvest wines. At least one firm – the Royal Tokaji Wine Company – disapproves of this, on the grounds that the region should have as its priority the single-minded re-establishment of the world reputation of Aszú. Adding Late-harvest wines to the spectrum of products, they argue, simply confuses the customer and distracts attention from Aszú. While this may have a grain of truth, nobody who has discovered the wonderful quality of the Tokaji late-harvest wines would wish to see them disappear.

ASZÚ GRAPES

Grapes are affected by botrytis individually, rather than as whole clusters, and they are individually picked by harvesters who make a pass through the vineyard up to three or even four times during a period of almost a month, traditionally starting between October 28 (SS Simon and Jude's Day) and November 11 (St Martin's Day). A good harvester can pick about ten kilograms (twenty-two pounds) of aszú berries a day, for which, in 2000, he would have been paid HUF230 (£0.55) an hour. The open market price for aszú berries in 2000 was between HUF1,200 (£2.88) and HUF1,500 (£3.60) per kilogram.

Almost every vintage will yield some aszú berries somewhere in the region. In 2000, aszú was plentiful in Tarcal (close to the River Tisza) but very scarce in Tállya (with minimal rainfall). However, in Tarcal acidity levels were low, while in Mád they were better. With everything dependent on unpredictable weather conditions, nothing can be taken for granted. In some years, some producers make no Aszú wine at all; Royal Tokaji, for example, made no Aszú in 2001. In good years, patient growers may expect between ten and twenty per cent of all their grapes to be affected by botrytis.

Aszú grapes are graded into three classes, established in 1979, for sugar content and quality. The following table explains how. Normally, between ten and fifteen per cent of aszú berries will be Class I; from sixty to seventy per cent Class II; and the remainder Class III. In 2000, an *annus mirabilis,* eighty-five per cent were Class I, and almost all the rest were Class II. Conidia are mould-like whiskers or fur on the surface of the grapes caused by *Botrytis cinerea.*

	Class I	Class II	Class III
Appearance	Chocolate brown	Chocolate brown	Brownish
Conidia	Partial	Less than Class I	None
Pulp	Yellow-brown without green. Greasy texture	Light brown without green	Yellow and green
Seeds	Yellow-brown without green	Light yellow	Yellow and green
Must sugar at 20°C	60%	50%	45 %
Mixture	100% Class I	5% Class III permitted	5% partially shrivelled permitted

THE MAKING OF ASZÚ

In this section we deal with the wines for which the region is most famous: Esszencia, Aszú, Forditás, and Máslás. Of these, quantitatively and commercially, Aszú is the most important. The others must rank as comparative rarities.

Esszencia. After harvesting, aszú berries are placed in containers, now generally made of stainless steel, with a perforated base. The berries begin to exude a heavy juice – almost a syrup – just from the weight of their pressing against each other. Class I berries may be kept for up to two months like this, but Class III berries, being less desiccated, cannot be kept as long. Traditionally, no pressure is placed on the aszú berries, although some older producers tread lightly over them wearing rubber boots to compact them and thereby reduce oxidation. Some producers additionally sprinkle them with a little sulphur, and cover the container to protect against vinegar flies and evaporation.

The nectar thus produced is Esszencia (or Natúr Esszencia), a name first documented in 1707. It is the easiest wine to produce in the whole world, because it makes itself. With a sugar content that can reach well in excess of 800 grams per litre, it barely ferments at all, and then only on its surface. Although this slight fermentation may continue for years, Esszencia seldom attains much more than four per cent alcohol. This is the supreme luxury product that became the gift of kings and emperors, aged in half-litre bottles for fifty or more years, during which the bouquet and flavours underwent a remarkable evolution of depth and complexity. Whether there is any limit to this development is not known, but it is clear that the high sugar and acid content of Esszencia makes it almost indestructible.

When young, however, Esszencia is something of a disappointment. It is opaque, with a heavy, viscous texture reminiscent of cod-liver oil, redolent of the pungent smell of botrytis and cooking orange marmalade, and intimidatingly sweet (for, although the acidity is high, this is completely masked by the high sugar level). People have been known to choke quite seriously on it. Esszencia is normally put into demijohns rather than wooden casks, although the Tokaji Kereskedőház has 1972 Esszencia – the vintage of the century – still in a wooden cask. In most cases, probably only a little will be stored away to be kept for eventual sale, or possibly to be offered to visitors to the winery as a curiosity, a final *bonne bouche*. Most, and sometimes all, will be ingloriously used to adjust and enrich blends of other Aszú wine. A lot of the mystique of Esszencia, it must be confessed, has now vanished. Even old, bottle-matured Esszencia can reveal the limitations of a wine that makes itself. A winemaker can achieve a proper balance of elements through his craft which blind nature, in its "take it or leave it" randomness, does not necessarily provide.

Aszú. There is now no standard way of making Aszú, but our starting point is the idea – a sort of primitive recipe – that lies behind the various methods employed today. Making allowances for over-simplification, which the qualifications and variations discussed below will correct, the basic idea is this. After Esszencia has been collected from the aszú grapes, they are made into a paste – traditionally by treading them, but usually now by using a mill with rubber rollers to avoid damaging the seeds. The paste is then added to a fixed amount of dry wine in which it is allowed to soak (to macerate) for a while. This mixture of dry wine and aszú paste is then pressed, and the resulting juice is put into oak casks and allowed to ferment naturally. (Commercial yeast is unusable because it cannot deal simultaneously with high alcohol and high sugar, so you do not get a smooth fermentation.)

The sweetness of the wine so produced (the Aszú) depends on the amount of paste added to the fixed amount of dry wine: the more paste, the sweeter the Aszú. The proportions were traditionally determined by adding various multiples of *puttonyos* to one *gönci* barrel of dry wine. A *puttony* is a traditional wooden harvesting hod that holds between twenty and twenty-five kilograms of paste (or of aszú berries), and a *gönc* or *gönci* barrel is a cask, named after the Hegyalja village in which it originated, which holds 136 litres of wine.

The currently recognized levels of sweetness are 3, 4, 5, and 6 *puttonyos*, the Hungarian plural for more than one puttony (although up to twelve were known in the past). However, above the level of Aszú made with 6 *puttonyos* of paste, but below Esszencia, there is an intermediate category called Aszú Esszencia – not to be confused with Esszencia (Natúr Esszencia). This is effectively the top grade of commercially available Tokaji Aszú, approximately equivalent to one made using eight *puttonyos* of paste. The number of *puttonyos* used appears on the label of each half-litre bottle of Aszú – except for Aszú Esszencia – as an indicator of its sweetness.

It will be immediately obvious that, as it stands, this traditional quantitative system of measurement is imprecise as a measure of sweetness, because the sweetness of the wine will vary according not only to that of the berries used to make the paste, but will be influenced by other factors such as the degree of alcohol of the dry wine base, and the length of maceration. Consequently, the different categories of Aszú have been standardized in terms of the legal minimum sugar content and the legal minimum dry extract content of the finished Aszú, while the notional number of *puttonyos* has been retained as an indicator. Thus:

	Sugar (g/l)	Extract (g/l)
Esszencia	250	50
Aszú Esszencia	180	50
6 *puttonyos* Aszú	150	45
5 *puttonyos* Aszú	120	40
4 *puttonyos* Aszú	90	35
3 *puttonyos* Aszú	60	30

At this point, it may be as well to mention other relevant legal limits. Total acidity must exceed seven grams per litre of tartaric acid; volatile acidity must be less than two grams per litre of acetic acid; free SO_2 must not exceed 60 milligrams per litre, and total SO$_2$ must not exceed 300 milligrams per litre.

Now we can consider the other factors that influence the character of the final Aszú wine. Over the course of three centuries, changes in vinification techniques have taken place, some of them now considered inappropriate, and even, in some cases, fraudulent. In the new atmosphere of freedom, especially with the arrival of foreign companies in Tokaj with different traditions of winemaking, the 1990s saw a tendency to re-examine these techniques to see if they had anything to offer to the contemporary winemaker. This experimentation has led to a diversity of styles of Aszú, and has also resulted in acrimonious discussion about the "true" style of Aszú. I shall comment on the search for this chimaera in a later section of the chapter.

One of the factors influencing the character of Aszú is whether or not the winemaker makes a paste of the aszú berries or, instead, uses them whole. A paste tends to yield more extract, and to result in Aszú with heavier aromas and deeper, more complex flavours than are obtained simply by using berries; the tannins from the seeds and skins also give the wine more body. Some winemakers, however, are looking for a lighter style and, by using whole berries, they trade off complexity and weight for fruitiness and elegance.

Another factor is the choice of base for the Aszú. For this, must, fermenting must, dry wine of the same vintage as the aszú berries (new wine), or dry wine of a previous vintage (old wine), or even Szamorodni (thought by many to be the "classical" preparation) have all been used at one time or another. In the eighteenth and nineteenth centuries, both must and wine were used, although the frequent use in the Hegyalja of the word *bor* (meaning "wine") to refer to must in documents of the late 1700s often makes it far from clear which is really meant.

In the first part of the twentieth century, however, the preference appears to have switched to using dry wine of the previous vintage, and this would be the clear preference of the older generation of winemakers in Tokaj today, because, they claim, refermentation of old wine with aszú berries produces Aszú with more colour, more intense aromas, and greater depth and complexity of flavour. However, this option clashes with EU norms, which preclude a wine being sold under one vintage date when it actually contains a greater amount of wine from a different vintage. Consequently, since 1994, the use of old wine has been illegal in Hungary – although it is only in the past few years that so-called traditionalists have reluctantly started to comply with the law. Those who would not in any case wish to use old wine say that they are looking for a more elegant result, and that while the alcohol in old wine brings out certain positive properties in the Aszú, it also tends to take out too many rough tannins from the skins.

The issue of whether to use must, fermenting must or new wine is quite complex. In the first place, even those who in general prefer to use must admit that, if you want to make a 6 *puttonyos* Aszú or an Aszú Esszencia, it is not technically possible to do so with must because the fermentation would be too slow and indefinite, and volatility would be in danger of becoming too high. The dilemma is that the use of unfermented must increases volatile acidity, but the use of wine increases the tannins. Again, especially in a poor year, it is better to use wine with Class III berries, because with must there are dangers of bacterial infection. In a good year, however, you might be able to use fermenting must (which gives a quicker fermentation than must). It is also preferable to use new wine with Sárga Muskotály aszú berries.

In the second place, the sweetness of the must or the wine will have some bearing on the amount of sugar extracted from the aszú berries or paste. Starting with grapes picked early on in the harvest and suitable for making a dry wine – whether they are used in the form of must or new wine – results in a final product quite different from starting with late-picked bunches containing overripe, shrivelled or botrytized grapes, whether they are used as a base in the form of must or wine.

Another factor affecting the outcome is the grape variety and the degree of acidity of the must or base wine, which makes up about eighty per cent of the final Aszú. When Furmint is used as the base, it gives a stronger and richer result, because it takes more flavour out of the berries, producing characteristic flavours of peanuts, raisins, and tobacco. Hárslevelű has a softer action on the aszú berries, and makes a more delicate wine requiring time to bring out its aszú character; flavours of banana and chocolate tend to develop. Sárga Muskotály is used chiefly for its aromatic qualities, although it does not impart any pronounced Muscat smell to the eventual Aszú.

All this clearly shows what should, perhaps, be obvious: that the winemaker has to adapt to the sort of aszú berries he has, and has to fine-tune his techniques, such as the period of maceration and the components he uses, to the sort of result he is aiming at.

Aszú wines are inherently unstable. Sometimes the fermentation will stop naturally (at about thirteen per cent), but the wine is liable to re-ferment if its environment changes. It is quite common for the wine-maker to block off fermentation at what he considers the optimum point, and this can be done by chilling the wine, or by using sulphur dioxide, or a combination of the two. This is a controversial issue, however, and levels of SO_2 in Aszú tend to be high – so high, indeed, that Hungary is seeking a special dispensation to exceed the EU norms in Article 65 (1) of Council Regulation No 822/87. Apart from preventing further fermentation, of course, sulphur helps to preserve the fruity character of wine and prevents oxidization, but many think that sulphur is used too much to achieve this end, to the extent of prejudicing the ageing potential of Aszú wines made in this way. Some French companies have argued that 400 milligrams per litre should be permitted, which is 100 milligrams above the present legal Hungarian limit. On the other hand, Royal Tokaji never exceeds 200 milligrams.

There are, however, other ways of stabilizing the wine. One, which has been illegal since 1991, is to block further fermentation by adding some alcohol to the Aszú. There are historical precedents for this, and in the nineteenth century, it was normal to add a little alcohol even to Esszencia. The Wine Act of 1936 also sanctioned the limited addition of up to four per cent alcohol (distilled from Tokaji) – later reduced to three per cent – but only to replace alcohol lost during maturation in partially filled barrels.

However, there is a difference between stabilizing a wine that has fermented to its natural limit, leaving large amounts of residual sugar, and using spirit as a substitute for natural alcohol in order to raise the level of alcohol while preserving a higher level of natural sugar in the wine than would otherwise be possible. The latter is now regarded as a corrupt practice, allegedly used during the Communist era, akin to making a fortified Aszú similar to port or madeira. Bootleg Aszú is still made in this way, totally illegally – and the price at which it is sold betrays the fact. Not only is such wine sold to tourists in the remoter villages of Tokaj, it can be found in supermarkets. In 2000, a well-known international supermarket was selling 3 *puttonyos* Aszú at HUF340 (£0.81) a half-litre bottle. Producers will tell you that a legal 3 *puttonyos* wine certainly cannot be prepared for less than double this amount, and that three times this amount would be the norm. This illegal use of alcohol is perhaps the most contentious issue in Tokaj today.

One has to ask why it is that the authorities appear to tolerate the production of impossibly cheap Aszú. Some say that telling how a wine has been made is difficult. István Szepsy explained the problem to me:

> "*After two years it is not possible to detect which way a wine has been made. Wines with higher alcohol tend to have less body and more raisin fruit, and the fruit (grape) sugar and glycerine proportions between the two wines will be different. But analysis of the wine is not a proof of how it has been made, because these proportions may be the result of a weaker terroir or a weaker vintage.*"

On the other hand, a former winemaker at the Borkombinát believes that it is possible to tell which wines have been made with spirit because you can feel it on your tongue and your nose. It has a certain bite. When you put old wine on the aszú berries it brings out the taste and flavour; when you put the spirit in the wine, it does not result in the same rich taste.

Pasteurization is yet another way of stablizing Aszú, and this was used by the Borkombinát and the Tokaji Kereskedőház up until 1999. It is not now used, as far as I am aware, by any Tokaji producers, although it is still legal to do so. While pasteurization normally drastically reduces, if it does not actually eliminate, the ability of a wine to develop in bottle, in the case of Aszú it took place after the wine had undergone its full cask development. Apparently it was considered that the high amino acid content of Aszú threatened the health of the wine in bottle, and the heat treatment – flash pasteurization at 83°C, followed by two to three weeks of being kept in isothermic containers at between 35° and 45°C – was designed not just to stablilize the wine but to counteract this specific threat. It was applied only after the proteins it was designed to remove had made their full contribution during cask maturation.[3]

This heat treatment was developed by Sandor Ferenczi and started at

---

[3] See Lambert-Gócs, M: "The Tale of Tokaji" in *The Underground Wine Journal*, October 2001, p. 39.

the Borkombinát in 1962. It is said that organoleptically, in the judgement of experienced tasters monitoring the development of Aszús subjected to this treatment, it had a favourable rather than an adverse effect on the taste of the wine, and did not impede it from undergoing considerable evolution in bottle. Nevertheless, the second part of the process is so akin to the *estufagem* (heating) process to which the lower qualities of madeira are subjected, albeit for a much greater length of time, that it is difficult to believe that it did not impart to the Aszú a little of the slightly cooked character it gives to madeira. And if alcohol was added before the heating process, the similarity to the method of making madeira is, if anything, more striking.

That the process did not prevent the wine's development, however, appears to be abundantly clear from the museum stocks of the Tokaji Kereskedőház, which amply testify that Aszús of the period have lost nothing of the astounding complexity they are inherently capable of developing. This complexity is due partly to the quality of the grapes used in making the wine, and partly to the way in which the wine has been made, but is primarily a consequence of the development of the wine in cask.

Before discussing cask-ageing, however, mention must be made of Forditás and Máslás. Neither is all that common nowadays, it must be said, but they are occasionally encountered. Forditás is made by macerating the pressings of Aszú must in fresh must, re-pressing, and fermenting the result. In other words, the aszu berries or paste are used for a second time. Máslás, on the other hand, is made by adding must to Aszú lees and fermenting the mixture. Forditás can, on occasion, make a reasonably sweet wine, but without the depth of an Aszú. The examples of Máslás I have encountered have been unimpressive: relatively dry, and usually lacking in body – which is, perhaps, why it is so seldom made now.

THE AGEING OF ASZÚ

Older winemakers often quote the golden rule that Aszú should be aged in cask for the same number of years as it has *puttonyos*. Thus, they say, a 5 *puttonyos* Aszú should spend five years in wood. A variant of this rule adds a further two years to the number corresponding to the *puttonyos*, which in this case would make the total seven years, although some makers say that in practice this is impossible without the use of alcohol. Other winemakers think there is, or should be, no rule at all, and that the length of cask-ageing depends only on the wine. At one time, apparently, one company wanted to make Aszú without any cask-ageing at all. The law, however, requires a minimum period of two years of cask-ageing, followed by one year in bottle before the wine is released for sale.

The object of cask-ageing is to develop the flavours and complexity of the wine by means of the gentle oxidation that takes place as the wine "breathes" air through the wood of the cask. However, during the period of the Borkombinát, many of the wines were not just oxidized in this way – a perfectly normal process in all cask-aged wines – but became excessively oxidized to the point of having disagreeable aromas and flavours. Oxidation of this sort happens, roughly speaking, when wine is exposed to too much oxygen too quickly. Currently, opposition to prolonged cask-ageing by some prominent producers appears to be as much a response to this as to anything else. Indeed, it is frequently alleged that the excessive oxidation of Borkombinát wines was the result not just of an excessive length of cask-ageing, but of poor practice, a failure to top up ullaged casks; it is even said that the allegedly "traditional" formula for cask-ageing was invented to rationalize this Borkombinát over-oxidation.

I am quite certain, however, that this is entirely false. The rule relating the length of cask-ageing to the *puttonyos* strength of Aszú was subscribed to by teachers at the Soós School in the 1960s – for example, by Dr László Gazday, chief instructor at the school for almost forty years – and by writers about Tokaji such as Dr Árpád Mercz, a respected veteran now in his eighties, as well as by János Pogácsás, the outstanding Tokaji winemaker of the 1970s. It was current when they were learning about winemaking.

In fact, in the *Album of the Tokaj-Hegyalja* of 1867, it is expressly recommended that casks be kept on ullage:

> "The natural good qualities of the Tokay wine, the charm of its delicious bouquet and taste are such as to ensure its keeping for a century, without it being necessary, as is the case with other wines, to fill up the cask again, or to have it carefully bunged again. On the contrary, it is necessary that during the process of its developement [sic], the casks

should never be filled up to the bunghole or too tightly bunged . . . [so that] the space above the wine is occupied by the carbonic acid, which, having a greater density than the atmospheric air, remains continually suspended above the surface of the wine, and prevents the free entrance of the oxygen of the air. Thus the Tokay wine is preserved from all danger of deterioration."[4]

While this advice is clearly linked to the instability of Aszú in the nineteenth century, and to the fact that there was no way of completely stopping fermentation, I also have to report that I have tasted Aszús in small private cellars like that of Mihály Hollókői, where wines that have been kept on ullage for many years have not exhibited a disagreeable oxidized character. Equally, I have tasted Aszús that have been in cask for up to twenty years that have a fresh and fruity character, with none of the notorious oxidized character. It is much more likely, in my opinion, that oxidized-tasting Aszú has resulted in the past from the widespread use of dry Szamorodni as a base wine, rather than from length of cask-ageing, regardless of whether or not the cask has been kept topped up.

One of the arguments against long cask-ageing is the danger of refermentation. When that happens, the sugar content is reduced as the alcohol increases. You need a very high level of sugar, therefore, to achieve stability, the minimum being 150 grams per litre of sugar, eight grams per litre of acid, and twelve per cent alcohol. Because of this, some producers claim that, short of the use of alcohol, it is in practice impossible to keep a 3 *puttonyos* Aszú (with sixty grams per litre of sugar) in cask for three – let alone three plus two – years. A 3 *puttonyos* Aszú that really has had three years of ageing will also have a very high percentage of alcohol, indicating that it probably started off with more than 3 *puttonyos*.

Some have argued that bottle-ageing can be a substitute for cask-ageing. However, although both types of ageing will enhance the aromas of Aszú, cask-ageing appears to develop a wider range of aromatic compounds, and it will develop *rancio* flavours (the term refers to a maderized Spanish white wine with a nutty flavour) and a degree of com-

[4] Szabó and Török, p. 91.

plexity on the palate not obtainable through bottle-ageing alone. That, in my view, is the whole point of ageing in wood, and the amount of time it takes will depend on factors like the amount of tannin in the wine, as well as variables such as dry extract, sugar, and alcohol levels. If an Aszú-Esszencia or 6 *puttonyos* Aszú has the right mix of elements to maintain stability, there seems to be no *prima facie* reason why the winemaker should not allow it to age in wood for as long or as short a period as he judges necessary to reach the style of wine he is aiming to produce.

TRADITION

"Tradition" is a word heard in Tokaj as often as "experiment". But what is tradition? It all depends on who you speak to, and for every view there appears to be someone who holds a contrary opinion. What emerges is a patchwork of often quite disparate elements – which, perhaps, casts doubt on whether an unequivocal tradition really does exist. Nevertheless, I have to report that so many of the older winemakers in Tokaj, as well as commentators familiar with the literature about Tokaji in Hungarian, insist so strongly on the existence of a classical tradition stretching back well before the advent of Communism (and quite separate from whatever malpractices there were in the Borkombinát) that, even if it appears to be impossible to reach agreement on all of its details, it is not something that can, or ought to be, dismissed out of hand – as many iconoclasts in Tokaj are apt to do. Too many knowledgeable people perceive that there was such a classical tradition for it to be just an illusion.[5]

[5] After this section of my text had been written, Miles Lambert-Gócs kindly drew my attention to an article by him called "Tokaji: Forever Amber" which has since appeared in the Summer 2002 issue of *Gastronomica* (published by the University of California Press), pp. 59–63, in which he attempts to demonstrate and document the elements of the classical Aszú tradition expressly to counter assertions that "nobody knows quite how they made Tokaji in 1900, or at any other period in the wine's long history". The essential elements of the tradition, according to Lambert-Gócs, are that Aszú has always been an amber-coloured wine that has undergone prolonged barrel maturation in partially empty casks to give it an oxidized character with an idiosyncratic *brodigság* (soft-bread) taste. See also the same author's "Tokay" in *The Journal of Gastronomy*, Vol 3, No 3, Autumn 1987, pp 16–29.

It is partly because there has been so much disagreement about what constitutes that tradition that there is so much debate about how Aszú should be made. The reader is now aware of all the variables in making Aszú, and how different permutations of these lead to Aszús of differing character. At one extreme, using an old base wine, a paste of aszú, and long cask-ageing give one style – rich, aromatic, and complex. At the other, the use of must, berries rather than an aszú paste, and minimal cask-ageing give a light, floral, and fruity style.

The supporters of these different styles have polarized into two very partisan factions. The former claim that their view is supported by tradition, while the latter claim that the former have espoused a false tradition of relatively recent origin, and that true tradition lies behind it (in the eighteenth and early nineteenth centuries). In its pettiest form, the way in which this debate is conducted descends to vulgar abuse, such as the often-expressed view that the French firms have abandoned tradition because they came to Tokaj only to make quick profits, and so do not wish to have money tied up in long ageing; or the counter accusation, already mentioned, that so-called traditions are rationalizations of previous "corrupt" Borkombinát practices. These assertions are as demeaning to the people who make them as they are unhelpful in trying to understand what is at issue.

Wine styles, wine fashions, and wine technology all over the world are in a constant state of evolution. They are not set in aspic. It is more accurate, therefore, to see traditions as continually developing and changing rather than as being "true" traditions challenged and displaced by "false" ones. It used to be traditional to add white wine to the blend of reds in Chianti; it was not traditional for Cabernet Sauvignon to be used for the blend. Changes in these traditions are now being accepted. New vinification techniques displace old ones; sometimes techniques of the past are revived when makers realize they have something to offer that has been overlooked – like, for example, the revival of interest in treading grapes in Portugal. Market conditions dictate change. Generally, across the world, most wines are being made to mature earlier, and more emphasis is being put on accessibility and fruit appeal. One sees this in wines as diverse as Bordeaux, port, and madeira.

Why should Aszú be an exception to all of this? *Vive la différence.* Happily, the law permits the maker enough latitude to make Aszú in both the old and new styles, and (increasingly) somewhere in between. In fact, there appears to be a certain amount of consolidation under way, and in vertical tastings it is noticeable that, in the wines of the early 1990s, there is a huge divergence in style and standards between the various companies that you do not find in later vintages. You can sense the uncertainty in the use of the technology at the beginning of the decade, whereas in later vintages there are, perhaps, the beginnings of some convergence in winemaking.

It may be that the appeal of the new style to the younger generation of Hungarians partly reflects the fact that under Communism few had any opportunity to experience Sauternes-style dessert wines. The new style Aszú, therefore, burst on them like a revelation. Equally, it may be that the attraction of the older style for me, who would naturally look to France and Germany for the best examples of sweet dessert wine, stems from knowing that the richer, complex kind of Aszú is unique, and has no equal anywhere in the world.

In all probability the market will, in the end, decide the issue, and it may be that the styles that are cheapest to produce will triumph. But I suspect that the market can accommodate a spectrum of styles, and I agree with Szepsy, who says, "We must find a range of styles for different occasions." Not all tastes have to be the same.

I hope that this diversity will soon be recognized by the Wine Qualification Board. There is a strong case for having a local committee to decide such matters, as in Eger. At the moment, the board is too reactionary in fighting the "new-style" Aszú, and too lax in not enforcing adequate quality standards at the lower end of the market. Difficulties with the board go back to 1995, when Aszú from Disznókő, Hétszőlő, and Szepsy were denied recognition although their wines received many prizes. Cynics began to say that the number of times your wine was refused by the board was a strong indication of its high quality! But the board's job, it seems to me, is properly to monitor quality – not to dictate style. The association called Tokaj Renaissance, comprising the leading local producers, is surely the right body to regulate these matters, enabling the region to take responsibility for its own quality standards and its own image.

THE PRODUCERS

SZEPSY BORÁSZATI MAGÁNVÁLLALKOZÁS

H–3909 Mád, Táncsics u. 37. Tel: +36–47 348349; Fax: +36–47 348724. *(a)* István Szepsy. *(b)* 20ha: F 10.2ha; H 9ha; SM 0.8ha. *(d)* István Szepsy. *(e)* Aszú, late-harvest. *(f)* Unspecified

Szepsy, now in his early fifties, has become an almost legendary figure in Tokaj. A workaholic, he has directed his energies into a passionate advocacy of Tokaji. He was the first managing director of the first Royal Tokaji Company, and it was the quality of his wine, according to Peter Vinding-Diers, that convinced him and Hugh Johnson to start the venture. He was instrumental in the formation of the increasingly influential Tokaj Renaissance Association (of which he has been chairman since 1998), and he is reponsible not just for his family firm but is a partner in a new joint venture, Királyudvar, which looks set to become a key firm in the development of the region. For younger Hungarian wine-lovers he is almost a cult figure.

Szepsy is descended from a small noble family that arrived in Tokaj at the turn of the fourteenth and fifteenth centuries, and gained its coat of arms in 1631, more or less when Laczkó Máté Szepsi, who is related to the family, was formulating the method of making Aszú wine. Szepsy's father, a cooperative chairman, was the largest grower in Bodrogkeresztúr before the Second World War, and the family, of which there were three branches, collectively owned more vineyards than the local Gróf.

Szepsy went to work in the Mád Cooperative in 1975, where he became the technical production manager in 1976. He rented his first vineyard in Mád in 1976, and by 1989 he had just over four hectares. After his brief involvement with the Royal Tokaji Wine Company, he became independent and started to build up his vineyard holding, including part of one of his grandfather's vineyards, the Szepsydűlő in Bodrogkeresztúr, where he was born. Szepsy's total holding in 2001 was twenty hectares, with plots in the following vineyards: in Mád – Király (5ha), Urágya (3.4ha), Danczka (3ha), Nyúlászó (1.5ha), Szent Tamás (1.4ha) and Betsek (1.4ha); in Tarcal – Nyúlas (1.8ha); in Rátka – Padihegy (0.5ha); and in Bodrogkeresztúr – Szepsy (2ha). Most are between fifteen and thirty years old, but Szepsydűlő was planted in 1962, while he himself planted Király in 1992. In his most recent planting he has a density of 5,500 vines per hectare, trained with a low (seventy-centimetre/twenty-seven-inch) cordon. He prunes short spurs with one eye. During the summer he practises bunch selection (according to their size) so as to have a yield of ten hectolitres per hectare, rising to a maximum of twelve hectolitres per hectare in a good year.

Szepsy started bottling and selling his Aszú wines in 1995, with two small gönci barrels of the 1989 and 1991 vintages. He sold 400 bottles of the former and 600 of the latter to sixty foreign purchasers, and showed it to innumerable wine-writers and journalists. With them he made his reputation, and has never looked back. His is a family firm, and his son and eldest daughter, both in their twenties, are studying oenology and marketing. While he continues to build up his own company, he has also formed a joint venture (Királyudvar, *q.v.*) with a Chinese-American, which gives him additional financial security. Királyudvar's high-tech winery contrasts oddly with his own basic set-up. He presses his grapes in the garage of his home with a thirty-year-old horizontal screw press, and the must is then taken to one of his cellars to mature.

The grapes for must or base wine are picked in the last week of the vintage, as late as possible. "I want to work with better and better grapes, as overripe as possible. The richness, complexity and harmony of the best grapes are necessary to produce wines with the most possibilities." So Szepsy's base wines are really all technically late-harvest wines, typically having, like his 1999 Late Harvest Furmint, twenty-six grams per litre of sugar and thirteen per cent alcohol. "In a good year, there is no dry wine."

Szepsy prepares his base must at between 8°C and 10°C. He then calculates the weight of aszú berries to add to the must, this being dependent on his analysis of the sugar content of the berries and the must. In terms of the old formula, as one puttony weighs a minimum of thirty-six kilograms, this means that to make a 6 puttonyos Aszú he has to add about 216 kilograms of berries to every 136 litres of must.

Esszencia is produced in the usual way. Szepsy bottled his 1996 Esszencia, but now he adds it to his wine. The aszú berries are not made into a paste. Szepsy used to do this, with a longer maceration time than he has now. By keeping the berries whole he gets less tannin; there may also be less taste, but you get more refined flavours. The maceration is for less than one day, and the mixture of berries and must is given minimal agitation; the tanks revolve only once or twice.

Szepsy prefers to use must whenever possible in making Aszú, but uses base wine when making an Aszú of 6 *puttonyos* or higher. All fermentation is done in barrels, even of the base wines; stainless-steel tanks are used only for settling. Szepsy wants to be able to separate the different tastes of the vintages from each other, and believes that the use of new oak helps to make them more easily distinguishable. However, he commonly washes out new casks with hot water to remove rough tannins, and when he is afraid he might damage the subtlety of his Aszú he uses second year barrels. He follows no formulae and likes to give Aszú what he considers the maximum possible ageing in wood before bottling.

Here is Szepsy's passionately held credo:

> "I am looking for better balance, more refinement, and more harmony than power or ageing potential. I want to produce complex, fruity wine with a certain level of ageing quality that puts a frame round the fruit but does not dominate the wine. But I am still only experimenting. I make many mistakes, but I am trying to find a direction for development, and to show the wide range of wines of which Tokaj is capable."

This is a reference to his late-harvest wines, produced under the name Tokaji Cuvée, which are in some ways even more remarkable than his Aszús – to be judged in world terms only by the highest standards. Szepsy's Aszús equally embody the aims of his credo. I respect their integrity and subtlety, and the fact that there is absolutely no compromise with quality, yet reluctantly, I have to admit that this is not the style that appeals most to me. I look more for depth and weight. Nevertheless, Szepsy's wines are remarkable, and the whole world must eagerly await the fascinating results of his future "experiments", not only under his own label, but that of Királyudvar. Appropriately (and some think belatedly), Szepsy received the accolade of Winemaker of the Year in 2001.

ÁRVAY BORÁSZATI KFT

H–3908 Rátka, Kossuth u. 101. Tel: +36–47 374025. *(a)* János Árvay. *(b)* 42ha:
F 25.2ha; H 14.7ha; SM 1.9ha; Zt 0.2ha. *(d)* János Árvay. *(e)* Dry wines,
Szamorodni, Aszú, late-harvest. *(f)* None

János Árvay is a remarkable man. Described by some as a dreamer, he is another of the winemakers of Tokaj who is dedicated to quality at any price. Árvay made wine in Tállya from 1975 until 1991, then, after a brief spell with the Borkombinát, he was chief winemaker for Disznókő from its inception until February 2000. Having been making wines for himself since 1979, he started his own business in 1996, and formed a limited company in 1998. His resignation from Disznókő coincided with the conversion of his own company into a joint venture with an expatriate Hungarian, with a minority interest in the company.

Expansion had been quite rapid even before he found his collaborator, because the six hectares he owned in 1998 had become fourteen by 1999. Now he has forty-two hectares. The rejuvenated company has purchased a large and potentially attractive building (it was once the town hall) in the heart of Tokaj, and this will become the vinification centre, with up-to-date technology, replacing the small facility Árvay previously used in Rátka.

Árvay can still scarcely believe his luck. "In one year," he says, "I have progressed as much as I might previously have expected to do on my own in twenty years." Better than that, he has the financial backing to produce specialty wines, where the amounts may be very small but the quality will be exceptionally high.

The company has eighteen parcels of vines in all, including a twenty-seven-hectare block in Padihegy, planted in 1992. Five hectares are planted with stakes in the traditional metre-square way, from which he gets two bunches per vine, and there are some sixteen hectares still to plant. These will have a density of 5,000 vines to the hectare, and Árvay hopes some will be stake-trained, even if it means they have to be completely worked by hand. He also aims to take less than one kilogram (2.2 pounds) per vine from those in the traditional plantations. His preferred training is a mid-height double-cordon, and he is trying to reduce the cordon height of some of his existing plantations to sixty centimetres (twenty-three inches).

Árvay believes that he is a true traditionalist, and appears to have read in depth about the making of Tokaji in earlier times. He much prefers using individual berries rather than a paste. If he has good aszú he uses fermenting must as the base, but for less good aszú, new wine is used. All his wine (including base wine) will in future be barrel-fermented, and he is comparing Hungarian oak casks made at Sátoraljaújhely (some of which are made of split wood) with casks made from American and French oak. The French oak, he thinks, gives the most elegant wine, the American oak the most perfumed wine, and Zemplén oak a richer traditional flavour and stronger acidity. His personal preference is for the Hungarian taste. He thinks that four years is the maximum one needs to age any Aszú in cask. "If it hasn't matured by the end of four years, it was a waste of time putting it in the cask to start with."

Many of Árvay's aims and practices are what have earned him his reputation as a dreamer, but it may well be that the amount of financial backing he now has will allow these dreams to become realities. The wines he showed me were all of outstanding quality, and I personally think that their richness makes them preferable to those of Szepsy. He may be the king in waiting.

DISZNÓKŐ SZŐLŐBIRTOK ÉS PINCÉSZET

H–3910 Tokaj, Pf. 10. Tel: +36–47 361371; Fax: +36–47 369138. *(a)* AXA Millésimes. *(b)* 100ha: F 60ha; H 28ha; Zt 10ha; SM 2ha. *(d)* Stéphanie Berecz. *(e)* Dry wine, Szamorodni, Aszú, late-harvest. *(f)* 80% of Aszú under Disznókő label (France, the US, and the UK)

The name of this company, founded in 1992, comes from one of its vineyards, recognized as a first growth in the original classification of vineyards in the eighteenth century. It means "rock of the wild boar", and is derived from a curiously-shaped rock said to resemble a recumbent boar in the middle of the vines. The estate belonged to the Rákóczi family in the seventeenth century, the Waldbott family in the nineteenth, and now belongs to the French insurance conglomerate AXA, owner of Châteaux Pichon-Longueville (Baron) and Lynch-Bages, as well as of Quinta do Noval. AXA has made Disznókő one of the showpiece properties of the region, with an architecturally striking and extremely well-equipped winery and a boomerang-shaped cellar – more accurately, one shaped so as to recall a *jurta,* a traditional native tent – both living in harmony with the classical old press-house, now converted into the Sárga Borház (Yellow Winehouse) restaurant, by the side of Route 37.

Of the vineyards, forty hectares of Furmint and two of Hárslevelű have been planted since 1994, and all are in production, while one hectare of Sárga Muskotály and eight of Zéta were replanted in 2001. The density of the new vineyards is 4,500 vines per hectare. The company plans on ten bunches of grapes per vine. The soil is volcanic, with more clay at the bottom of the slope, and a higher content of minerals at the top; two-thirds of the way up the slope is the best growing area.

The company makes a full range of wines. Before 1997, Disznókő selected the parcels of vines to be made into dry Furmint at the beginning of the harvest, but now the aszú berries are picked first and kept in store for about three weeks. The method of making the Aszú wine depends on the quality of the berries. The preferred method with Class I berries is to macerate them whole in fermenting must for from twenty to forty-eight hours, with constant tasting. This gives a more complete and powerful wine. Class II berries are made into a paste (with a pump) and added to a base wine, with a maceration period of twelve to twenty-four hours. In 1999, an experiment was made to see what difference using or not using a paste makes to the finished Aszú, and it was decided that there were no crucial differences.

During maceration, the berries are circulated by pumping them over. (The company does not like rotary drums, which it regards as commercial and difficult to control.) Fermentation is in stainless-steel tanks at 10°C to 15°C for several weeks. The more botrytis there is, the longer the fermentation. Varieties have been vinified separately since 1998, and are blended after two years. Three-year-old Sauternes barrels are used. Disznókő is considering the possibility of fermenting in barrels in future. When the fermentation is finished – by chilling to between 3°C and 5°C and using sulphur – the wines are racked.

Disznókő, in my opinion, makes very high-quality wines. I also think, having once mistaken one of its early Aszús for a Sauternes, that the style is really quite French in character. However, these are wines of substance and complexity that reflect the volcanic origins of the Disznókő soil, and they require one to take them seriously. Disznókő is one of the leaders in the Hungarian market.

GRÓF DEGENFELD SZŐLŐBIRTOK BT

H–3915 Tarcal, Terézia kert 9. Tel: +36–47 380173; Fax: +36–47 380149.
(a) Thomas Lindner. *(b)* 75ha: F 30ha; H 30ha; SM 15ha. *(d)* Sarolta Bárdos.
(e) Dry wines, Aszú, late-harvest. *(f)* 30% (Sweden, Germany, Japan, and Hong Kong)

This winery was established in 1996, and had its first vintage that year. The history of the firm goes back to the 1850s, when Imre Degenfeld headed the family and was considered one of the best wine producers of the region. He was one of the founding members of the Viticultural Union of Tokaj-Hegyalja, which was established in 1857. After the Second World War, the family went to Germany, but reclaimed its confiscated property at the time of privatization. When its original vineyard area was returned by the state, part of this included, somewhat unusually, physically the same vineyards it previously had.

The present Gróf Degenfeld-Schönburg is married to Marie, the daughter of Thomas Lindner, whose business in Germany is the largest manufacturer of needles in the world. Lindner is also the owner of the firm, and has just built a very modern winery, designed by Imre Makovecz – yet another of the architecturally exciting wineries of the region. Its clean-cut, contemporary lines are intended to be an image of the clean, direct wines made in it: a very wide range of fruity, crisp, reductive wines for the Hungarian restaurant trade and export, intended to be competitive on foreign markets with varieties like Chardonnay and Sauvignon Blanc.

The company owns forty hectares of vineyards and rents thirty-five which it sub-rents to its workers, from whom it then buys the grapes. Each year they replant five or six hectares. The old vineyards, twenty hectares of which are twenty-five-year-old Hárslevelű, are planted round the winery on the Terézia and Mézes Mály vineyards, and yield seventy to 105 hectolitres per hectare. The new plantations have a density of between 6,000 and 8,000 vines per hectare, and the aim is to take thirty-five to forty-two hectolitres per hectare (from one to 1.5 kilograms per vine) with over 20° of sugar.

The winery incorporates excellent vinification facilities, storage facilities, and the most modern bottling line in the Hegyalja. Underneath, there is a traditional cellar. For the table wines, the grapes are macerated after crushing for six hours at 8°C. After pressing, the must is fermented and then stored in stainless steel, stabilized and bottled under CO_2. Dry Hárslevelű is not produced: it does not make good dry wine. The firm is experimenting with Hungarian oak barriques to round down the acidity in the less good years. An unusual barrel-fermented Furmint, which is given a malolactic fermentation and aged for six months, is produced. It is by far the most interesting dry Tokaji Furmint on the market – but using barriques adds HUF100 (£0.26) to the cost per bottle, and because it sells no better than ordinary Furmint, its future is in doubt. The new wine has ten or eleven per cent alcohol.

Semi-dry and semi-sweet styles, to appeal to the home market, are made as well as late-harvest wines. The former are presentable examples of their genres, but the 1999 late-harvest and noble late-harvest wines show considerably more seriousness: high extract, excellent acid–sugar balance, and intensity of flavour. The Aszú wine is made by mixing fifty per cent aszú paste with fifty per cent new wine, and this gives a resulting wine of either 5 or 6 *puttonyos*. Esszencia is not added to boost sugar levels. The only Aszú known to me (1996, 5 *puttonyos*) is lightweight and rather hollow.

TOKAJ HÉTSZŐLŐ SZŐLŐTERMESZTÉSI ÉS BORÁSZATI.

H–3910 Tokaj, Kossuth tér 15. Tel: +36–47 352009; Fax: +36–47 352141.

(a) Grands Millésimes de France (Groupe GMF, France, 60%; Suntory 40%).

(b) 44.7ha: F 30.66ha; H 11.29ha; SM 1.2ha; Kv 1.59ha. *(d)* András Kanczler.

Dry wines, Aszú, late-harvest *(f)* 30% (through Barrière to France, Belgium, Germany, the UK, the US, Denmark, Switzerland, and Japan)

Hétszőlő is an estate with a long and distinguished history. It was first established and named in 1502 by the Garay family, who formed it by consolidating seven smaller vineyards (*hét* is Hungarian for seven), and it had a succession of celebrated owners, including Gaspar Károlyi (the first translator of the Bible into Hungarian), Gábor Bethlen, Prince of Transylvania, and (inevitably) the Rákóczi family, before being taken over by the Austrian crown, to be administered as an imperial property for almost 200 years. After nationalization it was allowed to languish until the 1960s, when some replanting was done. It was reconstituted as an estate at privatization in 1991. After having had a variety of shareholding owners, it now belongs entirely to Grands Millésimes de France (owner of Châteaux Beychevelle and Beaumont), itself partly owned by the Japanese firm Santory.

Viticultural excellence is synonymous with the name of Hétszőlő. The company's vineyards, impeccably maintained, are on the southern slopes of the Kopaszhegy, and seen from the road, they are an imposing sight, with the name of the estate painted on a retaining wall halfway up. The vines are planted with a double cordon, forty centimetres (sixteen inches) high. The planting has a density of 5,000 vines per hectare, and the cropping expectation is of 1.5 kilograms (3.3 pounds) from each vine. Kövérszőlő is grown on individual stakes. No herbicides are used, and the very minimum of chemicals. The company's slogan is "viticulture which respects the environment".

At the foot of the slope is the modern winery (built in 1992) and the adjacent warehouse (built in 1998), both with vestiges of alpine decoration to harmonize with a worker's cottage that forms the third component of the group. The impressively equipped three-level winery is built on the gravitational principle, with the bottling line and stock room on the lowest level. Dry wines are fermented for at least a month if possible, at a temperature of 18°C, to produce wines with 12.5 per cent alcohol. The aszú berries are macerated in must without having been made into a paste. The Esszencia is added to Aszú when necessary. All fermentation had been done in stainless steel, but in 2001, the company experimented with fermentation in 500-litre barrels, and has high hopes that with its new cellar it will have the capacity to do all its fermentation like this.

The aim of the company is to produce mainly Aszús, with only ten per cent dry wine. The company has 40,000 hectolitres of reserve wines, ninety per cent of which are Aszús. Surpluses of dry wines and grapes are sold to other producers such as Hilltop Neszmély. The company's view is that the grapes are too mature for dry wine by the time they are picked, and that late-harvest wines are a more appropriate product. It claims, indeed, to be the first company to have offered one in 1995. The style of Aszú that Hétszőlő aims to produce is refined, fruity, and supple. This is partly dictated by the situation of the vineyards in the south of the region, where the soil is loess and the wines are thus less acidic than many. It is easy to recognize the Hétszőlő style, which is the lightest and fruitiest in Tokaj – and the one, therefore, that most upsets the local traditionalists.

Hétszőlő has, notoriously, had a lot of trouble getting its wines accepted by the Wine Qualification Board. Its 1995 6 *puttonyos* Aszú was refused six times, although it received a gold medal in Bordeaux in 2000, while the 1996 5 *puttonyos* Aszú was refused three times, but was passed in December 1999; it also gained a gold medal in Bordeaux in 2000. These are wines of considerable quality, and it is absurd that obstacles should have been placed in the way of marketing them. There is no doubt that this is a highly successful company, and its wines have a very big following – especially among younger professionals. It is true that they are graceful and that they display floral, fruity characteristics with great elegance. I always enjoy drinking them. But, in the last analysis, anyone who champions strength and vigour in Aszú is likely, in my opinion, to find them lacking. Refinement is not the only quality in good wine.

TOKAJ-OREMUS SZŐLŐBIRTOK ÉS PINCÉSZET KFT
H–3934 Tolcsva, Bajcsy Zs út 45. Tel/fax: +36–47 384504/384505. *(a)* Bodegas Vega Sicilia. *(b)* 110ha, of which 65ha planted and 52ha in production: F 35.75; H 19.5ha; SM 3.9ha; Zt 5.85ha. *(d)* András Bacsó. *(e)* Dry wines, Szamorodni, Aszú, Forditás, late-harvest. *(f)* 50% (Spain, Finland, the US, Japan, and South America)

The company was founded on March 1, 1993. It belongs to David Alvarez, owner of Vega Sicilia, the famous Spanish wine company. Since its inception, the management of the company and its winemaking have been in the hands of András Bacsó, who directed the Borkombinát prior to privatization, and he and his Hungarian team run the company with minimal intervention from Spain.

The company's vineyards (some owned and some rented) are in four basic locations: Tolcsva (at Mandulás, Kútpatka, Lőcse, Szentvér, and Serédy-Vay); Tarcal (Deák); Tokaj (Máriassy); and Sátoraljaújhely (Oremus). The last of these is famous for being the vineyard from which Laczkó Máté Szepsi is supposed to have been the first to make Aszú wine. This vineyard, of five hectares, was replanted in 1999. The old vineyards, planted some thirty years ago, have a density of 2,700 vines per hectare. They give a yield, with green pruning, of thirty-five hectolitres per hectare. The new plantings have a density of 5,600 vines per hectare. They have a fifty-centimetre (19.5-inch) cordon. A yield of thirty-five to forty-two hectolitres per hectare means that each vine gives half the yield of the old plantations. Replanting should be completed by 2008.

Although the vineyards contain a little Zéta, it is a variety that the company does not much favour – which is sad when one remembers that this variety was formerly called Oremus.

The company's new winery (architect Péter Sugár) was completed in 2000. It has a pleasing contemporary design, with facings of natural yellow volcanic rock and matching locally-made bricks. It is built on a gravity-flow basis, and has 1999 Spanish Revinsa vinification equipment. There is bunch selection of grapes after delivery. Those with forty per cent botrytis or with sixty per cent overripe grapes are used for making late-harvest wine. The rest make dry wines, and after destemming are pressed and fermented for from seven to ten days. Aszú (and late-harvest) grapes are not pumped, but go straight to unique large, pot-shaped steel containers (called "*puttonyos*" by the firm). Must (generally Furmint) is added to them before they are decanted into maceration tanks, where they remain for twenty-four hours. The object of the steel *puttonyos* is to give the aszú berries gentle handling, and to avoid pumping them. Hence they return to the pot-shaped containers and are subsequently pressed pneumatically. The must is fermented in stainless steel at 18°C for forty to forty-five days in the fermentation hall below. Esszencia is made only in good years, the berries subsequently going into the steel *puttonyos* without being made into a paste.

The company uses *gönci* (136-litre) and *szerednyei* (200-litre) barrels, made in the region; in the long term, it intends to have its own cooper. It regards two years as the optimal period for cask maturation. The main cellar on the hill above the winery was started in the thirteenth century, although much altered and extended, and is carved out of volcanic soil. It is four kilometres (2.5 miles) long, on three levels, and has a capacity of 3,000 barrels.

Oremus makes an interesting range of wines. A 1999 dry Furmint from Mandulás that was given one month on lees in barrique with *bâtonnage*, has real personality, and, like Gróf Degenfeld's version, seems to me to point the way to making dry Furmint with an export future. The company also makes a feature of its late-harvest wines, which are of remarkably high quality. Oremus was among the first producers with its 1995 Late Harvest Furmint. One marketed under the Château Kurucz label is especially interesting. With vineyards on loess and on volcanic soil, Oremus has the possibility of making different styles of Aszú; nevertheless, I find them a little unappealing, with more barley sugar than butterscotch characters, which are possibly the result of the limited barrel-ageing they receive. That said, they have good acid–sugar balance and demonstrate the company's policy of ensuring that their vineyards give only the best quality fruit.

PAJZOS RT ÉS MEGYER RT

H–3950 Sárospatak, Nagy L. u. 12. Tel: +36–47 312310; Fax: +36–47 312320.
(a) Pajzos: CSGVT (a company in which Jean-Louis Laborde has a majority interest). Megyer: Jean-Louis Laborde. *(b)* Pajzos 64ha: F 30.7ha; H 25ha; SM 8.3ha. Megyer 83ha: F 37.4ha; H 18.3ha; Ch 12.9ha; SM 12.5ha; T 1.9ha. *(d)* Sándor Zsurki, Jr. *(e)* Dry wines, Aszú, late-harvest. *(f)* 66% (France, Belgium, Spain, the UK, the US, Japan, Canada, Russia, Czech Republic, and Poland)

This company comprises two separate properties, but they effectively have one owner, Jean-Louis Laborde, proprietor of Château Clinet in Pomerol, and they are run in tandem. Both estates were among the first to be privatized in 1991, and they share the same very well-equipped winery at Sárospatak. The cellars, however, are separate. Megyer has the Rákóczi cellar under the castle – 900 metres (2,925 feet) long and holding 800 casks, it is on two levels and was completed 500 years ago. Pajzos has three cellars: one under its vineyard, and two at Tolcsva.

The two companies have separate vineyards. Pajzos has a south-facing aspect, while Megyer faces south and southwest. Both have heavy volcanic clay, although that at Pajzos is lighter and more friable than that at Megyer. A certain amount of replanting is being carried out.

The technical director for both properties was, until 1999, a first-generation Canadian-Hungarian, Thomas Laszlo, who had been making Eiswein and late-harvest wines at the Henry of Pelham Estate Winery in Canada before he came to Tokaj in 1997. Now he acts as consultant, and since 1999, the winemaker for both properties has been Sándor Zsurki, Jr. The winemaker at Château Clinet helps with the blends, primarily at Pajzos, but does not influence vinification practices.

The winemaking at Pajzos, according to Laszlo, is still at an experimental stage. Their preference is to use the best aszú berries they can get. They make a traditional aszú paste, and for both properties use one hundred per cent Sárga Muskotály as the base wine. The volcanic soil makes the Sárga Muskotály very acidic, and gives it a citrus, almost

Riesling character. The Megyer wine is mostly tank-fermented, but twenty per cent is barrel-fermented. Half goes into new oak casks to mature, and none of the casks is older than 1993. For Pajzos, half of all the Aszú is fermented in cask, and nothing but new oak is used for maturing the wine. For both properties, only Zemplén oak is used. The best vintages are kept for up to four years in cask, but Laszlo believes that for a weak vintage, such as 1998, two years in cask can be too much.

The reason there are differences in practice between Megyer and Pajzos is because the wine of Megyer is neither as concentrated nor as high in sugar content as that of Pajzos. The fact that older barrels are used also gives it more of an oxidized style. This results in a taste that is more popular with the Hungarian palate – a sort of bridge between the old and the new styles. Pajzos commands highish prices; Megyer, at half the cost, is in a more price-friendly category.

Thomas Laszlo's expertise with late-harvest wines is evident in the very impressive issues from Pajzos in the past few years. The 1997 Muskotály Late Harvest (193 grams per litre sugar, fourteen grams per litre acid, 47.2 grams per litre dry extract) counts as one of the achievements of Tokaj in this category: a conjunction of fruit intensity, high sugar, and acid co-existing harmoniously in a Mosel *Trockenbeerenauslese* mould.

ROYAL TOKAJI BORÁSZATI KFT (THE ROYAL TOKAJI WINE COMPANY)

H–3909 Mád, Rákóczi út 35. Tel: +36–47 348 011; Fax: +36–47 348 359.

(a) Approximately 100 shareholders. *(b)* 110ha, of which 88ha in production: F 49ha; H 31ha; SM 7.8ha. *(d)* Károly Áts. *(e)* Aszú. *(f)* 90% plus (the US, the UK, Canada, Sweden, Italy, and Norway)

The Royal Tokaji Wine Company was originally set up in September 1990, before privatization became general in the region. Hugh Johnson and Peter Vinding-Diers were prime movers in the venture. Over sixty local growers participated in the formation of the company, into which they put some of their vineyards. Sadly, it was undercapitalized and had to be relaunched in 1993. Although the company still reflects its largely British origins, the shareholders now range across an international spectrum and include several Hungarians.

The new company currently rents back the vineyards it acquired from the previous company to their original owners, who cultivate them, and it buys aszú from them on preferential terms. At the moment, Royal Tokaji only makes Aszú wines. However, it hopes to buy the whole crop in future, and is considering what options exist with regard to the non-aszú grapes, such as the production of dry wine, grape juice, or concentrate. The first-growth vineyards owned by Royal Tokaji are in Szent Tamás, Nyulászó, and Betsek. The company also controls over twenty hectares in which cultivation is done by contract (11.7 hectares in Mézes Mály, eight in Nyulászó, and one in Szent Tamás), and has forty-eight hectares on leasehold.

A start was made on much-needed replanting in 2001, with five hectares in Szent Tamás and seven in Nyúlászó. The density will be 7,000 vines per hectare, with a sixty-centimetre (23.4-inch) cordon and a yield of one kilogram (2.2 pounds) per vine. In older vineyards the cordon height is seventy centimetres (27.3 inches), with yields of between 1.5 and two kilograms per vine (less in Mézes Mály). Some vineyards are cordon-pruned and others are single Guyot-pruned. The company aims to be self-sufficient in aszú within eight years.

Royal Tokaji was one of the first companies to market its Aszú under vineyard names. It admits that, before 1995, the authenticity of the vineyard origins could not be absolutely guaranteed, but since then the vineyard lots have been kept rigorously separate. Until 1994, when it was reluctantly forced to change its policy by law, the company preferred to use wine from the previous vintage for its Aszú base. Now it uses new dry wine – with a high alcohol content – because this takes more out of the berries than must. This base wine is normally made in stainless-steel containers, but new casks are twice used to ferment some of it in order to season them before they are used for Aszú.

The company aims to make 5 or 6 *puttonyos* Aszú with grapes from unclassified vineyards, and 6 *puttonyos* Aszú or Aszú-Esszencia from grapes of single vineyards. Aszú berries are pumped with some wine into maceration tanks and are kept together, depending on the vintage, for between seven and ten days – a much longer period than that used by any other firm – during which time the juice is racked two or three times a day. The residue is pressed at a maximum of 1.5 bar, and the juice is fermented in a mixture of *gönci* and *szerednyei* barrels for between three and sixteen months. If fermentation continues after the intended sugar-alcohol balance has been reached, it is stopped by refrigeration to –2°C and filtration.

The wines are aged in cask for at least three years, but there is otherwise no doctrinaire rule. The 1993 vintage was aged for four years, but some of the 1997 will not come out of barrel until 2002. It is company policy to market its Aszús with sugar levels well in excess of the minimum required by law for each *puttonyos* level. The company winemaker is Károly Áts, while Peter Vinding-Diers is in charge of blending the wines.

The style of Royal Tokaji Aszú is distinctive, owing a great deal, no doubt, to the long period of maceration given to the aszú berries: a rich but refined, full and complex, almost chewy, crème brûlée style, built round a spine of acidity. The wine is generally darker than average – one reason, according to the company, being that the amount of sulphur used in making the wine is minimal. The wine has no unpleasant oxidized tastes, and appears to me to display a serious character, closer to what I think of as the older style of Tokaji than to the fruit-driven style, without, however, sacrificing any fruit quality. If I may express a personal taste, this is the style that most appeals to me.

TOKAJ KERESKEDŐHÁZ RT

H–3980 Sátoraljaújhely, Mártirok útja 17, Pf. 229. Tel: +36–47 322133; Fax: +36–47 321603. *(a)* Hungarian Privatization and State Holding Company (Állami Privatizácós és Vagyonkezelö Rt). *(b)* 40.37ha (excluding 42ha Szarvas vineyard): F 24ha; H 16ha. *(d)* Lajos Kun. *(e)* Dry wines, sparkling, Szamorodni, Aszú, Forditás, Máslás, museum wines. *(f)* 30% (UK, Scandinavia, Germany, the US, Russia, Poland, Czech Republic, and Japan)

Tokaj Kereskedőház (Tokaj Trading House), started in 1993, is the metamorphosed form of the Borkombinát, the state farm that had a virtual monopoly of the region during the Communist period. Its transformation is described in the historical section of this chapter. It remains a state-owned and state-run organization (controlled by another state company). However, stripped of most of its vineyards, it has become a slightly top-heavy institution, and one whose continued existence gives rise to mixed feelings within the region. Some see it as a sort of champion of traditional values, guarding a precious legacy in the face of foreign attempts to undermine it. Others acknowledge that it fulfils a politically useful function, acting as buyer of last resort, and enabling the government to subsidize one of the poorest areas of the country. Of the opposite opinion are small producers who cannot expand their businesses because they cannot persuade their lazy neighbours to sell their plots because they are content with whatever, without effort on their part, the Kereskedőház will pay them for their grapes. Dispassionately looked at, the continued existence of the Kereskedőház in its present form requires further review.

For better or worse, however, it finds itself the custodian of two priceless assets. The first of these is the Szarvas vineyard, on the slopes of the Kopaszhegy by the side of the road from Tarcal to Tokaj. The second is the Museum Cellar, with its huge collection of old wine.

Confiscated from Ferenc Rákóczi II, *Szarvas*, the Hungarian word for "deer", became one of the Imperial and Royal Court Vineyards of the Habsburgs. Acknowledged as the finest of the Tokaj vineyards, it is virtually the most southerly of the region. Being reasonably close to the River Tisza, it produces a lot of aszú berries, and the grapes ripen earlier than elsewhere in the region.

After shameful neglect under the Communists, a start was made in May 2001 on replanting forty-two hectares which had had their vines removed in 1998. Until 1970, Szarvas had no terracing, and it has now been returned to its original state. The density is 4,750 vines per hectare, and *berlandieri* × *riparia* T.5C has been chosen as the rootstock. The training system will be Guyot Royal Cordon, with a height of seventy centimetres (27.3 inches), and the projected yield will be forty-two to forty-nine hectolitres per hectare (under two kilograms/4.4 pounds per vine). The planting of the entire programme is to be finished in 2005. A few wines from Szarvas have been made by the Kereskedőház since 1990. Of these, a rich but as yet undeveloped 1991 4 *puttonyos* Szarvas hints at the refined complexity that this vineyard has the potential to provide.

Associated with the Imperial Vineyard is the thirteenth-century Imperial Cellar at Tarcal, destined to be used once again to make the Szarvas wine. Above the cellar there is a fine baroque building, dating from 1771. It is presently used for the fermentation and maturation of Aszú, but modern fermentation equipment and a tourist reception centre will be installed in due course.

The Museum Cellar is at Tolcsva, close to Oremus. The cellar has two parts: the Constantine Cellar (so called because it belonged to the Greek royal family in the mid-nineteenth century) and – yes, another one! – the Rákóczi Cellar. The combined cellars are one kilometre (0.62 miles) long, with a cask capacity of 2,500 hectolitres and an historic collection of more than 500,000 bottles dating back to the beginning of the twentieth century. A few of these are released for sale from time to time. The high humidity of the cellar requires the replacement of the metal bands of the casks every seven years, and the alcohol loss is from 0.1 per cent to 0.17 per cent a year. Casks are topped up every two or three weeks.

The main winery is at Szegi, in a modern and very well-equipped building constructed between 1995 and 1996. This is where both dry wines and Aszú are made. Grapes are regularly purchased from over 3,000 growers, all under integration contracts. Since 1990, only Class I and Class II berries have been used. A pump tears their skins slightly, but does not make them into a paste, and after twenty-four hours' maceration with dry wine – must has only been used experimentally – they are pressed, with the residues being used to produce Forditás, Máslás, and pálinka, a brandy for the production of which the company has a regional monopoly.

The style of the company's Aszú has changed over the last decade towards the fruitier style favoured by many other companies, and it will be interesting to see if this trend continues under Lajos Kun, who became chief winemaker in 2001 after having spent six years at Oremus.

The company relaunched itself on export markets (the UK, the US, and Japan) in 2000 under the name Crown Estates. It markets dry Furmint and dry Hárslevelű under the name Castle Hill. These, unlike the dry wines for the home market which are oxidative, are made in a reductive style by New Zealand winemaker Tanya O'Sullivan, who is directed by Angela Muir (winemaking consultant). Some of the home market dry wines are also available under a special label for Hungarian supermarkets. The company also makes, for sale through its own shop in Budapest, two méthode traditionelle sparkling wines: Royal (brut) and Diplomat (demi-sec). The Aszú wines are sold in Hungary under the traditional Kereskedőház label, but special wines (at the moment a range of Szarvas wines) now appear abroad under the Crown Estates label.

It has become fashionable in Hungary in some quarters to denigrate the Kereskedőház Aszús just because of the company's association with the Borkombinát. In my opinion the company has moved a great distance forward since 1993, and recent releases of Aszú are on a par with, and mostly well above, average quality in the region.

PÁLL-SZOLG ÉS PINCÉSZET KFT

H–3915 Tarcal, Szondi ltp. 3/2. Tel: +36–47 380016; Fax: +36–47 380639.
(a) János Páll. *(b)* 15.5ha, of which 8.5ha in production: F 6ha; H 2ha; SM 0.5ha.
(d) János Páll. *(e)* Dry wines, Szamorodni, Aszú, late-harvest. *(f)* None

János Páll, previously a mechanical engineer, is steeped in local wine tradition. He made his first wine in 1963, when he was six, and started hobby winemaking in 1977. His father, grandfather, and great-grand-father were all winemakers, and his son Roland is studying to become one as well. When the reorganization of the Borkombinát took place in 1995, he began providing tractor services and started his present company. He only began to bottle his wine in 2000, and says that his business is just getting started.

Páll's vineyards are in Mád, Bodrogkeresztúr, Bodrogkisfalud, and Tarcal. The first (in Sajgó) was planted in 1964–5 by his father; the last (in Vinnay) in 2000 by him, grafting his own scions, and replacing seventy-year-old vines from which, in 1999, he made a remarkable dry Furmint and Hárslevelű blend with thirty grams per litre of dry extract. He aims at a yield of thirty to fifty hectolitres per hectare. At the moment he is mainly building up his stocks, and because he believes that long cask-ageing brings out the true character of Aszú – a rich, old taste – this is likely to take time. Páll's winemaking is "traditional" in other respects, too. He prefers to tread the aszú berries into a paste so as not to damage the grape seeds. He also racks all his wines each year. The oxygen they get from this makes his wine darker over a ten-year period. And, if the law allowed, he thinks it would be best to use old wine to make Aszú. These he considers to be authentic traditions because they go back as far as his great-grandfather, whose techniques of winemaking have been passed down within the family.

Páll's Aszús – most of which, in the nature of the case, I have tasted out of cask – seem to me to show the so-called traditional way of making wine in its best light. Despite long ageing, his Aszús show no unpleasant oxidation, and they have taken on the weight and complexity I miss in so many other Aszús.

OTHER WINE PRODUCERS

Baksó Pince. H–3932 Erdőbénye, Kossuth u. Mobile: +36–30 249 1747.
Tokajibor Bene Kft. H–3916 Bodrogkeresztúr, Felső u. 2. Mobile: +36–30 903
8448. *Bodnár Pincészet.* H–3980 Sátoraljaújhely, Balassi Bálint u. 31. Tel:
+36–47 321579. *COS Kft (Color Odor Sapor).* H–3909 Mád, Árpád u. 33. Tel:
+36–47 348050. *Demeter Tokaj Hegyaljai Borászat.* H–3910 Tokaj, Ady Endre út
4. Tel: +36–209377074. *Dereszla Kft (formerly Bodrog-Várhegy Kft).* H–3916
Bodrogkeresztúr, Felső u. 2. Tel/fax: +36–47 396002. *Dobogó Pincészet.* H–3910
Tokaj, Dózsa út 1. Tel: +36–47 348037. *Dusóczky Tamás-Tokaji Borászat.*
H–3918 Szegi, Dusóczky tanya. Tel/fax: +36–47 309058. *Erzsébet Pince.*
H–3910 Tokaj, Bem József út 16. Tel: +36–47 353014. *Evinor Bt (Evinor
Pincészet).* H–3950 Sárospatak, Bercsényi út 27. Tel: +36–47 311946; Tel/fax:
+36–47 312234. *Fitomark-94 Kft (Kiss István Családi Pincészete).* H–3934
Tolcsva, Arany J. u. 16/a. Tel: +36–47 384010; Fax: +36–47 384275. *Fürst zu
Löwenstein.* H–3910 Tokaj, Hegyalja út 15/b. Tel/fax: +36–47 352612. *Hollókői
Mihály.* H–3097 Tállya, Bocskai u. 10. Tel: +36–47 398054. *Imperial Tokaji Kft.*
H–3909 Mád, Rákóczi u. 15. Tel/fax: + 36–47 348750. Winery: H–3907 Tállya,
Rákóczi u. 2. Tel: +36–47 398061. *László Pincészet Tokaj-Tállya Kft.* H–3907
Tállya, Dobogó u. 47. Tel/fax: +36–47 398182. *Lauder-Láng Pincészete (Gundel
Restaurant Pincészete).* Lángastronómia Kft, H–1146, Budapest XIV, Allakerti út
2. Tel: +36–1 3213550/3430241; Fax: +36–1 324 2917/3430245. Winery:
H–3909 Mád, Árpád u. 37. Tel: +36–47 348383. *Lenkey és Társa.* H–3909 Mád,
Táncsics M. u. 29–31. Tel/fax: +36–47 548410. *MWB Pince Kft.* H–3881
Abaújszántó, Béke u. 11. Tel: +36–47 330567. *Monyók József.* H–3909 Mád,
Tácsics Mihály u.18. Tel/fax: +36–47 548033. *Olaszliszkai Borker.* H–3933
Olaszliszka, Kovács út 34. *Promontorbor Rt.* H–3909 Mád, Kölcsey u. 10. Tel:
+36–47 348000. *Ráski László Pincészete.* H–3529 Miskolc, Perczel Mór u. 45/b.
Tel/fax: +36–46 362324. *Royal Palatine Kft.* H–3918 Szegi, Dusóczky tanya.
Tel/fax: +36–47 309058. *Szabó Dániel.* H–3950 Sárospatak, Dobo Ferenc u. 65.
Tel: +36–47 312601. *Tokaj Hímesudvar Bt.* H–3910 Tokaj, Bem J. út 2. Tel:
+36–47 352416. *Tokaji Királyudvar Kft (Királyudvar Szőlőbirtok).* H–3915 Tarcal,
Fő út 92. Tel/fax: +36–47 380111. *Tokaj Kővágó Pincészet Borászati Kft.*
H–3917 Bodrogkisfalud, Várhegy. Tel/fax: +36–47 396001. *Tolcsva-Bor
Szőlőfeldolgozó és Kereskedelmi Kft.* H–3934 Tolcsva, Táncsics M u. 3. Tel/fax:
+36–47 384420. *Török Béla.* H–3900 Szerencs, Hegy u. 8. Tel/fax: +36–47
363835. *Úri Borok Pincészete Bt.* H–3909 Mád, Kossuth u. 40/a. Tel/fax:
+36–47 348601

The initials "MWB" stand for Márta Wille-Baumkauff. Born in Sárospatak, she is married to a German who operates a wine-distribution business in Braunschweig. Her company, MWB, was started in 1991. With 6.5 hectares of first-class vineyards and a sixteenth-century cellar with relatively modern equipment, MWB's stated aim is to make traditional wine in traditional ways, but to show that "technology can produce other aromas than those known before". Only Aszú wines are made, using various permutations of berries and paste with must and new wine. The winemaker is István Dorogi.

Many of the wines are frankly experimental, and in some ways come closest to the possible extreme of the new style – very fruity, with intensity of flavour rather than any of the toffee-apple, butterscotch richness of traditional Aszú. This is especially true of a reductively made 1998 Aszú grown on loess at Deák (Tarcal), for which great German wine was the model. Despite repeated Wine Qualification Board refusals, Márta Wille-Baumkauff resolutely refuses to alter the style of her (undoubtedly high-quality) wine.

Úri-Borok is a family company that started in 1993 under the care of Vince Gergely. He has fifteen hectares of vineyards, the best of which are in Szent Tamás, Danczka, Bojta, and Nyúlászó. His vast cellar on three levels in the middle of Mád is 300 years old and once belonged to the Orczy family. His equipment is fairly basic. Gergely, specializing in high-puttonyos Aszú and Aszú-Esszencia, uses must rather than wine, and makes a paste from the berries. The wines are barrel fermented. His wines are already receiving recognition, and his 1994 6 puttonyos Aszú stands out for quality.

Sándor Bodnár, for thirty-three years chief oenologist at the Borkombinát and Tokaji Kereskedőház, retired in 1994. He works six hectares, partly in the Vióka vineyard at Sátoraljaújhely. For his Aszú, Bodnár takes very little Esszencia from his berries, on the basis that skimmed milk makes poor cheese. A paste is macerated in a rotatank with semi-fermented wine for two to three days. The wine is matured in cask for the same number of years as its puttonyos rating. Good-quality, old-style wines, without excessive oxidation.

Zoltán Demeter got a spraying machine for his twelfth birthday, and has never looked back. For someone in his mid-thirties, his curriculum vitae is remarkable: winemaking experience in California and Beaune, the

British Wine and Spirit Educational Trust Diploma, and experience at Hétszőlő and Gróf Degenfeld before becoming winemaker at the recently established Királyudvar. He also works for himself, and made his first Aszú in 1997. He aims at maximizing the fruity character of the wine: "We must make wines for the new millennium: the soil and the variety must speak for themselves." He macerates whole berries in fermenting must. His wines have considerable elegance but, to my mind, rather lack weight. Monarchia has bought his entire 1999 vintage.

Tamás Dusóczky is a retired mathematician who previously lived in Switzerland. His father was a wine producer who purchased most of the Kővágó vineyard in Mád in 1930. Having belonged to the High Judge of Zemplén, who acquired it in 1563, the vineyard passed to the Rákóczi family in 1623, and then to the Máriássy family, who owned it until 1690. It was nationalized in 1951, then abandoned. In 1998, Dusóczky was one of a group, including a descendant of the Máriássys, that purchased it, since when it has remained un-replanted. Dusóczky makes small amounts of rather modest late-harvest and Aszú wines from 6.5 separately owned hectares at Szegi.

Evinor is a family business started in 1997 and run by Sándor Simkó, who was previously the general manager at Pajzos. He has thirteen hectares planted between 1960 and 1970 in Kincsem (at Tolcsva) and close to Sárospatak. His winery has modern technology, and he makes the full Tokaji range. In 2001, his 1995 5 *puttonyos* Aszú was still in cask – a reflection of his Hungarian customers' preference for an aged style. He also has a 1972 6 *puttonyos* Aszú, said to have spent twenty years in cask. All his Aszús are attractively fresh, and none I have tasted has had the least hint of excessive oxidation.

Gundel's (founded in 1884) is Budapest's most famous restaurant, now owned by RS Lauder, formerly US ambassador to Vienna and son of Estée Lauder (who was born in Sátoraljaújhely), and G Láng, the American proprietor of the famous Café des Artistes in New York. In addition to its winery in Eger, the company owns twenty-six hectares in Mád and a cellar dating from the thirteenth century. The Aszú wines are barrel-fermented using a paste and either must or new wine. These are basically commercial wines designed for everyday restaurant use.

József Monyók, a product of the Soós School in Budafok, worked in the Borkombinát and the Mád Cooperative, then in the Mád zeolite factory, until he became an independent, full-time winemaker in 1990. He has almost eight hectares, all in first-class vineyards, and aims to more than double this within five years. Since 1996, he has fermented varieties separately, using the same variety of base wine as the aszú, and favours long barrel-ageing with occasional oxygenation of the wine. He sells to top Budapest hotels and CorVinum.

Dániel Szabó has worked in the region since 1964, first in the Pincegazdaság, then in the Borkombinát, and finally as chief winemaker for the Hercegkút Cooperative. He has almost three hectares of vineyards in Hosszúhegy (at Sárospatak) and a winery at Károlyfalva. He started selling his wine in 1992. Szabó is an old-style winemaker, making Aszú with high alcohol levels. He ages the wines for three years minimum, racking them once a year. Szabó's Aszús are among those with the most heavily oxidized style to be found on the market at the moment.

Tolcsva-Bor is a third-generation family winery, run by Gábor Sajgó, whose grandfather was András Kassai, the winner of many competitions in the pre-Communist era. Sajgó started making wine in 1960, became a full-time wine producer in 1982, but founded the present company only in 1995, when the up-to-date winery was built. There are eleven hectares of vineyards, most of them in Tolcsva, around a quarter traditionally planted with stake-trained vines. Seventy per cent of the bottled wine is exported to Poland, and forty-five per cent of the total production is still sold in barrel. Aszú is fermented in stainless steel, but aged according to the "number of *puttonyos* plus two years" formula, and in any case for a minimum of four years in cask. Some impressive wines.

Two Budafok companies have satellites in the Hegyalja. Tokaj Kővágó Pincészet is run by Hungarovin, having previously been the Bodrogkeresztúr Cooperative. It has fifty-six hectares in the Kővágó vineyard, and buys from a further one hundred hectares. Supervised by László Romsics, the winemaker is János Puklus. Promontorbor, a satellite of the company in Budafok, has sixty-four hectares in Mád and Olaszliszka.

Bodrog-Várhegy was founded by the French company CANA in September 1992, but changed hands in June 2000, when François d'Aulan, former proprietor of Piper-Heidsieck, took a controlling interest on behalf of a family group with wine interests in France and Argentina. In October 2001, the company changed its name to Dereszla. According to the company, "We are starting a new epoch in which there will be a quest for much higher quality than before." The old winery and cellar, dating from the sixteenth century and once owned by the Széchenyi family, are on the banks of the River Bodrog at the bottom of the Dereszla Hill – previously used as a brand name, and now as the company's name. A new winery, built in 1993, was re-equipped with excellent vinification facilities in time for the 2000 harvest, which was made by a guest French winemaker. Château Dereszla has in the past had the refined, more delicate style associated with loess vineyards, although seldom attaining really top quality. How the new quest will turn out remains to be seen.

Because it takes time to mature Aszú wine, let alone to establish vineyards, a number of firms do not yet have their own Aszú to market (although in some cases they buy in other people's wine to sell under their own label). The following brief summary indicates some of the future players.

Tokaji Királyudvar is a joint venture between István Szepsy and a Chinese-American, Anthony E Hwang, which started in 1997. Its prospects are potentially the most exciting in the region. With 104 hectares of vines in first-class vineyards, eighty of them planted, and a new high-tech winery installed in a beautifully restored sixteenth-century building in Tarcal, this company looks set for success. Its large cellar is still pretty empty, but Aszús from the 1997 vintage onwards are gently maturing in it. The winemaker is Zoltán Demeter, and Szepsy acts as consultant. The first releases are planned for 2002.

Fürst zu Löwenstein, established in 1997, belongs to Alois Konstantin Fürst zu Löwenstein-Werthheim-Rosenberg, a lawyer and international financier. He has twenty hectares in Veresek, Betsek and Király, of which thirteen are newly planted, but as yet has no cellar. László Hornyák acts as his manager, and István Szepsy assisted in making his Aszús in 1999 and 2000.

Imperial Tokaji was a dormant company until it was taken over by a group of seven Hungarians in 1998, one of whom, Géza Schusztig, acts as general manager. Without vineyards, its new winery in Tállya, equipped with the most recent reductive technology, was completed in 2000. The winemaker is Norbert Kovács. The company is marketing dry table wines and, while its own stocks mature, is selling bought-in Aszú wines under its own label.

Royal Palatine, although it sold bought-in wine in 1999, now appears to be dormant. Started in 1995, and funded by Erzherzog Michael von Habsburg-Lothringen and Herzog Alois Löwenstein-Werthheim-Rosenberg in association with Tamás Dusóczky, this company has twenty-six hectares in first-class vineyards.

COS is owned by two Israelis, Willi Kizner and János Váry, who were inspired to get involved in Tokaji production by wines made by István Leskó, now their winemaker and vineyard manager. Founded in 1998, with five hectares planted (two in Nyúlászó) out of fourteen hectares owned, the company also has a well-renovated and equipped cellar with a smart-looking new press-house in Mád. COS made its first wine in 1999, and is currently selling Leskó's wines under its trading name "Aurum Vinum".

Gyula László, who was born in Transylvania, spent three decades in South Africa, and now spends half the year in retirement in Stellenbosch where, for fifteen years, he was chief cellar-master of the Bergkelder. The company is a joint venture between László, a Dutchman, and two Hungarians. It started in 1996 with one hundred hectares (eighteen of them planted), and in 2001 converted an old flour mill into a well-equipped modern winery, with South African dejuicers, which provide almost ninety per cent of the entire must yield as free-run juice. All dry wine is exported to Holland. No releases of Aszú yet.

Two other wineries founded in 2000 but not yet marketing their own Aszús are Baksó Pince, with fifty hectares, and Olaszliszkai Borker, with almost twenty-seven hectares.

Final Thoughts

Any attempt to foretell the future of Hungarian wine has to battle with imponderables such as how to estimate the effect of Hungary's accession to the European Union, and is likely to be a mixture of gloom and hope. So, in order to end on a happy note, let us deal first with the less-cheerful aspects of the situation.

The development of a healthy wine industry that is able to export successfully is of considerable importance to Hungary, because more than half of Hungary's GDP comes from its export trade. How unsuccessful the wine industry presently is in this regard can be seen from three depressing comparisons: (1) the average export price obtained for one litre of wine in 2002 was HUF217 (£0.52) as compared to the price in 1993, which was HUF279 (£0.67) – a drop in excess of twenty per cent over eight years; (2) the amount of Hungarian wine shipped to the UK in 2000 was 93,894 hectolitres, as compared to 121,600 hectolitres in 1998 – a drop of 22.8 per cent; (3) Hungary's overall share of the UK wine market has fallen further since then from 2.1 per cent in June 2000 to 1.2 per cent in June 2001 – a drop over a two year period, in real terms, of 42.8 per cent. Bear in mind, also, when contemplating these figures, that over fifty per cent of UK imports of Hungarian wine originate from just one company: Hilltop Neszmély.

The explanation of this catastrophic drop has less to do with the quality of Hungarian wine, and more to do with poor marketing. Companies with adequate advertising budgets, like Hungarovin, generally do well. Such companies usually turn out to be western, or they are companies with access to marketing know-how. But there are many small producers – similar, in some ways, to the boutique wineries one found in New Zealand in the late 1980s – who simply do not know where to turn to for help. The state, which ought to be playing a leading role in creating favourable conditions for export, is failing them dreadfully. Overseas agencies tasked with creating publicity and giving marketing support are starved of funds which, scarce though they are, appear to be squandered on unproductive projects through inefficiency, mismanagement or – if rumours have any foundation – worse.

Part of this book has dealt with the plight of small growers who, cut off from the benign protection of the old cooperative system, are daily giving up what they see as the unequal struggle against rising costs, falling profitability, and the crushing burden of paperwork imposed by the excise controls introduced in August 2000. This paperwork is no less for the small winemaker than it is for the big producer, and he is unlikely to have a computer to help him.

Elsewhere in the book I have tried to show the precarious financial state of the cooperatives which, against the odds, manage to keep on going. Hitherto, the government, without much evidence of a coherent policy on wine, has appeared to act in a pragmatic way, simply trying to keep the show on the road. A large part of the problem has been that policy regarding wine has been mixed with policy on social issues – as witness the subsidy for growers in Tokaj-Hegyalja, the poorest region in the country. This was largely due to the Independent Smallholders' Party which, right from the start of the new political system, formed part of the government coalition and always made protection of the interests of small growers and small farmers the price of its cooperation. As a result, the government was prevented from firmly grasping the nettle of a directed and targeted wine-development policy. However, in the elections that took place in April 2002, there was a shift in leadership leading to a left-wing coalition between the Socialist Party (MSZP) and the Free Democrats (SZDSZ). The Independent Smallholders' Party, which split into two parts in 2001 and has been plagued with financial scandals during the last two years, far from forming part of government, failed to obtain a single seat in the parliament. Whatever the consequences of this, it is thought by many in the wine trade that the (ex-Communist) socialist leaders may be rather more open to influence from the beer and spirits lobby, and will back big wineries rather than small private producers. Time will tell.

When I started to get more seriously interested in Hungarian wine and began to research this book, I had hoped to report that, ten years after the end of Communism, Hungary's wine industry was settling down to a period of positive development and rapid expansion. I discovered, however, that there are problems of an almost intractable nature that can only be sorted out over a period of many years: the replanting of old vineyards, for example, which in several of the regions has not really even begun. Good vines (virus-free, of the best clones, on the most suitable rootstocks) in well-maintained vineyards (with trellising suited to variety and climate) are the indispensible prerequisite of good wines. Yet, in Hungary, the government does not seem to see this as a priority; research effort is underfunded, and arguably rather diffused because of the fragmentation of the research institutes. Several people have compared the present situation unfavourably with the positive and urgent role the government played in the aftermath of phylloxera. Limited funds require better targeting, and should, in my view, be directed primarily at building up premier wine regions (even at the expense of others in which the basic conditions for producing high quality are not present).

Opinion is divided in Hungary about the merits of joining the EU. The certainty of some subsidies to help the wine industry, and of a rising standard of living – "more people will be able to afford to buy wine" – are counterbalanced by the realization that Hungarian wines of the lowest quality will face competition from imports on the home market. Some people are apprehensive of the EU, regarding it, with a sense of the continuity of history, as yet another foreign power exercising a form of economic colonization in succession to the Turks, the Austrians, and the Russians. Pessimistic commentators say that joining the EU will bring about at least a very necessary rationalization of the present situation, but one that will be difficult to control. An apocalyptic view – articulated by a government minister – foresees that, as a lot of small growers and producers go out of business as cheap EU wine from France, Spain, Italy, and Greece floods the domestic market, there will be widespread disillusionment among the peasantry, leading to its political radicalization and even to social unrest.

On the other hand, the optimists see entry to the EU as a necessary route to salvation, because there is insufficient capital in the country to bring about the investment in the wine industry necessary to overcome the problems rehearsed in Chapter Two, and only foreign capital can lead to long-term improvement. Moreover, although imports may kill off the inefficient in the domestic market, the enterprising and efficient will be presented with expanding markets abroad, and the fittest will survive. Sadly, most potential exporters I have spoken to have no conception of the savagery of international markets, although unhappy encounters with supermarkets in Hungary have given some of them an inkling of what might happen.

In fact, there is nothing incompatible about these two views, and doubtless what the future holds will be a reduction in the number of growers, with a healthy consolidation of small vineyard plots. Whether the EU will provide all the conditions for successful inward investment remains to be seen; the embargo on foreign ownership of property remains a big deterrent. What entry to the EU will provide, if the experience of the most recent entrants is any guide, will be rising standards of living with a growing sector of the population joining the middle-income bracket. This is precisely what is needed to provide the majority of wine producers with the economic stimulus to make better-quality wine.

Sensitivity to the advent of the EU is connected with nationalist sentiment, which has had an understandable resurgence in reaction to forty-five years of Russian-dominated Communist rule. Nationalism expresses itself in winemaking as much as in any other activity, and I see this as a healthy development except when it takes an isolationist form. There can be no place in Hungary for the sentimental nationalism that, setting its face against progress, turns back to a nostalgic past – and I am not thinking just about Tokaj here! Who in their senses would want to drink the Chianti of thirty years ago, mean and lean as it was? Well, some parts of Hungary will have to achieve an evolution of their wines comparable to that of Tuscany if they wish to reclaim their rightful place in the wine world.

By contrast, the nationalistic interest in promoting traditional native grape varieties on foreign markets is shrewd, because there is no point in trying to compete with other countries with better climates in producing international varieties that they are generally able to make to a higher standard – especially when interest in some of these varieties, such as Chardonnay, appears to be on the wane. Hungary can and should compete in world markets with wine made from its own varieties. I have seen (or rather tasted) enough in the past year to make me feel certain that they will succeed if – but it is a big if – the wines themselves are of a sufficiently high standard.

I am continually struck by the fact that the wineries which produce the best wines in terms of quality, and the most successful wines in terms of marketing, have either employed foreign consultants or have winemakers who have been lucky enough to have made wine in other countries. It is not so much that they have greater technical skills – although most of them have usually learned something new and useful while abroad – as that they have had the opportunity to taste the wines of at least one rival exporting country in some depth, and they return to Hungary with a more sophisticated perspective on the international scene. They know what they have to compete against. Happily, there seems to be an increasing number of younger winemakers who have a less parochial outlook on their craft than the older generation.

When I started to write this book I met with a certain amount of scepticism. "Are there really enough good wines and winemakers to write about?" This book must serve as my reply, and I hope that it amply demonstrates that, despite all the problems, there are indeed a lot of good winemakers, and even some potentially great ones. The renaissance of Hungarian wine is quite certainly under way: not a recreation of the past, but an evolution based on the past and pointing towards the future. It may take more time than we should all like, but the main thing is that it has begun.

Appendices

appendix I

Conventions, Weights, and Measures

This appendix is an *omnium gatherum* of miscellaneous information that, it is hoped, will be helpful to the reader.

Map of Alföld (The Great Plain)

To avoid undue fragmentation of the mapping of Kunság, which is included in this map on page 170, an element of simplification has been introduced by grouping some very small areas together into larger ones for clarity of presentation. For a completely accurate map, the reader is referred to *Magyarország Borvidékei – Wine Districts of Hungary*, published by Top-o-Gráf, H–1063 Budapest, Sziv u. 14. Tel/fax: +36–1 322 1410. Readers should, however, bear in mind that modifications of the areas of all of the wine regions are made on an almost annual basis.

Proper names

The Hungarian convention is to write surnames before given names (except in the case of foreigners, where the British convention applies). Because this is potentially confusing to readers, however, I have adopted the British convention throughout the book, except when proper names are used in the names of companies. In such cases, where the reader might encounter a proper name on a wine label, for example, it has seemed better to stick to the Hungarian convention.

Possessives

The addition of 'i' to a Hungarian name makes it possessive. Thus, Somlói means "of Somló", and Tokaji means "of Tokaj". Thus Tokaji sometimes means Tokaji Aszú – "Aszú wine of Tokaj" – or Tokaji bor – "wine of Tokaj".

Crop yields and must

Indications of crop yields have been expressed in hectolitres per hectare rather than in tonnes per hectare. Although volumetric yields vary according to a number of factors, I have adopted the convention that one tonne of grapes yields seven hectolitres of must.

Measurement of sugar

Hungary has its own way of measuring must sugar, known as *Magyar Mustfok*, or the Hungarian Must Scale, which is abbreviated to MM. The definition of 1°MM is that it is equivalent to one per cent of sugar by weight. Throughout the book, sugar measurements are expressed as °, and this is to be understood as "degrees MM".

Equivalences to other scales of measurement such as Oechsle, Beaumé, and Brix are difficult to express accurately because they are not linear. However, the following example will give an idea of the relationship between them:

MM	Oechsle	Beaumé	Brix	Sugar (g/l)	Potential Alcohol (% vol)
22	110	14.0	25.3	243	14.0

Meteorological information

Information about mean temperatures and sunshine hours is derived from meteorological stations in the regions, and averages measurements made between 1986 and 1999.

Currency

The Hungarian unity of currency is the forint, indicated by the abbreviation HUF. To illustrate values in sterling and US dollars, the rate of exchange used is the average of that current during the preparation of this book – that is, £1.00 = HUF417 and $1.00 = HUF288.

Technical terms

"Table Wine" and "Quality Wine" are used by the Hungarian Wine Law in a technical sense to indicate wines that conform to certain analytical standards. In ordinary English, however, "table wine" normally means still (as opposed to sparkling) or beverage wine, while "quality wine" would normally be understood to indicate wine of outstanding quality. To remove confusion, therefore, I have used upper case letters to indicate when these terms have their technical, legal sense, and lower case letters when they do not.

Supermarkets

Supermarkets, almost universally owned by western interests, have become virtually the primary means of distribution of food and bottled wine in Hungary. Familiar names like Tesco, Auchan, Julius Meinl, Cora, and Penny Market abound. Unless the context indicates the opposite, mention of specific supermarkets in the book refers to their domestic Hungarian operations.

appendix II

Vineyard Statistics

Until recently regional statistics for vineyard areas were recorded only by the National Council of Wine Communities, and were derived from data submitted by local wine communities. Such statistics were notoriously unreliable. To remedy this situation Act No 142 of 2000 empowered the Hungarian Central Statistical Office to carry out a census of all vineyards (a) of up to 500 square metres (5,380 square feet) – i.e. household plots – and (b) of more than 500 square metres (5,380 square feet) – i.e. actual or potential commercial vineyards (see Table 1). This survey was carried out between May 31 and November 15, 2001, in accordance with the provisions of Council Regulation (EEC) No 357/79, and from it a National Vineyard Register, reflecting the dispositions of Hungarian vineyards in 2001, is being compiled. Data abstracted from the survey are given below by courtesy of Dr Ernő Péter Botos, the Director General of the Kecskemét Research Institute for Vine and Wine, who has been in over-all charge of the project.

The areas given in Table 2 are for vineyards in full production, those that are planted with young vines not yet in full production, and those that are "not properly cultivated" (i.e. abandoned vineyards). Not included are vineyards planted with varieties that are neither recommended nor authorized by wine communities, American hybrids (which are now illegal, but still existed at the time of the census) or plantations of unidentified grape varieties. All of these come into a category referred to as "other vineyards" which, at a surprisingly high national total of 7,489 hectares, is included in the global total of Hungarian vineyards given in Table 1. Finally, the census took no account of vineyards for which permission had already been given for grubbing-up.

1. Total vineyard surface areas (in hectares)

Commercial vineyards of over 500 square metres, of all types of production (wine, table grapes, nursery stock, etc.)	91,421
Non-commercial vineyards of less than 500 square metres, of all types of production	1,688
Total	**93,109**

Of the total of 91,421 hectares of commercial vineyards, 80,042 hectares are used exclusively for wine production, of which 59,651 hectares (74.53 per cent) are white varieties and 20,391 hectares are red varieties (25.47 per cent).

Of the total of 80,042 hectares used for wine production, 72,946 hectares are within the twenty-two authorized wine regions, of which 54,305 hectares (74.45 per cent) are white varieties and 18,641 hectares (25.55 per cent) are red varieties – almost identical with total national distribution.

2. Vineyard surface areas (in hectares) by region

These figures refer to commercial-sized vineyards of more than 500 square metres which are used for wine production. The sequence of the regions corresponds to the numerical key used in the maps, with Wine Producing Areas and other non-classified vineyards at the end.

Region varieties	Total area	White varieties	Red varieties
Sopron	1,800	317	1,483
Pannonhalma-Sokoróalja	679	653	26
Ászár-Neszmély	1,601	1,484	117
Somló	315	311	4
Balatonfüred-Csopak	2,131	1,900	231
Badacsony	1,639	1,559	80
Balatonfelvidék	1,351	1,318	33
Balatonmelléke	921	878	43
Balatonboglár	2,663	2,030	633
Etyek-Buda	1,868	1,737	131
Mór	868	843	25
Kunság	25,935	20,273	5,662
Hajós-Baja	1,940	1,141	799
Csongrád	2,683	1,681	1,002
Mecsekalja	773	658	115
Szekszárd	2,149	495	1,654
Tolna	2,739	1,579	1,160
Villány-Siklós	1,801	651	1,150
Eger	5,080	2,197	2,883
Mátraalja	6,844	5,869	975
Bükkalja	1,504	1,072	432
Tokaj-Hegyalja	5,662	5,659	3
Wine Producing Areas	1,972	1,515	457
Non-classified areas	5,124	3,831	1,293
TOTALS	**80,042**	**59,651**	**20,391**

3. Percentages of vineyards by surface area (in square metres)

Up to 499	2.0%
500–999	7.0%
1,000–1,499	6.4%
1,500–4,999	16.0%
5,000–9,999	9.2%
10,000–24,999	12.4%
25,000–49,999	9.7%
50,000–74,999	6.4%
75,000–99,999	4.6%
100,000 and over	26.3%
Total	**100.0%**

appendix III

Wine Routes and Festivals

Wine tourism in Hungary is not for the faint-hearted. Although more and more wine routes are being established, in some cases the leaflets only give maps and descriptions of wine villages without indicating the names or addresses of wineries that are open to visitors. Generally, winery staff will be unable to speak English, although a smattering of German will carry you a long way. Details of wine routes may be obtained from the following offices:

Badacsony: Badacsonyi Borvidéki Borút Egyesület,
    H–8261 Badacsony, Római út 2.
    Tel: +36–87 431003
    Tel/fax: +36–87 531033/4
    E-mail: borutbad@matavnet.hu

Bükkalja: Bükkaljai Hegyközségi Tanács,
    H–3400 Mezőkövesd, Alkotmány út 5.
    Tel: +36–46 360627

Balatonboglár: Balatonboglári Borút Egyesület,
    H–8630 Balatonboglár, Erzsébet u. 11.
    Tel: +36–85 351311
    Fax: +36–85 350469
    E-mail: balatonboglar@somogy.hu

Eger: Eger Város Hegyközsége,
    H–3301 Eger, Déak Ferenc u. 51.
    Tel: +36–36 411943
    Egri Borvidék Hegyközségi Tanácsa,
    H–3301 Eger, Kőlyuktető, Pf. 83.
    Tel: +36–36 310533

Mátraalja: Mátraaljai Borok /tja Egyesület,
    H–3200 Gyöngyös, Fő tér 13.
    Tel: +36–37 311155 or 364012
    Fax: +36–37 313581

Mecsekalja: Mohács-Bóly Borút Egyesület,
Tourinform Bóly,
H–7754 Bóly, Erzsébet tér 1.
Tel/fax: +36–69 368100
E-mail: tourinform@boly.hu

Pannonhalma-Sokoróalja:
Kisalföldi Vállalkozásfejlesztési Alapítvány,
H–9022 Györ, Czuczor Gergely u. 30.
Tel: +36–96 316188
E-mail: info@kva.hu

Somló: Somlóvásárhely Hegyközség,
H–8481 Somlóvásárhely, Somlóhegy.
Tel: +36–20 293371

Sopron: Kisalföldi Vállalkozásfejlesztési Alapítvány,
H–9400 Sopron, Szent György u. 16.
Tel: +36–99 340220
Tel/fax: +36–99 340210

Szekszárd: Vino-Fer,
H–7100 Szekszárd, Hrabovszky u. 12/a.
Tel: +36–74 317490

Tokaj: Tokaj-Hegyaljai Borút Egyesület,
H–3915 Tarcal, Fő u. 57.
Tel/fax: +36–47 380146
E-mail: tarcal@matav.hu
Website: www.tokaji-borut.hu

Tolna: Tolnai Borút Egyesület,
H–7052 Kölesd, Kossuth tér 12.
Tel: +36–74 436013

Villány-Siklós: Villány-Siklos Borút Egyesület,
H–7800 Siklós, Kossuth tér 1.
Tel/fax: +36–72 352746
E-mail: borut@siklos.hu
Website: www.borut.hu

Annual wine festivals are held in all regions. Details and dates may be found in a booklet called *Diary of Wine Events in Hungary* normally published in English each year by AMC, a branch of the Ministry of Agriculture; it is obtainable from the

Hungarian National Tourist Office, which has branches in all large countries, and has a standard e-mail address:

ht***@hungarytourism.hu

in which you insert the name of the city whose branch you wish to contact in place of ***: for example, htlondon@hungarytourism.hu or htstockholm@hungarytourism.hu

Many of the festivals are very simple village affairs at which visitors have opportunities of tasting local wines at stands or in the cellars. Others are organized more like funfairs, and have sideshows and produce stalls that almost eclipse the wine aspects of the festival. A national wine festival is held in Budapest every year, but this is a very provincial affair when compared to national wine fairs in major European countries.

The following is a list of the main wine festivals and "open cellars":

April Bóly (Mecsekalja); Mór; Tapolca (Badacsony)
May Villány; Palkonya (Villány-Siklós); Hajós
June Szekszárd; Bogács (Bükkalja)
July Eger; Keszthely (Balaton/Melléke)
August Badacsony; Tokaj; Balatonfüred; Balatonboglár
September Budapest; Budafok; Eger; Somló; Badacsony; Pécs
October Villány

appendix IV

A Guide to Hungarian Pronunciation

Accents modify the pronunciation of vowels, and do not indicate stress, which is always on the first syllable. The umlaut ¨ modifies vowels in the same way in Hungarian as in German. The accent peculiar to Hungarian is ˝. It has the same effect as ¨, except that it is more intensive, and lengthens the sound slightly.

a   as in *bald*
á   as in *ham*
e   as in *bed*
é   as in *eight*
i   as in *if*
í   as in *reef*
o   as in *top*
ó   as in *bold*
ö   as in the French *oeuf*
ő   as explained above
u   as in *lunar*
ú   as in *too*
ü   as in the German *früh*
ű   as explained above

The following consonants are pronounced as in English: b, d, f, h, k, l, m, n, p, r, t, v, y, z. The following consonants and clusters differ:

c   like *ts* in *tsar*
g   as in *golf* rather than *rage*
j   like *y* in *young*
ly   like *yi* in *yippee*
ny   like *ni* in *onion*
s   as in *sugar* rather than *suck*
ty   like *t y* in *got you*
w   like *v* in *van*

The following consonant clusters are regarded as individual letters in Hungarian, and appear as such in alphabetical listings:

cs like the *ch* in *child*
gy like the *dg* in *sledge*
sz like *s* in *sail*
zs like *s* in *pleasure*

Repeated letters, whether vowels or consonants, are separately pronounced, but without hesitation or emphasis. Thus, Bátaapáti is pronounced "Bah-taw-aw-patty".

Select Bibliography

I have made no attempt to include the vast literature in Hungarian in this bibliography which, with few exceptions, confines itself to texts written in English. For a bibliography of books about Hungarian wine in Hungarian, see Halász (1), below.

Alkonyi, László. *Tokaj – A szabadság bora.* (Hungarian and English text). Alkonyi: Spread Bt, [Budapest], 2000.

Alkonyi, László, ed. *Birtokok és Borok 2001–2002.* Borbarat, n.p., n.d. [2001]

Anon. (1) *Tokay.* Berry Bros & Co, London, 1933. (2) *Borongoló: Wine Roads in Hungary.* [Hungarian Viticultural Foundation.] N.p., n.d.

Bakonyi, K., Bakonyi, L. and Kocsis, L. "Zsigmond Teleki, his life and results" in *Horticultural Science–Kertészeti Tudomány*, 1996, 28 (3–4), pp. 87–91.

Berend, Ivan T. *The Hungarian Economic Reforms 1953–1988.* Cambridge University Press, Cambridge, 1990.

Blom, Philipp. *The Wines of Austria.* Faber & Faber, London, 2000.

Csepregi, P. and Zilai, J. *Quality Varieties of Hungary.* MMM Ltd, n.p., n.d.

Csizmadia, László, ed. *The Wines of Eger.* Hungarian Picture Publishers Ltd and House of E. Szelényi, n.p., n.d. [?1997, ISBN 963 8155 82 5]

Douglass, Sylvester. "An Account of the Tokay and Other Wines of Hungary" in *Philosophical Transactions of the Royal Society of London,* 1773; reprinted by the Rare Wine Co, Sonoma, California, 1998.

Gombár, Csaba et al, eds. *Balance: The Hungarian Government, 1990–1994.* Centre for Political Research, Budapest, 1994.

Gunyon, R.E.H. *The Wines of Central and South Eastern Europe.* Duckworth, London, 1971.

Halász, Zoltán. (1) *Hungarian Wine Through the Ages.* Corvina Press, Budapest, 1962. (2) *The Book of Hungarian Wines.* Corvina Kiadó, Budapest, 1981.

Hare, P.G. et al, eds. *Hungary: A Decade of Economic Reform.* George Allen and Unwin, London, 1981.

Howkins, B. *Tokaji.* International Wine & Food Society, [London], 1999.

Hulej, von Endre and Kovács, Josef Ö. *Ede Weber in Helvécia: Ein Schweizer in Ungarn.* N.p., n.d. [Published by the Helvéciai Állami Gazdaság, ISBN 963 02 4752 6]

Hulot, M. *Vins de Tokaj.* Éditions Féret, Bordeaux, 2001.

Katona, József. *Pocket Guide to Hungarian Wines.* Hungarian Wine Traders' Association, Budapest, 1995.

Laposa, József. *Villány: A Magyar borvidékek ékessége.* (Hungarian and English text.) Magyar Borkereskedők Egyesülése, Budapest, 1995.

Laposa, J. and Dékány, T. (1) *Pincejárás: From Cellar to Cellar.* Mezőgazda Kiado, Budapest, 1999. [Summary in English]. (2) *Villány – Borvideékek Ékessége – The Jewel of Wine Regions.* Aduprint Kiadó és Nyomda Kft, n.p., 2001. [Hungarian and English text]

Moulton, K. and Botos, P. "Evaluating Privatization in Hungary's Wine Industry: A Framework for Analysis" in *Agribusiness,* Vol 10, No 3, 1994, pp 198–203.

Rohály, G. and Mészáros, G., eds. *Rohály's Wine Guide: Hungary.* Borkollégium, n.p., 2002. [Wine-tasting notes of the College of Wine, Hungary; published annually]

Sailer, Michael. *Das Tokajer-Buch.* Michael Sailer Verlag, Nürtingen, n.d. [ISBN 3–9802951–2–5]

Szabó, Joseph and Török, Stephen, eds. *Album of the Tokay-Hegyalja.* Pest, 1867. Reprinted (without map), n. p., 1984.

Tőkés, Rudolf L. *Hungary's Negotiated Revolution.* Cambridge University Press, Cambridge, 1996.

Tőttős, Gábor. *A Szekszárdi Szőlő és Bor.* (With a short summary in English and other languages). Módos Ernő, Szekszárd, 1987.

In addition, the reader may wish to consult the web-pages of individual firms and organizations available on the internet under the heading of Hungarian Wine (try www.winesofhungary.com), and may also be interested in a series of CD-ROMs on Hungarian wine regions published by Archimedia: www.archimedia.hu

A Glossary of Hungarian Terms

Állami. State (-owned).
Állami Gazdaság. State Farm.
Aszú. Botrytized; wine made from botrytized grapes.
Asztali bor. Table wine.
Bor. Wine.
Borászat. Viniculture/winery.
Borászati. Wine production.
Borház. Tavern.
Borozó. Wine pub.
Borvidék. Wine region.
Bt (Betét társaság). Deposit company.
Comecon (Council for Mutual Economic Assistance). Trade agreement among Soviet bloc countries.
Családi. Family.
Cuvée. Blend.
Dűlő. Vineyard; locale.
Édes. Sweet.
Egyesült. Amalgamated.
Egyesület. Association.
És. And.
Fehér. White.
Fél. Semi: e.g. félédes: "semi-sweet".
Fia. Son.
Gazdaság. Farm.
Gönc. A town in the Hegyalja; the name of a 136-litre cask.
Gróf. Count.
Hegy. Mountain.
Hegyközség. Wine community.

Hordó. Cask, barrel.
Kék. Blue.
Kereskedelmi. Commercial, trading.
Késöi Szüretelésű. Late-harvest.
Kft (Korlátolt felelősségű társaság). Limited. (Limited liability company).
Kht (Közhasznú társaság). Public benefit company.
Király. King.
Királyi. Royal.
Kkt (Közkereseti társaság). Partnership with unlimited liability.
Kombinát. Combine.
Környéki bor. Country wine.
Magyar Borszövetség. Hungarian Winegrowers' Association.
Mezőgazdaság. Agriculture.
Mezőgazdasági. Agricultural.
Mezőgazdasági Termelő Szövetkezet (MGTSZ). Agricultural Production Cooperative.
MGTSZ. See under Mezőgazdasági Termelő Szövetkezet.
Minőségi bor. Quality wine.
Must. Must.
OBB (Országos Borminősítő Bizottság). National Wine Qualification Board.
OBI (Országos Borminősítő Intézet). State Wine Qualification Institute.

OMMI (Országos Mezőgazdasági Minősítő Intézet). National Institute for Agricultural Quality Control.

Palack. Bottle.

Palackozás. Bottling.

Pálinka. Brandy distilled from any fruit.

Panzió. Guest house.

Pezsgő. Sparkling wine.

Pince. Cellar.

Pincesor. Cellar row.

Pincészet. Wine cellar, winery.

Piros. Red.

Pogácsa. Small cheese scone served with wine.

Puttony. A wooden hod holding up to 25 kilograms of grapes.

Rozé. Rosé.

Rt (Részvénytársaság). Joint-stock company.

Sárga. Yellow.

Siller. Wine with a colour intermediate between rosé and red.

Söröső. Beer bar.

Száraz. Dry.

Szőlészet. Viticulture.

Szőlő. Grapes, vineyard.

Szőlőbirtok. Wine estate.

Szőlőfürt. Bunch of grapes.

Szőlőskert. Vineyard.

Szőlőtermelő. Vine-growing.

Szövetkezet. Cooperative.

TSZ. See under MGTSZ.

Tájbor. Country wine.

Termelő. Production.

Tőke. Vine.

Törkölypálinka. Brandy distilled from wine marc.

Ernyő. Umbrella.

Út. Road.

Utca. Street.

Vállalkozás. Enterprise, venture.

VPOP (Vám és Pénzügyminisztérium Országos Parancsnoksága). National Customs Authority.

Zöld. Green.

Index

The page references in bold print indicate the main sections dealing with each topic.

A

acacia trees, 15, 135, 198
Alföld (see also Great Plain), 46, **169–96**, 321
Alkonyi László, 271
Antinori, Ludovico, 143, 243
Apponyi family, 211, 214
Ászár-Neszmély, 4, 30, **87–92**, 130
aszú grapes, (see also botrytized grapes), 70, 265, 270, 274, 275, **276–7**, 278–83
Aszú (see also Tokaji), 41, 167, 265
Aszú Esszencia, see Tokaji
Australia, xiv, 114, 131, 139, 140, 213, 242
  wine regions of,
    Barossa Valley, 114
    Hunter Valley, 76
Austria, xii, 3–4, 5, 28, 31, 47, 50, 51, 52, 57, 58, 59, 73, 75, 76, 79, 85, 117, 118, 150, 159, 211, 219, 220, 221, 226, 297

B

Badacsony, 46, 56, 108, **116–26**, 127, 128, 129, 132, 135, 138, 177, 178
Baja, 171, 183
Bakonyi, Károly, 45, 111
Balatonboglár (region), 131, **138–47**, 153, 155
Balatonfelvidék, **127–34**
Balatonfüred, 10, 105, 110, 113
Balatonfüred-Csopak, **105–116**, 127
Balatonmellék, 127
Balatonmelléke, 127, **134–7**
Balkans, 51, 52, 57
barrique technology, 66–7
Batthyány family, 220, 234
beer, 17, 48, 49
Berényi family, 163
Berry Bros & Rudd, x, 272

Bikavér, see wine, types of
Borbarát, see wine, periodic publications about
borkombinát, 10
Botos Ernő,323
botrytis cinerea, 87, 139, 220, 261, 265, 268, 276, 278, 300
botrytized grapes (see also aszú grapes and wine, botrytized), 39, 82, 144, 184
Buda, 46, 148
Budafok, 5, 10, 17, 44, 140, **148–56**, 166, 192, 310, 311
Budapest, xii, xiii, 5, 6, 19, 27, 45, 46, 98, 100, 112, 120, 122, 144, **148–56**, 157, 173, 193, 195, 228, 230, 233, 251, 255, 264, 306, 310, 311
Bükkalja, 237, **261–3**
Bull's Blood, see wine, types of, Bikavér
Burgenland, 73, 166

C

California, 78, 224, 226, 260, 309
Cladosporium cellare, 269
Csongrád, 169, **186–9**
chaptalization, 39, 58, 96, 253, 261
Chile, 131, 153
climate, xii-xiii, 74, 82, 87, 96–7, 108, 117, 120, 134, 135, 136, 138, 151, 157, 169, 171, 182, 184, 186, 191, 198, 211, 214, 215, 220, 237, 238, 253, 261, 265, **322**
collectivization, 7, **8–11**, 25, 94, 96
Comecon, xiv, 11, 12, 14, 15, 17
command economy, xv, 13, 20
Common Agricultural Policy, 42
communist regime (see also Hungarian political parties, Communist Party), xv, **6–19**, 22, 36, 37, 49, 54, 87, 101, 103, 108, 149, 163, 169, 171, 173, 178, 186, 187, 190, 198, 199, 211, 220, 237, 238, 272, 282, 287, 304, 317

compensation vouchers, 21, 22, 26, 129, 202
Confuron, Jean-Pierre, 225, 227
conidia, 276–7
cooperatives (see also producers), 7, **8–16**, 19,
    20, 21, 22, 24, 25, 26, 28, 29, 30, 31, 57,
    60, 64, 82, 84, 95, 96, 134, 135, 143, 163,
    165, 171, 172, 174, 175, 186, 187, 192,
    211, 212, 215, 253, 272, 315
crawling wine, **xvii**, 261
Croatia, 5, 134, 135, 136, 217
currencies, 322
cuvée, **70**, 121, 242, 255
Czech Republic, 31, 150

D
Debrő, xiii, 56, 237, 250
Dél-Balaton, 138
distillation, 41, 42, 161, 162

E
economics of wine production, **26–31**
education (see also wine, courses on), **43–5**,
    research institutes, **45–7**, 245
        Ampelographical Institute, 45–6,
        Eger Research Institute, 46, **47**, 54,
        Kecskemét Research Institute, **46**, 323
        Pécs Research Institute, 46–7
    schools, **43–4**, 202, 244
        István Soós Food Industry Vocational
        School, **44**, 154, 167, 183, 285, 310
    universities and colleges, 44
        Georgikon Faculty of Agriculture, **44–5**,
        58, 96, 130
        Horticultural University of Budapest, **44**,
        46, 92, 109, 112, 113, 114, 128, 153,
        154, 160, 167, 176, 179, 204, 230, 248,
        254
        Kecskemét University College, 44
        Szent István University of Gödöllő, **44**,
        206
        University of Gyöngyös, 44, 202
        University of Veszprém, 44
Eger, xiii, 10, 45, 50, 54, 57, 151, 155, 156,
    173, 199, **237–51**, 253, 254, 261, 289, 310
Erdődy family, 94
Esszencia, see Tokaji
Esterházy family, 94
Etyek, xiii, 54, 148, 151, 152
Etyek-Buda, 148, **157–63**
Europe, xi, xii, xvii, 5
European Union, xvi, 38, 42, 260, 280, 282,
    314, 316, 317, 323
exports, see markets.

F
Fehérvári family, 94
Festetics family, 44, 140
First World War, 5, 105
five year plans, 9, 10, 11
forint, see currencies
France, xi, xii, 38, 54, 59, 67, 174, 213, 214,
    221, 224, 228, 243, 282, 289, 311
    wine estates in,
        Ch Beaumont, 298
        Ch Beychevelle, 298
        Ch Clinet, 301
        Ch Haut-Marbuzet, 221
        Ch Lynch-Bages, 294
        Ch Pichon-Longueville (Baron), 294
        Clos des Jacobins, 221
        Vosne-Romanée, 225
    wine regions of,
        Arbois, 275
        Beaujolais, 226
        Bordeaux, xii, 43, 226, 228, 231, 248,
        288
        Burgundy, xii, 238
        Côte d'Or, xi
        Graves, xii
        Madiran, 223
        Pommerol, 221
        Sauternes, 295

G
Garay family, 297
Garay János, 199
Germans (see also Swabia),117, 73, 192, 193,
    220, 229, 309
    expulsion from Hungary, **6**, 74, 157, 163,
    211
Germany, xvii, 3, 6, 17, 18, 19, 38, 59, 105,
    174, 184, 194, 213, 256, 289, 296
grape growing, economics of, 24, 28, 29
Great Plain (see also Alföld), 4, 8, 24, 28, 29,
    30, 36, 46, 50, 56, 60, 62, 153
guilds,
    Guild of Eger Wines (Egri Bormíves Céh),
    240
    Guild of Pannonian Wines (Pannon Bormíves
    Céh), **43**, 120
Gyöngyös, 179, 185, 212, 241, 252, 253, 257
Győr, 82, 86
Gyürky family, 91

H
Hajós, 47, 182
Hajós-Baja, 169, 171, **181–5**, 258
Haller family, 253–4

Treaty of Trianon, 5, 73, 264
Turkey, xii, 3–4, 57, 94, 138, 169, 199, 219, 220, 270

U

Union of Grape Growers and Winemakers of the Hungarian Great Plain, 172
Union of Hungarian Wine Producers, 27, **42–3**
USSR, see Soviet Union
universities, see education

V

Vega Sicilia, 113, 299
Villány, xiii, 54, 58, 59, 67, 76, 79, 142, 155, 190, 193, 194, 195, 196, 197, 198, 199, 201
Villány-Siklós, **217–35**
vine,
  bench-grafts, 143, 223, 243, 255–6, 259
  cross breeds, 53, 58
  diseases, 63
  eastern varieties in general, 12, 52–3, 58, 118, 190, 317
  pests, 63
  pruning, 4, 46, 60, 62–3, 99, 118, 121, 128, 131, 151, 187, 222, 225, 130, 231, 303
  rootstocks, 46, 54, **59–60**, 243, 256, 305
  species of,
    American direct producers, 38, 59, 135, 323
    Vitis berlandieri, 59
    Vitis riparia, 59
    Vitis rupestris, 59
    Vitis vinifera, 4, 51, 59, 177
  training systems, 4, **60–3**, 95, 171
    Geneva double curtain, 60, 62
    Guyot, 60, 129, 136, 145, 214, 222, 225, 230, 231, 243, 246, 268, 303, 305
    Lenz Moser, 60, 62, 76, 82, 92, 102, 109, 136, 139, 144, 164, 254, 268
    single curtain, 60, 82, 114, 151, 164, 175, 268
    staked, 4, 57, 60, 95, 164, 171, 187, 204, 243, 293, 298
    umbrella, 60, 76, 82, 88, 93, 109, 112, 114, 118, 123, 124, 139, 151, 164, 167, 188, 204, 225, 254
  ungrafted, 169
  variety of, xiv, **50–8**,
    Aranysárfehér (or Izsáki), 52, 56, 60, 173, 179
    Attila, 95
    Bakator, 119
    Bianca, 71, 173

Bibor Kadarka, 57, 71
Blauburger, 53, 58, 71, 238
Blauer Limberger, see Kékfrankos
Blauer Portugieser, see Kékoportó
Blaufränkisch, see Kékfrankos
Budaizöld, 52, 71, 126
Cabernet, xii, 239
Cabernet Franc, 29, 51, 54, 173, 185, 186, 199, 222, 224, 238
Cabernet Sauvignon, 29, 51, **54**, 71, 76, 84, 108, 126, 138, 173, 184, 199, 206, 221, 222, 224, 238
Cardinál, 71
Chardonnay, xi, 13, 51, 53, 54, 71, 84, 96, 128, 129, 130, 145, 151, 158, 164, 173, 179, 192, 196, 214, 238, 253, 256, 317
Chasselas, 71
Cinsaut, 71
Cirfandli, 52, **56**, 190, 225
Corvinus, 53, 58
Csabagyöngye, 52, 56, 71
Cserszegi Fűszeres, 45, 53, 58, 71, 111, 179, 186, 192
Ezerfürtü, 71
Ezerjó, 51, 52, **56**, 60, 71, 95, 164, 165, 173
Favorita, 71
Furmint, 51, 52, 56, 71, 95, 221, 268, 274, 281, 294
Gamza, 57
Gewürztraminer, see Tramini
Gohér, 52, 56, 71, 268
Grüner Veltliner, see Zöld Veltelini
Hárslevelő, xiii, 29, 52, 56, 71, 95, 96, 237, 238, 250, 256, 268, 281, 295, 296
Irsai Olivér, 53, 57, 71, 160, 179
Isabella, 82, 87
Italian Riesling, see Olaszrizling
Izsáki (see also Aranysárfehér), 71, 173
Juhfark, 53, **56**, 71, 95, 96, 100, 101, 192
Kadarka, 51, 53, **57**, 60, 71, 171, 173, 199, 204, 206, 221, 238, 239, 243
Kékfrankos, 28, 29, 51, 52, **55–6**, 71, 75, 76, 84, 112, 126, 171, 173, 177, 178, 184, 186, 190, 199, 202, 206, 208, 214, 221, 238
Kékmedoc, 238
Kéknyelő, 52, 53, **56**, 71, 117, 119, 126, 221
Kékoportó, 28, 51, 52, 55, 71, 173, 193, 199, 221, 225, 238
Kereklevelő, see Chardonnay

W

wages, 13, 15, 27–8
Waldbott family, 294
Walloons, 3
water curtain, **66**, 176, 194, 209
Weber, Ede, 177–8
wine,
  bio-wine, 122, 147
  botrytized (see also Tokaji, Aszú), 119, 125, 126, 165, 270
  categories of, legally defined, **38**, **322**
    Country Wine, 38, 123, 141, 144, 153, 181, 234, 241, 251
    Museum Wine, 19, 166, 241, 242, 260, 284, 305–6
    Quality Wine, 30, 38, 141, 234, 251
    Superior Quality Wine, 39, 40
    Table Wine, 38, 141, 181, 241, 251
    Wine of Protected Origin, 39
  cellars, **47**, 158, 182, 200, 211, 253–4, 268–9, 301, 306
  certificates of origin, 37, 38, 41
  communities, **35–7**, 39, 41, 50, 69, 70, 173–4, 187, 211, 323
    National Council of Wine Communities, 36, 50, 69, 323
  competitions, 19, 48,
  courses on,
    College of Wine, 45
    CorVinum, 156
    House of Hungarian Wine, 45
  culture,
    Hungarian, 47–9
    manorial, 4, 220
  distributors,
    CorVinum, 156, 160, 311
    Demijohn, 90
    Monarchia, 77, 79, 100, **156**, 205, 227, 235, 245, 248, 310
    Montrade, 257
  duty on, see taxes on
  fake, **30–1**, 88, 172, 211, 260
  festivals, 327–8
  laws, 10, 36, **37–40**, 42, 73, 97, 270, 282, 323
  makers, see winemakers
  marketing of, 314–5, 318
  museums,
    Bozóky, 166
    Keszthely, 129
    Szőlőskislak, 139
    Villány, 233
  organic, 120
  periodic publications about, **45**

quality, 11, 18–9, **39–40**, 48, 151, 171, 174, 181, 224, 239, 252, 272–3, 289
producers (see producers)
regions (see also under individual names), xvi, 35, 50, 69–70, 324
retailers (see also supermarkets),
  Budapest Wine Society, 99, 204
  La Boutique de Vin, 227
routes, 326–7
taxes on, 40
tradition, **47–9**
types of,
  Ausbruch, 17, **184**
  Bikavér, 40, 41, 57, 199, 204, 205, 206, 209–10, **238–40**, 243, 245, 247, 248, 249, 250
  Eiswein, 124, 125
  fortified, 18
  late harvest (see also Tokaji), 56, 109, 115, 118, 119, 126, 133, 136, 137, 253
  pezsgő, see wine, types of, sparkling
  rozé, 39, 124, 203
  siller, 39
  sparkling, 17, 39, 54, 95, 102, 131, 140, 150–1, 152, 154, 155, 171, 173, 178–9, 195–6, 263, 306
  Trokenbeerenauslese, 167, 302
Winemaker of the Year, 43, 88, 110, 206, 230, 231, 233, 244, 247, 292
winemakers (see also wine, producers), 318
  foreign,
    Hall, Stephen, 242
    Hartnell, Clive, 140
    Laszlo, Thomas, 301, 302
    Milne, Kym, 140, 256
    Muir, Angela, 306
    O'Sullivan, Tanya, 306
  Hungarian, xvi, xvii
    Gádor Dénes, 18, 141, 146
    Figula Mihály, 109–10, 162
    Gál Tibor, 54, 113, **214–5**, 221, 243–4
    Kamocsay Ákos, 88, 89
    Szeremley Huba, 118–20, 178
wine-producing areas, **38**, 114, 127, 187, 324
wine regions, see Hungary
Women's Association of Friends of Wine, **43**, 160

Z

Zala, 127, 134
Zemplén Forest, 67, 264
Zichy family, 94, 167